D1707322

AFTER WILSON

THE

STRUGGLE

FOR THE

DEMOCRATIC

PARTY,

AFTER

1920–1934

WILSON

DOUGLAS B. CRAIG

The University of North Carolina Press

Chapel Hill & London

Library of Congress

Cataloging-in-Publication Data

Craig, Douglas B. ✓

    After Wilson : the struggle for the Democratic ✓

Party, 1920–1934 / Douglas B. Craig.

        p.   cm.

    Includes bibliographical references and index.

    ISBN 0-8078-2058-x (cloth : alk. paper)

    1. Democratic Party (U.S.)   2. United States—

Politics and government—1919–1933.   I. Title.

JK2317   1992

324.2736–dc20   92-53629

                                        CIP

CONTENTS

Acknowledgments   vii

Introduction   1

1. The Politics of Disintegration: The Campaign of 1920   15

2. The Rise and Fall of William Gibbs McAdoo, 1920–1928   30

3. The Politics of Despair: The Campaign of 1924   51

4. The Struggle for the National Organization, 1920–1928   75

5. Looking to Houston   92

6. The Problem of Al Smith   112

7. A Businessman Comes to Politics: John J. Raskob   131

8. "Wall Street Likes Al Smith": The Election of 1928   157

9. The Politics of Money:
   John Raskob and the DNC, 1929–1932   181

10. In McAdoo's Steps: Franklin D. Roosevelt, 1928–1932   205

11. The Coalition Responds:
    Nominating a President, 1930–1932   225

12. The Ideology of Antiprohibition:
    From the AAPA to the American Liberty League   248

13. The Politics of Consistency:
    The American Liberty League, 1934–1940   274

Conclusion   296

Notes   307

Bibliography   369

Index   393

A section of illustrations can be found following page 214.

ACKNOWLEDGMENTS

Like most books, this one has had a long gestation and many midwives. Professors David A. Shannon and William H. Harbaugh of the University of Virginia, as doctoral supervisors, provided essential guidance and criticism during this work's earlier life. Professor Harbaugh later provided unfailing encouragement during the long transition from dissertation to book. I am profoundly grateful to both men. Professors Robert D. Cross, Michael F. Holt, Joseph F. Kett, James Sterling Young, and Olivier Zunz also provided analysis and advice, for which I thank them. I also acknowledge a great debt to Professor Elliot A. Rosen, whose help on the conceptualization of this project came at a crucial time in its development.

Grants from the Corcoran Department of History and the Graduate School of Arts and Sciences at the University of Virginia were generous and sustained, allowing me to undertake most of the archival research for this book. I have also been generously assisted by the Australian American Educational Foundation, the Franklin D. Roosevelt Foundation, the Hagley Museum and Library, the University of Sydney Travelling Scholarship Fund, and the Gowrie Trust Fund.

The librarians and archivists at the University of Virginia, Yale University, the University of Kentucky, Wright State University, Connecticut College, the Australian National University, the Franklin D. Roosevelt Library, Hagley Museum and Library, the Library of Congress, the New York State Library, the New York Public Library, and the National Library of Australia all provided patient and expert advice, for which I am very grateful. I am also grateful to the copyright and physical-property owners by whose permission quotations from manuscripts appear in this book.

The staff at the University of North Carolina Press have been pillars of strength and patience through a protracted revision and production process. Lewis Bateman, Sandra Eisdorfer, and Craig Noll, especially, have played major roles in bringing this work into existence. My sincere gratitude goes to them and to all the staff at Chapel Hill.

Along the way I have accumulated innumerable personal debts. The Crystals of Richmond, Mrs. Olive Jones of Lexington, Kentucky, the Newells of Bethel, Connecticut, Mrs. Esther Bradley of Hyde Park, New

York, Robert McCord and Leigh Jackson of Washington, D.C., the Speakmans of Greenville, Delaware, and Ian Meakin and Jane Cooper of New Haven all provided accommodation which stretched a tight research budget further than I had any right to expect. Malcolm and Barbara Crystal, Neill and Alletta Bell, Paul Field, Diana Brock, Elizabeth Van Beek, Ann Merritt, Margaret Newell, Catherine Wilcoxson, John Kirn, Tania Ewing, Richard Button, and many other friends took time from their own concerns to help me with mine. My heartfelt thanks go to them all. Margaret Thomson was patient and supportive through it all, and I am grateful for the sacrifices she made to see this book completed. I also wish to express my gratitude to all my colleagues in the Department of History, and to Dr. John Hart of the Political Science Department, at the Australian National University. They have been unfailing sources of both intellectual stimulus and companionship for the past two years.

I owe the greatest thanks to my family. My parents have been meticulous proofreaders and constant supporters throughout this and all previous endeavors. Andrew, Hugh, and Mary Louise have contributed both directly and indirectly to this book, and their youngest sibling is profoundly grateful. The least I can do in return is to absolve them, and all others, of responsibility for this book's content. That responsibility belongs to me alone.

Department of History, the Faculties
Australian National University
Canberra
September 24 1991

AFTER WILSON

INTRODUCTION

This book is about a political party passing through the wilderness of defeat, and the way in which the Democratic party's organization and leaders were affected by that experience. The Democrats had to endure failure again and again during the 1920s. The policies and electoral strategies of the previous twenty years had to be scrutinized and analyzed in the unforgiving light of demonstrated inadequacy. The national party in the 1920s was faced with problems not unlike those which confronted the Democratic leadership of the 1980s. Had the party lost touch with the pressing concerns of the electorate? Had demographic and economic changes permanently eroded its old bases of support? Was the party wasting away into irrelevance? Unlike the Democrats of the 1980s, however, those of the 1920s could not console themselves with the thought that their performance in congressional elections remained as an indication of organizational vitality. The Democrats lost their House and Senate majorities in 1918 and would not regain them until 1930 and 1932 respectively, and all three of their presidential nominees during the 1920s suffered landslide defeat.

Historians of the party have generally argued that the party reacted to its electoral losses by descending into rancorous cultural conflict. Bereft of the cohesion afforded by national power and patronage, the fragile alliance of farmers, urbanites, and southerners that Woodrow Wilson had assembled fell apart. "The prohibitionist collided with the cockney and the liberal," David Burner wrote of the 1924 national convention in his landmark *Politics of Provincialism*; "Protestant glowered at Catholic, the East Side jeered the Nebraska spread, and Smith battled McAdoo to a 100-ballot stalemate."[1] Burner's ethnocultural interpretation has since become orthodox; in 1974 Peter L. Petersen described the party of the 1920s as an unholy and unhappy alliance of "immigrants and Klansmen, Catholics and Protestant fundamentalists, rednecks and shanty Irish, bosses and antibosses, wets and dries."[2]

The emphasis of recent works on the party has been to assess the relative importance of these conflicts; whether, for example, prohibition or Catholicism was the main factor in Smith's defeat for the presidency in 1928, or whether congressional Democrats manifested a rural-metropolitan division in their voting behavior.[3] Few historians, however, have questioned the central assumption of Burner and his school that ethnocultural conflicts were the only significant factors determining Democratic party history after 1918.[4]

In studies of the 1920s as a whole, however, different organizing themes have been used, ranging from Robert H. Wiebe's metaphor of the breakdown of "island communities" to Ellis Hawley's organizational revolution.[5] Recent studies of the fourth party system have also explored the possibility that the ethnocultural political patterns that held sway in the years before 1896 had considerably changed by 1910.[6] Richard L. McCormick, in his *Party Period and Public Policy*, noted that the ethnoculturalists had failed to connect voting behavior with policy change; no satisfactory explanation, for example, had been put forward for the lapse of time between the realignment during the 1890s and the important legislative changes of 1905–15.[7] In search of such a connection, McCormick observed, political historians were rediscovering ideology and the socioeconomic origins of political alignments.[8]

This book aims to contribute to that rediscovery by examining the philosophy and activities of conservative Democrats within the party's national organization during the 1920s and early 1930s. Its central hypothesis is that behind the more spectacular cultural conflicts lay an equally profound ideological turmoil which contributed to the party's chronic failure to unify around a coherent set of principles between 1920 and 1932. While the party was engaged in bitter disputes over prohibition, urbanism, and Catholicism, it was also torn apart by a fierce struggle between conservatives and liberals for control of the party's economic and social policies. This division has passed almost unnoticed by historians intent on exploring the cultural schisms within the party. To the existing ethnocultural catalog of splits between wets and dries, urbanites and rural dwellers, Catholics and Protestants, and immigrants and natives, this book adds a fifth division between liberals and conservatives.

The party's ideological disputes ran both parallel to and across its lines of cultural cleavage. Those Democrats who supported national prohibition generally saw themselves as progressives, dedicated to the maintenance of Woodrow Wilson's legacy of reformist activism. Those who opposed prohibition were generally less identified with Wilson and progressivism, preferring instead to direct the party toward a more accommodating attitude toward big business and negative statism. Prohibition therefore became both a cultural and an ideological issue, for it encompassed a division not only between rural and urban Democrats but also between those who wished to reverse the tide of government regulation of industry and control of individuals' private conduct and those who supported extensions of government regulation in the name of public welfare. The leaders of the "rural group"—William Jennings Bryan, William Gibbs McAdoo, and Franklin Roosevelt—were also the leaders of the liberal group who opposed conservative and urban Democrats led by Al Smith, John Davis, and John Raskob. At times, however, ideological divisions cut across cultural lines. The frankly urban Al Smith gave behind-the-scenes support to the southerner Oscar Underwood at the 1924 convention in order to defeat the progressives arrayed behind McAdoo; the very northern and very wet John Raskob attempted to forge an alliance with the dry southerner Harry Flood Byrd in 1932, and McAdoo, perceived to be the Klan's candidate in 1924, supported the Catholic Thomas J. Walsh for the presidential nomination in 1928.

Historians have long recognized an ideological dimension to Democratic disputation in the periods that preceded and followed the 1920s. The split over economic policy between Cleveland's Gold Democrats and Bryan's free-silver Populists has been fully explored,[9] as has the relationship between Wilson's progressives and their more conservative Democratic colleagues.[10] The political alignments of the 1930s have also been seen in socioeconomic terms.[11] Although the 1920s fall neatly between these two eras, the lack of a study of the divisions between liberal and conservative Democrats during that decade gives the impression that the ideological disputes within the party during the period 1895–1918 and 1932–40 disappeared between 1920 and 1932. To show that they did not is a primary purpose of this book.

The party's ideological travails during the 1920s are detailed in this book. I examine the formation, composition, and policies of a loose coalition of northeastern economic conservatives who won control of the national party's nominating process and organization in the years after 1920. The Democratic party entered that year as a political body responsible for reforms that had significantly expanded federal power in areas such as banking, industry regulation, and labor law. In the twelve years be-

tween 1920 and 1932, however, new platforms were devised which emphasized the Democrats' solicitude for the interests of the corporate sector and
disavowed the federal interventionism and activism of the Wilsonian era.
They now leaned toward the negative statism and economic conservatism
of Grover Cleveland. The liberals within the party were too disorganized
to mount effective opposition to this takeover until 1928. There followed
an intense struggle for control of the party's 1932 platform and presidential nomination, culminating in the defeat of the conservative wing of the
party by the forces which coalesced behind Franklin Roosevelt between
1930 and 1932. This struggle centered upon the party's prohibition and
economic policies and proved to be a precursor of the division between
conservative Jeffersonian Democrats and the New Deal in the 1930s.

The protagonists of the 1920s were men who occupied the most senior
positions within the party. The conservative wing was led by James M.
Cox, John W. Davis, and Alfred E. Smith, the three presidential nominees
of the decade, as well as John J. Raskob (Democratic national chairman
between 1928 and 1932) and Jouett Shouse, the head of the Democratic
Publicity Bureau from 1929 until 1932. Arrayed against this group was a
loose coalition of former Wilsonians and other liberals who gathered first
behind McAdoo, who had been Wilson's secretary of the treasury, and
then behind Franklin Roosevelt.

A study of the ideological turmoil of the Democratic party during the
1920s adds to an understanding of antiprohibitionism and the later conservative reaction to the New Deal. The Democratic conservative coalition
was intimately connected with the Association Against the Prohibition
Amendment (AAPA) and later the American Liberty League. Leaders of
the AAPA and the Liberty League, such as Pierre and Irénée du Pont
and William Stayton, although not Democrats, worked toward the same
broad policy ends as did the Raskob wing within the national Democratic
party. Historians such as Elliot Rosen and David Kyvig have noted the
similarities between the three groups' leadership, political philosophies,
and organizational methods, but studies of the Democratic party during
the 1920s have not developed this theme.[12] The Raskob group attempted
to use antiprohibitionism to engender hostility toward all government
regulation. Worried by the interventionist and centralist implications of
national prohibition, and concerned that the depression would encourage
economic radicalism, the conservative coalition attempted to avoid a plat-

form of far-reaching economic reform in 1932. It was the Raskob wing's aim to win the 1932 election on the issue of prohibition alone and thus to avoid a mandate for economic change. In this way the demands of the economically distressed could be sidetracked to the prohibition issue, while government policy could be tailored to suit the demands and interests of the corporate sector.

Analysis of the conservative coalition during the 1920s also questions the accepted view of the American Liberty League's crusade against the New Deal during the 1930s. The leaders of the Raskob group were prominent in that organization, and their complaints against the New Deal were based upon the same states' rights, small government, and negative state ideology that underlay the AAPA, which Cox, Davis, Smith, and Raskob had tried to impose upon the Democratic party between 1920 and 1932. The revolt of the conservatives against the New Deal can therefore be placed in the broader context of Democratic party history since 1920. By showing this continuity, another blow also can be struck against the old conception of the 1920s as a self-contained historical era which separated progressivism from the New Deal.[13]

This book also challenges the common perception that the 1920s and 1930s were marked by the triumph of corporatism in American social and political life. Robert Wiebe's conception of a "new middle class" and its vision of modern industrial society as an interdependent community of specialized, bureaucratically organized, and disinterested experts has engendered much interest among historians of the interwar period.[14] So too has Ellis Hawley's interpretation of the 1920s as a decade which witnessed the emergence of an "associative state" stemming from the organizational stimulus occasioned by national mobilization during World War I.[15] Hawley argued that a new form of liberalism, which stressed the value of organization as a bulwark against the declining importance of the individual, emerged during and after World War I. First private and then public bureaucracies, as well as voluntary interest group organizations, assumed increasing importance in an era which marked the death of what Felix Frankfurter described as "romantic individualism."[16]

The Democratic conservative coalition, however, did not share this associative vision. James Cox, John Raskob, John Davis, and Al Smith remained firmly wedded to nineteenth-century romantic individualism throughout their lives. Although Cox, Raskob, and Davis, in particular, rose to wealth and prominence through their understanding of and expertise within highly structured and tightly organized business organizations, their corporatism did not extend beyond the factory door. In politics they remained intensely distrustful of centralization, planning, and bureaucracy and staked their reputations and fortunes in defense of what they saw as individual liberties and the free market. They refused to accept either the Hooverian or the Rooseveltian vision of the state as an arbiter of competing interest groups or of the allocation of social resources.[17] The men who sought to control the Democratic party and its policies between 1920 and 1932 were determined, paradoxically enough, to prevent the translation of the organizational ethos that had served them so well in business into the political sphere. They therefore stand as a warning against overstating the degree to which the associational vision molded the national political agenda after 1920.

Robert F. Burk, in his examination of the political activities of Pierre, Irénée, and Lammot du Pont between 1925 and 1940, has argued that the du Ponts were corporatists because they were champions of the business corporation as an "organizational construct."[18] Although they had welcomed those aspects of the progressive movement that had elevated managerial expertise and efficiency as essential national virtues, Burk argues the du Ponts retained a "pre-Jacksonian" vision of an America governed by the propertied class and through a limited, property-based franchise.[19] The du Ponts' political enemies were the "rural insurgent populists" and those progressives who argued for the extension of governmental power to redress social wrongs and economic inequalities.[20] Pierre du Pont and his brothers fervently believed in what Burk describes as the corporate state as it had existed during the 1920s, because their position in that state had been dominant. They therefore bitterly attacked the "broker state" as it emerged during the New Deal, with its recognition of the claims of labor, consumer, and agrarian interest groups and its increasing separation from private industrial bureaucracies and corporate concerns.[21]

This book uses a broader definition of corporatism than that implicitly adopted by Burk and thereby arrives at a different conclusion as to the appropriateness of the term to the du Ponts and their conservative Democratic allies. In this work "corporatism" is taken to encompass a general organizational trend, extending beyond the creation of successively more complicated business structures to most forms of social, political, and personal activities. Although the Democratic conservative coalition shared the du Ponts' dislike of the Roosevelt's broker state, they cannot be called corporatists in the broader sense. Nor, it is argued, can the du Ponts be so characterized if corporatism is defined beyond the business sphere. Although Burk argues that the du Ponts wrongly described themselves as Jeffersonians, it is argued here that both the conservative coalition and the du Ponts did subscribe to what can be called the conservative interpretation of Jefferson's thought, which stressed the primacy of individual concerns and aspirations over organizational and class interests.[22] Whereas Burk argues that the du Ponts did not oppose centralization as long as they could direct that process to serve their own purposes, and that "If they and their allies could not *control* the machinery of economic stabilization, then it was better that the machinery be dismantled than be operated by their enemies," it is the argument of this book that the social and political vision of the du Ponts and the conservative coalition was flawed by an unresolved conflict between the corporatism they practiced in the private business sphere and the individualism and negative-state ideology they espoused in public affairs.[23]

The methodology of this book is clearly not consonant with John Vincent's complaint in 1966 that too much political history is written about the tiny subculture of party politicians who are assumed to be representative of the political concerns of the nation as a whole.[24] In fact this book's approach is clearly at odds with the "new political history"— and its stress upon voter behavior and the politically disenfranchised and its disdain of party platforms and leadership machinations—that has so dominated the field since Vincent passed judgment. Recently, however, some political historians have questioned the assumption of voter sovereignty over public policy which underpinned much of the political history written in the 1970s and 1980s. This questioning has been led by Richard McCormick, as noted above, Samuel Popkin, and Thomas Ferguson.[25] Ferguson argued in 1983 that the degree of control exercised by voter coalitions over political parties had been exaggerated and that it was "high time" that new approaches to political parties were developed which would give prominence to the role of "business elites" and party institutions. Blocs of major investors, and not the rank and file, were the major determinants of party policies and candidatures, Ferguson claimed, and it was up to political historians to recognize that fact of political life.[26]

As will be seen, the activities of the Democratic conservative coalition in the 1920s provide supporting evidence for the investment theory and for the continuing relevance of political elites in the fabric of political history.

A study of political leadership groups during the 1920s is also appropriate because of the frequently noted decline of popular interest in politics after World War I. Unlike the Gilded Age, when high turnouts and closely fought campaigns attested to the powerful influence of politics and partisan loyalty upon citizens' lives, the Jazz Age brought other distractions. Frederick Lewis Allen, in *Only Yesterday*, devoted less than a page of his three-hundred-page work to the campaign of 1924 and only three and a half to that of 1928. He gave an entire chapter, in contrast, to the Florida land boom of 1922–26. "The opportunities to make money were so ample," Walter Lippmann observed of the 1920s, "that it was a waste of time to think about politics."[27] In Robert and Helen Lynd's Middletown, 87 percent of eligible voters voted in 1888, while only 46 percent bothered to do so in 1920.[28]

In these circumstances party leaders during the decade were given, by default, great power over the political process. The absence of strong popular interest or rank-and-file pressure allowed small groups within the party's organization to control policy with little fear of a mobilized grass-roots movement to challenge their power. This was particularly true concerning the Democratic party's economic policy, because what interest Democrats had in their party was largely dissipated in endless cultural disputes. The 1920s, therefore, are particularly suitable for an analysis of the activities of political elites.

The terms "ideology," "conservative," "liberal," and "progressive" are used frequently in this book. They require definition, despite the difficulties of that task. Ideology, in particular, has presented philosophers, sociologists, political scientists, and historians with great problems. In 1964 Clifford Geertz complained that social scientists at that time had not developed "a genuinely nonevaluative conception of ideology." Ideology had itself become ideologized, becoming freighted with pejorative associations and connotations. Ideology once meant simply "a collection of political proposals," but Geertz noted that even Webster defined it in 1964 as "the integrated assertions, theories, and aims constituting a politico-social program, often with an implication of fictitious propagandizing."[29] The term seemed to many writers to be a relic of discredited Marxism, or of Nazism, or at the very least simply a justification for the exercise and maintenance of political power.[30] By the middle of the 1960s, in Reinhard Bendix's view, "ideology" was in "such bad repute that writers on the subject are either apologetic about using it or prefer to substitute another term like 'belief system.'"[31]

After World War II many intellectuals questioned whether the notion of ideology was appropriate to the modern Western political and social context. In the 1960s and 1970s it was argued that the importance of ideology had declined because of the lack of popular interest in politics, the acceptance of welfare capitalism across the political spectra of developed nations, the sustained economic prosperity of those nations, and the discrediting of both Nazism and Communism.[32] In 1971 Seymour Lipsett went so far as to say that the old ideologies had lost their power to mobilize citizens in the West because "the fundamental political problems of the industrial revolution have been solved." Conservatives had accepted the welfare state, and liberals had recognized the dangers of an all-powerful state.[33]

This writer neither apologizes for nor avoids using "ideology." The passing of the polemics and iconoclasm of the 1960s has also brought a lessening of the ideologizing of ideology. The 1988 edition of Webster does not include the reference to propaganda in its definition of ideology that Geertz noted in 1964, although it does retain a reference to ideology's "idealistic, abstract, or impractical" nature. It now seems possible to accept a less pejorative working definition of ideology. In this book the term is used in accordance with the definition proposed by James MacGregor Burns in 1966: "Ideology is a set of major values and of modes of cognition and perception, all of which relate to one another and to social and economic forces and institutions in varying degrees of reinforcement and antagonism. Political ideologies are those ideologies concerned mainly with the distribution of political power—for example, the legitimacy of authority, recruitment of, and access to, leadership, constitutional forms and procedures."[34]

Putting to one side the accuracy or otherwise of the "decline of ideology" hypothesis for U.S. society in the 1960s and 1970s, it is clearly not relevant to the political culture of the 1920s and 1930s. The work of ethnocultural historians such as Burner has shown the existence of a matrix of cultural values, prejudices, and reactions such as anti-Catholicism, anti-urbanism, and xenophobia that was prevalent during the 1920s and which can be described as an ideology. What needs to be done is to examine other aspects of the Democrats' worldview to take into account equally pressing contemporary concerns about the role of the state in an industrialized economy. As this book will show, there was at that time no consensus over the value of welfare capitalism, or of the welfare state itself. Political debate both within and outside the major political parties was sharply polarized between two broad conceptions of the role of government in society and of the degree to which individuals should be let alone to solve their own problems and to take responsibility for their own economic and social welfare. These broad conceptions are subsumed under the term "ideologies" in this book, thus borrowing from Daniel Bell the view that "ideology is the conversion of ideas into social levers."[35]

The definition of "conservatism" has presented fewer problems to political historians. Clinton Rossiter identified political conservatism as "a sense of satisfaction and identity with the status quo" as it exists in legal, social, or economic practice, and the desire of "someone who has something substantial," in the form of property, status, or power, to defend against "the erosion of change."[36] Its distinctive features, he argued, were traditionalism, constitutionalism, religiosity, individualism, and a stress on the sanctity of private property.[37] Conservatives, Rossiter argued, think of liberty as something to be preserved and defended, whereas liberals view it as being capable of improvement and enlargement.[38] Fundamental to the difference between the two philosophies is the position and power of the state in society.

The most distinctive feature of conservative political thought during the 1920s and 1930s was antistatism.[39] The greatest danger to economic and therefore human liberty, conservatives believed, lay in the abuse and extension of governmental power. The purposes of government were primarily negative, revolving around the protection of citizens and their property from each other and the removal of obstacles to individuals' quest for material advancement.[40] Antistatism manifested itself in two main ways during the 1920s and 1930s. The rights of the states as opposed to the powers of the federal government were emphasized in the belief that state power was more easily tamed when it was exercised in local communities. The federal government was too remote from most of the population to be entrusted with greater powers. Conservatives of this period were also determined to prevent any redistribution of income away from the wealthy to less-privileged members of society. It was not the state's role to confiscate the possessions of the worthy to assist the shiftless, for such measures were futile attempts to remove the natural and beneficial differences between people. Social progress was not made through governmental planning and state coercion, but rather through what William Graham Sumner described as "the force of mutual selfishness of individuals."[41] Liberalism, conservatives thought, attempted to replace individual initiative with state paternalism. Calvin Coolidge described it as "the claim in general that in some way the government was to be blamed because everybody was not prosperous, and because it was necessary to earn a living."[42]

"Liberalism," which Rossiter described as "the stickiest word in the political dictionary," is much harder to define.[43] Historians have long noted the ascendancy of what is termed the "liberal spirit" in American political thought, loosely defined as a forward-looking, capitalistic, and optimistic vision of the ability of individuals to prosper economically and morally under a free government.[44] This "liberal spirit" seemingly encompasses both conservatives and their ideological adversaries, for the meaning of "free government" is open to many interpretations. As Merrill Peterson has pointed out, this is at least partly due to the position of Thomas Jefferson as the great hero of American political thought.[45] Jefferson's precepts were so diverse and so contradictory that they are capable of inspiring conservatives and liberals alike. Conservatives approve his strict constructionism, his championing of states' rights, and his emphasis upon the rights of the individual, while liberals adopt the sweeping language of the Declaration of Independence and its author's faith in the efficacy of the popular majority's will to control the direction of government.[46]

Liberalism, in its early nineteenth-century form, was a largely negative political faith. Liberals opposed entrenched economic privilege, religious absolutism, and political authoritarianism. Laissez-faire in economic, social, and political life became a liberal catchcry because it promised freedom from societal structures that stunted the prospects of the many in order to protect the privileges of the few. Because it was largely in the hands of a hostile establishment, the state in early nineteenth-century England and the United States became the great enemy of liberal reformers.[47] As the nineteenth century wore on, however, many liberals began to rethink their earlier hostility to the state. To some extent this was caused by the triumph of liberalism itself. Once liberals won control of the state, they often found it less threatening than they had perceived it to be when they were outsiders. By the end of the nineteenth century, too, many liberals began to worry that the increasing complexities of modern industrial society had made laissez-faire ideas obsolete. From its origins as a doctrine of reformers and outsiders, laissez-faire had, by 1880, become the doctrine of conservatives.[48] Conservatives and liberals, in both England and the United States, radically changed their views of the state. Conservatives had begun the nineteenth century defending state coercion against the voluntarist and individualist liberal credo; they ended the century by championing individual freedom and liberties against what they saw as liberalism's increasing reliance upon state coercion.[49] Well might Herbert Spencer complain in 1884 that liberals had become Tories.[50]

Politicians of the 1920s continued to muddle the definition of liberalism. In 1924 the political scientist Arthur Holcombe noted that in New York a liberal was one who believed in the personal liberty to buy and consume alcohol, while in Kansas a liberal was one who supported national prohibition. Rural liberals sought to use the power of the federal government to raise the prices of agricultural products, while their urban counterparts fought to keep food prices low. "Conservative and Liberal and Radical are relative terms which have no standardized significance," Holcombe warned; "their meaning must be discovered by investigating the interests of those who use the term."[51]

Holcombe's warning is pertinent to any attempt to delineate ideological conflicts during the 1920s. Conservative Democrats such as John Raskob and John W. Davis described themselves as liberals, and they decried their opponents' use of the term to denote centralizing and economically interventionist policies. Davis, aghast at the expansion of federal power into both private business and state prerogatives undertaken by the "liberals" of the New Deal, argued that they had perverted the meaning of liberalism. "Nothing disturbs me more," he wrote to a friend in 1934, "than the use which is made of the fine old term 'liberal.' Properly understood, a Liberal is one who believes in human liberty and who is willing to shape all his policies to that end. It is in this sense that Thomas Jefferson has been properly called 'the greatest Liberal in the modern world.' In the mouths of some only those can be called Liberals who are in favor of increasing the control of government over human action."[52]

This book does not use Davis's definition of liberalism, which was borrowed from John Stuart Mill, the Manchester school, and Herbert Spencer.[53] Instead, I use the more modern meaning espoused by William Gibbs McAdoo and Franklin Roosevelt during the 1920s. The fundamental difference separating liberals from conservatives during the period 1920–40 concerned the acceptable limits of governmental activism. Liberals were willing to expand the role of government in order to redress imbalances in economic privilege or material distress; their conservative opponents were not. Liberal Democrats perceived the power of government, and especially that of the federal government, as a positive force that could use public policy to redistribute income from the rich to the poor and to exercise a strong regulatory influence over the conduct of private enterprise.[54] Ramsay Muir's description of liberalism is an accurate one in the context of Democratic politics between 1920 and 1934: liberalism is "a readiness to use the power of the state for the purposes of creating the conditions within which individual energy can thrive, of preventing all abuses of power, of affording to every citizen the means of acquiring mastery of his own capabilities, and of establishing a real equality of opportunity for all. These aims are compatible with a very active policy of social reorganization, involving a great enlargement of the functions of the state."[55]

The definition of "progressive" has also caused much debate among historians. The concept of a progressive "movement" has come under fire from those who argue that the process of reform between 1900 and 1920 was so complex and diverse that it cannot be satisfactorily labeled as a single movement.[56] This militates against an exclusive definition; before 1916, Woodrow Wilson's progressivism had strong anticentralist tendencies, distrusting big government almost as much as big business. In 1916, however, his administration pushed through nationalistic legislation outlawing child labor, setting working hours for railroad employees, and creating a rural credits scheme.[57] Some progressives retained the distaste for government and politics that they had developed during the seamy days of the Gilded Age; others enthusiastically embraced the opportunity to use state and federal governmental power to redress society's wrongs.[58] By 1920 the concept of progressivism had become as muddied as that of liberalism; even Warren G. Harding could describe himself as a "white-haired progressive."[59]

Among Democrats of the 1920s, however, such distinctions were largely moot. "Progressives" were identified as those who had supported Wilson's administration, and "progressive" and "liberal" were used synonymously.[60] In the interests of clarity and in order to keep as closely as possible to the usage of the period, I adopt this practice. The capitalized "Progressive" is used only to refer to the organization upon whose ticket Robert M. La Follette ran for the presidency in 1924.

The chapters that follow reexamine the Democratic party between 1920 and 1934 within an organizing theme of ideological division rather than cultural conflict. The major events and campaigns of the period are examined from the previously unexplored perspective of the conservative coalition. This is done by interspersing chapters dealing with specific events and issues with biographical studies of both the conservative leaders and their opponents. Thus chapters 1, 3, 5, 8, and 11 cover the presidential campaigns of 1920, 1924, 1928, and 1932, while chapters 2, 4, 6, 7, 9, and 10 continue the argument by examining the roles of William McAdoo, the national committee Democrats, Al Smith, John Raskob, and FDR in the struggle for control over the party's policies. These chapters interrupt the sequence of the more temporally specific chapters so as to highlight the longer-term changes which occurred within the party between 1920 and 1934. Chapters 12 and 13 conclude the argument by broadening still further the context of conservative activism in the 1920s and 1930s. By incorporating the Association Against the Prohibition Amendment and the American Liberty League into the related struggles within the Democratic party, the book aims to provide a coherent and inclusive treatment of Democratic party activities between the presidencies of Woodrow Wilson and Franklin Roosevelt.

THE POLITICS OF DISINTEGRATION

THE CAMPAIGN OF 1920

The 1920s were plague years for Democrats grown accustomed to national power. The decade began with an overwhelming national defeat in the presidential and congressional elections of 1920. Reunited and invigorated by their victory against the League of Nations, the Republicans reasserted their majority status and swept back to power. For the Democrats, divided over the league and suffering from a lack of leadership from their ailing president, the 1920 campaign was marked by depression and defeatism. Few in the party expected victory; the predominant concern was to minimize the extent of the anticipated defeat.

Developments within the party during the first six months of 1920 added to Democrats' forebodings of imminent defeat. Both Herbert Hoover and Henry Ford, whose allegiances to the party were doubtful, were widely mentioned as possible Democratic presidential nominees; then rumors that Woodrow Wilson himself desired a third nomination circulated. This increased the sense of desperation within the party, for the president was scarcely a safe choice. Not only was the two-term tradition a potent liability, but the president himself had become increasingly unpopular because of his insistence upon the league as the overriding issue of 1920. The president hoped to be drafted by the convention in San Francisco to do battle on behalf of international peace. He even went so far as to draft an acceptance address.[1]

Secretary of State Bainbridge Colby and Postmaster General Burleson acted as agents for Wilson at the convention, keeping in touch with the White House by a system of coded telegrams. The Colby-Burleson plan was to await the strategic moment and then try to stampede the delegates by a dramatic presentation of the president's name.[2] The moment never came, due in part to Wilson's more sober admirers who feared that his renomination would kill not only the president but also the party.[3] In the end only 2 delegates out of a total of 1,094 at San Francisco cast their votes for Wilson.[4]

The uncertainty over Wilson's intentions for 1920 did more than increase Democrats' gloom as they prepared to do battle with a reunited GOP. It also hampered and then scuttled the prenomination campaign of the front-runner of the Wilsonians, William Gibbs McAdoo.[5] The former secretary of the treasury was also Wilson's son-in-law, and he was anxious not to run across the president's ambitions. McAdoo spent 1919 and the early months of 1920 waiting for an endorsement from his father-in-law. This was not forthcoming, and McAdoo conducted his campaign in an agony of indecision and caution.[6] The former secretary's vacillation did not seem to affect his popularity; a *Literary Digest* poll undertaken during the months before the convention placed him as the clear leader among Democratic hopefuls, with over 100,000 ballots. His nearest rival was Woodrow Wilson, with 67,500.[7] The suspense proved too much, however, and McAdoo decided that it was not sensible to risk Wilson's enmity by throwing his hat in the ring. On June 18, the same day that press reports had hinted that Wilson would be a candidate, he declared his "irrevocable" decision not to allow his name to go forward. He seemed, however, to waver on the eve of the convention; the secretary would, reports suggested, be receptive to a draft.[8]

Although abortive, McAdoo's candidacy had momentous consequences for the party in the short and long terms. His rising star alarmed Democratic leaders in the Northeast and Midwest, who were determined that the nomination should go to a man who was not closely connected with the Wilson administration. McAdoo, as the best known of Wilson's cabinet and the president's son-in-law, was unacceptable to these leaders. During the early months of 1920 a discernible anti-McAdoo group began to form, led by the urban bosses with whom Wilson had uneasily coexisted since 1912.[9] Charles F. Murphy of New York, Tom Taggart of Indiana, Ed Moore of Ohio, and George Brennan of Illinois combined forces to encourage support for other candidates.[10]

These men found the prospect of McAdoo's nomination profoundly disturbing. He had earned Tammany's enmity by distributing federal patronage in New York independently of the Hall, and as a prominent Wilsonian he would be associated in the public mind with the unpopular league issue.[11] McAdoo was also a firm supporter of the newly ratified prohibition amendment, which was as unpopular as the league among urban ethnic constituencies. In addition—and most significantly for the party during the next decade—McAdoo was perceived by the urban Democrats to be tainted with radicalism. He had presided over the railroads during the period in which they were under federal management and in the process had alienated business opinion by appearing to be too partial to labor unions and to the concept of permanent federal control.[12] His support came from the West and the South, rather than from the more economically conservative East, which had championed Alton B. Parker in 1904, opposed Bryan in each of his three presidential campaigns, and exercised passive resistance to Wilson's reformist agenda after 1912.[13] McAdoo, in short, attracted a conservative backlash even before the convention met.[14]

It was under this set of inauspicious circumstances that the 1920 Democratic convention was called to order in San Francisco. The early ballots for the presidential nomination revealed three main contenders: McAdoo, whose support came from southern and western delegates; Attorney General A. Mitchell Palmer, whose nucleus of support lay in Georgia and Pennsylvania; and Governor James M. Cox of Ohio, who had become the anointed candidate of the northeastern bosses.

Like McAdoo, Palmer had been a highly visible member of the Wilson administration, having served as custodian of alien property during World War I and then as attorney general. Although he had been a thorough-going progressive as a Pennsylvania congressman between 1908 and 1914, he based his nomination campaign upon a platform of superpatriotism. To this end he could point to his notorious "Palmer raids" against suspected radicals and his sweeping injunctions against striking workers.[15] These actions earned him the enmity of labor groups, who would not hear of his nomination. The balloting ground on, with none of the three leaders able to attain two-thirds of the 1,090 convention votes necessary for nomination.[16] Finally, however, the combined votes of Ohio, Indiana, New York, and Illinois wore down the supporters of Palmer and McAdoo; Palmer withdrew after the thirty-seventh ballot, and Cox achieved a two-thirds majority on the forty-fourth. The man whose candidacy Bryan had described as a disgrace was to be the party's standard-bearer in a contest that few thought he could win.[17]

CANDIDATE JAMES M. COX

James M. Cox, whom Geoffrey Perrett described as "mildly liberal, mildly wet, mildly able," was a self-made millionaire who had built up a chain of newspapers in Ohio.[18] A great admirer of Grover Cleveland, Cox appealed most strongly to the business-orientated conservative Democrats who had deserted Bryan over the free-silver issue. "The fact that I had achieved some measure of success in the business conduct of newspapers," he noted, "inspired conservative Ohioans with a certain confidence in me. They regarded me as a 'safe' kind of liberal."[19] With such qualifications, Cox was elected to the governorship three times—in 1912, 1916, and 1918—becoming the first Ohioan to be accorded this honor. He was also one of only two Democratic incumbent governors of northeastern states who survived the Democratic electoral collapse of 1918.[20]

Cox's record as governor was a competent one, but it hardly justified his judgment of himself as a "rather advanced political progressive."[21] In many ways his gubernatorial achievements were similar to those of Al Smith in New York. Although he did push through a workman's compensation law against strong opposition from insurance companies in 1913, Cox concentrated on reforms of the governmental structure, including the revamping of the prison system, the streamlining of tax collection procedures, the installation of an executive budget, the centralizing and rationalizing of the functions of state bureaus, and the overhauling of the state's rural school system.[22] He was careful to justify these reforms in language that soothed conservatives. Reorganization of governmental procedure and structure, for example, was designed to "place the financial affairs of Ohio on a businesslike basis" and would result in a more economical government. Anxious that his party shed its antibusiness image, he urged Woodrow Wilson in 1916 to accede to business demands for the creation of a nonpartisan tariff board.[23] He espoused a strong states' rights philosophy, opposing federal worker's compensation laws and federal aid to education.[24] He firmly upheld the principle that business should be left largely alone in the conduct of its own affairs. His credentials as a conservative candidate in 1920 were strengthened by his failure to ally himself with the Wilson administration and by his opposition to national prohibition.[25] Thomas J. Walsh, the progressive Democratic senator from Montana, noted as early as May 1920 that McAdoo seemed strongest among labor groups, while Cox was "mentioned mostly by the business men."[26] When Senator Carter Glass of Virginia visited Woodrow Wilson during the convention the invalid president expostulated, "Oh! You know that Cox's nomination would be a joke."[27] All in all, Speaker Joe Cannon noted in 1920, James Cox "would make a damn good Republican if he weren't a Democrat."[28]

Although Cox was a "safe" candidate for those troubled by McAdoo's Wilsonian and reformist credentials, he was an uninspiring choice to lead the party into a desperate battle. In the words of Geoffrey Perrett, he "cut an immediately forgettable figure," and he seemed only slightly more capable than his Republican opponent.[29] H. L. Mencken was even more cutting; assessing both Harding and Cox after the conventions, the acid-tongued columnist claimed that "no one but an idiot would argue seriously that either candidate is a first-rate man, or even a creditable specimen of a second-rate man."[30] That he had also earned the opposition of liberals who had supported McAdoo, of the dries who objected to his antiprohibition past, and of Wilsonians who objected to the sabotaging of their plans by the hated bosses made Cox's task even harder.

The platform adopted at San Francisco did little to soothe the feelings of those progressive Democrats who were disenchanted by Cox's nomination. Progressives had pushed for a far-reaching reform manifesto in 1920. In 1919 Franklin Roosevelt, then Wilson's assistant secretary of the navy, put forward a set of platform recommendations which included the further development of federal farm loan policies to assist farmers, the complete reorganization of railroads under federal control, guarantees of labor's right to organize, the imposition of heavier inheritance taxes, and the use of public works programs during times of unemployment.[31] William Jennings Bryan went even further. In January 1919 he outlined a new program of reform to carry America into the postwar age, including the provision of a national highway system; the permanent federal ownership of railroads, telegraphs, and telephones; federal insurance of bank deposits; the ratification of the female suffrage amendment; and the strict enforcement of national prohibition, which was to come into force in 1920.[32]

The San Francisco platform dashed these hopes of a new reformist age for the Democratic party, and it provided further evidence that the Wilsonians and the Bryanites were losing control of the party. Although the party committed itself to the League of Nations, it also declared that "we do not oppose the acceptance of any reservations making clearer or more specific the obligations of the United States to the league associates."[33] This seemed close to the spirit of the Lodge reservations, against which the president had fought so stubbornly.

On other issues, too, the platform moved several steps from the concerns of progressives. The taxation plank promised to undertake a "searching revision" of the War Revenue Acts, with a view to reducing the level of taxation, and no mention at all was made of the future of inheritance and excess-profits taxes—measures that were close to many progressives' hearts.[34] Although the labor plank recognized that both labor and capital had an "indefeasible right of organization," the platform was careful to declare that the right to strike was in no way paramount to public welfare.[35] Cox made no explicit appeal to labor during the campaign and instead worked to reassure the electorate that no repeat of the industrial turmoil of 1919 would be tolerated.[36] Concerning the railroads, a crucial issue for those progressives who wished to see them kept under federal control, the platform counseled a "fair and complete test" of the Esch-Cummins Law, which had recently returned them to their former owners.[37]

Progressives were thrown a few sops at San Francisco. Besides lauding their previous efforts, the platform promised a "comprehensive study" of farm conditions, promised cooperative federal assistance to the states to improve educational facilities, and pledged itself to the continuation of federal aid for road-building. It was clear, however, that the party would go into the campaign with few trappings of its recent reformist past. Cox did choose Franklin Roosevelt, who had served in both of Wilson's administrations, as his running mate, but his choice seemed based more upon Roosevelt's famous name and the slim chance that he might deliver New York than upon a desire to appease progressives.[38] Although H. L. Mencken dismissed the GOP platform as one resembling "words scrawled on a wall by feeble-minded children,"[39] it was scarcely more conservative than that put forward by the Democrats.

Many reformist Democrats were disappointed in both the candidate and platform of 1920. William Jennings Bryan was alienated by Cox's acceptance speech, in which he criticized national prohibition as an effort to make the population "moral by statute." The platform's economic planks also angered Bryan; Cox's taxation policy seemed to be nothing less than a redistribution of wealth from the "consuming public" to the "profiteers."[40] Dismayed by the platform's shying away from any hint of his reform agenda, William Jennings Bryan spoke for his supporters, and many progressives besides, when he summed up his feelings after the convention. "The nomination of Governor Cox signalizes the surrender of the Democratic party into the hands of the reactionaries."[41]

Bryan was not the only prominent Democrat to express his disapproval of Cox. Even as the delegates at San Francisco were casting their ballots, word of Wilson's deprecating comments about Cox's fitness for the nomination leaked out. The candidate made an aggrieved telephone call to the White House, pointing out that he had always supported Wilson's league policy and that he deserved better. He would, he concluded, "leave it to the President's own sense of justice as to how the matter should be handled."[42] Although Wilson denied the comment, Cox received little or no help from him during the fall. Given his platform and studied distance from the administration, it is hard to see how Cox could have expected full-blooded support from Wilson, but certainly the silence from Washington was deafening.[43]

A LACKLUSTER CAMPAIGN

Largely left to their own devices by the party's established leaders, Cox and Roosevelt ran an active but incoherent campaign. The governor traveled over 22,000 miles through thirty-six states, delivering four hundred speeches, while his running mate covered 18,000 miles and spoke at a rate of ten speeches a day. Harding, in contrast, ventured from Marion, Ohio, only seven times to deliver speeches.[44] The peripatetic nature of the Democratic campaign was matched by Cox's inability to settle upon a fixed agenda of issues. He began by attacking the GOP's allegedly huge "slush fund," with which they aimed to subvert the league by buying the election. This attempt to make a virtue out of the Democrats' penury misfired when he could not substantiate his charges.[45] Cox then moved to the league and declared that he would, after all, dedicate his campaign to the achievement of the president's dream. This conversion was said to have come about after Cox and Roosevelt visited the ailing Wilson in the White House, but the candidate always claimed that it represented a personal conviction rather than a tribute to a president who had snubbed him.[46]

Cox's strategy was to build upon the electoral votes of the South, which were considered safely Democratic, with those of any northern and eastern states which could be won over. This strategy, which was to be repeated in the presidential elections of 1924 and 1928, was a modification of the Gilded Age Democratic strategy of concentrating upon the "swing states" of Ohio, Indiana, and New York and adding them to the solid South.[47] It was in sharp contrast to the Wilsonian electoral strategy of combining southern and western electoral votes into a majority. In 1920 it was hoped that Roosevelt could win New York and New Jersey; Cox had a chance in Ohio, and perhaps in its neighboring states through the efforts of Taggart in Indiana and Brennan in Illinois. These northern states were considered to be hostile to prohibition, and Cox steadfastly refused to make any declaration of support for the Eighteenth Amendment in the hope of winning votes in these areas. This represented an abandonment of the West, which was predominantly dry, and with it any hope of winning Bryan's support. Thomas L. Chadbourne, long a supporter of Bryan and one of McAdoo's backers for the nomination, implored Cox to support the rigorous enforcement of the new amendment. "I do not believe you will win New York or New Jersey," Chadbourne wrote Cox in September 1920; "your chances lie in the Middle and Western states. . . . Why, then, not make this appeal to the West when it is sound and right?"[48]

Robert Woolley joined the chorus of Wilsonians protesting the abandonment of the electoral coalition which had served the party so well in the previous presidential election. Woolley warned Cox at the outset of the campaign that he should not be "deluded" into thinking that he had a chance to carry either New York or New Jersey. "Of course, we must go through the motions, but no money should be risked. We have got to win this fight where we won it in 1916."[49] Cox was unmoved, reasoning that the West was lost to the Democrats, and instead staked his hopes on an appeal to the East. When he found time to elucidate his economic program, he stayed true to both his strategy and his personal predilections. His calls for the minimum of governmental interference in business and for the replacement of the excess-profits tax by a sales tax were scarcely designed to appeal to the sulking Bryanites and Republican progressives of the West.[50]

Cox's campaign was to some extent the victim of its own inconsistencies. Although they had earlier agreed that the West was unsympathetic to their cause, Cox and Roosevelt made two trips each through the region, extolling the league, despite warnings that it was an unpopular subject there. Steve Early, FDR's advance man in the West, reported from Washington State that the league was a dead issue because "the Republican propaganda has been most effective." The candidates' strong stand on the league had identified them, ironically enough, with Wilson, who was extremely unpopular because of his agricultural policy.[51] Undeterred, Cox proceeded to link these unpopular issues by declaring that crop prices were low because of the Republicans' failure to allow the United States into the league.[52] When the votes were finally counted, Cox did not win a single electoral vote in the eighteen western states.[53]

The campaign in the East was equally beset with contradiction. Although Cox's attitude toward prohibition was designed to appeal to ethnic voters, his stress upon the league further inflamed their resentment of the terms of the treaty, causing defections that far outweighed any gains that he might have made over prohibition. In so doing, he alienated the only power base he had outside the solid South: the same urban bosses who had made his nomination possible became increasingly concerned lest the league cause a revolt among their constituencies. In order to protect their own power, Murphy, Taggart, and Brennan began to distance themselves from the national ticket and concentrated instead on electing their local candidates. Charles H. McCarthy, FDR's campaign manager, warned his boss in early October that Tammany Hall was sitting on its hands and that "if they have not sent out the word to lay down they might as well do it, because not even a meeting in Brooklyn or New York City has been called by them."[54] Reporting to FDR on a visit to New Jersey the following week, McCarthy noted that everywhere he went in the state the democratic leaders "taboo the discussion of the League. . . . Of course, I refused to discuss anything but the league."[55] It was no wonder that Louis Howe, stationed in Washington as assistant to the assistant secretary of the navy, complained fretfully at the end of September that "I can't make head or tail about this madhouse of a campaign."[56]

The organizational weakness of Cox's campaign was also debilitating. Although the governor inherited a national organization which had been idle from 1918, the Cox forces did little to revivify it.[57] The candidate's choice for chairman of the Democratic National Committee (DNC), George White, was a loyal supporter but an ineffective organizer. The campaign began badly at the DNC. Homer Cummings, who had been chairman before the San Francisco convention, offered to remain in that post for the duration of the campaign. It was only after some weeks that Cox decided to replace him with White.[58] Funds were slow to come in, due partly to the disaffection of wealthy Wilsonians and the defeatism of the rank and file. Louis Antisdale, a wealthy donor who was editor of the *Rochester* (New York) *Herald*, replied to FDR's appeal for funds in June of 1920 by declaring that he would not consider assisting "the incompetent, dishonorable and wholly discredited organization known as the Democratic National Committee." Cox and Roosevelt would have as much chance of victory, Antisdale concluded, if "the National Committee were to close its offices and permanently disband."[59] Joe Tumulty, who had been Wilson's postmaster general, bluntly informed Cox that "the campaign, so far as the National organization is concerned, is a complete and tragic failure."[60]

Cox's campaign exacerbated these difficulties. In September Robert Woolley, Democratic national committeeman from Washington, D.C., cabled the candidate that it would be "only with the greatest difficulty" that the campaign headquarters in New York could be kept open until

November. The party's wealthy benefactors, and especially Thomas Fortune Ryan and Cleveland Dodge, were reluctant to support the campaign unless Cox came out definitely against any modification of the Volstead Act. "In God's name," Woolley concluded, "at this eleventh hour please heed an earnest warning. You must realize moral forces arraying against us means disaster."[61] Cox remained silent, and by election day the Democrats had raised only $900,000, far short of the Republican war chest of $8,000,000.[62] Charles McCarthy reported to FDR that "the real work around Headquarters . . . is being done by the revolving electric sign which has the pictures of Cox and Roosevelt on it. . . . When all is said and done you cannot win an election without money."[63]

Although affairs at the New York headquarters were bad, they were worse at the western headquarters at San Francisco. Here, Nevada senator Key Pittman oversaw the campaign in the huge area encompassed by all the states west of Kansas. By the middle of September, he had received just $10,000 from the national committee, necessitating the use of his own funds to meet the payroll.[64] At the end of his tether, Pittman closed his western headquarters on September 30, effectively conceding that region to Harding.[65] If Cox was to win, he told White, it would have to be in New York, New Jersey, Ohio, Indiana, and Missouri.[66]

In such fashion the Cox campaign limped to election day. Torn apart by ideological differences before the campaign had even begun, handicapped by underfunded and incompetent management, and scuttled by an illogical strategy, the Democrats could scarcely hope for victory. The final indignity came on the very day of the election. Reporting to work on the morning of November 2, workers at the national campaign headquarters in Manhattan's Grand Central Palace found themselves locked out. The national committee had defaulted on its rent.[67]

ANALYSIS OF THE DEMOCRATIC DEFEAT

With hindsight, Democrats tended to point to two reasons for their defeat. At first they blamed foreign policy for the party's poor showing. "The truth is," Josephus Daniels declared of Harding's victory, which had cost him his job as secretary of the navy, "that we lost the election in Paris." The great blocs of ethnic voters—the Irish, the Germans, and the Italians—had all been offended either by American involvement in World War I or by the peace treaty which followed.[68] This disaffection began in the presidential election of 1916, during which Irish and German voters, upset at what they saw as the pro-British bent of Wilson's foreign policy, refused to support the Democracy with their usual enthusiasm.[69]

This interpretation provided the standard explanation for the defeat of 1920 among both Democrats and their historians for many years. James M. Cox remembered his campaign in defeatist terms. Because of the ethnic disaffection with Wilson, Cox argued in his memoirs, "no matter what the candidates might say or do, the die was cast."[70] In Missouri, the state treasurer of the party reported that on election day in LaFayette County, "Every German who was eligible to vote and could walk, crawl or be carried to the polls marked his ballot. . . . The result was not only a Republican victory in 1920, but a permanent transference of the county to the Republican column."[71]

This explosion of anger was most damaging to the Democrats in the heavily ethnic urban electorates in the Northeast. In Massachusetts, for instance, Irish and Italian voters, the backbone of the Bay State's Democracy, simply went on strike. Harding won the state by over 680,000 votes, leaving Cox with a mere 28.9 percent of the two-party vote. Cox won only 39.7 percent in Boston, and 29 percent in Massachusett's other thirty-eight cities. Although Wilson had not carried the state in 1916, he had won 48 percent of the state vote and had won Boston with 60.2 percent.[72] In New York City predominantly immigrant districts which had given Wilson 49.3 percent of their votes in 1916 gave Cox only 19.9 percent. Germans, who had voted 57 percent for Wilson in 1916, gave Cox only 28 percent; the Democrats' share of Irish New York votes dropped from 64 percent to 47 percent, and their share of the Italian vote declined from 63 percent to 47 percent. Among Jewish voters the drop was even more precipitous: 55 percent supported Wilson, but only 19 percent voted for Cox.[73] In Chicago Cox failed to win a majority of any major ethnic group's votes, with the exception of the Lithuanians, who gave him 53 percent.[74] "What we will do in this land of mixed peoples is a problem," wrote Wilson's secretary of interior Franklin K. Lane after the election, "Our policies now are to be determined by Fiume and Ireland—not by real home concerns."[75]

A second explanation was also put forward for the defeat of 1920. As William Jennings Bryan was quick to remind the party, the presidential election of 1916 was won in the West and the South, sections where immigrant and first-generation voters were fewest.[76] Wilson, indeed, won a second term without the benefit of the electoral votes of New York, Illinois, Michigan, New Jersey, Pennsylvania, or Massachusetts. As David Sarasohn has shown, the winning Democratic coalition of 1916 had a "deceptively rural complexion" because of Irish and German defections in the cities and the popularity of Wilsonian progressivism in areas outside the Northeast.[77] Recognition of this fact gave rise to a different theory as to why the Democrats lost so badly in 1920. Instead of foreign policy, more recent historians have stressed domestic economic policy as the prime contributor to the landslide that buried James Cox.[78]

The years 1917–19 witnessed an erosion of Democratic support in the West, due chiefly to the vagaries of Wilson's agricultural policy. By controlling the price of wheat while allowing cotton prices to rise with increasing wartime demand, Wilson alienated western growers.[79] On August 30, 1917, the price of wheat was fixed at $2.20 per bushel in Chicago, even though prices at that time were well above that figure. In 1918 the price was set at $2.00, further inflaming wheat growers, who were convinced that their produce could fetch up to $5.00 per bushel on an open market.[80] In the congressional elections of 1918, voters in the ten largest wheat states voted in twenty-two new GOP candidates and only two new Democrats.[81] The southern and western coalition was shattered, and Democratic fortunes sank further through the loss of northeastern and midwestern industrial workers' support because of the economic dislocation stemming from World War I. Retail prices doubled between 1915 and 1920, and the cost of living in 1920 was 102 percent above that of 1914.[82] Although rapid demobilization and the cancellation of war orders did not create acute unemployment immediately after the war, by October 1920 at least four million workers had lost their jobs.[83] The great strikes of 1919 were the result; 3,600 stoppages in that year directly affected more than four million workers.[84] Seattle was gripped by a general strike; Boston suffered a police strike. In September 300,000 steelworkers walked out, and in November northern bituminous coal miners struck.[85]

The shift of western and midwestern voters away from the Democrats in 1920 was as dramatic as that of ethnic metropolitan voters. Of the 105 congressional races in the Midwest, Democratic candidates won only 3, and only 5 of the 53 contests in the West in 1920.[86] In Colorado, Cox's 35.9 percent of the total vote was nearly 25 percent below that given to Wilson four years before, and in California he lost over 22 percent. In Ohio, Michigan, Iowa, and Kansas Cox ran between 15 and 22 percent behind Wilson. In the twelve states of the Midwest (those lying between Ohio and Kansas), Cox's 29.8 percent share was well below the 46.9 percent garnered by Wilson. In the thirteen western states the difference was even more striking: Wilson secured 51.1 percent there in 1916, while Cox could muster only 29.8 per cent in 1920.[87]

This combination of eastern, midwestern, and western disaffection spelled disaster for the Democrats: Cox won only 38.8 percent of the national vote to Harding's 55.5 percent and lost every state west of the Mississippi except Texas.[88] Even the solid South showed a crack. Cox and his running mate Franklin Roosevelt lost Tennessee and won Kentucky by a mere four thousand votes. The party's Senate and House tickets did somewhat better, running 8 and 4 percent respectively ahead of Cox, although the party suffered a net loss of fifty-nine seats in the House. The Democratic share of the House votes nationwide was 42.3 percent, while those of Democratic senatorial candidates was 46.7 percent. In 1916, by contrast, Democrats had won 51.2 percent of the votes cast for House candidates and 49.7 percent of the Senate vote.[89]

Although this tale of Democratic woe has been told with increasing detail and analytic sophistication by historians, other questions regarding the impact of this defeat upon the party and the balance of power between regional and ideological groups within it have received little attention. Yet the nature and outcome of the 1920 campaign were to have profound effects upon the conduct of the national party organization for the next twelve years. Cox's nomination and defeat hastened the disintegration of the Wilsonian group which had steered the party to two successive presidential victories. These Wilsonians—among them the president himself and such luminaries of his cabinet as Newton D. Baker, William Gibbs McAdoo, Josephus Daniels, and Homer Cummings—occupied the highest positions of authority and influence within the party. They had succeeded in controlling the party's ideological direction for eight years, and in the process they had shepherded an impressive agenda of banking, tariff, and social reform into law. Until 1918 their power within the party had seemed secure, and their ability to influence the party's platform and candidacies in 1920 went largely unquestioned.

By 1920, however, much of this power and influence had gone. Cox's campaign completed the collapse of the Wilsonian alliance of West and South. The poor showing of the western Democracy left in its wake demoralized organizations which proved incapable of wooing back voters, even in the face of declining farm prices throughout the following ten years. William Jennings Bryan had crowed in 1916 that the presidential election of that year had been won "BY THE WEST AND SOUTH WITHOUT THE AID OR CONSENT OF THE EAST. The scepter has passed from New York, and that is sufficient glory for one year."[90]

In 1920, the scepter was passed back, for although the eastern Democrats had also suffered a setback, they would soon regain the allegiance of the ethnic voters who had deserted them under the pressure of issues arising from the war and the League of Nations. When those voters returned in the 1922 elections, the eastern wing of the party regained and then augmented its strength. From that time on, the party was dominated by the ever-present southern wing and a growing eastern wing.[91] The consequences of this change were far-reaching. The strategy of forming a coalition of East and South, attempted in a chaotic and contradictory way in 1920, would be repeated in 1924 and 1928. With this new alignment came a new leadership group whose electoral base lay in the growing urban centers of the Northeast, and whose political ideology reflected the concerns of urban finance capitalism rather than those of western rural activism. Concomitantly, those Democratic leaders whose power lay in western and southern regions, and whose political agenda reflected the issues and causes of their constituencies, suffered a diminution of prestige and power during the following decade. No one demonstrated this process more clearly than the crown prince of the Wilsonians, William Gibbs McAdoo.

2

THE RISE AND FALL OF

WILLIAM GIBBS McADOO

1920–1928

Apart from Woodrow Wilson, William Gibbs McAdoo was the most prominent Democrat in the United States in 1920. He had been ubiquitous in the Wilson administration and had been associated with the most successful of the Democratic policies between 1912 and 1920. McAdoo, it seemed, was the great success story of the administration. He was reputed to have Wilson's ear on all major issues and was even the president's son-in-law. There seemed little doubt that he was the heir apparent to the control of the party that Wilson would relinquish in March 1921.

Despite their promise, however, the 1920s were years of disappointment and frustration for McAdoo. His two campaigns for the presidential nomination failed, and even his attempts to be a promoter of nominations came to nothing. Despite his prominence and national following he failed to influence the ideological direction of the national party. Historians have generally held that he was largely responsible for his own decline. John M. Blum described him as a "victim of his own ambition," who "curdled his own disposition and integrity."[1] Newton Baker admired his former cabinet colleague for his energy and drive but worried about his ruthless use of any power that came his way.[2] In search of political power and money, this argument has it, McAdoo was fatally undiscriminating. He accepted a huge retainer from oilman Edward Doheny and so became embroiled in the Teapot Dome scandal; he courted the Ku Klux Klan in his bid for the nomination in 1924 and thereby allied himself with a poisonous influence in American life. McAdoo, in short, squandered his preeminent position in the party through his own greed.

Yet if McAdoo's fall can be explained solely by the company he kept, how was it that Al Smith could prosper so spectacularly, despite his close alliance with the unsavory Tammany Hall? McAdoo's involvement with both the oil scandal and the KKK may have been unethical, but it was not illegal. Why were they fatal to his political career while Smith, although openly breaking the nation's prohibition laws, prospered? The answer lies in the ideological and cultural divisions within the party during the 1920s. McAdoo, to be sure, was hampered by his own lack of discretion and by his political expediency, yet the causes for his decline lay deeper than his personal failings. As a prominent Wilsonian and self-proclaimed leader of the progressive Democrats of the South and West, the secretary found himself on the losing side of the battle for control of the Democratic party that raged during the years between the presidencies of Woodrow Wilson and Franklin Roosevelt. McAdoo was the most famous political casualty of the ideological struggle that rent the party during the 1920s. His rise and fall thus provides insight into the nature of that conflict.

SECRETARY OF THE TREASURY

William McAdoo was born in Marietta, Georgia, in 1863. His parents were loyal Confederates, and they paid for that allegiance soon after William's birth. Sherman's army destroyed the family plantation on its march through Georgia, plunging the family into severe poverty. In 1877 the family moved to Knoxville, where McAdoo's father was appointed professor of history and English at the University of Tennessee. McAdoo himself attended that institution and then trained for the law. He was admitted to the Tennessee bar in 1885.[3] As a young man, he quickly demonstrated the entrepreneurial and acquisitive traits that would contribute both to his making and to his downfall in later years. An avid promoter of urban transit development, he risked all his savings in a street railway venture in Knoxville in 1889. After the failure of this scheme in 1892, the young lawyer moved to New York City. His fortunes thereafter rose quickly in the city which he would later condemn as "rooted in corruption, directed by greed and dominated by selfishness."[4]

Although he resumed the practice of law in New York, McAdoo's interests still lay in urban transit. The half-completed railroad tunnels underneath the Hudson River, designed to connect New Jersey with Manhattan, attracted his attention. Construction had begun in 1874, but a cave-in six years later had forced their abandonment. A second attempt in 1890 pushed the tunnels to within two thousand feet of completion before the depression of 1893 brought down their promoters.[5] In 1900 McAdoo resolved to complete the job. By assiduous promotion he raised the necessary funds from such industrial titans as E. C. Converse and E. H. Gary of U.S. Steel, and on March 4, 1904, the first tunnel reached Manhattan. McAdoo, who had arrived almost penniless from Tennessee only eleven years before, now found himself president of the New York and Jersey Railroad Company at a salary of $50,000 a year.[6]

Before 1910 McAdoo's chief political interest was in the fight for women's rights. His New York and Jersey Railroad instituted equal pay for women, and he was active on behalf of New York teachers in the same cause.[7] He was much taken by Theodore Roosevelt, despite his fears that TR's policies were insufficiently punitive of trusts. "All the powers of the nation," he believed, "should be exerted to preserve competitive conditions."[8] By 1911 he had transferred his loyalties to Woodrow Wilson. He went to work as a Wilson fund-raiser in 1911 and 1912 and managed to collect, on his own estimation, $200,000.[9] At the Baltimore convention of 1912 he was one of the few Wilson supporters in the New York delegation, defying Tammany Hall and its strong preference for Champ Clark.[10] He was rewarded by his appointment as secretary of the treasury after the election.

"Not since the time of Washington and Hamilton," McAdoo's campaign biographer declared in 1924, "had there been the combination of a great President and a great Secretary of the Treasury."[11] The Federal Reserve Act was a landmark of Wilson's first administration, and the secretary played a prominent role in its passage and implementation. He portrayed the act as a great democratic advance which stripped the titans of Wall Street of their financial supremacy and returned to the people control of their economic destiny.[12] McAdoo assumed the role of crusader against the power of these vested interests; convinced that the New York banks were purposely depressing the value of U.S. Treasury Bonds, he publicly excoriated them for defying the will of the people.[13] With characteristic exuberance, he portrayed himself as the champion of the people against the forces of greed and plutocracy. "There has been going on since I have had this office a titanic struggle," he wrote in 1914, "with certain selfish interests in this country, a struggle which . . . is just as essential . . . [to] make as it was to fight the War of 1861 for the preservation of the Union."[14]

McAdoo seized every opportunity to promote himself during World War I. He seemed to be everywhere during 1917 and 1918: secretary of the treasury, director of the Liberty Loan drive, ex officio head of the Federal Reserve Bank, supervisor of the Farm Loan banks, manager of the soldiers' insurance scheme, head of the Public Health Service, and director general of the railroads. "The greatest son-in-law on Earth," ran a popular ditty of the time, "I don't believe he ever hid/A single thing he ever did."[15] He undertook several national Liberty Loan tours, which brought him into contact with Americans in every section of the nation. He continued his "titanic struggle" with Wall Street by his insistence that half the cost of the war should be met through taxation revenues, rather than from the issue of bonds, which not only would pay interest to wealthy investors but also would transfer the cost of the war to the next generation.[16] In this he was only partially successful; bonds accounted for two-thirds of the funds for the war effort.[17] Yet McAdoo had again been ostensibly associated with the interests of the average American against those of the large bankers and investment houses.

The war provided opportunities for McAdoo to apply his faith in the efficacy of state intervention in the economy. American dependence upon the British merchant marine, for example, became painfully obvious almost as soon as England began to requisition her ships for her own war effort. The U.S. merchant marine was far too small to transport the belligerents' war needs across the Atlantic. At the end of 1914 McAdoo proposed that the federal government establish a shipping corporation to purchase, construct, and operate cargo vessels. Although his first proposal involved total government ownership of this corporation, he later modified his scheme to allow for a minority of its stock to be held by private interests.[18] Refusing to heed the accusations of private shipowners, who attacked his proposal as socialistic, McAdoo went on a national speaking tour to argue the merits of his idea. The Shipping Board Bill was finally shepherded through Congress in 1915 and signed by the president in September.[19]

The secretary's greatest wartime contribution, however, came during his tenure as railroad commissioner. During the severe winter of 1917–18 the railroads almost ground to a halt, starving the eastern seaboard of much-needed war materials.[20] The railroad operators refused to integrate their lines so as to facilitate the movement of goods, and some even refused to open their lines to the locomotives of rival lines. The federal government came under increasing pressure from agricultural shippers, the military departments, and the railroad brotherhoods to take over the entire system. On December 5, 1917, the Interstate Commerce Commission formally recommended a federal takeover, prompting Wilson to act. He announced that the government would assume control of the railroads effective January 1, 1918, and that McAdoo would oversee the whole operation.[21]

As railroad commissioner, McAdoo had control over a nationwide transportation network which employed 1.8 million people on a bewildering array of lines. Working at feverish pace, he restored order to the chaos that he had inherited and then set about using his enormous power to bring reforms to the railroad system. Federal control of the railroads, he hoped, would serve as a demonstration of the efficacy of governmental intervention to solve problems which had proved insurmountable to private enterprise.[22] As an adept politician, too, he saw how his responsibilities as commissioner could create a power base for his political future.

Accordingly, he set about improving the conditions of employment for railroad workers. His General Order No. 8 of 1918 forbade discrimination against employees because of membership in labor organizations, and General Order No. 27 increased wages by 40 percent at the lower end of the pay scales, with smaller raises for higher-paid workers. General Order No. 27 also instituted equal pay for equal work for the railroads' female and black workers. By the end of the war railroad employees enjoyed the benefits of an eight hour day, time and a half for overtime, and recognition of collective bargaining.[23] These reforms made McAdoo the hero of organized labor, and they won him the admiration of progressives everywhere. Here, they thought, was government activism and reform at its best: combining efficiency with humanitarianism and economic justice. Even Walter Lippmann, no admirer of the secretary, conceded in 1920 that "his administration of the railroads will probably be regarded as a piece of heroic and successful intervention in one of the worst crises of the war."[24]

McAdoo resigned from the administration at the end of 1918, citing his desire to earn more money. It is likely, however, that Wilson's increasing unpopularity contributed to his decision to leave. If the administration's ship was to sink, McAdoo had no desire to be on board.[25] Consequently he avoided involvement in the League of Nations fight and maintained his high reputation with labor by distancing himself from the administration during the bitter labor disputes of 1919.

UNDER A CLOUD OF SCANDAL

The outcome of the San Francisco convention in 1920 convinced McAdoo that his political future did not lie in New York. Tammany's opposition to him meant that he could not hope to build a political foundation for a national candidacy in that city. It ill behooved one who wished to continue the Bryanite and Wilsonian coalition, furthermore, to center his operations in New York. He moved to California in 1922 and set up a law practice in Los Angeles.[26] From his new base of operations in the West, the Georgia-born and Tennessee-raised McAdoo set out to unite his new section and the South against the "reactionary East."

In contrast to 1920, there was never any doubt that he would be a candidate in 1924. Between 1921 and 1924 he busied himself in activating his network of supporters in preparation for his preconvention campaign.[27]

In this he was assisted by a group of lieutenants led by Daniel Roper of Washington, D.C., who had served as assistant secretary of the treasury under Wilson; Thomas Chadbourne, a New York lawyer; David Ladd Rockwell from New York; Hollins Randolph from Georgia; and George Fort Milton of Tennessee. Bernard Baruch and Chadbourne provided the funds necessary for disseminating publicity and organizing delegate slates.[28] So efficient was this group in drumming up support for their candidate that McAdoo was able to concentrate upon building up his law practice. Particularly helpful was an annual retainer of $25,000 from Edward L. Doheny to act as "special counsel."[29]

At first it seemed as if the McAdoo forces could do no wrong. The size of Cox's defeat in 1920 strengthened McAdoo's position because Cox's avowedly eastern candidacy was widely perceived as a reason for his failure. The McAdoo strategy between 1921 and 1924 was to point to his progressive credentials, national prominence, and strong support from organized labor. He was also the favorite of the still-powerful prohibitionists.[30] A *Literary Digest* poll of Democratic senators, congressmen, governors, mayors, and other officeholders taken in June 1923 confirmed that he could look to 1924 with confidence; of the 2,000 ballots received, 706 showed the secretary as first choice, as opposed to 231 for Henry Ford, 204 for Oscar Underwood, and 128 for Al Smith.[31] A wider poll conducted by *Collier's Magazine* at the same time showed that among ordinary voters McAdoo ran behind only Harding and Henry Ford as the most desirable presidential timber in the field. Harding's death in August 1923 and Ford's declaration for Coolidge at the end of the year left McAdoo as the Democratic front-runner.[32] "Nearly everything" west of the Mississippi, the *Louisville Post* reported in September 1923, was "McAdoo country," and the South was equally promising.[33]

Campaign headquarters under David Ladd Rockwell were established in Chicago, and generous donations from Baruch and Chadbourne ensured that the preconvention campaign had adequate funding.[34] Nearly five hundred delegates were assumed to be for McAdoo even before the first primary ballots were cast, and 60 percent of the DNC were thought to be supporters.[35] "Unless there is some radical change," McAdoo wrote his friend Claude Bowers on January 11, 1924, "I think that the outcome of the Convention is not at all in doubt."[36] On the same day David Rockwell wrote his boss from headquarters that "everything is going extremely well, and if there is any fear in the matter it is that things look too good."[37]

But it would be Rockwell's doubts rather than McAdoo's hopes that would be realized during the first half of 1924. The candidacies of Al Smith and James Cox were making inroads into the Northeast, making it increasingly unlikely that McAdoo could win the necessary two-thirds majority at the convention. Since both Smith and Cox were avowedly anti-McAdoo candidates, a deadlock seemed inevitable. The selection of New York as the convention city came as another blow to the McAdoo camp; the candidate himself described the city as "an environment naturally hostile to me, so far as big business and Wall Street influence is concerned."[38] To compound these setbacks, the death of Woodrow Wilson on February 3, 1924, removed any hope that McAdoo might have entertained that his recalcitrant father-in-law would endorse his candidacy.[39]

The most devastating blow, however, came from the sensational developments in the Teapot Dome scandal that emerged in the first days of February 1924.[40] Edward L. Doheny admitted to bribing secretary of interior Albert Fall in order to win the right to tap the naval oil reserves at Teapot Dome, Wyoming. Under questioning from Republican senator Irvine Lenroot of Wisconsin, Doheny also revealed the existence of the retainer that McAdoo had accepted in 1922.[41] Lenroot's questions had been fed to him by James A. Reed of Missouri. Although a Democrat, Reed was a conservative and a bitter opponent of McAdoo. The timing of Doheny's revelations, just before the primary season, created a strong feeling in the McAdoo camp that Reed had tried to sabotage the secretary's campaign.[42] Reed had announced his own candidacy for the nomination a few days previously.[43]

The secretary responded to these revelations in a less than forthright manner. On February 7 McAdoo explained that Doheny had originally retained his firm of McAdoo, Cotton, and Franklin in 1919, shortly after he had resigned from the cabinet, and that his personal retainer had been activated after he had moved to California.[44] He rightly pointed out that his relationship with Doheny concerned only the oilman's Mexican properties and that he had had nothing to do with the illegal transactions concerning Teapot Dome. McAdoo's task was to persuade the U.S. government to use its influence with Mexico to prevent the nationalization of its oil resources, some of which were owned by Doheny. It seemed more plausible, however, that Doheny was more interested in McAdoo's ability as an influence peddler than as a lawyer. This suspicion was strengthened by McAdoo's failure to disclose that his contract with Doheny included the prospect of a "contingency fee" of $900,000 in the event that his work was successful. McAdoo's total fee from Doheny could thus have exceeded $1 million, far larger than the $100,000 which Albert Fall had received. This emerged after he had claimed to have disclosed all the relevant facts of his arrangement with Doheny.[45]

The fact that McAdoo's name was now so prominently associated with the Teapot Dome scandal had worrying implications for the party in the event of his nomination. With the nonfarm economy booming in 1924, unemployment declining, and purchasing power of wages increasing, it appeared that Republican corruption would be the major, and perhaps the only, weapon in the Democrats' arsenal during the coming campaign.[46] Doheny's revelations meant that the scandal now involved both parties, severely limiting its effectiveness for the Democrats.[47] If the Democratic candidate was implicated even indirectly in Teapot Dome, the party's major issue would be lost. McAdoo had become vulnerable not only on grounds of personal character but also in terms of electoral viability.

Subsequent developments further weakened McAdoo's ability to run a strong campaign against corruption in the federal government. In March and April of 1924 reports emerged that the secretary had accepted employment which involved arguing cases before the Treasury Department during 1920. This was so soon after his resignation as secretary of the treasury as to arouse suspicions of influence peddling.[48] This, again, did not contravene the law, but it seemed improper. Thomas J. Walsh, who had once thought that McAdoo could rise above the Doheny revelations, considered that McAdoo had further compromised himself and that "it was most unfortunate that you accepted such employment."[49] The combined effect of the Doheny retainer and McAdoo's appearance in tax cases, the Montanan believed, was to create "a load too heavy for you or your friends to carry."[50]

Walsh was not alone in his criticism of McAdoo's conduct. Many Democrats expressed great reservations about the secretary's character and his fitness for the presidency. Some even doubted that he was a committed progressive. Professor William Dodd of Harvard considered him to be a demagogue, arguing in 1925 that "McAdoo is not a genuine progressive, never having thought out social problems. He is simply ambitious and able and willing to be progressive."[51] Walter Lippmann shared Dodd's feeling that McAdoo's primary motivation was not political principle but popular opinion. Noting that the secretary was seldom at the forefront of thorny and unpopular issues, Lippmann concluded that "he is not fundamentally moved by the simple moralities. He is liberal but worldly, he is brave but not selfless."[52] With backhanded praise, Lippmann summed McAdoo up as "a statesman grafted upon a promoter."[53]

There was, indeed, something disingenuous about William Gibbs McAdoo. He never ceased to refer to his small town origins in Georgia and his ties to the old South, using these as qualifications for his long crusade against "Wall Street," yet he had spent thirty years as a corporate lawyer in New York. Although he never hesitated to proclaim his heartfelt commitment to Woodrow Wilson and progressive reform, he resigned from the cabinet at a time when the ailing president was under political siege from all quarters and in desperate need of support from his appointees. George Creel spoke for many of his colleagues when he declared to Daniels that "Mac has never been largely concerned in anybody but himself."[54]

McADOO'S ECONOMIC PLATFORM

Although many of his opponents doubted the secretary's commitment to his professed political principles, McAdoo did put forward a coherent and distinctive plan for the party's future. This vision diverged markedly from those offered by more conservative Democrats such as James Cox and Al Smith. McAdoo's political philosophy was based upon two interrelated premises: that he was the proper guardian of the reformist legacies left to the party by William Jennings Bryan and Woodrow Wilson, and that his natural constituencies were in the West and the South. These groups, he thought, could be united by a reformist program developed from the one which had swept Wilson to power in 1912 and 1916. "In the alignment between the West and the South," his friend Daniel C. Roper had written to Wilson in 1916, "we have united the two real Democratic sections of the country and eliminated the plutocracy of wealth."[55] McAdoo set out to repeat that feat.

McAdoo saw in the 1920s ample cause to rededicate the party to the removal of economic privilege. This theme was almost as old as the party itself, conjuring up memories as diverse as Jackson's fight against the Bank of the United States, Bryan's populist crusade against the trusts, and Wilson's New Freedom. While John Davis and Al Smith, his rivals for the 1924 nomination, invoked Thomas Jefferson's dicta of minimalist government and local autonomy, McAdoo preferred to remind the party of Andrew Jackson's use of governmental power to further the cause of economic justice.[56]

The secretary's most serious contribution to the debate as to the meaning of Jefferson to the Democrats' future direction came in 1926. In a speech to the Co-operative Club International at Des Moines, Iowa, he provided a tightly reasoned and often brilliant interpretation of the legacy of this Democratic idol. In so doing, he launched a frontal attack upon the conservative eastern Democrats' uses of Jeffersonian thought to justify their own agenda for the party. Given McAdoo's aim of providing a theoretical rebuttal of the political philosophies of James Cox, John Davis, and Al Smith, it was fitting that the secretary's talk was entitled "States' Rights and the Jeffersonian Idea."

McAdoo began his speech by discussing the paramount importance of cooperation in modern industrial society. The advent of railroads, the telegraph, and large-scale manufacturing had tied formerly isolated and autonomous regional and economic groups together into an integrated national economy. This interdependence had created a corporatist society in which economic and social interest groups had organized themselves to maximize their economic and political power. Individual companies had merged to form national corporations; farmers had organized into producer groups and the "farm bloc" in Congress to try to buttress crop prices; workers had developed trade unions to represent them more forcefully in the workplace. "So long as the principle of co-operation is not adopted by any group or interest in the community," McAdoo argued, "that group or interest will be at the mercy of other and better organized interests."[57]

What was to be done if some groups, by reason of their small size or geographic dispersion, could not effectively organize themselves to protect their economic or political interests? McAdoo argued that the federal government should prevent the exploitation of such groups. Because society was interdependent, the economic health of the whole nation depended upon fair and equal interaction between its component parts. This was a legitimate function for government to perform, since government was "merely the servant of the people for their common purpose." Of all

American statesmen, Thomas Jefferson best understood this fundamental tenet of republicanism.

In McAdoo's opinion, Thomas Jefferson was both the most profound and the most misunderstood of American philosophers. His thought had fallen victim to partisanship and willful misinterpretation by conservatives uneasy with the implications of the sweeping language of the Declaration of Independence. Although the sage of Monticello "is often represented today as a dogmatic believer in a theory of governmental inactivity," this was not a fair representation of his views. Such a view stemmed from a failure to appreciate the political and economic context of Jefferson's day, and from an unwarranted conflation of economic and political rights.

Jefferson wrote and practiced political theory during a time when government was not yet fully democratic. Suffrage was limited, and the organs of government were subject to the control of small but powerful economic cliques. Furthermore, the preindustrial America of his day did not require the same degree of interdependence and cooperation that modern industrial societies demanded. In an empty land people could realistically be presumed able to protect their own economic and political interests without governmental assistance. In the modern world, however, this presumption was no longer valid, since each man was now "economically dependent upon thousands of other men who he has never even seen or heard of, and upon whom, as an individual, he can bring no pressure to bear for his own protection." Individualism, as Thomas Jefferson knew it and Democrats like John W. Davis imagined it, was dead.

Would Jefferson persist in his dislike of governmental action if he were alive in the modern world? To McAdoo this was inconceivable because Jefferson himself distinguished between the "political and civil liberties" of men and their economic liberties. Political liberties—the rights of free speech, religion, and assembly—were still best protected by prohibitions upon governmental interference. The protection of economic rights, however, "frequently requires an interference with the economic activities of some." McAdoo did not define what these economic rights were, but he implied that they involved the protection of the economically weak against those who might oppress them by their superior economic resources. The degree of governmental interference necessary to protect the people's "economic rights" was "purely relative to the needs of each specific situation," but it was clear that "it increases in direct ration [sic] with the integration of national commerce and industry." McAdoo believed that Jefferson never intended that his dictum that civil rights were best protected by governmental inaction should be extended to matters concerning economic rights.

How could Jefferson condone federal activism while remaining true to his belief in the reserved powers of the individual states? Again, McAdoo argued, it was necessary to remember the context of Jefferson's time and to bear in mind the distinction between political and economic rights. Jefferson's strong adherence to states' rights sprang from the Federalists' attempt to foist the Alien and Sedition Acts upon the states. In the economic sphere, however, things were very different. In a direct rebuttal of the states' rights arguments put forward by the business conservatives and antiprohibitionists of the eastern wing of his own party, McAdoo argued that Jefferson "would have been the last man to invoke it . . . as a protection for great interstate monopolies or for great systems of national traffic of an anti-social character with which the individual states are impotent to cope."

Jefferson and his colleagues who founded the nation knew better than the conservatives of McAdoo's day who clung to the doctrine of states' rights as a protection against federal regulation of business. By including the commerce power in the Constitution, the Founding Fathers anticipated the development of an integrated national economy. Because modern economic life did not respect state boundaries, the secretary argued, "state governments are no match for the great combinations which . . . are bidding for unregulated license." Only the federal government was capable of adequately regulating giant interstate concerns so as to ensure the protection of the people's "economic rights."

McAdoo disposed of the conservatives' argument that federal activism would create an oppressive bureaucracy which, in its own way, would inevitably erode the people's liberties. This argument was fallacious, the secretary countered, because "the truth is that under modern conditions every great organization, whether of government or of private business, must operate through large staffs of officials and employees." By minimizing governmental activity, Americans would not be minimizing the impact of bureaucracies upon their lives. They would rather be simply replacing governmental bureaucracy with "a host of private bureaucracies employed by the corporations." Such being the case, it was far preferable to have a governmental structure which was accountable to elected officials and representatives.[58]

The conservatives had willfully misinterpreted Jefferson's states' rights doctrine to serve their own ends. Knowing full well that the states were not capable of adequately regulating modern business, they were hiding behind the doctrine so as to avoid any regulation at all. To the secretary, nothing demonstrated better the inconsistency of the conservative apologists for untrammeled business than their attitude toward the Fourteenth Amendment. Although this addition to the Constitution was "the most nationalistic provision" in the entire document, allowing the federal judiciary to set aside state legislation deemed to contravene due process of law, no complaints against it could be heard from the conservative champions of states' rights. It was too useful for removing unwanted state regulation of business. "The importance of the states' rights doctrine is primarily as a guarantee of political liberty," he concluded, and "it is being twisted to an alien purpose if it is invoked to defeat the right of the people to protect themselves against economic tyranny."[59]

Here, in forceful terms, was McAdoo's rebuttal of the political ideology of the conservative Democrats who wished to assume control of the Democratic party. During the 1920s he staked his political career upon the translation of this theoretical opposition into concrete policies for the future direction of the Democratic party at the national level. As the self-professed guardian of Wilsonian progressivism, McAdoo promised to protect and extend the achievements of the administration in which he had so prominently served. His policy manifesto for 1924, accordingly, leaned heavily upon the legislative landmarks of the Wilson years. The Federal Reserve system, he claimed, had fallen prey to "the grip of Wall Street" and was now being administered for the benefit of the large bankers rather than for average depositors and borrowers. He promised to reduce the current Fordney-McCumber Tariff rates of 1922 back to the levels of the Underwood-Simmons Tariff of 1913 and to extend the Federal Farm Loan system that had been established during the Wilson years.[60] He made a vague promise to reform the railroads so as to reduce freight rates but did not give details as to how this was to be achieved. His promises to ensure federal control of water-power sites that lay on public lands, to support the ratification of the child labor amendment, and to sponsor laws preventing the abuse of injunctions during strikes did, however, reveal in him a progressive's desire to see an active federal government intervening to regulate economic relationships.[61]

In three important areas, however, he found it prudent to shrug off the Wilsonian mantle. Since 1918 he had been vague on the thorny question as to whether the United States should enter the League of Nations. As the secretary pondered his platform at the end of 1923, he could see that he would have to commit himself during the coming campaign. Thomas Chadbourne, one of his main financial backers, strongly advised him to duck the issue by advocating a referendum on the matter after the election. "We had a better argument in favor of the League in 1920 than we can possibly have in 1924," Chadbourne wrote McAdoo in November 1923. It defied logic to expect that the party could win in 1924 with a strong mandate to join the league.[62] McAdoo agreed and endorsed the idea of a referendum. "Among the great body of the American electorate there is a strong revulsion against Europe," he replied to Chadbourne. "We must not shut our eyes to facts nor butt our heads against stone walls, just for the fun of having our brains ooze out."[63]

McAdoo also saw the need to adjust his Wilsonian ideas to the political realities of the new decade in some areas of economic and fiscal policy. Although he had advocated in 1920 that the railroads remain under government ownership for an additional five years, he had moved away from this by 1924.[64] The return to private ownership was by then an accomplished fact, and he had no wish to be seen as advocating a return to federal control. Instead, he promised to increase the power of the Interstate Commerce Commission to prevent destructive mergers and to reduce freight rates to help the nation's beleaguered farmers.[65]

The secretary also moved away from his earlier support of the excess-profits tax, a Wilsonian initiative that had long been anathema to business groups.[66] His chief financial supporter, Bernard Baruch, was especially keen for his candidate to disassociate himself from this measure. McAdoo seems to have listened; less than two weeks after the financier had written the secretary asking him to oppose any attempt to include an excess-profits tax in the party's 1924 platform, McAdoo asked his friends to announce that he was "absolutely committed" against the measure.[67] "I think business is solidly against the excess profits tax," he wrote Daniel Roper in a rare concession to the big-business interests he so frequently attacked. "I have been very much in hopes that the Party . . . would find some other form of taxation which would be more equitable, more easily administered and less objectionable."[68]

If McAdoo made some strategic retreats from his Wilsonian past, he did maintain a general willingness to use the powers of the federal government to remold society. This was particularly apparent in his willingness to use fiscal and economic policy to effect some redistribution of the national income. He supported the early payment of the soldiers' bonus, arguing that the soldiers were primarily responsible for ending the war earlier than expected. This had saved the U.S. Treasury at least $22 billion, making it only fair to give the veterans back a little more than 7 percent of the amount they had saved the American people.[69] He was prepared to use federal law and the federal treasury to redistribute revenues taken from the wealthy to the generally less privileged veterans.

On other fiscal issues McAdoo was consistent in advocating the use of federal policy for income redistribution. He continued to support high inheritance taxes to prevent the perpetuation of an American plutocracy. To make it quite clear that his target was only the very wealthy, the secretary proposed that inheritance tax rates should be kept low for estates less than $100,000 but that after that figure they should be sharply raised.[70] On the matter of federal income taxes, a burning issue in 1924, McAdoo maintained his stand that taxes should perform a social function as well as the purely fiscal one of raising revenue. He attacked Secretary of the Treasury Mellon's tax proposals as grossly beneficial to the rich. Mellon's reductions would save the 172,359 taxpayers with incomes over $10,000 approximately $141 million in taxes, while the 6,489,000 Americans with incomes less than $10,000 would be saved only a similar amount. Mellon's proposed flat tax of 25 percent on all incomes above $100,000 also struck his predecessor as regressive, and he roundly criticized the proposal to eliminate the surtax of 25 percent on such large incomes.[71]

McAdoo suggested an alternative program that would tax unearned income at a higher rate than that levied upon wages and salaries. In addition, he advocated the retention of high income taxes upon the very wealthy to pay for further reductions of the taxation burden on the majority of taxpayers and for the soldiers' bonus. His most imaginative proposal, however, was clearly designed to benefit those sections of the electorate upon which he based his political hopes. Instead of reducing federal revenues by cutting the income taxes of the rich, he argued, tariff rates should be reduced. This would cut the cost of living for millions of consumers and give material assistance to farmers by reducing the cost of farm equipment.[72] Thus income would be redistributed from the wealthy to the industrial workers and farmers whom he hoped to unite behind his candidacy.

OUTMANEUVERED BY THE CONSERVATIVES

The ideological nature of McAdoo's challenge to the conservatives of his own party and of the nation as a whole did not go unnoticed. The distrust of business groups engendered by his conduct as secretary of the treasury and railroad commissioner had not been diminished either by the passage of time or by his retreat on the excess-profits tax. At the end of 1923 Tom Chadbourne was deeply concerned about his friend's low standing among business circles. McAdoo had baited Wall Street for so long that Chadbourne feared he would be overwhelmed by retaliatory attacks if he was nominated.[73] Many other Democrats felt the same; Benjamin Carter, a Washington, D.C., lawyer, believed that McAdoo's nomination would further alienate the business community from the Democrats. "My propositions were (1) that on no account whatever ought William G. McAdoo, or a man of his habit of mind, be President of the United States; (2) that the mere nomination of McAdoo would be a serious disturbance to sound business and might arouse a radical sentiment all over the country which business men and property owners would find it their duty to combat at high cost in money and labor, and therefore he ought to be beaten before the national convention meets."[74]

Although Colonel Edward M. House found the secretary's prospects to be rosy in January 1924, his optimism was tempered by his observation of "the intense antagonism" that emanated from "business people." If McAdoo was successful at New York, House predicted to Breckinridge Long, "there will be almost as determined a fight made upon him by this element as was made upon Bryan in his campaigns."[75] From Memphis, Tennessee, R. M. Barton wrote the secretary during the New York convention that "there has been broadcast in this state, and I expect everywhere, among business men the idea that your progressivism amounts to radicalism, and that your election would be dangerous to all business interests, and that you would go to any limit to favor the demands of certain classes, especially labor unions."[76] In its survey of the Democratic candidates for nomination on the eve of the convention, the *Portland* (Maine) *Press Herald* noted that McAdoo was "tainted by radicalism, which has made many Democrats realize that he is an unsafe man to be named as the standard bearer."[77]

For his part, McAdoo was not averse to portraying himself as a liberal champion besieged by the forces of economic privilege. The armies of reaction and corruption were united against him, he wrote U.S. senator Luke Lea of Tennessee in April 1924. "I am standing today for what Mr. Wilson stood, fighting . . . for the supremacy of the decent and progressive forces within our Party as against corrupt bosses who are subservient to the formidable wet and selfish interests in the country and who have allied with them the great financial and business interests represented by Wall Street."[78]

Having portrayed the struggle in these terms, McAdoo refused to withdraw from the 1924 nomination contest in New York. Soon after the Doheny revelations became public, he called a meeting of his closest advisers to discuss the situation. "What I am concerned about is not McAdoo," he wrote them in an uncharacteristically modest mood. "My political life is of no consequence as compared with the cause of Progressive Democracy. That cause must be preserved and made victorious at any cost or individual sacrifice."[79]

It was not surprising that many of his friends urged him to continue the fight, for the secretary was preaching to the converted.[80] Others were more skeptical. To John W. Davis, the whole exercise was one of self-justification. "Today Brother McAdoo assembles his division commanders in Chicago," he wrote his law partner Frank Polk on February 18. "No doubt they will give him a hearty cheer. It seems to me, however, that when the captain of the boat, after denying that she has been torpedoed, calls the crew together to consider how many hours she will float, it is not calculated to improve the morale of the passengers."[81] In fact, many of McAdoo's lieutenants did decide that McAdoo's candidacy was hopeless; Daniel Roper, Tom Love, Bernard Baruch, and Tom Chadbourne all urged him to step aside and let some other progressive wage the fight in New York.[82] But McAdoo, David Ladd Rockwell, and George Milton would not be swayed; no other progressive enjoyed the secretary's prominence or qualifications, and the conservatives could not be allowed to win by default.[83] His campaign therefore continued, funded by the long-suffering Baruch and the more hesitant Chadbourne.[84] McAdoo's hopes even flickered again after his overwhelming victory at the Texas Democratic Convention at the end of May, at which he won an instructed delegation.[85] In the primary elections of 1924, he won 456,733 votes, or 59.7 percent of all votes cast. Smith, by contrast, won only 16,459 votes, although his name did not appear on any primary ballot paper.[86]

McAdoo's supporters stressed the theme that McAdoo was the progressives' only hope at New York. At the end of May, Breckinridge Long wrote his fellow Missouri delegates that "Mr. Smith has extended and increased his influence and has become the leading figure in the opposition to Mr. McAdoo and the candidate behind whom the ultra-conservative and so-called 'wet' influences are amalgamating their votes. Under these circumstances, the fight developes [sic] in the persons of Mr. McAdoo and Mr. Smith; between the forces of progressive Democracy and those of reactionary Democracy. You are quit [sic] familiar with the influences behind the candidacy of each individual. . . . Mr. McAdoo represents the great broad spirit of progressive Democracy with no entanglements from any special interest, class, or faction of our society."[87]

When defeat came at the 1924 convention, the secretary was in no doubt that he had been a victim not of his own indiscretions and political liabilities but rather of an unholy alliance between the urban bosses and "Wall Street."[88] His subsequent hopes of rising from the wreckage of 1924 on the strength of a southern and western crusade for prohibition and progressivism did not eventuate. In his home state of California he was at the forefront of a fierce dispute within the party during 1926 which split the state organization along wet and dry lines. This was fatal for whatever hopes he had for a candidacy in 1928, because it meant that he could not count on united support from his own state organization.[89]

From this position of political impotence McAdoo was forced to watch the further consolidation of the northeastern group's power within the national party. Davis's defeat in 1924 further convinced him that "the Eastern strategy is dead, because New York and the east is becoming each year more hopelessly reactionary and, therefore, more inflexibly anti-Democratic."[90] After 1924 McAdoo changed tactics in his battle against the eastern group within the party. Instead of stressing economic policy, he emphasized the need to defend prohibition against its growing opposition. The political logic of this course seemed attractive to him. The increasing prosperity of the decade made it unlikely that a progressive economic policy of state intervention would receive national electoral support. In prohibition, however, McAdoo had a moral issue that served several important political purposes. It was an issue that appealed more to the South and West than to the East, and it remained popular among those who had followed both Bryan and Wilson.

Prohibition enforcement also implied opposition to the urban machines of the East and Midwest, which were notorious for their disregard of the Eighteenth Amendment. McAdoo also made frequent reference to the strong interest in prohibition repeal exhibited by many representatives of big business. He argued that repeal was a Wall Street plot designed to curtail federal activism in all forms of business. His advocacy of prohibition enforcement was therefore consistent with his earlier crusades against "sinister forces" which aimed to sabotage the great achievements of populist and progressive reform.[91] Finally, McAdoo saw in prohibition enforcement an ideal way to attack Al Smith, who had made no secret of his desire to be the 1928 presidential nominee. Smith had become the most famous wet politician in the country by signing in 1923 a bill that repealed New York's prohibition enforcement act.[92] McAdoo's strongly dry stance further widened the political and philosophical gap between the two men.

McAdoo's equation of antiprohibitionism and economic conservatism was borne out by Smith's nomination and John Raskob's selection as chairman of the DNC in 1928. McAdoo's warnings that the conservatives wished to reduce the party to a mere echo of the GOP in order to make the party safe for business went largely unheeded as Smith and Raskob took control of the party. McAdoo found it impossible to regain the stature he had once held within the party. His reputation as a splitter and a poor loser, gained during the campaigns of 1920 and 1924 and strengthened by his activities within the Californian state party, made Democrats everywhere wary of entrusting their party's destiny to him. Doheny and the Klan had lessened his much-vaunted electability; his new crusade on behalf of national prohibition only hardened the northeastern wing's opposition to him. The conservatives and urbanites had been strong enough to deny him the nomination in 1924; it was certain that they would and could do so again. McAdoo had lost his battle with the "sinister forces" within the Democratic party.

This, then, was the rise and fall of William Gibbs McAdoo. His campaigns to unite the South and West on a platform first of economic progressivism and then of prohibition enforcement failed to win him national party leadership. He had presented a genuine ideological challenge to the emerging northeastern conservative wing of the party. Until 1924 he was this group's most prominent opponent, putting forward a platform which went to the heart of the ideological issues that divided Democrats throughout the decade. As such, he was the obvious target for those who wished to steer the party along lines that diverged markedly from the party's recent Bryanite and Wilsonian past. In order to make good their drive to control the party, the conservatives were obliged to defeat McAdoo and to prevent him and his allies from controlling the party's agenda. Even without the emotive issues of the Klan, Doheny, and Tammany's dislike of McAdoo, the fight was inevitable.

The secretary was therefore both the master and the pawn of his political fate. It was his misfortune to be the leading progressive at a time when conservatism, both within the Democratic party and the nation at large, was on the ascendant. He performed the unprofitable role of lightning conductor for the ideological turmoil of the party. The dominance of the conservative northeastern wing was sufficiently long-lived to extinguish his ambition to lead the party, but it did not outlast the decade. When the northeastern group faltered, however, it would not be McAdoo but rather Franklin Roosevelt who would be the beneficiary. By keeping progressive concerns alive and by providing a dissent against the conservative drift of his party, McAdoo had performed an important holding action during a conservative decade. Yet he ultimately proved himself incapable of leading his forces to victory. The great opportunist had created opportunities only for his successor.

3

THE POLITICS OF DESPAIR

THE CAMPAIGN OF 1924

       Few events in Democratic Party history during the 1920s have been as exhaustively analyzed as the convention that met at Madison Square Garden in 1924. This interest can be attributed not only to the sheer spectacle of the event itself—the 103 ballots, the two weeks of acrimony, and the portentous arrival of radio broadcasting to political events—but also to the convention's seemingly perfect encapsulation of the ethnocultural cleavages that historians have traditionally seen as the paramount factors determining the party's history during the decade. In the circuslike atmosphere of Madison Square Garden, this interpretation has it, Catholic fought Protestant, wets fought dries, and urbanites fought farmers in an embarrassingly public display of the fundamental

divisions within the party. "My God," Theodore Dreiser wrote Claude
Bowers soon after the convention, "is this the meaning of Democracy?"[1]
With the tumult of the convention still ringing in his ears, William Allen
White argued in 1924 that the convention cemented the division between
the two great antagonistic forces in American life: rural Protestants and
urban Catholics.[2] For more than sixty years this interpretation has been
the standard analytic framework for historians of the party. David Burner,
the foremost historian of the cultural conflict school, described the convention as one in which the "poorly assimilated strands of city and country tore apart in open disintegration," and few subsequent analysts have
disagreed.[3]

The explosion of cultural antagonism at Madison Square Garden was
both real and dramatic, but it has obscured more subtle ideological
struggles within the party. Little is known, for example, of the jockeying
for power between liberals and conservatives as the convention neared, or
of the reaction of progressive Democrats to the eventual nomination and
campaign of John W. Davis, or of the electoral strategy pursued by the
candidate in his ill-fated quest for the White House. These issues will be
examined in this chapter.

DAVIS AND THE DEMOCRATIC PLATFORM

Even before Edward L. Doheny had tainted William
McAdoo's liberal credentials with the oil scandal, more conservative
Democratic leaders had made plain their determination to block the secretary's ambition to be the Democratic standard-bearer in 1924. The objections of the conservatives to McAdoo's close identification with Wilson's
administration, his antipathy to big business, and his close ties to labor
were as strong in 1924 as they had been in 1920. It was therefore appropriate that James M. Cox should enter the fray as an avowed block-McAdoo
candidate. Cox allowed his name to be entered in the Ohio primary, which
he won easily.[4] He then resolved to use Ohio's delegation as a basis upon
which to build support as the convention wore on.[5]

Cox was not alone in his desire to derail McAdoo and the progressivism
that he represented. Oscar W. Underwood, U.S. senator from Alabama, attempted to forge a southern candidacy in opposition to McAdoo's impres-

THE CAMPAIGN OF 1924 : 53

sive support in Dixie. Although Underwood had been a loyal supporter of Wilson and had even served as majority leader in the Senate during the Wilson years, he had never been a committed progressive.[6] His conception of reform owed more to Grover Cleveland, his lifelong hero, than to more modern notions of the value of an active federal government. The great goal of the Democratic party in the 1920s, he believed, should be to return to its "Jeffersonian fundamentals" of states' rights, decentralization, and minimalist government.[7] There was nothing unorthodox about this, but in some ways Underwood was a very unusual southern politician. Although as a congressman he represented the burgeoning steel city of Birmingham, he refused to advocate protective tariffs or to support labor organizations.[8] In 1923 he took the even more unusual step of denouncing the Ku Klux Klan, despite the strength of that organization in Alabama.[9]

Underwood's political obsessions were states' rights and limited government. The protective tariff, he argued, was a subsidy to the industrialists paid for by farmers and consumers. Federal child labor laws were intrusions into the private domestic and business arrangements of citizens.[10] Nothing, however, offended his view of the proper role of the federal government more than national prohibition. Like the Fifteenth Amendment, the Eighteenth was to him not only obnoxious but also unenforceable.[11] Aware of the popularity of prohibition in his own section, and exasperated by southerners' failure to comprehend their own inconsistency in supporting the Eighteenth Amendment while at the same time effectively nullifying the Fifteenth, Underwood moved closer to the northern conservatives who had put Cox forward in 1920 and Smith in 1924. "It is a strange condition of our own times," he mused in 1928, that the "great cities of the East, with their foreign populations," were the bastions of "the true tradition of Thomas Jefferson." In the West and South, in contrast, states' rights seemed to have been forgotten, despite the "Revolutionary blood and Protestant . . . religion of those sections."[12]

Although he began his political career as a free-silver advocate, Underwood quickly moved away from William Jennings Bryan. By 1924 he was firmly within the conservatives' camp; Bryan dismissed him as a tool of eastern business interests.[13] Underwood had little time for McAdoo's policies or philosophy. Accordingly he set out to capture the South as base from which to join forces with the Smith group so as to deny McAdoo the nomination. He had little trouble in winning Alabama's convention votes, but in Georgia, Texas, Mississippi, and Florida his stance on the KKK, his support of Mellon's tax reductions, and his opposition to prohibition ensured easy victories for McAdoo.[14] Underwood's failure to win the South deflated tentative plans made with Taggart, Brennan, and Smith to mount a combined effort in New York.[15] Underwood died in 1928, but the goal of a conservative East-South coalition that his candidacy represented would affect Democratic party history for another decade.

In Indiana, Democrats gathered around the standard of Senator Samuel Ralston. Ralston's economic views were conservative, but not to the extent of disqualifying him as an acceptable compromise for McAdoo's supporters. Although Indiana was a center of Klan activity, the elderly senator had not attracted that organization's enmity.[16] He was also personally dry, although his backers in New York were most decidedly not. Consequently he was billed as an ideal compromise candidate, able to harmonize the discordant ideological and cultural groups within the party. Louis Howe noted with mirth that Ralston's slogan was, "He is a second Grover Cleveland." "If he can live that down and get away with the nomination," Howe wrote FDR, "I take my hat off to him."[17] Even William Jennings Bryan had mild praise for the Hoosier; upon surveying the field of candidates, he wrote Wayne Wheeler of the Anti Saloon League that "both McAdoo and Ralston are dry and, of course, on this subject would be better than Underwood or Smith, and they are better, also, on economic grounds."[18]

Cox, Underwood, and Ralston all entertained hopes that they would emerge victorious after McAdoo had succumbed to a war of attrition at the convention. Al Smith, on the other hand, set upon a more active campaign to block the secretary's presidential ambitions. He was predisposed to view McAdoo with disfavor; not only had the secretary opposed Murphy and Tammany Hall during the Wilson years, but also the strong backing lent to McAdoo by the Klan made him anathema to Smith and his Catholic and immigrant power base.[19] There was also a significant philosophical divergence between the two men; Smith had little sympathy for McAdoo's Wilsonian and agrarian reformism, and on his side McAdoo considered Smith to be too close to the "reactionary" forces of Wall Street and Tammany.

Although Smith had gained much stature since 1920, it is doubtful whether he or his backers realistically expected him to win the nomination in 1924. He had, it was true, proved himself an able campaigner by regaining the governorship in 1922 against the incumbent Nathan Miller. Yet with growing prominence had come controversy; in 1923 he signed the Culliver Bill, which repealed New York's prohibition enforcement law. He thus became the hero of the nation's wets but also the great enemy of its dries. This was a powerful liability, which, when added to his Catholicism and Tammany origins, created a matrix of negative associations for many Bryanite and Wilsonian Democrats.[20] His campaign therefore aimed at blocking McAdoo and thereby ensuring a more acceptable nominee. By putting himself forward as the champion of anti-Klan, antiprohibition, and anti-Wilsonian Democrats, Smith also consolidated his power base in anticipation of a more serious attempt at the nomination in 1928.[21] This strategy was no secret to his opponents. George Creel, a strong McAdoo supporter, was sure that Smith did not believe that he could be nominated; he was instead "merely a gun man to kill off any Democratic candidate with progressive ideas."[22]

Smith's conservative support gathered strength as the prospect of McAdoo's nomination became more real. Although the secretary had been weakened by the oil scandal, the absence of a strong alternative candidate made conservatives worry that he might still win by default. Smith, as a nationally known candidate, offered the best hope of preventing this. Norman E. Mack, the Democratic leader of Buffalo, New York, wrote to Smith at the beginning of 1924 that his best platform would be the twin precepts of "personal liberty" (a euphemism for antiprohibitionism, which was also attractive to conservatives concerned about the possibility of another outbreak of reformist business regulation) and "states rights." Both themes were eminently suitable for distinguishing the governor from McAdoo's record of federal activism.[23]

Three months later, an attorney from Ogdensburg, New York, wrote Smith that McAdoo's nomination would ensure defeat in November. "Entirely aside from his connection with the oil scandal," George Van Kennan wrote the governor in mid-April, "he could not command the support of many conservative people. His action in connection with the Railroad Administration has alienated every important investor in railroad securities."[24] Another New Yorker, G. N. Orcutt of Hornell, wrote in the same vein. The only way to stop McAdoo, Orcutt advised the governor, was to "unite on someone who is pretty close to the people." Smith was doing well, Orcutt thought, because of a general feeling that "you are the logical candidate because, while you are conservative enough to satisfy the conservative men of the country, you are human enough to satisfy men who are not so conservative."[25] Even Alton B. Parker, whose 1904 campaign for the presidency had made him a byword for Democratic pro-business conservatism, declared himself in favor of Smith's nomination.[26]

The ultimate beneficiary of the anti-McAdoo movement, however, was John W. Davis. Although dismissed by Harold Ickes as "the original 'poor little barefoot Wall Street lawyer,' "[27] he was by any measure an extraordinarily talented individual. Born in Clarksburg, West Virginia, in 1873, he was a country schoolteacher at 19, the floor leader of the West Virginia legislature at 25, a congressman at 38, the solicitor general of the United States at 40, the ambassador to the Court of St. James at 45, and the president of the American Bar Association at 49. "Even in modern democracies, with their wealth of opportunity," a biographer marveled, "it is seldom that one man, in so short a space of time, rises from humble beginnings to a place of equal eminence."[28] Newton D. Baker, who had been a contemporary of Davis at Washington and Lee University, later declared to James Cox that "If I were granted reincarnation of the soul and could supply specifications of the new edition of myself, I would ask the Almighty to give me the legal mind of John W. Davis."[29]

Davis considered himself to be a "true liberal," and by nineteenth-century standards he was. He defined himself as one who "believes that [men] can govern their own individual destinies more wisely than others can do for them."[30] The great tension in American political life, he believed, had always been between the forces of centralization and those of individualism, and his own age was no different. "With the aid of constitutional amendments and the great powers to regulate commerce, to tax, and to make war," he argued in 1929, "the Federal Government has advanced its frontiers everywhere. And it always advances, it never retreats." With this advance came an inevitable struggle between paternalism and individualism. Paternalism, "the transcendental faith in the power and the wisdom of the State and the human agencies it must employ," was antithetical to individual liberty and individual sovereignty.[31] States' rights, he thought, was the only way to check further federal intrusion into citizens' lives. Not surprisingly, he was profoundly worried by the implications of the Sixteenth and Eighteenth amendments, which had so dramatically increased the scope of federal power.[32]

Davis's chief political aim was to return the Democratic party to what he saw as its traditional, Jeffersonian precepts of limited government and laissez-faire liberalism. He declared to DNC Chairman Cordell Hull in May 1923 that the party had strayed too far from these cornerstones since 1896. "It is the historic function of the Democratic party to represent this great body of opinion, the liberal thought of the country,—those who detest privilege, in whatever form; those who seek an equality of opportunity for every citizen; who wish for each individual the greatest liberty consistent with the public welfare; who deny the right to levy taxes for any other purpose than the support of the Government; who believe in the rule of the majority, but would not take from the minority any right to which it is entitled; who believe that public office is a public trust, who are willing to bear either at home or abroad their due share of responsibility for the peace and order and progress of mankind."[33]

In turning to specific issues, Davis always kept these "fundamental principles" in mind. He regarded the use of taxation to redistribute income as a prime example of the tyrannical implications of an active state. "There is no definition of human liberty from which you can omit the right of the individual to do as he will with his own," he told a group of Democratic women at the beginning of 1924. "When the government seeks to take from the citizen any portion of that which he owns, the sum of his rights and liberties is engaged in that subtraction."[34] The proper Democratic position, he concluded, was that taxation should be collected "solely for the support of the government," rather than to "give privilege or advantage to any man, nor to confiscate the property of any man."[35] If income redistribution offended his conception of natural and inalienable rights, so too did governmental action abridging "freedom of contract." Although he was prepared to accept some health and safety laws, and special protection for female and juvenile labor, Davis's labor policy was to leave "adult citizens to make their own contracts in their own way as to the terms and conditions on which their labor is to be performed."[36]

John Davis possessed an incisive yet instinctively conservative mind. Despite the magnitude and depth of his legal talents and experience, he was never interested in law reform, and he detested the new schools of legal relativism and realism.[37] He remained a strict formalist all his life. Two world wars, a depression, and the advent of a highly mechanized, corporate economy were insufficient to force him to change his "fundamental

principles" of laissez-faire, minimal taxes, and negative statism. His critics charged that his philosophy was self-serving and materialistic and that
he valued money too highly. Although his fees as a corporate lawyer to
J. P. Morgan and other clients averaged $400,000 per annum during the
later 1920s, he never ceased to rail against the moderate income taxes of
the Mellon years, and he even refused a seat on the U.S. Supreme Court
in 1923 on the grounds that he could not afford the cut in salary that
such promotion would entail.[38] Felix Frankfurter, who considered himself to be the guardian of the legal profession's conscience, was horrified
at this. "There is humor and there is humor," he fumed to a friend in
1924, "The 'humor' that disinclines a man to take a place on the Supreme
Court because it involves 'poverty' betrays a pernicious sense of values,
and at bottom it is the kind of thing that makes the leaders of the bar the
mischievious [sic] influence that you and I think they are."[39]

One of Davis's "fundamental principles" was the importance of public
service, and it was this conviction that led him into electoral politics. His
prominence as Wilson's solicitor general and then as ambassador to the
Court of St. James had created much pride in his native West Virginia, a
pride undiminished by the fact that by 1921 he had made his home on a
luxurious estate on Long Island. It was as a West Virginian favorite son
that he allowed his name to go forward, although his preconvention campaign remained an inactive one. "It seems to me," he wrote a supporter
in September 1923, "that it would still be premature to start any formal
movement. . . . I am quite convinced that if I am nominated, it will not
and cannot be as an active candidate."[40] Accordingly, he avoided any public comment on the issues of the day and refused to allow his supporters
to seek convention delegates. Clem Shaver, the head of the Davis movement, was forced to confine himself to the enlistment of the West Virginia
delegation and to quiet negotiation with other delegations to ensure that
Davis would be their second choice in the event of a deadlock.[41]

Privately, however, Davis saw much that worried him within the Democratic party. The rise of McAdoo, especially, concerned him greatly. He
was in no doubt that he and McAdoo were poles apart philosophically.
Writing at the end of 1923 to Robert Lansing, Wilson's former secretary
of state, he declared that "when I hear those who seek to lead, like our
friend McAdoo and Hirum [sic] J. and others, start again the dreary cries
of 'progressive' and 'reactionary,' the 'classes' and the 'masses,' I long for

a political bank which offers to pay its obligations in real coin, instead of tokens which are not only spurious but have been worn so smooth by use that even their original device is now illegible. What do we sow but dragon's teeth when we teach the people to believe that governments are made not to promote equality of right but equality of possession and achievement?"[42]

Others, too, found Davis to be limited in imagination. Woodrow Wilson summed him up as a "fine man, but he is a formalist. If you want a standstill, he is just the man to nominate."[43] Hiram Johnson observed that the only difference between Coolidge and Davis was "whether the entrance to the office of J. P. Morgan and Company should be on Wall Street or Broad Street."[44] William Jennings Bryan declared, "I have no personal objection of any kind to Mr. Davis. He is a man of high character. So is Mr. Coolidge. There is no difference between them."[45] The same could never have been said about Davis and William Gibbs McAdoo.

The story of the nomination battle in New York is well known.[46] The voting pattern at New York had a clear geographic polarity; McAdoo won the votes of 61.4 percent of southern and border delegates, 73.4 percent of delegates from the mountain states, 52.8 percent of the northcentral states' representatives, and 100 percent of Pacific states' delegates. Smith, on his part, won 80.2 percent of eastern delegates, 15 percent of the mountain states' votes, and only 0.6 percent of southern and border votes.[47] Smith and McAdoo could not agree on a compromise candidate; Smith suggested Oscar Underwood, but McAdoo rejected him as too conservative.[48] McAdoo proposed Ralston, and then Meredith, but neither were acceptable to Smith.[49] The ballots dragged on without compromise, until McAdoo released his delegates after the 99th ballot. Samuel Ralston appeared to be the consensus choice of the convention, before he disqualified himself on the grounds of poor health.[50] Physically exhausted by New York's summer heat and financially straitened by high accommodation costs, the delegates finally anointed Davis after the 103rd ballot. Whatever hopes the party had entertained of winning the election had been shattered. After such a public and acrimonious airing of its internal tensions, the party could not hope to win the confidence of voters in November.

Although the election was already lost, McAdoo's failure to win the nomination was a significant turning point in the battle for control of the national party. The notion that Davis's nomination was a victory

for the conservatives is borne out by the reaction of contemporary observers. H. L. Mencken found much merriment in the ticket that eventually emerged from the carnage at Madison Square Garden. The pairing
of the conservative Wall Street lawyer Davis with the agrarian reformer
Charles Bryan—a ticket as ideologically incompatible as it was culturally
incongruous—was almost too much for him. William Jennings Bryan had
become a figure of pity, Mencken wrote immediately after the convention,
because "they not only shoved his archenemy Davis down his throat; they
shoved his brother, the Nebraska John the Baptist, after Davis, and so
made it impossible for him to yell." This spectacle made the long convention worthwhile; "I shall be snickering over it for many long years."[51] The
McAdoo forces failed to see the joke and instead reacted bitterly to Davis's
victory. To them, the convention wasted any chance of a Democratic victory. For this they blamed the eastern bosses, who had sponsored Smith's
candidacy for the sole purpose of preventing McAdoo's nomination.[52]

The platform adopted at New York also revealed the struggle between
Wilsonian progressives and more conservative Democrats for control over
the party's philosophical direction and policy agenda. Each side could
point to specific victories within the document, but neither could properly claim that it represented a victory for their respective causes. The two
most bitter fights concerned the Ku Klux Klan and the League of Nations.

It is quite clear that the northeastern conservative faction which backed
the candidacies of Smith, Cox, and Davis in 1924 regarded McAdoo as the
Klan's candidate. They therefore saw it as imperative to oppose the secretary's nomination, for such an event would be disastrous in the urban
constituencies of the northeastern Democracy. Nothing could be more
certain to alienate the Catholic and immigrant voters in the northern cities
away from the Democracy than the nomination of a candidate who was
less than completely hostile to the KKK.[53] McAdoo, with his goal of align-
ing the West and the South against the East, represented a major threat
to the eastern strategy. Even without the Doheny revelations or the other
doubts as to McAdoo's fitness for the nomination, he was sure to face
strong opposition from those in the party who wished to see the East
assume a more powerful role within the national party.

As the requirements of the eastern strategy necessitated opposition to
McAdoo over the Klan, McAdoo's own strategy of uniting the South and
West led him inexorably toward a more accommodating attitude toward

it. In the South, his most significant opponent was Oscar Underwood. To secure as many convention votes as possible from the southern and western states, where the Klan's strength was greatest, McAdoo had only to maintain a discreet silence. The organization had been rebuffed by Underwood, and it could scarcely support the Catholic Smith. By a process of elimination, therefore, the secretary became their preferred candidate.[54]

If McAdoo's preconvention strategy incorporated a subtle wooing of the Klan, the rough and tumble of the convention itself required a more active approach. The vote on the Klan plank preceded those for the presidential nomination and was widely seen as a preliminary test of strength between the secretary and his opponents. McAdoo's floor managers therefore worked tirelessly to see that their delegations voted solidly against naming the Klan. When Hollins Randolph, one of McAdoo's most trusted lieutenants, heard that two members of his Georgian delegation planned to vote in favor of the minority plank denouncing the KKK by name, he bullied them into changing their minds. He told one dissident that such a vote would be tantamount to "stabbing McAdoo in the back," while to the other he reported that "this is a direct request from Mr. McAdoo. . . . Your vote may lose him the Presidency."[55] Both objectors changed their minds, and indeed there was a strong correlation between delegation votes against the minority plank and those for the nomination of McAdoo.[56] The McAdoo forces did manage to prevent the naming of the Klan, substituting an innocuous plank affirming the constitutional rights of freedom of speech, religion, and assembly. Their margin of victory—one vote— was so slight, however, as to be largely meaningless.[57]

The Smith forces won their victory on the League of Nations, when the minority plank calling for a Democratic pledge to bring the United States into the league was defeated by a much larger margin.[58] Instead, the New York platform called for a referendum on the league issue which would be "advisory," rather than binding, upon the administration.[59] Debate on both these issues was bitter and intense; it was an indication of the atmosphere of the convention that the gentle Newton Baker's plea for a commitment to enter the league was answered by Key Pittman in the most brutal terms. "With the tears in his eyes and his broken down, slobbering body across the rail," Pittman warned the delegates, Baker was "trying to appeal to your sympathies, not to your judgment."[60]

In its other aspects the platform largely divided the spoils between the

Wilsonians and the conservatives. Progressives were heartened by the inclusion of calls for federal aid to education, the elimination of lame-duck congresses, the holding of referenda before declarations of war, the limitation of private contributions to electoral campaigns, and the "vigorous enforcement" of antitrust laws. The farm relief plank was something of a compromise. Although it made a vague promise to create policies which would ensure that the huge farm surpluses would not be permitted to depress the price of crops, it made no specific reference to the far-reaching McNary-Haugen proposal, which was rapidly becoming the most durable political issue of the 1920s.[61]

The McNary-Haugen scheme envisaged a dual price for agricultural produce. American farmers would be protected by high tariffs on foodstuffs, thus allowing for higher domestic prices. Surpluses would be dumped overseas for whatever price they could command, and the difference between the domestic and foreign prices would be recouped by means of an "equalization fee" levied upon those producers who sold at the higher domestic price. The first version of this scheme, deliberated upon by Congress in 1924, covered eight commodities: corn, wheat, flour, cotton, wool, cattle, sheep, and swine. The "ratio price," or domestic price, of each commodity was calculated from the very high prices of the period 1905–14. Wheat, for example, sold for $1.16 a bushel in August 1924; the proposed ratio price under McNary-Haugen would have assured it of a price of at least $1.40.[62]

Led by George N. Peek and Hugh Johnson, the McNary-Haugen movement won many converts among economically depressed farmers in the West, but southern farmers, still influenced by free-trade ideas, were less impressed.[63] Conservatives opposed the scheme as a subversion of the free market and as an unwarranted extension of government control of business.[64] Urbanites objected to the scheme's contemplation of higher domestic food prices. Given that the fundamental problem afflicting American farmers was overproduction, it is difficult to see how McNary-Haugen, with its implied acceptance of the permanence of massive surpluses, could have provided a satisfactory method of relieving agricultural distress.[65] The proposal was defeated in the House in 1924 and again in 1926. The McNary-Haugen supporters finally triumphed in 1927 and 1928, but both bills were vetoed by Calvin Coolidge.[66]

Water power was also a vital issue to both liberals and conservatives during the 1920s. At issue was the control of the huge Muscle Shoals project in Alabama, originally built by the federal government to produce nitrates during World War I. Since then, however, the dam's considerable potential for generating hydroelectric power and manufacturing fertil- izer had been wasted. Liberals wished to see Muscle Shoals developed and operated by the government as a means of providing cheap power to the impoverished rural South; conservatives advocated the leasing of the entire project to private interests, most notably Henry Ford.[67] The New York plank concerning Muscle Shoals advocated its use for the production of fertilizer, but it did not mention the thornier issue of public generation of power. The party also pledged itself to further reductions in taxation, albeit along more equitable lines than the Mellon Plan, and the platform fell short of advocating the return of the railroads to federal control.[68] The platform was a compromise; William Jennings Bryan could describe it as the best the party had ever devised, while the eminently conservative John W. Davis could campaign on it.[69]

DAVIS'S HAPLESS CAMPAIGN

As they pondered the significance of the tumultuous events in New York, some of McAdoo's supporters perceived that they had been outmaneuvered by the Smith forces. The Klan issue, they believed, had been largely trumped up by the governor's backers in order to split the progressives' ranks, thereby destroying the cohesion of McAdoo's sup- port. George Fort Milton expressed this view to Senator Thomas Walsh soon after the election of 1924. Milton argued that the Klan issue was ini- tiated by "political tricksters who cared little about the merits of the issue" but who wished "to destroy the progressive candidate whose victory they feared for economic and social reasons. The big trouble with the Klan politically," he concluded, "is that its mere existence allows a vicious band of re-actionaries [sic] to shelter behind the anti-Klan cry, and to attract to them the assistance of right-thinking people everywhere."[70] When Urey Woodson, Kentucky's DNC member, asked George Brennan of Illinois why the Klan issue was raised at the convention, Brennan's reply strength- ened the suspicions of the McAdoo group. "It was the only thing we had left to stop McAdoo," Brennan answered, "and by God it worked."[71]

This argument, however, was weak in several respects. It ignored the fact that McAdoo had already lost some of his support before the convention met. Men such as Walsh had long before decided that the Doheny revelations and McAdoo's unseemly haste in arguing cases before the Treasury Department had put the former secretary out of contention. The theory that the Klan issue was a sham also sidestepped the embarrassing fact that the same delegations which had fought against naming the Klan during the platform fight were also those who fought most tenaciously for McAdoo's nomination. In fact, neither side could avoid a Klan fight once it was mooted; the Smith delegations had to fight in order to maintain the loyalty of their constituents, and the McAdoo camp had to fight in order to prevent a northeastern victory on this issue.

Other progressives were also critical of Davis's nomination and unanimous in the belief that it represented another setback to their cause. Claude Bowers, for one, considered that Davis's nomination was "the most inexplicable blunder at the wrong time in all our party history." Davis would be another Parker, nominated by conservatives and destined to defeat. "Our one chance this fall," he wrote James Cox straight after the convention, "was the nomination of a pronounced Progressive, and our one remaining hope is to convince the people that we have named one. Just between us, I have no doubt but that Davis is a reactionary at heart."[72]

The progressives' great fear was that Davis's nomination would increase the vote of Robert M. La Follette's Progressive party, which was formed soon after the Democratic convention. The nomination of J. P. Morgan's lawyer meant the virtual abdication of the progressive vote to La Follette, who now enjoyed a monopoly of that section of the electorate, while Davis undertook a futile contest with Coolidge for conservative support. This seemed to be confirmed by the actions of Senator Burton K. Wheeler, Democratic senator from Montana, who took an unauthorized leave of absence from the party in order to become La Follette's running mate. Bidding adieu, Wheeler declared that by nominating Davis, the Democratic party had "forfeited any right it may have had to the support of the progressive voters of this country. Between Davis and Coolidge," Wheeler concluded, "there is only a choice for conservatives to make. . . . I am a Democrat, but not a Wall Street Democrat."[73] Felix Frankfurter could not hide his disgust at the Democrats' folly, noting that after 1921 Davis had devoted his talents "exclusively in the service of those big interests which are already over-represented in the affairs of the nation." The Harvard professor declared that Davis's liberalism was a "campaign discovery."[74] Like many others of his ideological bent, Frankfurter voted for the La Follette ticket in November.[75]

It was Davis's misfortune to inherit a party already bitterly divided over issues which predated his nomination; yet it was also at least partly his fault that the divisions were even greater in November than they had been in June. This was caused by his selection of campaign issues, his electoral strategy, and his failure to incorporate all the ideological factions of the party into his campaign. As a dark-horse candidate unfamiliar with the concerns of the rank and file of his party, Davis needed help quickly to define the issues upon which he should run his campaign. On July 22, 1924, he sent a circular letter to every delegate to the convention, asking each to describe the principal issues in his or her respective state. Over 270 replies are preserved in Davis's correspondence, and from these a clear picture of the pressing concerns of Democrats across the nation can be gained. The most salient issue was that of corruption in the federal government, followed by the tariff, farm relief, the need for further reductions in taxation, economy in government, the League of Nations, the KKK, social welfare, and prohibition.[76]

This agenda, however, changed markedly region by region. Among delegates from the western and mountain states, the need for a strong labor policy to offset the appeal of La Follette's Progressive ticket was paramount. Farm relief was also a pressing issue.[77] Delegates from the South, in contrast, stressed the league, taxation, and tariff issues, while advising silence on the Klan and prohibition.[78] Those from the Midwest tended to make particular reference to the issues of corruption and economy in government, as well as to the political attraction of strong farm relief and labor policies.[79]

Davis received a different message as to the proper priorities of his campaign from those delegates who hailed from New England. These respondents evinced little interest in the league or farm relief, stressing instead the need to denounce the Klan by name, to advocate the modification of the Volstead Act so as to allow the sale of beer and wine, and to promise further cuts in taxation.[80] Those from the metropolitan Northeast supported a similar set of priorities. Governmental extravagance, corruption and activism, especially in prohibition, internationalism, and taxation, were singled out for criticism.[81]

Armed with this intelligence, Davis planned his campaign. The decisions he made over issues and electoral strategy reflected a distinct regional bias, heavily weighted toward the Northeast. This was a result not only of strategy but also of personal preference; the conservative policies of tax reduction, economy in government, and antiprohibition were those which best fitted with his own philosophy. As a successful Wall Street lawyer, he was not equipped to ignite the South and West by a crusade against monopolies or a far-reaching program of farm relief. Instead, he stressed the traditional Democratic concerns of tariff reduction and states' rights, and the need to reduce taxation further after trimming federal expenditures.[82] He made no attacks upon the concentration of financial and economic power in the hands of large corporations and banks, provided no specific programs for farm relief, ignored all calls to commit himself to a policy of assisting the unemployed, and largely avoided the contentious League of Nations issue.[83] He did not even mention Teapot Dome until the middle of September, despite the salience of this issue in the West.[84] Although he made few specific statements on prohibition, he made it plain that the Eighteenth Amendment offended his conception of the proper role of the federal government in matters that had traditionally belonged to the states.[85]

As Cox had done in 1920, and as Smith would do in 1928, Davis and his advisers staked their campaign on the premise that victory could be achieved by winning the East and adding the electoral votes of the solid South. In 1924 Smith had calculated that he could win more than the 266 votes required for victory in the Electoral College by carrying the old Confederacy and winning Missouri, Connecticut, Illinois, Kentucky, Maryland, Massachusetts, New York, New Jersey, Rhode Island, and West Virginia.[86] Davis simply adopted this strategy when the lightning struck him in New York.

It was clear from the outset of the campaign that Davis would concentrate upon the East. When Clem Shaver, the newly appointed campaign manager, was asked if the candidate would venture as far as the Northwest on his first campaign swing, he seemed surprised and replied: "That's the other people's country, isn't it?"[87] Although the Nevadan Key Pittman was in charge of Davis's itinerary, he could make little headway against the eastern strategy. After one desultory trip West of the Mississippi, Davis largely ignored that region. "I am very much embarrassed by the fact that it will be impossible for Mr. Davis to go to Nevada, or even to go West again," Pittman wrote a constituent eager to see the candidate in person. "His campaign committee have noted such a change in Illinois, Indiana, New Jersey . . . and even New York that they have determined that he shall concentrate his fight in those states."[88] Those Democrats who had supported McAdoo were quick to realize that their western and southern constituencies, and, by implication, their influence within the party itself, were to be largely ignored by Davis's strategy.[89] When McAdoo's friend and supporter Breckinridge Long offered his support to the campaign, his telegrams were not even acknowledged by Davis's headquarters. "The persons surrounding him do not wish him to have contact with McAdoo leaders," Long noted in his diary. "So be it."[90]

Davis's eastern strategy brought with it two rude shocks to McAdoo's supporters in the course of the campaign. The first was the decision to run primarily against the La Follette Progressives rather than against the Republicans. This followed from the eastern strategy, for all reports indicated that La Follette was so strong in the West, and even parts of the Midwest, that it was advisable to concede these areas to him.[91] Assuming that these assessments were valid, the Davis strategy was to campaign against La Follette in the East, arguing that Coolidge had no hope in the West or the South. If easterners voted Republican, this argument went, the result would be that each candidate would win a section: La Follette the West, Coolidge the East, and Davis the South. This would result in the election being decided in the House, where the western and southern agrarians could impose their candidates upon the North. Because Davis was assured of the South, therefore, easterners should vote for him so as to give him victory in the Electoral College on the basis of eastern and southern votes.[92]

Davis therefore focused his criticism upon La Follette. He portrayed the senator from Wisconsin as a dangerous radical, bent upon drastic restructuring of the American economic system. The Progressive plank calling for a constitutional amendment to empower the Congress to override Supreme Court decisions on constitutionality of legislation came under special attack from the strict formalist West Virginian.[93] In other ways, too, Davis sought to distance himself from the Progressives. Although he had been warned by his correspondents that La Follette was forging an alliance with organized labor in the West, Davis did little to prevent this. He made only perfunctory mention of the burning issue of labor injunctions and refused to modify his controversial views on the need to preserve freedom of contract as a fundamental American liberty. When William Jennings Bryan suggested that he promise to appoint a representative of labor to the Federal Reserve Board, Davis declined. Such an "occupational test" would, he told the Great Commoner, "greatly narrow the field of choice without furnishing any positive guide by which the fitness of men may be tested."[94] His coolness toward organized labor was nowhere more apparent than in his conduct toward AFL president Samuel Gompers. Although he wrote to Gompers after the convention to request a meeting, he refused to interrupt his vacation to bring this about. Davis suggested that Gompers submit a list of pertinent questions instead. Offended by this slight, Gompers later advised his members to vote for La Follette.[95]

The single most dramatic act of Davis's campaign further soured relations with the McAdoo wing. At Sea Girt, New Jersey, on August 22, 1924, he denounced the Ku Klux Klan by name. The only major victory won by the McAdoo forces at New York had at one stroke been rendered null and void. This was as much a product of the eastern strategy as the decision to concentrate Democratic fire upon La Follette, for it was essential to keep Catholic and immigrant voters loyal in order to win the East.[96] However, no more symbolic a blow could have been struck against a western and southern wing already smarting at an electoral strategy that consciously snubbed them.

As the acknowledged leader of the southern and western wing, William Gibbs McAdoo watched with increasing restiveness as the Davis campaign further eroded his position in the national party organization. The eastern strategy seemed to him to be as foolish in 1924 as it had been in 1920, and even more so now that La Follette was conceded a monopoly of progressive sentiment and votes. "I hope the Democratic party won't entirely disappear in the northwest," he wrote a Minnesota supporter in October 1924. "What a pity this highly progressive and liberal force was deliberately rejected by the bosses in the New York Convention!"[97]

While the campaign dragged on and Davis's chances became steadily more slender, McAdoo could not resist an "I told you so" attitude toward his conservative victors. Never free from self-righteousness, the secretary seemed content to let the party suffer under Davis's and the conservatives' leadership in the hope that it would learn its lesson. To his faithful retainer George Fort Milton, McAdoo could scarcely restrain his glee at the sight of Davis's travails on the stump. "Our campaign seems to be in a pathetic condition. I am not responsible for the present situation and there is really no reason why I should respond to the Macedonian cries for help from those who created the situation and destroyed all prospect of a Democratic victory. They have finally discovered that the strength that my nomination would have brought to them is the very strength that is necessary to victory."[98]

McAdoo therefore did little to help Davis and his flagging campaign. He declined to give speeches in favor of the ticket because his views and those of Davis were so different on such key issues as trusts, labor, and taxation that he considered it futile to try to reconcile them.[99] He was finally prevailed upon to make an address on behalf of the ticket on the eve of the election. He did so, but only halfheartedly. His seven-page script mentioned Davis by name only twice and concentrated upon the evils of the GOP rather than the virtues of the Democratic candidate. He was also at pains to point out that the chief object of the campaign was the removal of Coolidge and, in a subtle attack upon Davis's strategy, declared that "I would infinitely rather see the La Follette–Wheeler ticket go into power than see the election of Coolidge and Dawes."[100] McAdoo's inactivity was contagious. Davis's papers are replete with references to the failure of the secretary's backers to support the ticket.[101] McAdoo's critics were quick to point out after the election that in the three states where McAdoo was strongest—Kentucky, Tennessee, and California—Davis's vote dropped precipitously below that polled by Cox in 1920.[102]

The Democratic campaign staggered on through the fall. Davis himself struggled valiantly, but his style and message were ill suited to the rough-and-tumble of a national campaign. His carefully worded, precise speeches were not the stuff of oratory, especially for a candidate running a poor second in a three man race. "There is pleasure in the reading of his polished English," Claude Bowers remarked of Davis on the stump, "but he must slug more and purr less if he is to make an impression on these times."[103] But the leopard could not change his spots; a lifetime spent in quiet and meticulous courtroom argument had left its mark. For Davis to have transformed himself into a fire-and-brimstone orator was too much for even the most optimistic Democrat to hope.

If Davis was no crowd pleaser, there were plenty of Democrats who were. Their services, however, were not used effectively because of the chaotic state of the campaign organization. Although the general expectation of defeat among Democrats and the bitterness of the convention had left Davis with an unpromising task, his own decisions increased his problems in mobilizing the party. His campaign chairman, Clem Shaver, proved to be an unmitigated failure.[104] Quiet and unaggressive, Shaver was incapable of providing the dynamic leadership that his candidate so badly needed. Publicity was ineptly handled, and campaign funds belatedly solicited. By the beginning of October, the GOP had raised $1.7 million, while the DNC had collected only $300,000.[105] By the end of the campaign, the Democrats had raised a total of $1.3 million through contributions and loans, compared to Coolidge's war chest of more than $4 million.[106] Overall, Colonel House observed with disgust, "The result is about the worst managed and most confused campaign that I have ever had knowledge of." [107]

Although beset by difficulties, Davis refused to give up. Under no illusions about the result of the contest, he persevered with both his strategy and his campaign organization in the face of rising protest from significant sections of his own party. A pall of futility and despair, however, hung over all his activities. The Democrats had lost their audience; La Follette's Progressives had taken the spotlight because of their novelty and their adventurous platform, and Davis's attempt at me-tooism left him almost indistinguishable from Coolidge. To the Progressives, the Democratic campaign was merely a pale imitation of the Republicans'; to the GOP, Davis was scarcely a credible opponent when compared to the genuine ideological challenge presented by La Follette's candidacy.[108] By the end of August H. L. Mencken had identified the malaise that would afflict the Davis campaign until election day. "LaFollette [sic] is belaboring Coolidge, and the friends of Coolidge are belaboring LaFollette," he observed, "but no one seems to think it worthwhile to belabor Davis. He is simply concealed in the crowd, like a bootlegger at a wedding." [109]

DEMOCRATIC POSTMORTEM ANALYSIS

John Davis remarked to his friend Jouett Shouse of Kansas soon after the 1924 campaign, "I believe that I have been a fair success in life except as candidate for President."[110] The electorate seemed to agree, for the Democratic presidential ticket went down to resounding defeat. Coolidge and Dawes received over fifteen million votes to Davis's and Bryan's eight million; in the Electoral College the vote was 382 to 136. La Follette, whom the Democrats once feared as the master of the West, won less than five million votes and only Wisconsin in the college. Coolidge won 48.9 percent of the electorate, Davis 36.1 percent, and La Follette 15.0 per cent. In what amounted to a repudiation of Davis's leadership, the presidential ticket ran 11 percent behind Democratic candidates for the House and 13.7 percent behind those running for Senate.[111] Even James Cox, running against the dead weight of an unpopular Wilson administration and the explosive issue of the League of Nations, had managed to win 38.8 percent of the vote with 9.1 million ballots in 1920. Although Davis had won 136 electoral votes to Cox's 127, the difference lay only in a game of musical chairs; Cox won Kentucky but lost Tennessee, while Davis won Tennessee and lost Kentucky.

The election results seemed to show that the eastern strategy had failed again. Davis won no eastern state, and his share of the total northeastern vote showed a decline of 1.6 percent against that of Cox.[112] In almost every state in this region Davis ran behind his predecessor. In New Jersey the margin was 1 percent; in Massachusetts it was 2.9 percent; in Delaware 5.3 percent; in Connecticut 5.5 percent; in Pennsylvania 8.1 percent; in Michigan 9.2 percent, and in Ohio it was 14.9 percent.[113] Only in New York and Rhode Island did he run ahead of Cox, by margins of 2.1 percent and 3.7 percent respectively.[114] In the congressional races, Democrats performed disappointingly. The midterm elections of 1922 had been a minor triumph, in which the party had won 51 percent of the House vote and 50.5 percent of the Senate vote. In 1924, however, the Democratic share dropped to 47.4 percent and 49.8 percent respectively.[115]

Even the South was unenthusiastic about Davis. Along with Kentucky, he lost the three border states of Maryland, Missouri, and his own West Virginia, and he won Tennessee by a scant thirteen thousand votes. It was in the West, however, that the most bitter harvest of the eastern strategy was reaped; the Democratic share of the vote dropped from Cox's 29.8 percent to 16.8 percent.[116] In Kansas, Davis won 23.6 percent, down 8.9 percent from 1920; in Iowa he won 16.4 percent, down 9.1 percent; in Colorado his 23.0 percent of the vote represented a drop of 12.9 percent from Cox's performance; and in California the Wall Street lawyer won a mere 8.2 percent of the vote, running 16.1 percent behind Cox.[117] In Minnesota and North Dakota Davis won less than 9 percent of the vote.[118] "The fact is," the *Nation* commented after the votes were tallied, "that the Democratic Party is practically wiped out beyond the Mississippi River."[119]

It seemed clear that the bulk of La Follette's votes had come at the expense of the Democrats. The fact that Davis had run so far behind his ticket suggested that the Progressives had benefited from Democratic ticket-splitting, and in seven western states and Wisconsin the combined vote given to La Follette and Davis exceeded that given to Coolidge.[120] In the seventeen states west of the Mississippi (barring Missouri), La Follette won over 1.8 million votes on a ticket presented by a party only four months old. John Davis, heading a party that was over a hundred years old, won only 957,000.[121] "The party of Jefferson," the *Omaha World-Herald* declared in its survey of the results, "deserves to look like something better than what the cat brought in."[122] Davis's strategy had backfired badly; he had alienated progressive voters in the West, but La Follette had failed to win this section from Coolidge. For his part, Davis had failed to win the East. These failures allowed Coolidge to win both the West and the North, and in the process to amass a formidable majority in the Electoral College.

Democrats were quick to pass judgment upon this debacle. For James Cox and the other northeastern conservatives, the defeat of 1924 demonstrated that the road to recovery was a long and arduous one. The East, rapidly urbanizing and increasing in electoral power, must be won if the Democrats were to regain national power, but the damage wrought in the region by more than two decades of William Jennings Bryan and now William Gibbs McAdoo could not be rectified quickly. Those who advocated a return to the western and southern alliance of Woodrow Wilson had conveniently forgotten that Wilson won in 1912 only because of the split within GOP ranks, and again in 1916 because of the potent antiwar sentiment of that year.[123]

In a letter to a fellow Ohioan soon after Davis's defeat, Cox maintained that the last two Democratic victories which occurred in normal circumstances were those of Cleveland in 1884 and 1892. These victories, he argued, "came about largely in consequence of the sober thinking business classes having confidence in the Democracy." That good work was undone by Bryan in 1896, 1900, and 1908, when he "performed a very skillful surgical, political operation; he separated the business man . . . from the Democratic party." Cox concluded that it was now necessary to persevere in the return to the old liberal principles of Cleveland and John W. Davis and in the extirpation of the more modern federal activism and reform represented by Bryan and now McAdoo.[124] The implication of Cox's counsel was that the eastern strategy was essential to the *long term* success of the party; no matter how severe its defeats had been in 1920 and 1924, it would surely succeed once the unpleasant memories of Bryan's crusades and Wilson's perceived antibusiness measures had receded into distant memory.

Cox's ideological opponents within the party had a very different interpretation of the meaning of the 1924 defeat. To them, Davis's poor showing had demonstrated for the second time in as many elections the folly of the eastern strategy. Brice Claggett, McAdoo's private secretary, wrote George Fort Milton that the blame for the defeat lay squarely at the feet of the candidate. Davis was faced with the choice between carrying the West or carrying the East. He was advised by the McAdoo forces that he had a chance in the West if he was prepared to "hammer Wall Street, and adopt a liberal attitude on the railroad and similar questions." Instead, Davis chose to throw in his lot with Tammany Hall and to try to win the East by means of an economically conservative campaign and a repudiation of the platform on the Klan. The result, Claggett argued, was that the West was sacrificed in order to undertake a futile quest for eastern votes. The two outstanding facts of the defeat were that Davis lost the West because he "deliberately neglected" it, and that it was utterly impossible, "as alignments now are fixed," for the Democratic party to succeed in the northeastern states.[125]

Other progressives came to similar conclusions. In an exchange of letters with Senator Walsh of Montana at the end of December 1924, George Fort Milton argued that the lesson of 1924 was that "the real division in our party . . . is economic. The South and West, preponderantly agricultural, have a natural conflict with the industrial east." It was therefore pointless to attempt an electoral strategy that attempted to hitch the South and East together. The only route to success was to revive the Wilsonian and Bryanite coalition of South and West.[126] Replying a few days later, Walsh expressed complete agreement with Milton's views. "It seems to me too plain for disputation that the hope of success lies only in concert of action between the South and the West. However seductive it may appear, I am confident that any attempt to secure a victory through a union of other forces, in either or both sections mentioned, with those of the highly industrialized northeast, would result in the future, as it has twice in the past, only in disaster. . . . The interests centered in the city of New York will be, as a rule, for the Republican candidate. . . . It is idle for us to attempt to secure their support by accommodating the policies of the party to their views, even though those charged with its destiny were base enough to make the surrender."[127]

Intensification of the turmoil that had beset the party since 1920 followed Davis's defeat. On the conservatives' side there arose a determination to try the eastern strategy again, but this time with a more charismatic urban candidate. On the progressive side there emerged the resolve to reclaim the party before it was too late. Despite the bloodletting of Madison Square Garden, the divisions of the campaign, and the demoralizing defeat, Democrats were still unafraid of another fight. Both sides were convinced that the Democrats could combat the Republicans effectively only after they had purged their own party of its discordant ideological elements.[128] The campaign over, the antagonists soon continued their struggle to control the national party, this time within the Democratic National Committee.

4

THE STRUGGLE FOR THE

NATIONAL ORGANIZATION,

1920–1928

Both the Democrats and the Republicans maintained a structure of committees designed to provide organizational continuity between national conventions and congressional sessions. Local committees, led by precinct leaders and captains, oversaw the conduct of campaigns in most of the nation's 115,527 precincts.[1] Both parties had state committees, whose membership varied between twenty and eight hundred. Members of state committees were generally elected by delegates to the state conventions, although in some states they were part of the primary ballot. State committees raised funds for campaigns, distributed election material, and organized state conventions.[2]

In Washington, congressional committees, made up of one member from each state represented in Congress, were primarily responsible for the conduct of midterm elections. A senatorial committee, with seven members serving for two years, performed the same function in the upper house.[3] Although these committees were overshadowed by the National committee during Presidential election years, they performed an important task in planning electoral strategy and deciding party policy in the years between.[4] The collective voice of the congressional and senatorial committees was also decisive in coordinating House and Senate election campaigns during presidential years.[5]

Both parties also maintained national committees. The Democratic National Committee (DNC) was created in 1848, and eight years later the infant Republican party established the Republican National Committee (RNC).[6] The DNC was originally made up of one committeeman from each state and territory, but in 1920 it responded to the passage of the Nineteenth Amendment by doubling its size to admit committeewomen on an equal basis. The RNC followed suit in 1924.[7] National committee members served four-year terms, having been chosen by primary elections, by the delegates of their state at the preceding national convention, or by state conventions.[8] Neither the DNC nor the RNC met frequently during the 1920s; the average was three meetings per quadrennium.[9] The principal duties of the national committees were to organize national conventions, to conduct presidential campaigns, to recommend temporary officers for each convention, and to deal with the deficit invariably produced by each national campaign. The national committees also exercised the often contentious power to decide the method of apportioning delegates to each national convention.[10] Given the infrequency of their meetings and their unwieldy size, the important work of the national committees was largely done by their chairmen.

In theory the national committee sat at the top of the national party structure. Although it had no authority over the state and local committees, the DNC was designed to be an influential coordination body, charged with bringing organizational coherence to a diverse national institution. This was especially true in those years during which the Democrats possessed neither the White House nor congressional majorities. An incumbent president would naturally take control of the party organization, and the White House would provide the bulk of the party's publicity effort. Congressional committees, too, thrived on power; majority leaders and speakers of the House found it easier to gain national audiences and attention than when their party was in the minority. During the 1920s, without the White House or control of the Hill, the party was bereft of this leadership.[11] Although defeated presidential candidates often thought of themselves as titular leaders of the party, their influence was in practice largely ignored. Theoretically, therefore, the DNC stood alone as the national voice of the party during its years in the wilderness.

In many ways, however, the term "national organization" was hyperbolic as applied to the Democratic party between 1920 and 1928. During the first six years of Wilson's presidency, the DNC had functioned as an organized national headquarters, managing campaigns and disseminating publicity. After the 1918 elections, however, it had subsided into inactivity and disorganization.[12] Yet even in its weakened state, the DNC quickly became a battleground for the competing ideological forces that were tearing the party apart throughout the 1920s.

The results of the election of 1920 had barely been declared official before the McAdoo forces began a movement to depose George White, Cox's choice for chairman of the DNC. A successful businessman, White had also served in the U.S. Congress. An Ohioan, he had managed Cox's preconvention campaign before his promotion to the chairmanship of the DNC. He was a failure in both roles and quickly became a target for those who had opposed Cox's nomination. If White could be removed from the chairmanship, the McAdoo forces reasoned, a new chairman whose sympathies lay with the progressive wing of the party could be installed. In this way a beginning could be made to the task of rescuing the party from the northeastern conservative wing. An important step toward McAdoo's nomination in 1924 could also be made.[13]

Accordingly, the McAdoo wing began to undermine White's position. The leaders of this group were Carter Glass of Virginia, Tom Amidon of Kansas, Tom Love of Texas, and Robert Woolley of Washington, D.C., all prominent McAdoo supporters.[14] Their chief tactic was to convince a majority of the DNC that a change was in order and then to use this ma-

jority to force White's resignation. Their chief charge was that White was
an inadequate leader for such trying times and that the party could not
hope to make progress while he was at its helm. Carter Glass was especially damning, blaming White for an "exhibition of docility which seems
to have characterized the Democratic organization in recent months." [15]
For his part, Robert Woolley made several trips through the southern and
northwestern states to drum up opposition to White.[16] Cox and his northeastern allies, for their part, rushed to White's support. They recognized
the movement against the chairman for what it was: the first round in the
fight for the 1924 nomination.[17]

At first it seemed as if inertia might save White. Yet the forces against
him were so powerful as to make his job untenable. At the beginning of
September 1921 Bernard Baruch came out in favor of White's departure.
"George White is a nice fellow," he wrote Joe Tumulty on September 2,
1921, "but he is not the man for the job. . . . I will not contribute money
to be spent through an organization of which he is head. If you only knew
how much money I gave at his solicitation which was wasted, you would
feel the way I do." [18] This was a crucial defection, for Baruch was a major
contributor to the party at a time when its finances were low. White and
his allies finally gave in, and the chairman resigned on September 21, 1921.
Although the McAdoo forces had won a significant victory in forcing
White's resignation, they did not succeed in naming his successor. They
had wanted to install either Tom Chadbourne or Daniel Roper, both of
whom were closely identified with McAdoo. Instead, they were forced to
accept the appointment of Cordell Hull as a compromise acceptable to
both the northeastern and the McAdoo factions.[19]

Cordell Hull's appointment encountered no significant opposition because of his impressive record within the party. As a congressman from
Tennessee, he had sponsored the federal income and inheritance tax legislation during Wilson's administrations, and he had long been a champion
of progressive taxation as a means of replacing revenue lost through tariff
reduction.[20] A lifelong opponent of protective tariffs, he had been influential in the drafting and passage of the Underwood-Simmons Tariff of
1913, which had slashed rates to an average of 14 percent and greatly expanded the free list.[21] As a moderate dry, he had not been identified with
either extreme on that volatile issue, and he had been careful to remain
aloof from the McAdoo-Cox struggle of 1920. Best of all, he had time

to devote to the chairmanship, as the Harding landslide had swept him from office.[22] Well aware that he owed his appointment to his reputation for neutrality, Hull made it clear that he would not tolerate the use of the DNC to escalate further the battle between McAdoo and his opponents.[23]

Forswearing ideological battles, Hull concentrated instead on building up the party's finances and organization. He became the DNC's first full-time chairman, hiring a secretary and a newspaperman to manage both the DNC and the Democratic congressional committee.[24] A much more pressing priority was to raise funds, and it was on this task that the new chairman set to work. It was a depressing job. When Hull took over the chairmanship, he found the DNC to be $186,000 in debt, and in the entire month of December 1921 only $788 came to the committee in contributions.[25] "I am having a most frightful experience in getting our Democratic friends to co operate in the work of financing the current expenses of the Committee," he wrote Woodrow Wilson at the beginning of 1923, "even to a very modest extent."[26]

If the task was great, so was Hull's determination to put the party back on a sound financial footing. He spent $30,000 of his own funds in this cause and undertook vigorous fund-raising campaigns directed at the party's state and local organizations.[27] Yet during the whole of 1922 only 652 Democrats contributed funds, despite the fact that over 14 million had given their votes in the 1922 polls.[28] The following year brought only $38,553.50 to the DNC, of which more than 40 percent came from New York alone and 83 percent from the six states of New York, Illinois, Indiana, Ohio, Connecticut, and Missouri.[29] Despite Hull's efforts, the DNC's deficit still stood at $173,480 at the beginning of 1924. A further effort in anticipation of the 1924 campaign brought in over $130,000 between January and June, which, when added to New York City's contribution as the convention city, enabled Hull to hand over the chairmanship with a small surplus of funds.[30] By keeping the DNC out of the ideological disputes within the party during these years, Hull had made good his promise of 1921 to eliminate the deficit.

Following tradition, John W. Davis picked his own national chairman after the 1924 convention. Like Cox, Davis chose an old friend who had managed his preconvention boom. And again like Cox, Davis chose the wrong man for a delicate and important job. Clem Shaver, from West Virginia, was an inadequate organizer, a lackadaisical fund-raiser, and an incompetent leader. "All the King's horses and all the king's men couldn't make Shaver a capable national chairman," Robert Woolley noted, "though he was undoubtedly the best West Virginia coal operator that ever tried to be one."[31] For a party which had undergone a traumatic convention, a demoralizing campaign, and a devastating defeat, Shaver's chairmanship was unwelcome. Unlike White, however, he refused to take the hint and resign. Instead, he stayed at his post and did nothing. The deficit that Hull had so painstakingly eliminated reappeared after the 1924 campaign, and this time it showed few signs of disappearing. On January 1, 1925, it stood at $383,000; a year later it was still $243,000, and the debt actually grew during 1926.[32]

Shaver's ineffective leadership was compounded by John Davis's refusal to take an active role in party affairs after the 1924 election. The circumstances of his nomination and the severity of his defeat combined to make him reluctant to exercise any form of leadership. Davis prided himself on not being a politician, and his assessment was correct.[33] The bitterness of the convention and campaign had made the McAdoo forces distinctly unwilling to have anything to do with Davis, a fact which would have severely limited his usefulness to the party as it attempted to rebuild.[34] Fearful of another damaging fight for control of the DNC, Finance Director Jesse Jones decided to work slowly to erase the campaign deficit. The presence of the debt, he hoped, would make the fight less attractive to either the Smith or McAdoo groups.[35] With neither an effective chairman nor an active former nominee, however, the national committee resumed its drift after 1924. Consequently it soon foundered in the turmoil between the McAdoo and eastern groups.

THE FAILURE OF THE McADOO CAMP

The McAdoo forces and other progressive Democrats wasted little time after Davis's defeat in attempting to replace Shaver with a more active chairman of their own choosing. The names of J. Bruce Kremer of Montana and Breckinridge Long of Washington, D.C., were mentioned in the press and among McAdoo's circle as possible replacements.[36] Shaver, however, aided by the acquiescence of the Smith forces to his continued chairmanship, turned a deaf ear to calls for his resignation.

The lethargy of the DNC therefore continued, much to the distress of the McAdoo camp. By the end of 1925 it had become too much for Homer Cummings, one of the few easterners who was in McAdoo's circle. Cummings resigned from the DNC in disgust. Arthur Krock wrote to James Cox that "our friend in Connecticut" left the DNC "because the Eastern democracy is determined to have nothing more to do with McAdoo representation because of its involvement with Klan and anti-Saloon connections."[37] Cummings's departure marked a further distancing by the McAdoo elements of the party from the national organization, which was seen as increasingly eastern and conservative under Shaver's ineffectual leadership.

Having decided to assail the national organization from without, McAdoo's supporters set to work. Their goal, as always, was to facilitate a new West-South alliance of progressive elements to wrest control of the party from the eastern bosses and conservatives. Surveying the Democratic scene in April 1925, the *New York Times* noted that "there is hardly any concealment of the plan to make a McAdoo drive for the control of the next Democratic Convention," based on an alliance of the South and West, "while the Middle West and the East are to be left hopelessly joined to their Republican idols. Upon the folly of such a program it is needless to dwell."[38]

The McAdoo wing put forward three suggestions. The first was to bypass the national committee altogether and to create a rival organization of progressive Democrats. This idea was first mooted by George Fort Milton soon after the 1924 election. In a letter to Brice Claggett, McAdoo's secretary and then law partner, Milton appended a plan of action for Democratic progressives. There were two options, he believed: the first was to "let things drift along as they are" until Shaver and his allies gave up the seemingly hopeless task of paying off the deficit. They would then vacate the national organization, leaving the progressives to take charge and to redirect the party along more liberal lines in time for the 1928 campaign.

The second suggestion was to "cleanse the party of its present ineffective or reactionary management, and then install a vigorous liberal one, and go forward," by means of "our friends on the national committee and an independent group apart from it." Milton preferred this approach, for it avoided the necessity of "making war on the national committee." It was the Cox group's debt, and they should have the responsibility of repaying it. If they succeeded, the progressives could then take control, for clearing the debt "does not give them any title to the ownership of the party." If, however, the conservatives could not eliminate the debt, this would provide yet more evidence of their inability to lead the party. In this case Milton suggested the formation of a group of western and southern leaders to disseminate progressive Democratic doctrine while the DNC persisted in its folly. He felt sure that the progressives could easily raise the money that such an organization would need.[39]

While Milton worked to gather support for his separate organization, he and other members of the McAdoo group were also pursuing a second line of attack. This involved attempts to make procedural changes to the party's organization so as to make it more responsive to the progressive voices of the West and the South. Milton had argued even before the 1924 campaign that "we ought to start a scrap within the Party after November for the abolition of the two-thirds rule and the unit rule, and that through such a fight we can re-encourage the progressives in the Party."[40]

In an article published by the *Virginia Quarterly Review* at the beginning of 1927, Milton expounded his views on the Democratic party rule requiring presidential and vice-presidential nominees to have the support of two-thirds of national convention delegates. The rule, he argued, was from its birth a "child of hate," created by Jackson to prevent Calhoun from receiving the vice-presidential nomination in 1832. Since then it had prevented Douglas from defeating Buchanan in 1856, and in more recent times it had led to the doomed nominations of Cox in 1920 and Davis in 1924.[41] The two-thirds rule had become, in effect, a one-third rule which afforded a veto to a well-organized minority of delegates at national conventions. It had made nomination contests akin to a "battle royal" in boxing, in which half a dozen fighters enter the ring. Although they are unequal in strength and skill, the strategy of the fighters is to pick on the strongest until he is eliminated, and then move to the next strongest until the weakest, least acceptable fighter (and candidate) is left.[42]

Milton's most pointed criticism of the "one-third rule" struck directly at the changing regional balance of power within the party. Although the rule had traditionally been a protection for the South against the nomination of candidates who threatened to interfere with that section's racial policies, this was no longer the case. The population growth of the East had reduced the power of the South so that it could no longer command a third of the delegates to conventions. In 1924 the "solid South" had 278 convention votes out of a total of 1,098. This was 89 short of the 367 votes required to veto a nomination. Even if West Virginia, Oklahoma, and Maryland could all be persuaded to vote with the old Confederate states, their combined tally would still be 37 votes below one-third plus one of convention delegates.[43]

The "solid North," in contrast, had so benefited from demographic changes that it now had a veto over the nomination process. The combined votes of Connecticut, Delaware, Illinois, Indiana, Maine, Massachusetts, New Hampshire, New Jersey, New York, Ohio, Pennsylvania, Rhode Island, Vermont, and West Virginia totaled 472 votes at the 1924 convention—105 votes more than one-third. Even if the "reactionary forces" managed to assemble only the votes of the New England states (90 votes), the Atlantic seaboard (200), Illinois (58), and Indiana (30), this total of 378 would still be enough to exercise a veto. The two-thirds rule was therefore the ally of the "boss-ridden portion of the Democratic party" and the "best friend of the Tammany Tiger."[44]

Abolition of the two-thirds rule would break the bosses' veto and encourage a clear-cut battle to decide whether the party was to be conservative or liberal in its outlook and direction. "With the one-third rule out of the way, one of the two vigorous affirmative groups now calling themselves Democratic would emphatically establish its title to control of the party. If the defeated group were irreconcilable, it could seek a more fitting alignment. This would be a move toward honest politics. Nomination by affirmation, rather than by exhaustion, will re-establish Jefferson's child as somebody's party, instead of nobody's party."[45]

The third approach taken by the McAdoo camp toward the problem of reshaping the party's national organization was to attempt to increase the power of the West and the South within the party. Immediately after the 1924 election, Hollins Randolph of Georgia wrote to McAdoo suggesting that delegates from states "which go Democratic in National elections at least some of the time" should be afforded extra power in drafting platforms and choosing candidates. This would avoid the present situation, in which states with the largest number of convention votes—New York, Ohio, Illinois, Indiana and Massachusetts—could impose their candidates upon the rest of the party despite the fact that these states invariably went Republican on election day.[46]

In a second letter to McAdoo two days later, Randolph was more spe-cific in spelling out the geopolitical implications of his plan. Leaving aside the "split year" of 1912, New York, New Jersey, and Connecticut had given their electoral votes to Democratic candidates only twice in the forty years since 1884. Ohio and Illinois had done so only once, and Maine, New Hampshire, Vermont, Massachusetts, Rhode Island, and Pennsylvania had never gone Democratic during this period. Montana, Nevada, Califor-nia, North Dakota, Nebraska, Kansas, New Mexico, Missouri, Oklahoma, Utah, Idaho, and Colorado, however, had voted Democratic on at least three occasions since 1896. The South, of course, had gone Democratic in every election with the exception of Tennessee in 1920 and Kentucky in 1924. This was proof, Randolph concluded, that "the West has more often sided with the South . . . than has been the case with the East," and that "for anybody to undertake to say . . . that the South ought to 'line up' with the East in the face of these figures . . . is sheer nonsense."[47]

Randolph's proposal to stack the deck in favor of the South and West and, it was hoped, for the progressive elements of the party in those sec-tions, received support from others of his persuasion. William Jennings Bryan suggested a similar plan in January of 1925, which the *New York Times* dismissed as "pure bedlam doctrine."[48] At the end of January 1925, John Dickinson of Harvard University's Division of History, Govern-ment, and Economics sent McAdoo a detailed plan to reapportion con-vention strength along these lines. In his covering letter, Dickinson noted that "I never really realized how hopeless was the plight of the party in the East until I prepared the enclosed memorandum. It is at present a corpse, unburied and troublesome."[49]

None of these three movements was successful. Milton's plan for a sepa-rate organization of progressives foundered upon the harsh reality that progressives were in a state of disarray after their defeats in 1920 and 1924, and the funds needed for such an organization were not forthcoming. Although it was reported that the Smith camp was also in favor of doing away with the two-thirds rule, the two sides refused to join forces on the issue.[50] Shaver laid the matter to rest at the end of 1926 by declaring that a majority of the DNC favored the retention of the rule.[51] A survey of the DNC by the *New York Times* in May of that year had revealed that twenty-six members were publicly opposed to the rule, and only seven were prepared to support it. The other members of the committee did not publicly divulge their views, although the *Times* estimated that forty-eight—almost half—of the DNC privately opposed the two-thirds rule.[52] Even if the DNC were unanimous in opposing the rule, however, it did not have the power to make such a change. Each convention had exclusive power to alter its own procedural rules.[53] The suggestion regarding the reapportionment of delegates was so clearly self-serving to the McAdoo interests that the Smith forces would not hear of it. Franklin Roosevelt described it as an "idiotic idea." "The Democratic party must be a party of the entire country if it is to succeed," he wrote a Baltimore correspondent in 1925. "The minute it becomes the mouthpiece of any section, east or west, it ceases to be a national party."[54]

Other less visible factors played a role in the defeat of the McAdoo faction's attempts to restructure the party's national organization. The western Democracy had been shattered in 1918, in 1920, and again in 1924; its remnants were hardly a promising base from which to join hands with the South to gain control of the party. The progressives' dream of uniting the South and the West was also under increasing threat from economic and political change from within the South itself. Although the election of 1916 had shown that westerners and southerners could combine to elect a president, the less happy experiences of the 1918 elections had shown how fragile that alliance was. Could western progressives really cooperate on a permanent basis with those of the South? Were the economic interests of the two sections as coextensive as the McAdoo forces assumed? These questions were largely ignored within McAdoo's circle, but they became more pressing as the decade wore on.

Breckinridge Long, for one, did recognize the problem. Writing to Hollins Randolph in Georgia, he mentioned his concern that "divergences of thought" between western and southern Democrats were "the greatest obstacle we have to overcome." On matters such as racial policy and states' rights, the South and West had different concerns, and a few southerners like Oscar Underwood were even beginning to see the political use of the northern antiprohibition sentiment as a bulwark against unwelcome extensions of federal power into local social matters. In economic policy, too, the South seemed in danger of drifting toward the East; the growing industrial interests of Dixie were encouraging support for protective tariffs similar to those enjoying favor among eastern Democrats.[55] This "divergence of political philosophy" between the South and West, he believed, further weakened the prospects for an effective progressive alliance within the party. McAdoo's conservative opponents' eastern strategy was showing increasing signs of success. "The manufacturing influence in the East seems able to effect a sufficient number of votes in the South and to convert to their economic theories a sufficient number of persons in the Middle Western States to defeat our nominees with a too consistent regularity."[56]

FDR'S EFFORTS AT REORGANIZATION

While McAdoo and his supporters sought to attack their ideological opponents by pushing for procedural and organizational changes in the national party, another reorganization campaign was under way. Franklin Roosevelt had been concerned about the party's national organization since 1920, when it had been his misfortune to figure so prominently in Cox's chaotic campaign. At the end of 1920 Roosevelt wrote to a well-wisher that "our chief difficulty this year was in having to start things practically from the ground up in July."[57] A year later he was still concerned; writing to Cordell Hull to congratulate him on his election to the chairmanship of the DNC, FDR suggested that party leaders from all the states should meet at least once a year to devise election strategies and to coordinate fund-raising efforts.[58] As one of Al Smith's campaign managers during the 1924 convention, Roosevelt saw at first hand the divisions within his party and its continuing lack of organization. After Davis's defeat, he decided to take action.[59]

Toward the middle of December 1924, each delegate to the New York convention and every state Democratic leader received a circular letter from Hyde Park. Franklin Roosevelt had a problem, and he needed their advice. "A number of acknowledged leaders of our Party," he wrote, "have asked my opinion as to what should be done to make the Democracy a stronger and more militant organization nationally." Before he could give an informed opinion, he wanted the "counsel and thought of representative Democrats throughout the country." FDR put forward five "fundamental truths." These were that the DNC and its executive machinery should operate on a full-time basis and not simply during presidential election years; that it should be brought into closer cooperation with state Democratic organizations; that the DNC should be adequately and permanently funded; that the committee's publicity work should be "greatly expanded"; and that there should be frequent conferences of party leaders from all over the country to "exchange views and plan for united party action." As an additional "fundamental truth," FDR concluded that the Democrats had always been "the party of progress and liberal thought" and that it should spend the next four years not in fighting over candidates but rather in "presenting our own logical and progressive program."[60]

In a private memorandum FDR was more explicit about his plans for reorganizing the party. Integral to his conception of party organization were the various state Democratic committees. The national committee, he believed, should become the "child and servant" of the state committees, for it was at the local level that votes and funds had to be won. State committees would be recognized as the official organ of Democrats in their respective states, and they would have control over patronage matters. The DNC would be funded by an "equitable pro rata assessment" upon each state, and the DNC would solicit funds only through the state committees.

Roosevelt's ideas for the party's organization were designed to achieve the second "fundamental truth" of his circular letter—that of the need to bring the DNC into closer contact with the state committees. To bring this about, he suggested that a new body be formed to take the place of the DNC, the members of which would be appointed by the various state committees. This new body would conduct the affairs of the national party. These new arrangements were to be agreed upon at a conference of state and national leaders to be held by the middle of 1925.[61]

The proposed conference of party leaders was the lynchpin of FDR's proposals, and he took great pains to organize it so as to avoid an acrimonious battle between the McAdoo and Smith groups. He conferred closely with Senator Thomas J. Walsh on this issue, and between them they devised a plan to prevent an imbroglio. The conference was to be kept as small as possible, and incendiaries such as William Jennings Bryan were to be excluded. This was to be done, FDR explained to Walsh, by *not* inviting former presidential or vice-presidential candidates. Yet John Davis could come as the titular head of the party, James Cox on a proxy from the

Ohio state committee, and Franklin Roosevelt could attend as "temporary chairman."[62] Bryan's exclusion, Roosevelt hoped, would help to avoid the degeneration of his conference into a brawl over prohibition.[63]

The hundreds of responses that came from Democrats all over the United States represented a snap-shot of party thinking at a time when Democratic fortunes seemed at their lowest. None of the respondents cared to quibble with FDR's "fundamental truths." Roosevelt's respondents were much keener to use his letter as an opportunity to air their thoughts and complaints as to the party's past behavior and future direction. Senator William Cabell Bruce of Maryland encapsulated the view of the eastern conservatives.

To make the Democracy a stronger organization, the Party should:
1. Get back to the fiscal and financial ideas and policies of Grover Cleveland, which, except as to the tariff, differed very little from the present fiscal and financial policies of the Republican Party, and set its face like flint against the economic fallacies and paternalistic notions of the Bryan West. The old clash between the North and the South was a clash over the single issue; namely the true scope of state sovereignty under the terms of the Federal Constitution. The present conflict between the Democratic East and the Bryan West is essentially nothing else than a conflict between two wholly different systems of government. . . .
2. The Party should also get back to the ideas and policies of Thomas Jefferson relating to personal liberty, governmental interference with private industry, personal initiative, enterprise and self-reliance, and the proper line of partition between the authority of the national government and state authority. . . .
Conservatism with a whiff of national liberalism should be the leading trait of the party.[64]

Liberals, on the other hand, were wary of me-tooism. "There is no place in this nation for two conservative parties," Representative William Ayres of Kansas wrote FDR. "The Democratic party is essentially a progressive party."[65] From the West and the South came many complaints against Tammany Hall. The New York convention had shocked many Democrats from these areas into the belief that their party had been taken over by corrupt urban bosses.[66] Throughout all the replies, however, there ran a common refrain: the Democratic party was without money, without direction, without organization—but it was not yet without hope.[67]

Armed with these replies, FDR wrote Shaver at the beginning of March 1925 to request that a conference be called to reorganize the party's national machinery "at some central place in the Middle West not later than the last of June."[68] The chairman's unenthusiastic response mirrored the feelings of many of his national committeemen. Roosevelt had been less than tactful in his comments on the activities of the DNC as it was presently constituted. His circular letter did not include even a passing acknowledgment of the activities of the committee and its chairmen since 1920. Homer Cummings pointed out that none of the five "fundamental truths" were in any way new; every chairman since 1912 (including Cummings himself) had tried to implement them, each time to be frustrated by the party's lack of money.[69] Cordell Hull, whose efforts as chairman had been unstinting, was especially hurt. "Some of us," he noted sharply to Hollins Randolph, "both preached and practiced to the fullest extent of our ability the proposals Mr. Roosevelt suggests and many others in addition."[70]

If Hull was hurt, Clem Shaver must have been doubly so, for FDR's premise was that the DNC in 1924 was in incompetent and inactive hands. His proposal of a conference and then a new body of state-appointed leaders seemed a thinly veiled ploy to put Shaver out of a job. The chairman was therefore unwilling to be rushed into endorsing the idea of a conference; Louis Howe reported to Roosevelt that it took two "very long" interviews to persuade Shaver to announce his "sympathy" with the idea.[71] As subsequent events would show, even this victory proved pyrrhic.

FDR's attempts to revive the party's structure met the same fate as that which had befallen attempts by McAdoo's supporters' to remake the DNC. In the press there was much skepticism that the proposed conference would turn out to be a constructive affair; the opinion of the *New Republic*'s T.R.B. was that "the way to promote harmony in the Democratic Party is to keep the leaders apart, not bring them together."[72] The *New York Times* reported that congressional reaction to the proposal was decidedly cool; the senators and congressmen shared a feeling that it was still too soon after the convention for a common effort to repair the party's machinery.[73] Louis Howe agreed, pointing out to FDR that congressmen were the most conservative of all Democrats on such issues, because they were concerned in the most direct way about their own political futures.[74]

In the final analysis, FDR's proposals failed not because of the wounded feelings of the DNC or the skepticism of the press but because of the divisions within the party itself. McAdoo and his friends reacted sarcastically at the sight of Roosevelt as the peacemaker and constructive party statesman, for had it not been the same Roosevelt who had worked so hard for Al Smith in New York? George Fort Milton was predictably biting; the circular letter, he wrote Homer Cummings, was nothing more than an attempt to secure a "reorganization of the machinery from a Tammany viewpoint."[75] In his *Chattanooga News*, Milton thundered that "Mr. Roosevelt, who has been known as a man of some ability, by this move proves himself the possessor of unlimited gall." FDR's calls for harmony between the progressives and Tammany were dangerous and futile. "Should a man sleeping in a room with an open gas jet harmonize with the gas in the room?"[76]

McAdoo himself agreed with Milton's view that the whole exercise was both a Tammany plot and a cunning attempt by FDR to keep his name before the party. "When I hear that Franklin Roosevelt is attempting to essay the role of Moses to lead us out of the wilderness into which he and Tammany and the bosses drove us in the last election," McAdoo wrote a supporter in South Dakota, "I begin to feel that either he assumes there is no intelligence left in the Democratic rank and file of the country or there cannot be any, if he is taken seriously."[77] In the face of such opposition, the proposed conference failed to eventuate. Buttressed by McAdoo's surprising support, Shaver hurriedly disavowed his earlier sympathy for FDR's ideas, and Roosevelt himself accepted defeat at the end of June 1925. It was clearly too early, he conceded, to think of harmony between the two main factions.[78] Even Roosevelt's charm and sizeable mailing list could not moderate the ideological battle raging around him. In time, his suggestions would be implemented, but by a very different chairman, and for purposes very different from those that FDR or McAdoo had contemplated in 1924.

The political ramifications of the ideological schism within the party had created an impossible climate for any real reform of the party organization.[79] Each side suspected the other of using reorganization as an attempt to grab power within the party. It seems likely that such an intention did, indeed, lie behind the suggestions put forward by the McAdoo camp. It is less clear that such motives lay behind FDR's ill-timed attempt to "essay the role of Moses," but it was obvious that there could be no significant reform of the party's machinery until one side gained a clear victory over the other, and until the necessary funds could be raised. To the progressives' discomfort, the campaign of 1928 would provide both the funds and the opportunity for such a reorganization.

5

LOOKING TO HOUSTON

Even in December 1925, George Fort Milton was still bitter and despairing about the New York convention that had adjourned nearly eighteen months before. Convinced that McAdoo had been stabbed in the back by the reactionary East, he wrote to his friend Homer S. Cummings in a gloomy mood. "As I see it," he wrote Cummings, "we are in for a knock down and drag out fight in 1928, between the east on the one hand, and the south and west on the other, to determine whose party it is anyway. I think it is conceivable that it may turn out to be Al Smith's party, although I do not think it more than conceivable. In any event the Democratic party as today constituted is a mechanical mixture rather than a chemical affinity, and perhaps the best thing that could happen would be for it to dissolve into two component parts, the wet reactionaries of the east on the one hand, and the dry anti-Tammany progressives of the south and the west on the other. If this should occur as the outcome of the 1928 convention, I for one would not sorrow over the fact."[1]

Yet the party would prove Milton wrong, and Al Smith received the presidential nomination at Houston after the first ballot.[2] How could this "mechanical mixture rather than a chemical affinity" produce such a quick and seemingly painless decision in favor of a man whose very name and platform were anathema to the Democrats who followed McAdoo to Armageddon in 1924?

Historians of the party have paid surprisingly little attention to this question. David Burner largely avoided the issue in his *Politics of Provincialism*, attributing the unusual calm of the Houston convention to Smith's well-oiled preconvention campaign and his lack of significant opposition. Even so, Burner could not refrain from concluding that the ease of Smith's nomination represented "an impressive victory, astounding in contrast to the previous convention."[3] Other historians have alluded to a sense of exhaustion arising from the ordeal of 1924, which predisposed the party leaders and rank and file to avoid another convention mêlée at all costs.[4] All point to the preeminence of Smith—elected four times to the governorship of the nation's most populous state—which dwarfed the stature of any other contenders.[5] Perhaps the most enduring explanation was that proposed by the *New Republic*. Smith was nominated, the editors wrote on July 11, 1928, because "the Democrats believed that they had a chance to win with Smith, and none at all with anyone else."[6]

These explanations, however, beg the question as to *why* Smith had no significant rivals by the time that the delegates congregated in Houston.[7] Also unaccounted for is the fact that, far from being exhausted, the party resumed its squabbling almost as soon as the convention had finished. The party seemed to coalesce for a brief moment in order to anoint its 1928 nominee and then returned to its old ways to make his election most unlikely.

Smith's qualifications were impressive but scarcely unprecedented in party history. In 1924 he had already won the governorship of New York twice, yet this did not put his rivals out of contention. His Catholic, wet, and Tammany ties remained constant. Although Smith's supporters were enthusiastic and well funded, McAdoo, too, had assembled a dependable network of support. As Champ Clark and General Leonard Wood discovered to their cost, the mere possession of ample preconvention funds, an efficient organization, and a plurality of delegates was by no means a guarantee of victory in either party. Politicians—especially those as committed to opposing Smith as were McAdoo's supporters in 1924—do not give presidential nominations away lightly, especially to their archenemy. Why did they do so in 1928? Unraveling this mystery requires a reconstruction of the scenario facing Democratic leaders as they prepared for Houston.

McADOO'S EFFORTS TO STOP SMITH

Of the two major protagonists of the 1924 convention, McAdoo had the more difficult job keeping in the public eye after 1925. Unlike Smith, he held no public office but was occupied in legal practice in Los Angeles and Washington. Although he observed the proprieties of denying any presidential ambitions in the period 1925–27, it is quite clear that he sought to avenge his defeat at the hands of those he described as eastern reactionaries. His pronouncements on public issues, and especially upon prohibition, maintained a clear delineation between his views and those of Smith. Addressing the national convention of the Women's Christian Temperance Union in October of 1926, for instance, he established himself as a hard-liner for the dry cause, rejecting any amendment of the Volstead Act and calling for much greater enforcement of both state and federal dry laws.[8]

McAdoo's strategy for 1928 was to be a repetition of that of 1924—to unite southern and western progressives upon a Wilsonian agenda of agricultural relief, taxation reform, and tightened business regulation against the eastern business interests lined up behind Smith. So confident of success was the McAdoo camp in 1925 that there seemed little need to rush toward an open candidacy. Hollins Randolph advised his "Chief" that the best policy was to "sit steady in the boat, saw wood, and say nothing," while all the while quietly adding western and southern recruits. "We should be the ones to make the arguments giving the facts and figures to prove that the South and the West have exactly the same economic problems to overcome, both sections being agricultural; and . . . we should be the ones to present the deadly figures of the performance of the Eastern States—from Maine to Minnesota and to Maryland—since 1860. . . . It should be easy to convince the people of the west that the people of the East are joined to their idols, to-wit: Republican principles of privilege and preferment to the classes as against the masses."[9]

Yet it was not as easy in practice as in theory. McAdoo had not fared well in 1924, and his support seemed to erode further in 1925 and 1926.[10] He had flirted too intimately with the now rapidly declining Klan, his role in the imbroglio of Madison Square Garden was perceived as unduly intransigent, and his lukewarm support of the Davis-Bryan ticket did little to endear him to party regulars.[11] For all these reasons, and in the face of Smith's prominence as governor of New York, McAdoo's drive for the nomination stalled.

As Smith became seen as the front-runner for the nomination, the frustration in the McAdoo camp became more apparent. An article by Bruce Bliven in the *New Republic* of March 23, 1927, which lauded Smith as the "only thorough-going progressive" on the Democratic horizon brought forth an angry response from George F. Milton. "It makes me hot every time I see it," he fumed to McAdoo; "the Smith crowd seems to have been able to sell stupid intellectuals with the idea that he is a real progressive."[12] Soon after, Frank Hampton, secretary to Senator Furnifold M. Simmons of North Carolina, reported to McAdoo that Smith was now the favorite of the Wall Street interests. They, he thought, were really Republicans but were throwing their support to Smith in the hope of installing a beatable opponent for the Republican nominee. Hampton scarcely needed to remind McAdoo that the Democratic party had listened to the wishes of Wall Street in 1904 and 1924, and in both cases "these men were beaten much worse in New York and its adjacent territory than was Mr. Bryan himself in his Free Silver campaign."[13]

By the middle of 1927 McAdoo was so pessimistic about his chances of defeating Smith that he was ready to abandon his unannounced candidacy for the nomination. His closest political ally, George F. Milton, was horrified. The recent withdrawal of President Coolidge from the 1928 contest had so changed the political landscape that it was premature for McAdoo to abandon the field to Smith. Before the president announced his intentions, Milton argued, few Democrats had given their party much chance for 1928. Now the situation seemed brighter, yet McAdoo's retreat threatened progressive Democrats everywhere with oblivion. "How can they help but feel that their leader has deserted them, that he has gotten tired

of the fight and is not sufficiently interested in the principles for which he
and they were fighting to continue the battle?" he inquired.[14]

McAdoo was not convinced, and he replied to Milton that his letter
rested upon a "fundamentally erroneous assumption" that the progressive
forces of the party were an army which recognized him as its leader. Progressive Democrats recognized no single leader, he lectured his old friend,
and "as a matter of fact, my leadership has been resisted by a large body of
those whom I might naturally have looked to for support." There would
be no money for a progressive campaign comparable to that available to
the Smith faction, and McAdoo believed that he had sacrificed enough
of his effort and money for the cause. New leadership would have to be
found. "There is an extraordinary apathy and indifference in the ranks of
the progressive Democrats which is difficult, if not impossible, to overcome," he told Milton. "There seems to be no enthusiasm in our wing
of the party. Everywhere there is an apparent disposition to let things go
by default."[15] "Where is our ammunition?" he asked Milton, "We can't
fight a highly organized and entrenched and equipped opposition with
bare hands when they have machine guns, poison gas, and everything
else."[16] On September 17, 1927, his decision to withdraw became public
and final.[17]

McAdoo's decision did nothing, however, to diminish his determination that Al Smith should not be the nominee in 1928. As early as April
1927, Louis Howe reported to Franklin Roosevelt that McAdoo had realized that he would not be a viable opponent to the New York governor
but that he and his supporters would "try one man after another until
they find a live one" to stop Smith.[18] McAdoo and Milton even harbored a
hope that Smith would follow his rival's lead and withdraw in the name of
party harmony, but this proved to be wishful thinking. "We cannot expect
a pig to understand lyric poetry," Milton observed to his mentor.[19]

If Smith insisted on making the race, the tactics of the McAdoo group
were to block him by encouraging alternative candidates who might prevent the governor from achieving a two-thirds majority of delegates.
McAdoo himself played a leading role in this strategy. In a letter to the
editor of the *New Hampton* (Iowa) *Tribune* at the end of November 1927,
he argued that "the republicans can nominate a wooden Indian sign next
year and elect him. We have no chance at all." Under such circumstances,
the issue of the nomination became one not so much of victory or de-

feat but rather of ensuring that the party maintain itself in good shape for more auspicious contests in the future. The nomination of Smith, to McAdoo's mind, would be a disaster for the party. "Cox gave us a body blow," he wrote editor Feuling, "and Davis a complete knockout. I am afraid that Smith's nomination would finish the job." Smith's antiprohibitionism, his Tammany affiliation, and "the public's feeling that he is a tool of Wall Street despite all of the progressive claims made for him" would doom his candidacy in the South.

If the South was lost, McAdoo argued, the future of the whole party would be put in serious jeopardy. The nomination of Senator Thomas J. Walsh of Montana would, however, cut this Gordian knot: a dry Catholic, his impeccably progressive credentials and long experience as a lawmaker would at once still fears of a religious bar to the presidency and keep the South loyal.[20] It was for these reasons that Walsh, whose investigations of the Teapot Dome scandal had proved so damaging to McAdoo's presidential ambitions in 1924, became McAdoo's favored candidate.[21]

Thomas J. Walsh was in many ways a shrewd choice. His Catholicism was a convenient means by which McAdoo hoped to dispel any suspicion of religious bigotry that still attached to him from 1924, as well as a way in which southern Democrats could show that their objections to Smith rested not on religious but rather on ideological and policy grounds.[22] Few could challenge Walsh's qualifications for the nomination.[23] As the permanent chairman of the 1924 convention, he had achieved great prominence as a peacemaker, and it was only his adamant refusal that prevented a rush to nominate him at Madison Square Garden. As a western dry, he was eminently acceptable to the McAdoo forces, and it was hoped that his Catholicism would console Al Smith's disappointed urban eastern power base. Furthermore, Walsh and McAdoo had been friends and allies for many years.[24]

For his part Walsh was in a receptive mood at the end of 1927, but he never exhibited much hope that the lightning would strike him. "I am still pursuing a policy of watchful waiting," he wrote a correspondent in November. "Not a little mention of my name has been made in connection with the nomination, but there has not been such a response . . . as to lead me . . . to countenance any active campaign on my behalf."[25] The senator showed no embarrassment at McAdoo's sponsorship, denying that this new relationship took the luster from his investigation of the Teapot Dome affair.[26] No admirer of the conservative northeastern group backing Smith, Walsh saw himself as a logical heir to McAdoo's shattered presidential ambitions. On March 3, 1928, he announced that he was allowing his friends to put his name forward in South Dakota, Wisconsin, and California.[27] Assuming McAdoo's mantle, he announced that "it is known to all men that for at least thirty years . . . there have been two elements in the Democratic party as there have been in the Republican party, generally referred to as progressive and conservative. That division or classification exists today. Mr. McAdoo was supported in the 1920 and 1924 conventions by a very large contingent of the Democratic party. . . . It is quite reasonable to expect that the same elements which supported Mr. McAdoo . . . would look with favor now upon my candidacy."[28]

Walsh's availability aroused mixed emotions among Democrats. The Smith forces saw in it a cynical attempt to capitalize on the religious feeling against their candidate. This thought prompted Louis W. Hickey, an engineer from Dallas, to accuse Walsh of being a "hiding hole" for religious prejudice, and to wonder how he could stomach acting as a stooge for McAdoo's revengeful scheming.[29] Albert E. Barnett of Nashville, Tennessee, in contrast, welcomed Walsh's candidacy as a "real service to the Democratic party, especially in the Southern States." Barnett described himself as opposed to Smith because of his prohibition views, but he had earlier resolved to vote for Smith because "the silly position assumed by [Senator Tom] Heflin [of Alabama] and others of his stripe have made me willing to sacrifice my prohibition views in order to give what rebuke I can to . . . religious intolerance." The emergence of dry, Catholic Walsh gave Mr. Barnett and perhaps many other southerners a way out.[30]

This clever compromise did not eventuate. Despite a concerted effort by Walsh's supporters in South Dakota, the Montanan failed to win a clear victory over Smith in that rural, dry state.[31] The inadequate response that Walsh had sensed at the end of 1927 became a reality during the primaries. On May 1 he ran a distant third behind Smith and James A. Reed in the California primary and withdrew from the race four days later.[32] Walsh probably still entertained hopes that he would be nominated in the event of a deadlock at Houston. In the meantime it was clear that his withdrawal was yet another defeat for McAdoo.[33]

Four other candidates were mentioned with some seriousness during

1927 and 1928. Cordell Hull seemed at least quietly responsive to overtures from McAdoo supporters. George F. Milton became Hull's unofficial manager during the early part of 1928, and the two exchanged letters
almost daily.[34] Hull, however, was unwilling to be the means by which the
McAdoo element could split the party. He had prided himself as a peacemaker during his tenure as chairman of the DNC, and had no wish to lose
that reputation by engaging in a divisive race for the nomination.[35] He
consequently limited his activities to his own state of Tennessee, as well as
neighboring Kentucky and Mississippi. His goal was not to win the nomination on an early ballot but rather to position himself as a compromise
choice should Smith fail to achieve a two-thirds majority.[36]

Governor Albert C. Ritchie of Maryland was also a presidential hopeful during the early months of 1928. In May of that year he told a Senate
committee investigating preconvention expenditures that although he had
not expected his name to be mentioned in connection with the nomination, "I will say that I am pleased at it and would be delighted if it
came my way." He assured the senators, however, that he had no formal
organization at all and that no funds had been spent on his behalf.[37] Nevertheless he was considered an active candidate until his formal withdrawal
on June 18, 1928. "We must present a united front," he warned the party,
and promptly endorsed Al Smith.[38] This was scarcely surprising, for the
two governors shared a strong antipathy to prohibition, to governmental
interference with business, and to William Gibbs McAdoo.

Senator James A. Reed of Missouri, Edwin Meredith of Iowa, and
Newton Baker of Ohio were also mentioned as possible nominees. Reed
had become prominent as an anti-Wilson Democrat who appealed
strongly to wets and economic conservatives.[39] He was reported to have
been pleased at the result of the 1920 election because it marked the end
of Wilson's influence upon the party.[40] Such opinions made him unacceptable to McAdoo and his group. A keen admirer of Smith, Reed withdrew
his candidacy in favor of the New York governor. Meredith, an Iowa publisher who had served briefly as Wilson's secretary of agriculture, came
under pressure from McAdoo's group to oppose the Smith juggernaut.
A firm prohibitionist, Meredith had little time for Smith and his wet
views. Yet he found it impossible to mobilize support either for himself
or any other dry candidate. "It is the same old proposition," he wrote to

McAdoo, "of not being able to beat someone with no one." Despairing of his own chances, Meredith endorsed Baker, who was at least moderate on the prohibition question.[41]

Newton D. Baker was never sure about the desirability of the 1928 nomination. In September 1927 he wrote to his ardent backer Ralph Hayes that, although Smith himself would loyally fall behind any nominee, he doubted whether the Happy Warrior's supporters, "who would follow him to the stake," would do the same "if they felt the nomination had been denied him." "In other words," Baker concluded, "I see no prospect of any other candidate than Smith in 1928 with the slightest assurance of a fair chance."[42] He therefore steadfastly refused to enter the race, despite Meredith's persistent attempts to persuade him otherwise.[43] With McAdoo out of the race and Walsh, Hull, and Meredith without broad-based support, who would save the South and West and keep alive the Wilsonian heritage? "Surely," George Fort Milton exclaimed in an *Independent* article entitled "Progressive Democrats in a Quandary," "the party fathered by Thomas Jefferson will not be murdered by Al Smith."[44]

SMITH'S QUIET CAMPAIGN FOR THE NOMINATION

In stark contrast to the depression and disarray of the McAdoo wing of the party, Al Smith and his advisers were confident as they planned their strategy for 1928. Belle Moskowitz, the governor's most trusted aide, found the prospects encouraging even in 1925. The 1924 convention had provided Smith with much publicity, and the Klan seemed to be losing membership quickly. In addition, the death of Bryan and the eclipse of McAdoo had left progressive Democrats without an acknowledged leader. She saw the possibility of strengthening the North-South alliance that had been mooted in the national campaigns of 1920 and 1924. "The Southern democratic politicians, out of power for ten years, were becoming anxious once again to occupy the seats of the mighty. They must look for some one who would appeal to the powerful northern and eastern states with large blocks of votes in the Electoral College. I began to think about the votes needed to secure the nomination and to figure roughly where our strength might lie. Suddenly I realized that there was a certain inevitability about the situation and felt sure we could do the trick this time."[45]

It was upon this basic strategy that the Smith campaign was waged between 1925 and 1928. Even Franklin Roosevelt conceded to his old boss Josephus Daniels in June 1927 that "I do not believe that the farmers of the West will vote the Democratic ticket in sufficient numbers even if they are starving."[46] It made more sense to craft a campaign around an appeal to the South and North, a Pennsylvania Democrat wrote FDR in 1925, than to rely on radical western agrarians. "Northeastern Democracy is conservative and Southern democracy is conservative. I do not see any reason for these two branches of our party disagreeing. The matters that have split them up until this time have been the petty aspirations of religious mountebanks. If we . . . return to the propogation [sic] of the fundamental principles of our party, 'that government governs best that governs least,' our party will be successful."[47]

Wooing the South required both tact and patience, and the Smith pre-convention campaign remained discreet until the start of the Houston convention. "No man ever got the nomination by going out and looking for it," Smith told the New York Times in October 1925; "I know I would never get the nomination unless party leaders came to the conclusion that I was the only one who could win."[48] The governor rarely strayed from his duties at Albany, and he steadfastly resisted calls to speak on national matters. As long as he was governor, he argued, his first obligation was to the people of New York, and Democrats in other states would have to assess him on his record in state affairs.[49]

Smith's supporters, in contrast, were busy spreading the gospel among state leaders across the South and, to a lesser extent, the West. Attempts to abolish the two-thirds rule were resisted by the New York leaders. Smith, it was said, would not countenance any change of the rules which might give the impression that he was not playing fair. He would win the nomination under the same rules as had applied to every Democratic nominee since Van Buren. Although it was by no means their first preference, the governor's group did nothing to oppose the choice of Houston as the 1928 convention site, the first time a southern city had been so honored since 1860.[50]

The Smith forces were similarly circumspect in their quest for delegates.

As early as September 1926 FDR counseled the governor to avoid being seen as "an open out and out candidate for 1928." He warned Smith that some of his supporters were running too aggressive a campaign for him in states still under McAdoo's influence. This, Roosevelt believed, simply gave "the old McAdoo crowd and the know-nothings a reason for organizing against you." The governor should instead announce that he had appointed no manager and that he was doing nothing to promote his own candidacy. "You are gaining in the esteem and confidence of people in every state and as long as things are going well along that line, it is better to saw wood and keep out of the political side of things."[51] Joe Tumulty issued the same warning to James Hoey, an active Smith booster. Hoey should restrain those Tammany spokesmen who were singing their governor's praises, Tumulty urged in July 1926, because "any attempt by undue pressure from the East to force Al Smith on the Democracy will be resented. . . . His own friends in New York have but to sit in the bleachers, remain silent and watch the procession."[52]

This softly-softly strategy was followed throughout the South and West. Particular care was taken not to alienate favorite-son movements or to threaten entrenched McAdoo supporters in state organizations. The creation of Smith organizations in states that were formerly for McAdoo was invariably seen as a threat to existing ones, Louis Howe warned FDR in 1927, "whereas if they were left in peace, McAdoo now being an admittedly dead cock in the fight, they would in a great many instances be open to quiet conversion and conviction, when the time comes." Such diplomacy seemed to pay dividends. As early as 1926 Howe was surprised to hear from Congressman William A. Oldfield of Arkansas that Smith sentiment in the South was increasing, on the reasoning that the New York governor stood the best chance of election in 1928.[53]

Integral to this policy of appeasement of southern Democrats was an attempt to improve Al Smith's image in Dixie. The McAdoo forces were convinced that the sight and sound of Smith in person would permanently alienate southern support from him. Brice Claggett, McAdoo's secretary, told George Milton at the end of 1924 that the Smith forces faced an insoluble dilemma. In order to nominate Smith, his friends would have to send him out into the country, and as soon as they did that the rural electorate would resile from his accent, his manners, and even his style of dress. The very attributes that appealed to his constituency in New York would lose him support elsewhere. "He appeals to all the traits that the shanty Irish love most," Claggett observed, "liquor, loudness, cheapness. Thank God that the rest of the country is not New York City—they will never stand for Smith."[54]

Louis Howe was aware of this, and he constantly advised Smith to tone down characteristics that were picturesque in New York but embarrassingly foreign elsewhere. When Smith's wife, Katie, returned from a European trip in 1925, she proudly recounted stories of a special audience with the pope, in which the pontiff referred to the governor as his beloved son. "She is talking too much for Al's good," Howe grumbled to FDR.[55] Three years later he was again concerned that newsreels of Smith's daughter's wedding, at which Cardinal Spellman of New York presided, would hurt Smith's cause in the South. "I hope the young couple won't have to kiss the Cardinal's toe as part of the ceremony," he wrote.[56] Joe Tumulty, for his part, took James Hoey to task for releasing a particular picture of the Happy Warrior to the press. "The attached is a very bad picture," he wrote in February 1927, "good for home consumption but very bad in its effect beyond the East Side. Cannot someone suggest to the Governor that when posing, he do so without a cigar and without too prominently showing his gold teeth?"[57]

The effect of such warnings is debatable. Smith saw no need to change his manners or demeanor, and even if he had, it is doubtful that such cosmetic changes could have erased southern doubts as to his religion or his suitability for the social demands of the presidency.[58] Similar attempts were made to lessen the identification of Smith with Tammany Hall, an anathema to progressive Democrats. "Do you not think, my dear friend," McAdoo wrote to George Milton in Chattanooga, "that it would be an insult to Walsh, Wheeler, . . . McAdoo, Glass, Meredith and practically all of the members of the group of dry and progressives which have been making the desperate fight against the official and election corruption to nominate a life long member of Tamany [sic] Hall?"[59] Tammany Hall and Smith had been linked for too long for his friends to do much in the way of mollifying this hostility. Hints were dropped, nevertheless, that the governor did not see eye to eye on many issues with George Olvaney, the new leader of the Hall after Murphy's death in 1924, and moves to make Tammany a national organization by the creation of chapters outside New York were quietly scuttled by Smith's friends.[60]

Smith's allies were also anxious not to raise the ire of the South by conducting an extravagant preconvention campaign. Southerners, in particular, were suspicious of Smith's close connections with New York corporate interests, and too lavish a display of eastern funding would have deepened this suspicion. Consequently the Smith camp made as little fuss as possible in raising the funds necessary to further Smith's candidacy. George Van Namee, Smith's personal secretary and chairman of the New York State Democratic Committee, testified to the Senate committee investigating campaign expenditures that the Smith forces made no general appeal for funds before the convention. A small group of Smith's wealthy friends, including William F. Kenny, James W. Gerard (who would later become treasurer of the DNC), and Herbert Lehman, provided the bulk of the necessary money.[61] Kenny was a particularly generous backer, giving or lending a total of $50,000 to the Smith camp by May of 1928.[62] The preconvention total disbursements of the Smith campaign—$144,248.96—were by far the largest amount spent by any Democrat, but they were far less than the $380,151 spent by the Hoover forces to secure the GOP nomination.[63]

In these ways Al Smith was "sold" to Democrats between 1926 and 1928. Unhampered by organized or effective opposition, adequately but not ostentatiously funded, and perhaps helped by judicious image modification, the governor came to the Houston convention as the clear favorite. Yet few observers predicted the ease with which he achieved his triumph: after only one ballot the nomination was his after Ohio switched its vote. Although no attempt was made to make his selection unanimous, it was a stunning victory. Evidence scattered throughout the major manuscript collections bearing on party affairs, however, suggests that the disappearance of opposition to Smith was not as miraculous as it seemed. That evidence allows us to reconstruct the Democratic leaders' mind-set as the 1920s drew to a close.

DEMOCRATIC REASONS FOR SUPPORTING SMITH

As party leaders looked ahead to 1928, they faced a depressing prospect. Many thought that the selection of another compromise candidate in 1928 would mean only another defeat for the Democrats. To have any chance at all, the party would have to choose a man who already commanded the loyalty of a large section of the rank and file. "The worst thing the Democratic party has to fear," Senator Simmons of North Carolina wrote to the editor of the *Winston-Salem Journal* and *Star* in January 1927, is "the nomination of another immaculate gentleman whom nobody has anything against and in whom nobody has any interest and for whom nobody will fight."[64] Both Cox and Davis had been foisted upon the party by brokered conventions, and both had lost. The time had come for the Democratic party to face the fact that, as the minority party, it had to present nationally known figures in order to have a chance.[65]

Putting to one side the actual identity of this hypothetical candidate, many party leaders privately wondered whether any Democrat, no matter how strong or nationally known, could win in 1928. Among McAdoo's supporters there was grave doubt as to whether the 1928 prize would be worth anything to their man. As early as November 1925 Mark Sullivan wrote to Brice Claggett with the opinion that, so long as the current prosperity continued, nothing could deny the Republicans a victory in 1928.[66] It is likely that such thinking at least partially influenced McAdoo in his decision not to seek the nomination. Franklin Roosevelt also had profound doubts about the party's likelihood of success. "Strictly between ourselves," he wrote Josephus Daniels in the middle of 1927, "I am very doubtful whether any Democrat can win in 1928. It will depend somewhat on whether the present undoubted general prosperity of the country continues."[67] Although it was not politic to shout such views from the rooftops, it is likely that many Democrats agreed with him.

Under such circumstances, party leaders from all positions along the party's geographic and ideological spectrum had party health and unity rather than electoral success on their minds as they pondered possible nominees. From this perspective 1928 presented difficulties of unusual severity. "The party situation is of course rather perilous," Cordell Hull wrote to a constituent in January 1928; "we should naturally strive to win this year; but if dissension should render this impossible, we should bend every effort . . . to enable [the party] to live in the future as a truly national organization."[68] The problem thus facing prominent Democrats was to decide not so much how to win the 1928 election, but rather how to manage the consequences of defeat. The decision that most had reached by the end of 1927 was arrived at from three different directions, but the result was that Smith's nomination was made almost certain before the first primary ballot was cast.

The first line of thought can best be described as the sectional argument. This was based upon the North-South strategy, and it held that it was vital for the long-term health of the party to keep the burgeoning northern urban vote loyal to the Democracy. As FDR had pointed out, the mechanics of the Electoral College voting system meant that a victory such as that enjoyed by Woodrow Wilson in 1916, in which the West and the South were united against the East, was increasingly unlikely. The urban voters of the North had been disappointed once by Smith's defeat in 1924; if he were denied the nomination again, their alienation might become permanent. The South, in contrast, was so tightly bound up with the Democratic party as the guardian of white supremacy that its loyalty was more firmly based. The nomination of Smith, therefore, although threatening in the short term the loyalty of the old Confederacy, was necessary to cement the East to the party. "It strikes me that we are in this dilemma," Newton Baker wrote to Ralph Hayes in March 1928: "if Governor Smith is nominated, there is a danger that the party will break up in the states where it now has definite strength. On the other hand, if he is not nominated, there is certainty that the party will break up in the East."[69] William A. Comstock, a DNC member from Michigan, put this argument to southerners in May of 1928: "The leaders in the North and West realize the situation in the South. We realize that Governor Smith's candidacy is bad for your local conditions. The question which has to be decided at the Houston Convention is, therefore, WHAT IS BEST FOR THE PARTY IN THE LONG RUN. IS IT BETTER TO RENDER NORTHERN AND WESTERN DEMOCRACY IMPOTENT FOR A GENERATION, OR TO TAKE CHANCES TEMPORARILY IN THE SOLID SOUTH, KNOWING THAT PARTY DEFECTIONS ARE MORE EASILY CURED IN THE SOUTH THAN IN THE NORTH?" Comstock, for one, was sure that the latter course was the only one for the party to take.[70] Belle Moskowitz and FDR would have agreed, for it was upon this assumption that Smith's nomination strategy was based.

The second reason for Smith's nomination centered on the religious issue. If Smith was denied the nomination, so this argument went, it would be perceived by his supporters to be because he was a Catholic. This would alienate the millions of Catholic voters upon whom Democratic hopes for a permanent urban majority were based. Newton Baker could see little option but to nominate Smith so as to lay this suspicion to rest. "The kind of campaign which will follow his nomination fills me with sadness," he wrote Judge Joshua Alexander of Gallatin, Missouri, in January 1928, "and yet . . . it becomes [*sic*] to me that if the nomination were denied to Smith . . . the party would be judged to have denied it on the basis of religious prejudice, which would be a tragic inheritance for many years to the party."[71] FDR described this argument in much blunter terms, describing the mood of the South in the early months of 1927 from his vantage point at Warm Springs, Georgia. "Down here in the South there is, of course, still great opposition to a Catholic," he wrote his friend Will King in Oregon, but "there is a growing feeling by some of those who oppose Smith that the easiest and quickest way to get rid of this religious question is to give him the nomination, support him and get it off our chest once and for all."[72]

Behind this reasoning lay the feeling that 1928 was not destined to be a Democratic year, whoever the nominee turned out to be. It therefore seemed an attractive idea to use this opportunity to nominate a Catholic so as to establish the principle of toleration with little danger of it becoming a reality.[73] Smith—his religion, his wetness, his Tammany links, his conservatism and his embarrassing success—represented a problem to the party as a whole, and 1928 seemed the perfect time to exorcise it. The stage would then be set for a more acceptable and Protestant candidate in 1932, when conditions might well be more conducive to a Democratic victory. Colonel House explained his support of the nomination of Smith in these backhanded terms at the beginning of 1928: "I feel that it is the only chance the Party has for success, but that is not the moving desire to see him nominated. I want the religious question taken out of our politics. If he is not nominated we will have it in '32, '36 and heaven knows how much longer. If he is nominated and defeated he will not be like Bryan and Roosevelt, constantly agitating for renomination. He will go into business and disappear from the picture and the question will be settled. If he is elected, he will do for the nation what he has done for the state of New York and the question will disappear even in a better way."[74]

The third argument was a strategic one. By conceding the nomination to Smith in a year which promised little for the Democrats, some progressives argued that his defeat would leave the way clear for the nomination

of a more explicitly progressive candidate in 1932. Much the same thinking had muted William Jennings Bryan's criticism of the nomination of
the conservative Alton B. Parker in 1904.[75] This argument was widely held
by McAdoo's supporters. George Fort Milton described this sentiment to
McAdoo in August 1927 as a desire to rid the party of the eastern "menace" by "nominating Smith and letting him have the terrific trouncing he
is doomed to get."[76]

This argument was very attractive to dries such as McAdoo and Cummings, who longed to portray the 1928 campaign as a referendum on
prohibition. Smith's stand on the Eighteenth Amendment played into
their hands, allowing them to link his likely defeat with the neglect of the
strong dry sentiment that they had always alleged to exist in the South and
West. That anticipated defeat could also be used as an argument against
further Tammany control of the party, and in favor of a more explicitly
Wilsonian program of regulation of big business than Smith was prepared
to countenance.

These three arguments were never as self-contained as this analysis
might suggest. Smith's opponents combined them into a plan of conceding the nomination to him. The individual cases of two prominent
Democrats, one from North Carolina and one from Connecticut, demonstrate this conflation. Josephus Daniels, formerly Wilson's secretary of the
navy and Franklin Roosevelt's superior, had returned in 1921 to his *News
and Observer* in Raleigh, North Carolina. Daniels had begun his political career as a devoted free silverite and had been a relentless critic of
big business.[77] During the 1890s, however, he turned against the North
Carolina Populists because of their biracial platform. In 1898 Daniels and
his newspaper led a campaign for white supremacy which culminated in
the passage of North Carolina's disfranchisement law in 1900.[78] An ardent
dry who believed in an active federal regulatory state, he had been a strong
supporter of McAdoo at both the 1920 and 1924 conventions.[79] As 1928
neared, however, he regarded Smith's rising star with despair. He had no
time for the governor's wet views and considered Tammany Hall to be a
blight upon the party. Furthermore, he was dubious about the strength
of Smith's reforming or regulatory commitments. "This is the first time
in my life that I have felt so perfectly at sea as to what we ought to do
and what we can do," he wrote Roosevelt in 1927.[80] Daniels bemoaned
the lack of dry progressive leadership in the wake of McAdoo's seeming

lack of interest in the nomination. There seemed no one who could fill the breach.

"Just as long as the Democratic Party is willing to play second fiddle to big interests," Daniels declared to Claude Bowers toward the end of 1927, "just so long will it trail behind and deserve to trail behind." The real forces behind the Smith boom, he argued, were those who wished the "return of plenty of cheap booze" and "those who think his nomination will make it easier to ignore the domination of big interests" of American economic life.[81] But what could be done? Refusing Smith the nomination would ensure the survival of the religious issue and lose the party the votes of his Catholic adherents for years to come. Nominating Smith, however, would place him and his conservative eastern allies in control of the party machinery for four years and would also threaten local tickets and control of patronage throughout the South.[82] But in the absence of any more palatable alternative, and fortified by FDR's private opinion that 1928 would not be a Democratic year, Daniels reluctantly acquiesced to Smith's nomination, joining the group whom he described in 1927 as "those who are hopeless and say 'let him have it.'"[83]

Homer S. Cummings had long considered himself a misfit in Democratic politics, and with some reason. Wilson's former chairman of the DNC was a dry progressive, closely allied to McAdoo, who lived in the dripping wet and fanatically pro-Smith state of Connecticut. Like Daniels, Cummings grew increasingly depressed about the plight of progressive Democracy after 1920. He saw Smith as an economic conservative out of sympathy with the Wilsonian reforming heritage that Cummings held so dear. As a confirmed dry, he also opposed the governor's stand on prohibition.[84] From as early as 1925 he was convinced that 1928 would not be a Democratic year, and he advised his friend McAdoo not to make the race for that reason.[85] "I do not think the cause of progressive democracy is a lost cause," he wrote Edwin Meredith. "I think, however, it is under a cloud." That being the case, he saw little value in the nomination for the progressive wing of the party. "If I could see ahead the possibility of nominating a progressive candidate, and the possibility of electing such a candidate, it would be a different story."[86]

Believing that no Democrat could win in 1928, Cummings was prepared to see progressive Democrats vacate the presidential field so that their conservative brethren could nominate Smith with little fuss. He argued that the great mistake of 1924 had been to deny the nomination to McAdoo, the candidate with the single largest bloc of delegates, and to select a compromise candidate instead. The same reasoning applied to Smith in 1928. "Reflect for a moment," he wrote Vincent K. Miles, Democratic national committeeman from Arkansas, in 1927, "upon the burden which must be assumed by those who might succeed in defeating the Smith candidacy. They would probably get a candidate for whom they did not care very much and they would also be under obligation to finance the campaign. Thousands of disappointed and embittered Democrats would leave the party and the general result would be as disasterous [sic] as that of 1924."[87]

If Cummings did not consider 1928 to be worth the progressives' effort or money, he did hold hopes for 1932. In that year, he thought, prosperity might have declined to the extent that progressives could regroup and mount an assault upon the greed and materialism of big business. In that case, it was all the more important to let the conservatives have their day in 1928 and to keep Catholic Democrats loyal for another election when their support might well constitute the margin of victory. The nomination of Smith would suit both needs admirably. Writing to an Arkansas Democrat, he reported at the beginning of 1928, "Confidentially, I am inclined to state that I see no other nomination that the Democratic Party can make with the slightest hope of success. I do not know that that would be successful but I am rather inclined to the belief that if he is not nominated we shall be in for another overwhelming defeat and that the scars thereof will not be out of the way by 1932. If he is nominated and elected, then the nomination justifies itself. If he should be nominated and defeated, then the party would, I think, be in a pretty good position in 1932 to gather itself together under some new leadership."[88]

It was by such processes of reasoning that Al Smith could win his "astounding" victory at Houston. Yet his victory was a deceptive one, the product of an ideological and sectional cease-fire rather than of a genuine healing of the wounds of 1924. As the campaign of 1928 would demonstrate, many of those leaders who reconciled themselves, however reluctantly, to Smith's nomination would have second thoughts as the campaign wore on. If the eventual decision to hand Smith a first-ballot victory was necessary, it was nevertheless not a pleasant experience for those who had fought so hard just four years before against everything that Smith represented. George Fort Milton described his experiences at Houston to

Frank Gannett, the newspaper magnate, as a nightmare. More than half the delegates, Milton believed, did not want to see Smith nominated, but "so many of them had listened to their fears and had adopted the attitude that we must nominate him and get it over with or he would be a menace for the next twenty years."[89] In such inauspicious circumstances, the presidential campaign of Al Smith had begun.

6

THE PROBLEM OF AL SMITH

How many Al Smiths were there? He has presented a problem to two generations of biographers, who have grappled with a seeming inconsistency between his record as New York assemblyman, as governor, and later as strident critic of the New Deal. His running mate in 1928, Joe Robinson, remarked in 1936 that "somehow I think there must be two Al Smiths. One is the happy, carefree fellow behind whom we marched . . . in 1928. . . . Now we have this other Al Smith, this grim-visaged fellow in the high-hat and tails, who warns us that we are going straight to Moscow." [1]

This "fundamental dichotomy" interpretation argues two related cases. [2] The first is that Smith's liberal tenure as governor of New York was a rehearsal of the New Deal. The memoirs of prominent New Dealers support this view. Frances Perkins, for instance, reminisced that Governor Smith's policies were "the stones we now recognize in the foundations of the New Deal," and even Franklin Roosevelt argued that "practically all the things we have done in the Federal Government are like things Al Smith did as Governor of New York."[3] Many historians have agreed. In his 1970 biography of Smith, Richard O'Connor was in no doubt that "Smith's administration was a detailed preview of the New Deal. . . . It was the first hurrah, in effect, of the new politics."[4] Paula Eldot also saw in Smith's governorship a precursor of the New Deal and concluded that his four gubernatorial terms represented "a transitional stage between progressivism and the New Deal."[5]

The second part of the "fundamental dichotomy" argument is that Smith performed a volte-face from New Deal herald to New Deal critic. This is variously attributed to the disappointment of his 1928 defeat, to a personal feud with FDR, and to his susceptibility to the extreme conservatism of his business associates during the 1930s. Oscar Handlin believed that these factors contributed to make the Happy Warrior "lose his grip" after 1932.[6] But why should this be so? Why did Smith not undergo the same transformation after his defeat at the hands of Nathan Miller in the gubernatorial race of 1920? After that loss he had entered the business world as president of the United States Trucking Corporation under the tutelage of his millionaire friend William F. Kenny. Smith, however, retained his political constituency and won the governorship two years later. Why was he more susceptible to the views of the business establishment in 1929 than he had been in 1921?

As if to answer these questions, a handful of commentators have argued that Smith was consistently conservative throughout his public career. Walter Lippmann, for example, described the governor in 1927 as "the most powerful conservative in urban America,"[7] and even his campaign biographers maintained in 1928 that "he is conservative, in some respects, and always will be."[8] Smith's opposition to the New Deal therefore represented neither personal angst nor ideological self-betrayal but rather a reaffirmation of the conservative tenets of his political thought. Robert Moses, perhaps Smith's closest political friend, rose to defend his former boss in 1961 against what he termed "the theories of the head-shrinkers of the American Historical Society." Smith, according to his former secretary of state, was "honestly convinced that the New Deal was not his dish of tea." He was a "congenital conservative."[9] The "consistently conservative" interpretation, however, is not yet fully established, and it is almost overwhelmed by the numerous works by historians of the "fundamental dichotomy" persuasion.[10]

It is my contention that the conservative Democrats who supported Smith as a presidential aspirant in 1924, 1928, and 1932 did not mistake their man. They examined Smith's record as governor and found it consistent with their own political agenda. Smith's governorship did not show a general commitment to extensive reform along liberal lines. The fundamental precepts of his political thought and practice, and especially those on the role of the state and the limits of its proper power, the legitimate scope and nature of reform, and his ideal of American society, marked him as an enlightened conservative of the 1920s.

SMITH'S SERVICE IN THE NEW YORK ASSEMBLY

Alfred E. Smith's rise from the anonymity of the lower East Side to the governor's mansion in Albany is well known. Born in 1873 to poor but respectable Catholic parents, his education was cut short at the eighth grade by the death of his father. From that time on, his rise was through ambition and patronage rather through than education.[11] By the time of his first election to the governorship in 1918, he had served Tammany loyally for over twenty years as a subpoena server, assemblyman, leader of the legislature, and sheriff of New York County. It was his tenure in the state assembly (1903–16), however, that brought him into political prominence within the state.

Smith's early years at Albany showed no commitment to progressive reform. His opposition to the direct primary and female suffrage and his support of Sunday baseball attracted the ire of such watchdog organizations as the Citizens' Union. As late as 1914 it characterized Smith as an "experienced and resourceful leader of the Democratic minority, who seldom exerted his influence in behalf of desirable legislation."[12] William H. Allen, never a friend of Tammany or Smith, later described Assemblyman Smith as "the best trained chicken in a brood of trained chickens."[13] The prevailing Tammany attitude toward progressives before 1910 was later encapsulated by Jimmy Walker's definition of a reformer as "a guy who rides through a sewer in a glass-bottomed boat."[14]

Although Smith was too obedient to his Tammany masters for the reformers' liking, it was nevertheless true that Tammany itself was changing its attitude toward social reform. After the traumatic Triangle Shirt Waist Company fire of 1911, in which over a hundred employees perished, powerful voices were raised in support of a change in protective laws for labor. Under the leadership of Charles Murphy, Tammany Hall responded to this pressure and began to support welfare measures.[15] The "new Tammany" was born, and its two most prominent ambassadors were to be Al Smith and Robert Wagner. Propelled by public outrage at the appalling working conditions imposed upon sweatshop workers, and encouraged by the growing split within the state and national Republican parties between progressives and the "old guard," new alliances were forged between Tammany Hall, the state Democratic organization, and reformers.[16] Wagner and Smith even went so far as to forgo their personal objections to the Federal Income Tax Amendment and to the direct elec tion of U.S. senators—the two darlings of progressive reform—and to push their ratification through the state legislature.[17]

In company with social workers such as Frances Perkins, Smith and Wagner undertook a statewide survey of labor conditions.[18] Shocked at what he found, Smith concluded that state intervention through protective legislation was needed as a last resort to protect those members of the work force who were not adequately organized to protect themselves. As majority leader in the assembly, it was his task to shepherd legislation through the legislature. Smith's contribution to labor reform was therefore primarily procedural rather than conceptual; the ideas and formulations of the changes came from the social workers attached to the Legislative Investigative Commission. Between 1913 and 1914 forty-three bills were proposed, including measures relating to factory ventilation, the provision of adequate seating for female workers, medical examinations for working youths, and the limitation of working hours for women.[19] Smith fulfilled his tasks well; of these forty-three bills, only nine failed to become law.[20]

Smith's own conception of labor reform was essentially limited. It was confined to the protection of women and children, since he believed that men were able to look after their own interests. At the constitutional convention of 1915 he led an unsuccessful effort for a minimum wage amendment for women but at the same time dismissed the argument that this should be extended to cover men.[21] Women, as the mothers of the race, were entitled to special protection. Yet he stopped short of proposing the outright prohibition of child labor on the grounds that many poor families relied upon earnings from this source. That this lost income could have been replaced by higher wages or transfer payments from the state seems never to have occurred to him.[22] He did, however, argue for strict regulation of the hours and conditions of child labor.[23]

The measures which Smith ushered into law during this period did not radically alter the relationship between employer and employee, and he certainly did not see himself as a crusader against employers' freedom of contract. He believed, rather, that labor laws benefited employers by ensuring a more healthy and productive work force.[24] His investigations with the Triangle Fire Commission left him with a largely favorable conception of the integrity and humanity of employers as a class. The majority of factory owners would have implemented reforms without the prodding of the Legislative Investigative Commission, he thought, if only they had been more aware of the actual conditions under which their employees worked.[25]

In his pregubernatorial years Smith frequently championed the right of the state to intervene to protect especially vulnerable members of the community. Yet such intervention was to be strictly limited to specific areas of need; arbitrary or unlimited intervention was as unacceptable as the particular abuses at which it was aimed. He was prepared to borrow the ideas of reformers to the extent that these ideas provided workable solutions to concrete problems, yet he was not committed to far-reaching reform.

SMITH AS NEW YORK GOVERNOR

Smith was at the height of his powers during his four terms as governor. By 1928 he had steered New York through a difficult period of postwar adjustment and had presided over a reorganization of both the structure and functions of the state government. New York led the nation in its conservation of parkland resources and in its protection of female and minor labor. Its education system was now well funded, a program for the replacement of dangerous rail crossings had been implemented, and the prison and asylum systems had been reformed along humanitarian lines. The state's position at the center of American finance in the heady days before the crash of 1929 had been preserved, and Smith had even performed the seeming miracle of increasing state spending while at the same time reducing taxes. All this was achieved in the face of opposition from predominantly Republican legislatures eager to embarrass a Democratic governor. Oswald Garrison Villard hailed him in 1928 as "the best Governor, all in all, that New York has ever had,"[26] and thirty years later William E. Leuchtenburg could still describe him as "one of the ablest state officers in American history."[27]

New York under Governor Smith shared in a flowering in the quality and scope of state administrations across the nation during the 1920s. The governorships of Pennsylvania's Gifford Pinchot (1924–28), Tennessee's Austin Peay (1923–27), Alabama's Bibb Graves (1926–30), California's Clement Young (1926–30), Louisiana's John W. Parker (1920–24), Virginia's Harry Flood Byrd (1926–30), Texas's Pat M. Neff (1921–27) and Dan Moody (1927–31), and Cameron Morrison in North Carolina (1921–25) all represented the new spirit of "business progressivism" in state government that closely paralleled Smith's agenda in New York.[28] In the South, especially, the pressures of industrialization brought forth a revival of infrastructure development: roads, schools, and public health received heavy appropriations from legislatures acting with the encouragement of their governors.[29] Businessmen became more actively concerned with the process of government and pushed for extensive reforms of governmental structure in the interests of economy and efficiency. Every southern state adopted an executive budget system between 1918 and 1928, and all but Mississippi had adopted a system of state public welfare by 1927. Road-building and school improvements were the great priorities; in no southern state did the combined expenditure on roads and schools amount to less than 60 percent of the total budget.[30]

The application of "business principles" to government proved to be a durable theme of Smith's gubernatorial years. He also brought to the governorship the same inherently conservative precepts of government and statecraft as he had exhibited in the assembly. This was especially evident in his conception of the proper role of the state in society and of the acceptable scope and nature of reform. As governor, he took care to advocate state intervention only as a last resort. He frequently stressed that state power could not and should not be considered as limitless. In regard to business regulation, especially, he frequently repeated his 1919 warning of the folly of "irresponsible and wanton attacks on business," which were blows to "capital and labor alike."[31]

New York corporate interests were indeed little troubled by Governor Smith and his policies; private enterprise that was not grossly antisocial was sacrosanct.[32] Although crises like the coal and housing shortages of 1919 elicited from him a ready acquiescence to state regulation, he saw such steps as only temporary measures to alleviate short-term problems. He wasted little time in advocating the repeal of rent control legislation and coal rationing as soon as the emergency had passed.[33] He consistently advocated public ownership of water-power sites as the best means toward the conservation of a public resource, but he was careful to moderate his policies so as to avoid a wholesale attack upon private enterprise.[34] Although he proposed to the legislature in 1919 that the state should distribute power by means of a public corporation empowered to issue its own bonds, by 1926 he had modified his position to envisage residual ownership of power sites.[35] In this new position he was supported by Gerard Swope and Owen D. Young, respectively the president and chairman of General Electric.[36] Smith assured a campaign audience in Rochester in 1926 that "the State is not going into the business of dealing in electrical energy with the ultimate consumer."[37] It would be not Smith but rather his successor in Albany, Franklin Roosevelt, who would push most vigorously for public distribution of power.[38]

Smith displayed a similar uneasiness with the concept of extended state power by his actions during the Red Scare of 1919 and 1920. The new governor refused to take part in the hysteria and intolerance that seemed to capture other Democratic leaders. He strongly defended the rights of five Socialist representatives expelled by the New York Assembly in 1920, vetoed bills requiring a loyalty test for teachers, and refused to sign the six Lusk bills that would have effectively made the Socialist party illegal in New York.[39] Behind this defense of free speech lay a conviction that the state was in such cases interfering with personal liberty to an unwarranted degree. Criticizing the legislature in 1923 for countenancing such measures, he reminded the assemblymen of the Jeffersonian dictum that "the best government is the one that governs least."[40] A year later he attacked legislative censorship of motion pictures on the same grounds, arguing that "state interference with literary or artistic production beyond [the] prohibition of the criminal law is contrary to the fundamental principles of democratic government."[41] In 1927, however, the governor did sign a draconian "padlock law" against obscene theatrical productions, much to the displeasure of the American Civil Liberties Union. There were limits to this devout Catholic's tolerance.[42]

Smith's distrust of extensive state action led him to champion states' rights throughout his public career. Although he could countenance government intervention at the state level to address pressing problems, he was considerably less tolerant of federal activism. His desire for efficiency and flexibility in governmental functions did not dispose him to look kindly upon regulation from Washington. Expanding federal power brought with it a subsumption of individual and local interests into a huge and impersonal political bloc. Smith always held that the United States was too large a country, with too many different local interests, to be adequately governed by uniform federal laws.[43] Throughout the 1920s he advocated the repeal of the federal inheritance tax as an intrusion into the revenues traditionally reserved to the states.[44] Such diminutions of state control, he argued, "grow from a desire to do for the whole United States . . . what the different states can do for themselves, and because several have refused to do it, it is imposed upon them by a federal enactment."[45]

This antipathy to excessive centralization underlay Smith's enduring opposition to the Eighteenth Amendment. He thoroughly detested national prohibition as a coercive measure which represented an invasion by the federal government into the daily lives of its citizens. Like Pierre du Pont, John Raskob, and the other backers of the AAPA, he argued that liquor control was a purely local matter and strenuously objected to the situation under the Eighteenth Amendment in which the preference of some states was imposed upon the nation as a whole. It was not, he believed, "the function of law to jack up the moral tone of any community," for that was the proper domain of more private institutions such as the family and the church.[46] The organization necessary for the enforcement of dry laws, he told readers of the *New York Times* in 1920, carried distinctly un-American implications. "I would not submit myself to the enactment of a law that would send an army of spies among the people of the State harassing them and annoying them," he declared, for that would would be tantamount to "reproducing the conditions that exist today in Russia."[47]

Smith's view of the nature and scope of acceptable reform was also consistent with the views he had expressed as an assemblyman. The state government, he told a conference of social workers in 1927, "is divided into two branches, the strictly business side and the human," a division which created two corresponding classes of reform.[48] In practice, however, Smith tended to justify both categories in primarily business terms, adopting language that might have been used by a managing director about the need to revamp his company's corporate structure.

Smith's "business" reform was structural in character and was designed to increase the efficiency of government to make the fullest possible use of each tax dollar. He dwelt on the necessity for government to be run on "business principles," with emphasis upon efficiency and the establishment of a tightly integrated system of specialized areas of responsibility.[49] The linking of business principles and government practice was perhaps the most consistent theme of his governorship. This was especially so after his return to Albany after his two-year break as president of the United States Trucking Corporation between 1921 and 1923. His experiences in business, he reminisced in his autobiography, impressed him "with how much government is like business," and with how amenable problems of government were to the application of business solutions.[50] He saw the office of governor, for example, as being akin to "the head of the corporation or business organization that is the state."[51] His program for reorganizing New York's myriad of bureaus into nineteen departments overseen by secretaries responsible to the governor, and for an executive budget and cabinet, finally implemented at the end of his tenure, was vitally necessary because of the dictates of these "business principles." Smith explained to his constituents in a radio address in November 1924 that no modern business could be run on the same lines as their present state government. "The trend of modern business is to centralize and fix responsibility in department heads," he argued. "That is not true of the State Government."[52]

The governor undertook his "human" reform with a similar emphasis upon "business principles." The state's greatest asset was the health and strength of its people, and good business practice demanded that such an important asset be protected from abuse. Accordingly, Smith earnestly defended New York's workmen's compensation legislation against GOP attack, strengthened the state's Labor Department, and pushed through laws protecting working women and children.[53] He also won bond issues for the improvement of facilities for the insane and juvenile wards of the state, as well as for the creation of more state parks.[54]

Impressive as this agenda of reform was, it is difficult to perceive in it a commitment to fundamental change, much less the rehearsal for the New Deal that some historians have argued for. Smith's structural reforms, couched in the language of efficiency and economy, struck little fear into the hearts of even his most conservative constituents, and the difficulty with which they passed can be put down to Republican obstructionism. By stressing the savings created by his rationalization of the governmental structure of New York, the governor frequently justified them in terms of the tax reductions that such savings would bring.[55] His prison, asylum, and parks programs were primarily responses to the growth of population rather than attempts to redefine social and economic relationships or redistribute income.

Smith's labor policy, especially, reflected the essentially limited nature of his reform. His legislation was largely confined to the protection of women and children, by the same reasoning that he had expressed as an assemblyman.[56] Smith's attitude toward women in relation to protective legislation was echoed in other areas. He had been slow to support the ratification of the Nineteenth Amendment, and he eventually did so only out of a sense of political necessity. When a group of suffragists came to him in 1917 to seek his support, he reportedly spat a stream of tobacco juice toward a spittoon and told his visitors that as far as he was concerned a woman's place was in the home.[57]

However grudging his eleventh-hour conversion to the cause might have been, this consummate politician thereafter made women and their votes a target for special attention. Impressed by his record of support for female wage laws and protective legislation, women activists in New York flocked to his standard. Molly Dewson, later to become Franklin Roosevelt's chief female Democratic organizer in the 1930s, entered political life as a Smith partisan.[58] Smith's most famous and influential female supporter, however, was Belle Moskowitz, who became the most trusted political adviser that the governor ever had.

Smith and Moskowitz first met during Smith's campaign for the governorship in 1918. A social worker by training, Moskowitz spent her early years working in settlement houses and leading campaigns to raise the moral standards of dance halls.[59] Her real talents, however, lay in political strategy and analysis. Although she held no formal office in any of Smith's administrations, her influence over the governor was immense. She oversaw Smith's electoral campaigns, including those for the presidential nomination in 1924 and 1928, and conferred with the governor on state matters on a daily basis.[60]

Despite her intelligence and skills, Moskowitz maintained a consistently low profile. Contradicting the evident success of her own career, she declared that women were not "the intellectual equals of men." They could bring only an "intuitive sense" to politics which, when combined with "the thinking ability of men," made a "splendid working team."[61] Her self-effacing attitude was calculated to avoid threatening her male colleagues in what remained a man's world.[62] Certainly it sat well with Smith's own limits upon female assertiveness. "I always thought that, as a rule, men will take advice from a woman," Smith told FDR in 1928, "but it is hard for them to take orders from a woman."[63] Moskowitz never mistook the appearance for the reality of power. In her memoirs of the 1928 campaign, she recalled that she did not sit in on meetings of Smith's 'War Board,' "largely because I would have been the only woman present, and I had so much respect for the political pride of the men that I would never put myself in the position of attending these conferences."[64] She did not need to; everyone who knew Smith understood that Mrs. Moskowitz had the governor's ear on all major issues. Moskowitz's public attitude corresponded perfectly to Smith's ideas on women and their proper role in politics. She was an exception to his general rule that women belonged in the private sphere.

Smith's concern for working children was also in keeping with his broad outlook on reform and his adherence to welfare capitalism. He persisted in his refusal to advocate the abolition of child labor, urging instead, in the language of "business principles," for the regulation of their conditions of employment. It was the duty of the corporation-state to protect the precious asset that its young people represented, he told the legislature in 1918, for "the State that cares for them will have an investment bearing interest in human dividends, that will make it win in the long run."[65] He showed the same pragmatism when he urged the assembly in 1926 to pass an eight-hour-day bill for working women and minors. He argued that many employers were in favor of such a measure "because it was demonstrated to them that a reduction in the hours of labor resulted in increased production and increased efficiency." He was therefore in favor of the bill "having in view not alone the public welfare, but the beneficial effects on industry."[66]

In sharp contrast to the efforts of his former colleague Robert Wagner, by then in the U.S. Senate, Smith did little on behalf of male labor. Apart from protecting the workmen's compensation law, he limited himself during the 1920s to statements upholding the right to strike and vague declarations that injunctions were overused to break industrial stoppages.[67] He conceived of the state as having only a limited, conciliatory role in union-management disputes, with the minimum of interference with the bargaining powers of either side.[68]

Smith's professed faith in the efficacy of trade unions to protect their members from exploitation did not correspond to the reality of the times. Labor unions were notoriously ineffective, beset by judicial harassment and weakened by "yellow dog" contracts in what was essentially an employers' decade. Smith could not have been unaware of the hollowness of his faith in unions during this period. However he made no call for a constitutional amendment to confirm the state's right to regulate male labor, although the workmen's compensation law had been protected in this manner in 1913.[69] Nor did he call on the legislature to force the issue by passing regulatory legislation dealing with hours of employment for men. This suggests a fundamentally noninterventionist attitude to male labor, in the same way that his solicitude toward female labor revealed a deeper denial of the permanence of women in the work force and an affirmation of the traditional view of their place in society.

SMITH AND THE NEW DEAL

Having retired from the governorship in 1928, Smith entered private life after his defeat for the presidency. His political philosophy, however, remained remarkably constant, despite the changed economic situation after 1929. His Jeffersonian conception of the proper role of government remained unchanged throughout the depression. It was hardly surprising that the New Deal would strike him as unjustified federal expansion and activism. Just as he had objected to prohibition as a flagrant invasion by the federal government into the private affairs of its citizens, he found much to complain about in the scope of the New Dealers' intrusion into everyday life. Regarding child labor, for instance, he maintained his opposition to a blanket federal prohibition. This would, he argued, give the federal government "unwarranted and complete control over the lives and daily habits of every person below the age of eighteen. . . . Over a period of years, everyone would have a large part of his life regulated under it."[70]

The deep commitment to states' rights that marked Smith's years as governor remained with him throughout the 1930s. As one who had spent his entire career within state politics, the governor always retained a localized conception of politics which verged upon the parochial. He perceived in the New Deal a concerted policy of centralization which would lead to a dismantling of the traditional system of limited federal powers and reserved state powers. Furthermore, centralization created inefficiency and corruption.[71] "The New Deal," he complained in 1940, "doesn't want the American people to be self-reliant and independent."[72] Instead, FDR and his underlings aimed to create a planned society in which individuals would be allowed little freedom to use their own initiative to advance and prosper. "The Government," Smith maintained, "cannot solve all our problems and we should not expect it to."[73] America had been made by individual effort, and government's proper function was to foster this initiative rather than to replace it with a drab, Washington-directed uniformity.[74]

As it had done in his earlier years, Smith's strong sense of individualism underpinned his ideas as to the proper extent of government regulation of business during the 1930s. He continued to advocate the primacy of private and individual businessmen within the national economy. Business, rather than government, would lead the nation out of the depression, for only private capital could provide permanent mass employment.[75] "I can't possibly be wrong if I say that every workingman must be interested in the success of business," he told a campaign audience for Alf Landon in 1936, "because, after all is said and done . . . when capital is idle, everybody is idle."[76] The spirit of this declaration was identical to an admonition that Smith had made to the New York legislature during his first gubernatorial message in 1919. Warning legislators of the folly of "irresponsible and wanton attacks on business," the new governor had reminded them that "the prosperity of the working man depends in large part upon the prosperity of the employer."[77] Even as the focus of macroeconomic management moved away from Wall Street toward Washington, Smith clung tenaciously to his vision of an economy led by businessmen. In 1936 he argued that the New Deal was hampering businessmen's efforts to perform their proper function to provide relief from the depression, and instead precious time was being wasted through pointless experiments in social reform and government-led recovery. "In the meantime," he concluded, "the American businessman is certainly having a swell time of it getting kicked around all over the lot."[78]

Not all Smith's utterances during the 1930s were negative. In his more constructive suggestions, however, he was as faithful to his gubernatorial philosophy of government as he was when he criticized the New Deal. He again urged the rationalization of governmental structure in order to save money and to increase efficiency.[79] In 1932 he proposed a reorganization of New York City's administration, based upon his familiar themes of the elimination of bureaucratic inefficiency and the need for legislative allocation of responsibility to departments whose functions were clearly defined.[80] His concern that each tax dollar should be used effectively and frugally, along "business principles," did not lessen. In 1935 he blamed "the vast amount of superfluous laws, of red tape, of duplication and inefficiency" for making government "more than twice as extravagant and half as swift in its operation as comparable operations of private enterprise."[81]

The governor continued to support programs for the provision of low-cost urban housing.[82] If the private sphere could not manage this during the depression, he was prepared to see the state intervene as a last resort. He did not particularly like this thought, he wrote in the *New Outlook* in 1934, but he was prepared to accept it "if it were the only means of getting rid of one of the greatest curses of our civilization." On the whole, he thought, "it would be a whole lot better for government to invade this field . . . than to waste millions in other less promising experiments." As he had done as governor, however, he made clear that he envisaged a partnership between government and private capital in the creation of new housing.[83]

Smith also maintained his belief that the state was justified in rectifying gross injustices suffered by those members of society who could not adequately defend themselves. He continued to support labor safety laws and was worried that the sweatshop would reappear as tumbling wages and massive unemployment eroded workers' bargaining power.[84] Constant, too, was his belief that the states, but not the federal government, had a responsibility to ensure that equality of opportunity was preserved and that those who were incapable of protecting themselves were safeguarded from exploitation and "inhuman or unfair working, living, or sanitary conditions."[85] To this end he proposed in 1938 the creation of a state insurance scheme, brushing aside criticism that such a measure encroached upon private insurers. He pointed out that the scheme would only insure those individuals who could not afford private health insurance.[86] Although he was a persistent advocate of reduced government expenditures throughout the 1930s, Smith never allowed this to lessen his decades-old commitment to the improvement of educational facilities. "Time lost preparing our children to take their place in the world," he declared, "cannot be made up."[87]

In the face of these consistent themes in Smith's actions as governor and rhetoric as New Deal critic, it is difficult to sustain the hypothesis of the "two Al Smiths." This view seems to have been rooted in a misconception of Governor Smith as a doctrinaire liberal, a misconception that led both contemporaries and some historians to conclude that former Governor Smith turned his back on the tenets of his earlier political faith. Yet it was his very consistency that led him to leave the party with which his political fortunes had been tied for so long. It was the Democratic party—and not Smith—which changed. The party which he led to the polls in 1928 bore little resemblance in its orientation and philosophy to that which Franklin Roosevelt led in 1936. Smith was well aware of this ideological divergence; in 1940 he remarked that "within six months after the first inauguration of Mr. Roosevelt . . . [the New Dealers] had taken over the Democratic Party lock, stock and barrel."[88] Rather than two Al Smiths, in short, there were instead two Democratic parties.

SMITH AS A LIFELONG CONSERVATIVE

If there was only one Al Smith, how can he be best placed within the ideological context of his day? It is difficult to place him in an intellectual tradition of American conservatism, for Smith approached politics and problems of statecraft in a nonintellectual way. This at times verged on the anti-intellectual; he frequently boasted, "I never read a book for entertainment in my life," and he told the *New York Times* that "I was brought up in a tough political school where facts counted far more than theories. My training has been to distinguish between high sounding principles and actual results."[89] "His mind," Felix Frankfurter observed in 1928, "is fertilized by the concrete event."[90]

Despite his anti-intellectual bent, Smith in many ways did personify the antistatist conservatism that emerged in the years after the Civil War.[91] Smith's policies as governor and his criticisms of the New Deal reflected the same spirit that moved Herbert Hoover to complain of the "specious claim that hired representatives of a hundred million people can do better than the people themselves, in thinking and planning their daily life."[92] In his consistent support of state's rights, his opposition to social welfare that sought to impose equality upon society rather than to allow people's varying abilities to determine their place on the economic ladder, and his unvarying desire to apply "business principles" to the process of government, Smith exhibited a thoroughly conventional conservatism.[93]

As an urban Catholic, Smith also conformed to his church's perceived conservatism on social issues. Nathan Glazer and Daniel Moynihan noted in 1970 that the American Catholic hierarchy in general, and the New York church in particular, had long shown a "decided aversion" to the modern liberal state. This aversion had begun with the French Revolution and had been confirmed by the tumultuous events of 1848 and then Italian reunification. Catholic congregations had long been warned of the dangers of creeping socialism, and the bitter struggles over funding of parochial schools had left many extremely wary of state power.[94] Smith was clearly of this tradition, expressing the fears and cultural apprehensions that were part and parcel of many Catholics' perception of the world.[95]

But in equally pertinent ways Smith's conservatism defies ready classification. Although his conception of reform was limited, he by no means shared John Randolph's fear of the "maggot of innovation."[96] He never allowed his ideal of free and fair competition between citizens in their quest for material success to degenerate into the callous social Darwinism that was so popular during his lifetime. As early as 1915 he had criticized those who wished to "reduce the basic law to the same level of the caveman's law, the law of the sharpest tooth, the angriest brow and the greediest maw."[97] He was similarly distant from the antidemocratic bent that pervaded much American conservative thought. The concept of a ruling class was horrifying to this champion of an America in which success and leadership depended solely on talent, no matter how lowly its origins.[98]

The key to understanding Smith's political thought lies not in ideological traditions or intellectual categorization but rather in his outlook as a self-made man.[99] Like that of John Raskob, Smith's conservatism sprang from what he saw as the experience of his own life—"a plain story of a plain ordinary man who received during his lifetime, to the fullest possible extent, the benefit of the free institutions of his country"—an example of the triumph of Americanism.[100] Although he was native-born, Smith manifested an immigrant's gratitude for the blessings which the New World had showered upon him. He saw his own life as a fairy tale about the success that could come through hard work and determination, and he saw himself a guardian of the traditional ideals of his society which had made his miraculous rise possible.

Smith, like John Raskob, also serves to illustrate the point that corporatism had not completely triumphed in the 1920s. Strong strains of old-fashioned individualism persisted in his political thought, rhetoric, and action throughout his life. Although he was prepared to accept, virtually without cavil, what Ellis Hawley has described as the new individualism of business organizations and private bureaucracies, Smith never subscribed to the belief that individual economic or political autonomy had to be tempered to meet the demands of a new "associational" age.[101] Society existed, Smith believed, to further the rise and prosperity of individuals as free as possible from state intervention and bureaucracy.

Smith's desire to preserve the social and economic institutions which had afforded him so much opportunity marked him most firmly as a conservative. He could not tolerate any attempt, however well intentioned, to alter the fabric of American society in such a way that a future Al Smith might not be able to rise as he had done. What he saw as the hallmarks of the society in which he had prospered—social mobility, freedom of individual enterprise, and a deeply entrenched success ethic—created, he believed, the social climate best suited to aid the underprivileged. His humanitarianism led him not to espouse the welfare state but rather to reaffirm the status quo. The underdog, he believed, was best helped by safeguarding a free and open America unencumbered by an interfering state.[102]

Smith brought these views with him to the governor's chair, and he seldom missed an opportunity to reassert his desire to keep the paths of opportunity as open as possible. In 1924 he opposed the imposition of additional educational qualifications for accountants on the basis that accountancy required "ability and integrity" rather than formal education. "Are we not going a little bit too far?" he asked. "The first thing we know a fellow cannot be a truckman until he can show by college education he isn't going to break the truck."[103] "Suppose it was necessary," he asked a black audience in 1923, "to have a high school diploma to be Governor; where would I be? I never had the chance."[104] He maintained his opposition to a literacy test for immigrants seeking naturalization in the belief that there was no reason to believe that an illiterate immigrant could not be "just as good a citizen as the man with an unbroken line of New England ancestors."[105]

Governor Smith's most famous attack upon the unwarranted privileges of wealth came in connection with his long struggle for a state park system on Long Island. In 1924 he fought stubbornly—and in the end successfully—to appropriate a deceased estate on the island for a foreshore park in the face of concerted opposition from those he called "the wealthy residents and golf-club members" whose estates bordered upon the proposed park.[106] Well aware of the political value of this issue, Smith led a vocal attack on these groups, who feared an invasion of the city rabble "tramping over the country and leaving empty sardine cans behind them."[107] His concern was for equality of opportunity rather than equality of station. His fight was for the right of access to the countryside that had formerly been the preserve of the wealthy. He made no attack upon the right of the Long Island elite to maintain their retreats and hunting estates, but he insisted that less privileged New Yorkers had a right to share a small part of the pleasures of rural Long Island, if only for a day.

As a New Deal critic, Smith maintained the same vision of a fluid and classless society that he had cherished in his earlier years. Such initiatives as the massive public relief projects, the Social Security Act, the National Labor Relations Act, and the sharply progressive income tax scales seemed to him to be fraught with peril. The New Dealers were attempting to level America down rather than to allow the poor to rise up through their own initiative and talent.[108] He did not suddenly discover this danger during the New Deal; as early as 1919 he had attacked William Randolph Hearst as a cynical demagogue who deserved only contempt. "The man that preaches to the poor of this . . . community discontent and dissatisfaction to help himself . . . is a man as low and as mean as I can picture him," the new governor declared in almost exactly the same language that he would use thirteen years later to criticize Franklin Roosevelt's "forgotten man" speech.[109]

It was Al Smith's personal tragedy that he outlived his dream, which depended on prosperity to make it credible. His vision of America was based upon the assumption of a permanently expanding economy. The Great Depression, with its Hoovervilles, bread lines, and apple sellers, made a mockery of his ideal of an America in which all could rise to prosperity through their own efforts. Smith did not, and could not, see that his vision had become a nightmare for so many of his fellow Americans.

All this, however, lay in the future as Al Smith received the presidential nomination at Houston in 1928. Up to that time, his record was one of triumph rather than despair; his four terms as governor had been marked by electoral success and by concrete progress in the fields of administrative reform, infrastructure development, and conservation. There is little evidence, however, to support the view that his eight years in the governor's mansion were a prelude to the New Deal. If Smith was truly a committed and doctrinaire liberal, how could men as conservative as Pierre du Pont, John Raskob, and John W. Davis support him so wholeheartedly in 1928? It is clear that they considered him to be the best of both worlds: not only was his attitude toward the Eighteenth Amendment hostile, but his policies and attitudes on such matters of economic policy as business regulation and the proper extent of state intervention were eminently "safe." Al Smith had clearly earned his role as the darling of the northeastern conservatives; his qualifications as a beacon of liberalism and a herald of the New Deal were more dubious.

7

A BUSINESSMAN COMES TO POLITICS

JOHN J. RASKOB

"Don't breathe a word about it to anyone," James Hoey wrote to Joe Tumulty from Al Smith's campaign headquarters straight after the Houston convention, "but for your confidential information [I] would say the Governor is about to do the boldest and most courageous thing in the history of American politics."[1] Smith did, indeed, astound his party on July 11, 1928, by announcing that his friend John J. Raskob, a senior executive of the Du Pont and General Motors corporations and a self-identified Republican, would be his campaign manager and chairman of the DNC. No clearer message could have been sent that the Happy Warrior intended to court the businessman's pocketbook and vote in 1928, and no more obvious a sign could have been given to the party's progressives that economic conservatives were now at the party's helm. Perhaps only Raskob himself knew how significant his appointment was; neither his opponents nor his friends could have known that the new chairman was determined to leave his mark on the party and its ideological direction in a way undreamed of by his immediate predecessors. The era of "Raskobism" had begun.

Raskob's appointment was an important event in the development of the conservative coalition within the party during the 1920s. The campaigns of Cox and Davis had seen the party extend a more welcoming hand to businessmen and business interests, and this trend continued with the nomination of Smith. Raskob's appearance as chairman seemed to provide further evidence that the party was now more amenable to the businessman's point of view. In addition, his appointment marked an attempt to entrench the conservative northeastern group's power. Even if Smith should lose the 1928 election, Raskob's tenure would last until 1932. Unlike White and Shaver, furthermore, the new chairman was determined that he would not be a mere caretaker of a skeleton organization. John Raskob proved to be one of the central figures of the ideological struggle within the party, and thus he merits examination in his own right. What was his philosophy of business and government? Why did he join the party in such a dramatic way in 1928? Answering these questions gives an important insight into the development of the party faction in which he was to take such a prominent role.

JOHN RASKOB AND PIERRE DU PONT

Raskob owed his appointment to his friendship with Smith and to the lessons that the latter learned from the election of 1924. In that year, Smith told the press in 1928: "Hundreds and thousands of people here in New York who voted for me also voted for that cold fish, Coolidge. It puzzled me then, and I have thought a lot about it since. The only way I dope it out is that a whole lot of people who were willing to elect a Democratic Governor were afraid, for business reasons, of a Democratic administration at Washington. Jake Raskob will change all that. He's our best bet."[2]

Smith's "best bet" was born in Lockport, New York, in 1879. His father was an Alsatian cigar maker, and his mother was of Irish descent. Both were devout Catholics, and John was educated in parochial schools. After high school, he attended the Bryant and Stratton Business School in Buffalo, where he learned stenography and bookkeeping. His family had been poor, but not desperately so, until his father died in 1897. From that time on, Raskob had to give up hope of further education and instead find work to supplement his family's reduced income.[3] His first permanent job took him to Canada, as a bookkeeper for the Dominion Iron and Steel Company. In 1900 he applied for the position of Pierre du Pont's secretary and stenographer. Although his current employers paid him $100 per month, he wrote du Pont that he was prepared to accept a salary of $80, "and shall earnestly endeavor to merit an increase in a short time."[4] Twenty-eight years later, Raskob's personal fortune was estimated to be $100 million.[5] In Ernest Dale's estimation, Raskob was "probably the most highly successful 'assistant to' ever to work in an American company."[6]

Although Raskob and Smith were often described as self-made men, both owed their success to the tutelage of father figures. Smith was twelve when his father died. His place would later be filled by Charles Murphy of Tammany Hall, without whom Smith might never have reached the governor's mansion. In Raskob's case, Pierre du Pont provided the same support for his young secretary. Their friendship had an enormous impact upon two of the nation's largest corporations, the antiprohibition movement, and the Democratic party. The two men, in some ways, could not have been more unalike. Alfred Sloan, who knew them both intimately during the 1920s, thought that the two friends had fundamentally different, but not antagonistic, temperaments. Raskob was "brilliant and imaginative . . . and a man of big ideas," while du Pont was "steady and conservative." Du Pont was "tall, well built, and reticent," while his secretary was short and outgoing.[7] Doubtless aware of their differences, the two men combined their individual strengths and minimized their weaknesses by working in tandem in both business and political affairs.

Raskob quickly assumed duties beyond those normally expected of a personal secretary. In 1900 du Pont bought a failing street-railway in Dallas. Raskob became treasurer of that concern and then followed his mentor to Wilmington, Delaware, in 1902. The Du Pont Company was in the throes of a succession crisis; none of the older generation wished to take control after the death of company president Eugene du Pont. Pierre, T. Coleman, and Alfred du Pont eventually bought the company from their elders for $12 million, and Pierre was installed as the company's treasurer. John Raskob became his assistant, and together they set about creating a modern industrial giant.[8]

Du Pont and Raskob reorganized the company's accounting procedures, its internal structure, and its finances. They were at the forefront of the managerial revolution that swept American corporations after 1900.[9] The Du Pont Company came to embody, in Robert F. Burk's phrase, "industrial federalism." Management functions were largely decentralized to production divisions, but broad financial control was retained by powerful and centralized committees.[10] Raskob was appointed to the Executive Committee and then to the Finance Committee, and by 1914 he was the treasurer. It was World War I, however, that allowed the company to reap the maximum benefit from du Pont's and Raskob's efforts; the huge quantities of explosives needed by the allies and then by the United States had a dramatic effect upon Du Pont's size and profits. The company's productive capacity grew by a factor of twelve during 1917–18. In 1912, its best prewar year, its net earnings were $6.8 million; in 1916 this figure had jumped to over $82 million. Gross receipts and net earnings for 1916 alone exceeded the combined totals for the years between 1902 and 1915.[11]

Such huge profits needed to be invested, and the company again came to benefit greatly from Raskob's advice.[12] In 1914 he had bought five hundred shares of General Motors stock and persuaded Pierre du Pont to invest still more. GM had had a stormy history since its founding by William Crapo Durant in 1908. After losing control of his company in 1910, Durant had recovered his position by 1915 and was again undertaking an ambitious expansion program. By this time, both Pierre du Pont and Raskob sat on the board of directors. Firm believers in the rosy future of the automobile industry and of General Motors, Raskob and du Pont pushed their more reluctant colleagues at the Du Pont Company to invest part of their war profits into GM. In 1917 the company bought $25 million worth of stock, giving it nearly a quarter of the corporation's total share capital. This was the largest investment ever made by one company in another in a different industry.[13] By the beginning of 1921 the Du Pont Company was the largest single shareholder in GM, having bought a total of $47 million worth of shares.[14] Raskob's hunch proved to be very lucrative indeed; by 1945 the Du Pont Company's $47 million investment had a book value of $750 million.[15]

Events in 1920 increased the influence of the Du Pont Company and its senior executives in the affairs of General Motors. Durant's too-rapid expansion of his company threatened its viability, and the price of its stock plummeted. After losing his $20 million fortune in a fruitless attempt to buttress stock prices, Durant was forced to relinquish control to Morgan and Company and to the du Ponts. His departure marked GM's transition from "genius management" to that of systematic organization, and from a centralized structure to a decentralized organization of semiautonomous divisions.[16] Pierre du Pont became president, and he installed Raskob as chairman of the Finance Committee. After reorganizing and rationalizing the corporation's divisions, du Pont resigned in 1923, leaving Raskob as the second most powerful man in GM behind the new president, Alfred Sloan.[17] Revived by du Pont's reorganization, GM prospered mightily during the 1920s; its 1921 sales figures of nearly 215,000 cars more than doubled in 1922. In 1925 its earnings amounted to $116 million; three years later they were $276.5 million, the largest annual profit recorded by any company in the world before the end of World War II.[18]

Raskob's early years with General Motors revealed both his weaknesses and his strengths. As the Du Pont Company's chief representative at GM between 1917 and 1920, he had encouraged and abetted Durant's expansionary schemes at the expense of the corporation's short-term viability.[19] Although a brilliant financier, Raskob was indifferent to the less spectacular tasks of organization and administration. He was, in Alfred Chandler's phrase, an "industrial imperialist."[20] Raskob was not a corporatist in the sense of being part of Robert Wiebe's "new middle class" or Ellis Hawley's "associative vision."[21] Alfred Sloan and Pierre du Pont, in their obsession with organizational structure, lines of command, and detailed planning, conformed much more closely to this model. Raskob, on the other hand, was in many ways closer to the old, rugged individualistic school of "genius management." "It would be agreed, I think," Sloan argued in his autobiography, "that both Mr. Durant and Mr. Raskob had a strong desire to spend and had little inhibition about debt."[22] When GM's crisis came to a head in 1920, Pierre du Pont was forced to step in and repair the damage done by his ambitious and daring protégé. Raskob worked best as part of a team, in which his financial daring could be steadied by those with organizational skills.[23] Raskob was fortunate to have Pierre du Pont and then Alfred Sloan to provide that steadying influence in his personal and business life.

On the positive side, however, Raskob is generally credited as the guiding force behind the establishment of the General Motors Acceptance Corporation (GMAC) in 1919.[24] GMAC was, in essence, a finance company which allowed approved customers to buy GM automobiles on credit. GMAC was Raskob's greatest contribution to the firm because it dramatically expanded the market for cars. Banks had not generally lent money for the purchase of automobiles, thus leaving a gap in the market for GMAC to fill. Although the idea of corporations providing credit to their consumers was not a new one, GMAC was the first such venture into the automobile industry.[25] It proved to be a huge success; within ten years its volume had passed the $1 billion mark, and by 1927 two-thirds of all GM's car sales were financed through GMAC.[26] By 1939 GMAC had become the largest sales financing company in the world, with $400 million in assets, $720 million annual turnover, 5,400 employees, and annual profits of at least $12 million.[27]

By the end of World War I Raskob was a very wealthy man. Pierre du Pont was particularly helpful in Raskob's rise to riches by lending him money to speculate in stock. Raskob's financial skills enabled him to repay the money quickly and still generate enormous profits. In 1918, for example, he borrowed funds from du Pont to buy Chevrolet stock. By the time that he repaid the money in 1919, Raskob had made a profit of over $425,000.[28] The two men, linked by friendship, money, and occupation, grew steadily closer. In keeping with du Pont family practice, Raskob referred to Pierre as Daddy, despite being only nine years younger than his patron. Du Pont had no children of his own but Raskob behaved like a devoted and grateful son. When du Pont gave him the funds in 1916 to buy a large block of Du Pont stock, the younger man expressed his gratitude in a revealing way.

Dear Daddy,

It is hard for me to express myself in words under ordinary circumstances and it seems impossible to properly do so when my heart, always so full of love and affection for you, is filled to overflowing with the thought that you too really care so much for one who at times, I fear, has been very unruly and sorely tried your patience. . . .

. . . With me there has not been the slightest opportunity to fail because you just wouldn't let me and the magnified credit you always give me is really a reflection of you and your work in a mirror which you have succeeded in polishing after a great deal of hard work. Remember, Daddy, it is always possible to ruin mirrors through breaking them, and aren't you very afraid of spoiling me through your continued praise? . . .

Now I am going to build another monument by keeping your gift as a fund separately invested to grow and be used in the future in some way that will ever make me think of you in my endeavors to handle it in a way that I think will make my Daddy love me more if that is possible.[29]

The close collaboration of the two men in business and personal affairs continued throughout their lives. By 1928 they had added political activity to their long list of joint ventures. Both men had been active in the AAPA, and the nomination of the "wet" Smith led them to the Democratic party. Pierre du Pont contributed funds to the cause; Raskob contributed not only money but also his services as chairman of the DNC. In so doing, he became the decade's most prominent example of a "business man in politics." To be properly understood, he must first be seen in the context of the ideas about society and politics that business groups held during the 1920s.

BUSINESS ATTITUDES IN THE 1920s

The 1920s came as a relief to a business community alarmed by fifteen years of trust-busting, increased federal regulation, progressive reformism, and labor unrest. Progressivism increased the influence of the federal government in the everyday lives of its citizens, but the demands of the war effort between April 1917 and November 1918 still came as a rude shock. Mark Sullivan summed up those eighteen months as a time when "the state took back, the individual gave up, what had taken centuries of contest to win." Every male between the ages of eighteen and forty-five was subject to selective service; every person lost the freedom of speech; every businessman lost sovereignty over his factory and store; every wheat farmer lost control over the price of his crop. Railroads, telephones, and coal mines were taken over; producers of plows, paints, and even typewriter ribbons were suddenly subject to federal standardization.[30] Many complained, but there was a war to be won. As soon as the war ended, however, so too did businessmen's patience with federal control. "The crying need of the hour," Francis H. Sisson of the National Association of Manufacturers (NAM) declared during the last months of the Wilson administration, "is a business government for business people."[31]

This wish seemed granted when Warren G. Harding was elected to the presidency in November 1920. A new atmosphere pervaded Washington under the Republicans; the new president's cabinet included such prominent businessmen as Andrew Mellon and Herbert Hoover, and the federal regulatory agencies were increasingly led and staffed by men sympathetic to businessmen's desire to be left alone.[32] The business-government cooperation that had been fostered by such wartime measures as the War Industries Board, the Shipping Board, and the suspension of antitrust legislation carried over into the new decade and the new administration.[33]

Individual income taxes were progressively reduced, and the Internal Revenue Service was noticeably uncritical in its analysis of tax returns.[34] Antitrust laws were only sporadically enforced; of the 14,000 complaints of unfair trading practices lodged during the decade under the Clayton Act, 10,000 were summarily dismissed and 3,546 were dismissed after either an inquiry or a hearing. Only eight men were jailed for Clayton Act violations between 1920 and 1929, and five of those were labor leaders.[35]

The labor movement, which had grown accustomed to a favorable hearing from the federal administration after 1915, found in the 1920s a less congenial atmosphere.[36] The open shop movement, in the form of the "American Plan," grew rapidly in the early years of the decade, fueled by strong support from such business groups as NAM.[37] The AFL's membership slumped from 5 million in 1919 to 3.6 million in 1929.[38] In 1928 only 7.6 percent of the nation's work force of 47 million was organized.[39]

Although the Harding and Coolidge administrations desisted from openly espousing the American Plan or from condoning an all-out assault upon organized labor, the sweeping injunctions sought by Attorney General Daugherty against striking railroad workers in 1922 made it clear that labor could expect little from Washington.[40] From the Supreme Court came a string of decisions that gave substance to Chief Justice Taft's description of labor in 1922 as "that faction we have to hit every little while"; the decade saw the Court invalidate a national child labor law and a minimum wage statute in the District of Columbia, deny that labor organizations were exempt from the Clayton Antitrust Act of 1916, and strengthen restrictions upon picketing and boycotts.[41] Economic changes, too, seemed to conspire against organized labor; traditionally unorganized groups such as white collar, service, and female workers assumed greater importance within the work force; craft industries declined in the face of mass production firms, and the relative size of the antiunion South in the nation's industrial machine grew rapidly.[42]

Secretary of Commerce Herbert Hoover set the tone for the decade by assuring the NAM in 1922 that his department served "no regulatory function . . . minus a few inconsequential matters in connection with the safety of human life." It would, instead, be dedicated to the principle that its primary purpose was to be "of the greatest service" to business, and that its "whole relationship should be one of co-operation with our business public."[43] "Never before, here or anywhere else," the *Wall Street Journal* noted with satisfaction, "has a government been so completely fused with business."[44] Highly labor-intensive producers of textiles, steel, automobiles, and rubber had flocked to the Republican party in the 1890s in fear of labor unions, high taxes, and free trade, and the 1920s marked the high-water mark of this alliance. The GOP, funded by this coalition of major industries, was careful to keep its policies in line with the views of its major investors.[45]

Secure in their influence in Washington, America's large corporations continued their drive to consolidate their preeminent position in the nation's economy. In so doing, they moved further and further away from the classical nineteenth-century theory of competition. Increases in productivity and the growth of large-scale corporations demanded an expanding and stable consumer market and a new theory of competition. Price wars and destructive rivalries seemed increasingly dangerous as corporations became bigger and more diversified.[46] The 1920s saw the proliferation of cooperative oligopolies which were sustained by a continuing process of mergers, acquisitions, and trade agreements undertaken with the acquiescence and often approval of Herbert Hoover's Commerce Department.[47]

The Supreme Court gave its imprimatur to this new attitude toward business organization in the *U.S. Steel Corporation* case of March 1920. Under the "rule of reason" propounded in this decision, no merger was ipso facto illegal merely because of the size of the resulting business entity; an undue restriction of competition had to be demonstrated. The business sector responded to this with a rash of mergers; between 1920 and 1928 more than 1,200 mining and manufacturing consolidations took place, leading to the disappearance of 6,000 firms.[48] As Raskob and du Pont had done within the Du Pont Company, other business leaders restructured their companies to facilitate the flow of information, the allocation of responsibility, and the improvement of efficiency within their concerns.[49]

The increasingly oligopolistic business sector of the 1920s needed a stable and growing consumer market to sustain it. Schemes similar to John Raskob's GMAC proliferated so as to expand demand for the ever-increasing volume of goods produced through large-scale production. By 1929, fully 15 percent of all retail sales were made on an installment basis, and the phenomenon of margin trading of stocks became one of the decade's best-known characteristics.[50] No longer at odds with the federal government and increasingly dependent upon mass consumer demand, large corporations showed an increasing awareness that their success or failure was inextricably linked with that of the national economy as a whole. The era of reckless wildcatting and "public be damned" entrepreneurship had passed. In its place arose a new business philosophy that had two sides: a "soft" approach that stressed the need to improve business's image with the consuming public, and a "hard" line that was dedicated to maintaining the primacy of business interests in the nation's social and political agenda.

The "soft" side of business philosophy in the 1920s, often described as welfare capitalism, was predicated upon the proposition that the survival of any business was dependent upon the goodwill of its customers and of society as a whole.[51] Twenty years of muckraking, trust-busting, and progressive reform had left business, and especially big business, nervous that more restrictions upon its freedom of action would be imposed. Public relations campaigns aimed at improving the image of big corporations proliferated, and corporate philanthropy increased dramatically during the decade.[52] Trade associations redoubled their lobbying and public relations efforts in the hope of convincing consumers and legislators of the responsibility and utility of their respective industries.[53]

Louis Galambos's study of the public perceptions of corporations between 1880 and 1940 demonstrates that changes in political and economic life assisted the public relations efforts of large corporations.[54] After 1910 the antitrust and regulatory impulses began to wane, and middle-class Americans began to come to terms with giant corporations as permanent, and not necessarily evil, facts of life. The economic boom of 1914–19 benefited farmers and industrial workers, thereby weakening these mainsprings of populist and anticorporate activism. As the great tycoons of American industry—Gould, Vanderbilt, Rockefeller, and Carnegie—retired or died, their places were taken by less colorful managerial figures such as Sloan and E. H. Gary. This succession took away the instantly recognizable demons of the antitrust and populist movements and deflated the popular appeal of their activities. As the robber barons departed, so too did the terminology that they had spawned; "octopuses" and "trusts" fell out of popular usage, to be replaced by the less pejorative nomenclature of "corporations" and "firms."[55]

The demands of the war effort in 1917 and 1918 also improved the standing of business. Mobilization, war production, and Liberty Loan drives provided many opportunities for noisy displays of patriotism and public service. Companies apparently submitted to wartime restrictions and regulations without cavil, and prominent businessmen offered their services to the federal government for their much-advertised salary of a dollar a year. A corporatist culture, which championed the efficacy of organization and cooperation between societal groups, was also engendered by the growing interdependence in economic life and the demands of the war effort.

Welfare capitalism contributed to this trend not only by devoting resources to public relations campaigns but also by improving employees' conditions. From 1914 onward, those workers who were employed by large, prosperous, and capital-intensive corporations were increasingly exposed to a host of programs designed to increase productivity through use of the carrot rather than the stick.[56] The cessation of mass immigration, the demands of the war effort, and the advent of the eight-hour day combined to force major corporations to rethink their labor policies.[57] This was in keeping with their concerns about public relations and industrial stability, for each improvement in their employees' conditions bolstered their claim to be trustees of a wider community interest, while at the same time helping to create a more efficient and biddable work force.

Previously novel workplace schemes became commonplace in the years following 1914. Employee committees, insurance plans, stock purchase plans, and pension schemes proliferated; in the period 1924–28 over 300 companies instituted stock purchase plans, and by 1926, there were 432 corporations with employee committees.[58] The Procter and Gamble Company, for instance, had by 1928 instituted a profit-sharing plan for all its employees, a pension and benefit scheme, an "Employees Conference Committee" designed to give workers a voice in the running of their factories, and a guarantee of at least forty-eight weeks' employment per year in its soap-making operation.[59] Across the nation, 800,000 workers had invested in company stock-buying schemes by 1927, company insurance plans covered 6 million employees in 1928, and more than 350 companies had pension schemes in 1929.[60]

The chief executives of major corporations became public figures, expressing views on political questions and professing a philosophy that stressed their roles as trustees of the interests of their stockholders, their workers, and the general public. Owen D. Young and Gerard Swope of General Electric, Daniel Willard of the Baltimore and Ohio Railroad, John Raskob, Edward A. Filene, and Bernard Baruch became widely recognized figures, each preaching a new message of the pressing need for businesses and businessmen to be aware of their social responsibility. As Thomas Ferguson noted in 1984, most of these men represented large, capital-intensive firms which employed fewer workers than such labor-intensive giants as steel, textiles, and clothing. They therefore considered that they could afford to be generous to their work forces.[61] Young advocated stock distribution plans for employees and even lent tepid support to Al Smith's water-power policies, which envisaged state control of power sites. Willard maintained cordial links with the Wilson administration even after the Adamson Act, a most unwelcome piece of legislation for railroad owners that mandated an eight-hour day for their workers. Willard argued that railroads were "semipublic institutions" by virtue of their importance to the economic life of the nation and so required vigorous federal regulation.[62] Bernard Baruch was rarely silent on any political or social issue of importance, and as early as 1919 had publicly advocated profit-sharing schemes for employees, and even that "the working man must sit on the Boards of Directors."[63]

Edward A. Filene's views were typical of this group of prominent chief executives. In 1924 the Boston retailing magnate released a book entitled *The Way Forward*. The premise of this work was that social progress always depends upon cooperation between businessmen, government agencies, and the public. Business interests, Filene argued, had for too long denied the right of every citizen to "a decently adequate supply of the necessities of life." It was the responsibility of every business to supply its goods at the lowest possible cost and with the highest standards of hygiene and safety. Profiteering and exploitation by businesses were counterproductive, for such practices retarded social progress and therefore stunted the development of consumer demand.[64] "The whole idea of this book," he wrote, "is that good social policies are the surest recipe for big and continuous profits."[65]

Filene's conception of "good social policies" was even more adventurous than that of the most optimistic of the decade's political progressives. Just as the nineteenth century had seen the full flowering of political democracy, Filene thought, the twentieth would inevitably witness the triumph of industrial democracy. Workers would win the right to influence their corporation's policies and operations through their representatives on boards of directors, and their wages would have to increase at a rate faster than the cost of living so as to buttress consumer demand. A five-day working week, made possible by increases in productivity through increased mechanization, was inevitable. Through profit sharing and stock distribution the traditional distinction between employees and owners would disappear; in the future a true industrial partnership would emerge based on a genuine concert of interests.[66] "Commercial success and social welfare, in the days ahead," Filene predicted, "will stem from the same root."[67]

These rosy predictions made good copy, but the suspicion remains that they were little more than attractive public relations exercises designed to lessen public fears of huge business conglomerates.[68] Procter and Gamble's Employees Conference committees were, in practice, rubber-stamp affairs at which little of importance was transacted, and the company's attempts at welfare capitalism were transparent antiunion stratagems.[69] Employee representation schemes, which by 1929 had enrolled nearly two million workers across America, proved to be effective antiunion tools.[70] In a 1929 survey of welfare capitalism, Professor Sumner H. Slichter concluded that the new labor policies had contributed little to the large productivity increases or to the steep decline in industrial disputes that marked the years after 1920. Increasing mechanization and rising real wages had done far more to stabilize the employment market. Nevertheless, Slichter argued, welfare capitalism had significantly improved the morale of those industrial workers who had been exposed to it, and it had made the lot of the union organizer a more difficult one.[71] Welfare capitalism, with its comforting rhetoric of cooperation between business, government, consumers, and employees, sought to protect business dominance by humanizing it.

Other businessmen and their representative organizations, however, advocated a harder-edged business philosophy during the 1920s. Whereas the chief proponents of welfare capitalism usually represented the very largest and most capital intensive of the nation's corporations, representatives of labor-intensive industries and smaller firms tended to take a very different view of the proper interplay between employers, employees, and society.[72] Their views provided a balance to those of the apostles of the new corporate culture, as well as a warning to historians against too easily assuming that the new order of cooperation and corporatism was the consensus view of business during the 1920s. Organizations such as NAM, which drew the bulk of its membership from middling-size midwestern firms, stressed the need to maintain business freedom from government interference at all costs and extolled the virtues of individual endeavor and freedom.[73] In May 1924, for example, NAM released its "Platform of American Industry." It began its preferred agenda for the 1924 election with the thought that "the function of government is political—not economic." Government should not compete with its citizens in economic life, for this served only to "discourage initiative and lessen self-reliance."[74]

As it looked toward the election of 1924, NAM's platform strongly opposed the reform agenda proposed by those who would coalesce behind La Follette's Progressive campaign. The leaders of NAM vehemently asserted their faith in a "learned, courageous and independent judiciary" and warned that permitting Congress to reenact invalidated legislation, as

La Follette proposed, would make it "the master of its own limitations." Estate taxes, gift taxes, and surtaxes were also dangerous innovations, providing Congress with temptations to indulge in class legislation and demagoguery. "The taxing power," the platform maintained, "should never be employed to accomplish economic equalization."[75]

The NAM platform expressed its approval of existing Republican tariff policy, noting that a general downward revision of rates would create "uncertainty and instability." Although it advocated American membership in such international bodies as the International Court and Reparations Commissions, the platform opposed American involvement in the International Labor Organization. This body, it thought, would endanger the freedom of contract in the United States. The longest plank of the platform was entitled "Regulation of Combinations." Although it noted that "organization, rightly employed, is among the most useful and beneficial means of individual and social progress," the platform clearly limited this argument to trade associations rather than to labor organizations. The former deserved legislative encouragement; the latter should be subordinate to the open shop and to the public interest. The platform left little doubt as to its preferred candidate, quoting with approval Calvin Coolidge's famous dictum that "there is no right to strike against public safety by anybody, anywhere, any time."[76]

The cornerstone of this "hard" business philosophy of the decade was individualism. While Filene, Young, and others stressed the necessity for cooperation in a modern and interdependent economy, their more conservative colleagues emphasized the varied capacities and talents of each individual and the futility of attempts to create a society in which all enjoyed the benefits of modern prosperity. Human beings, these theorists held, were essentially selfish creatures, so that any ideology of cooperation was irrelevant and doomed to failure. Man is "a complete mental and physical machine within himself," Ben W. Hooper told the NAM Annual Convention in 1923, "adapted, it is true, to co-operative effort with other men, but such co-operative effort being always inspired primarily to obtain benefits and only secondarily to give them to others."[77]

Since human instinct was always directed toward the improvement of one's own and one's family's economic welfare, business individualists held, it was necessary to allow individual initiative the freest possible rein in society. The individual must be allowed to fight for success within only the most rudimentary rules of fair play. "We should not remain silent," President Julius Barnes of the U.S. Chamber of Commerce (USCC) urged his colleagues in 1923, "when theorists in public life propose to displace the sturdy philosophy of individual self-reliance and . . . accomplishment, with the easy theory of the care of the State." Society would prosper only in the absence of "artificial political and social restraints on the able and the ambitious."[78]

In keeping with this philosophy, the NAM and the USCC opposed most of the proposals put forward by Filene, Young, and Baruch during the 1920s. Shorter working weeks would decrease productivity by exposing workers to the corrupting influences of increased leisure time. Pension schemes, too, were injurious to individual initiative; by removing the responsibility from the individual for his or her own maintenance after retirement, such proposals threatened to stunt initiative, thrift, and industry.[79] Taxation rates should be devised to impose at least some burden upon all workers, and so bring home to them the fact that government cost money and that utopian schemes for the benefit of the unfortunate had to be paid for by their taxes. A general sales tax suited this purpose perfectly, and both the NAM and the USCC endorsed this source of revenue during the decade.[80]

Adherents to this branch of business philosophy had little time for an interventionist government. Regulation of industry was an artificial restraint upon the individual rights and initiative of employers and their workers. Business was too complicated for venal politicians to meddle with, and "natural economic forces" were adequate to ensure the smooth running of the economy. The primary functions of government were to protect personal and property rights and to ensure that individuals were given every opportunity to reap the most benefit from their own talents. This did not, however, involve intervention in economic affairs. "Law must in general be *negative*," Charles Fay of the NAM declared, "saying merely what shall *not* be done, in respecting the rights of others—but leaving to every citizen his liberty to do as he pleases, *up to the point forbidden*."[81] Businessmen of the NAM and the USCC distrusted government and the people who ran it. Politicians needed votes, and because the poor always outnumbered the rich, government was in constant danger of capture by the economically dispossessed. In order to avoid the dominance of government by the poor, therefore, it was essential to keep its powers to the minimum so as to give demagogues less to offer to their constituents.[82]

The basic elements of this side of business philosophy—elitism, materialism, individualism, and antipopulism—were incorporated in a book published by Julius H. Barnes in 1924.[83] Barnes argued that the basic rule for any government action was the "doctrine of fair play." This he defined as "a conception of perfect equality of opportunity for every individual." Every government act, he argued, should be judged by a single test: "Is this act necessary for the preservation of fair play between individuals?"[84]

In keeping with his colleagues, however, Barnes preferred to define fair play negatively. Fair play did not allow governments to undertake expensive spending sprees and expect wealthy citizens to pay the bill through heavy taxation; it did not allow politicians to change the value of the currency so as to penalize investors; it did not allow government corporations to go into competition with private concerns; and it did not allow trade unions and grower associations to be exempt from antitrust laws.[85] Most of all, Barnes argued, it was not fair play for "numerically strong" sections of society to "levy, through unequal and unwise taxation, and in a spirit of envy and resentment, an unfair burden, against those other groups more fortunate than themselves."[86] The fundamental purpose of fair play was to leave the field as free as possible for each citizen to prosper according to personal talents, and to avoid any laws which would "encase a man in the social stratum in which he has been placed by the accident of birth."[87]

THE TWO SIDES OF RASKOB'S BUSINESS THOUGHT

John Raskob's political philosophy neatly combined the "hard" and "soft" sides of business thought during the New Era. Like his friend Al Smith, Raskob considered himself a true Jeffersonian. Unlike William Gibbs McAdoo, however, Raskob declined to make a distinction between Jefferson's views on civil rights and those on economic liberties. Raskob believed that the political imperative of the 1920s was to return to Jeffersonian individualism and the belief that that government is best which governs least. This involved the reiteration of two ideological cornerstones: that government "shall operate equally for the benefit of every class, and never be used by one class for the economic exploitation of another," and that the powers of government should be "disseminated everywhere and not centralized intensively."[88] Much of his political thought during the 1920s corresponded closely with that of the NAM and USCC leadership.

This was especially the case with regard to the NAM and USCC view of an ideal society in which freely competing individuals determined their own economic rewards.[89] Raskob was particularly sympathetic to the NAM's deep suspicion of federal government activism. The most durable theme of his political thought was the need to maintain individualism against the encroachments of the federal government. The best way to limit government, Raskob believed, was to localize it. The aggrandizement of federal power at the expense of local communities and individuals worried him greatly. "The thing I object to," he wrote a fellow Democrat in 1931 concerning federal regulation, "is having another bureau in Washington that is going to regulate things having to do with the every day lives of our one hundred and twenty million people."[90] The worst examples of centralization were federal laws governing private and personal behavior. Such laws represented the most insidious means by which a remote government could impose not only conformity on but also control over its citizens' lives.[91]

Even local government, Raskob thought, should not regulate personal behavior. "I fear that we too often turn to our lawmakers to prevent wrong-doing," he declared to the DNC, "instead of demanding that our churches, homes and schools instill a strong sense of right and wrong in . . . our people."[92] The great danger of centralized governmental power was tyranny and then chaos. In a 1929 speech described by the *New York Times* as one of "adorable simplicity," he predicted the direst possible consequences of a further drift of power to Washington. This could "result in a revolution which will divide this country into two or three republics and our prosperity will then suffer the ills which the countries of Europe have suffered through jealousies, lack of trust, standing armies, etc."[93]

Raskob's views of the proper role of government bore strong resemblance to the "sum of good government" as described in Thomas Jefferson's first inaugural. Government, Jefferson held, should be "wise and frugal," limiting itself to restraining men "from injuring one another, which shall leave them otherwise free to regulate their own pursuits of industry and improvement, and shall not take from the mouth of labor the bread it has earned."[94] Raskob believed that both federal and state governments should limit themselves to the provision of defense and law, the protection of the individual's life and property, the fostering of trade, and the provision of nonprofit social infrastructure such as schools, roads, and sanitation. Government should not interfere with the normal functioning of the free market. To regulate business was to limit the expansion of industry and to retard the diffusion of prosperity. Regulation should be undertaken only on an ad hoc basis to correct palpable abuses. "If a utility is charging too much for power," Raskob lectured the DNC, "then society should deal with that particular case . . . and not attack the industry as a whole."[95]

"I am 100% in agreement with you in the matter of objecting to government ownership of anything operated for profit," Raskob wrote a correspondent. "Certainly anything the government owns and operates is bound to be operated by men who are more interested in holding their jobs than they are in the economical and successful operation of the property."[96] He also enthusiastically endorsed the NAM's emphasis upon the right of every individual to rise as high and as quickly as personal talents and determination would permit. In his case this theme was an intensely personal one; the example of his own life seemed to him to be a constant reminder of the benefits of a fluid society, open to young people with little money or family influence but with talent and ambition.[97]

Raskob perceived society as an organic economic unit dedicated to the achievement of the highest level of production. Labor and capital thus shared the same goals and aspirations; the two groups were interdependent, and upon that interdependence rested the economic and social well-being of society. "Personally," he wrote Charles Warner in 1924, "I think . . . the greatest danger facing us is the danger of the country being divided into classes . . . with the result that the selfish interests of these classes will eventually reach a stage of violence that will result in revolution."[98] In firm agreement with Al Smith's 1919 statement that "the prosperity of the working man depends in large part upon the prosperity of the employer," he railed against "the foolhardiness of attacking the rich or capital in the hope of aiding the poor or weak."[99] Such action, he thought, "tends to destroy that faith in each other so necessary to keep the machine in balance and running smoothly."[100] Accordingly he was an enthusiastic supporter of the antiunion and open-shop movements of the early 1920s. In 1919, the year of the great strikes, he wrote to his friend Owen D. Young that businessmen should prevent the "general unionization of industry." The solution to industrial unrest, he thought, was to "convince both capital and labor that their interests are identical, that neither can live without the other, that what is bad for one is bad for the other."[101]

Raskob's philosophy was as self-serving as that of the NAM in its view of government's proper role. Because the interests of capital and labor were identical, he argued, no "class-based" legislation should be enacted to benefit labor. Yet this reasoning did not apply to governmental assistance to capital, for he considered that the best way to help labor was to help businessmen achieve higher levels of production and productivity. Trade unions should receive no assistance or special protection, but industrialists should be given tariff protection and guarantees that their freedom of contract would remain unimpaired. To Senator Joseph T. Robinson he wrote in 1931, "I feel that it is not catering to capital to give capital that protection necessary to enable it to live properly, and in consequence profitably employ the masses."[102]

Few, if any, of these utterances would have raised even a murmur of disapproval from the NAM. In other moods, however, Raskob showed himself to be quite the equal of Edward Filene, Owen Young, and the other apostles of welfare capitalism and corporatism. Within the Du Pont Company and GM, he had shown himself to be a worthy ambassador for the human face of big business. His GMAC initiative had shown a brilliant understanding of the need to expand demand for expensive consumer goods, and the Du Pont Company had been a pioneer in the implementation of death benefits, unemployment compensation, savings plans, and paid vacations for its employees during Raskob's long association with the firm.[103] In 1919 he set up a savings and investment plan for GM employees which functioned as a kind of private bank for wage earners. In 1929 nearly 93 percent of the corporation's work force were enrolled in the plan, and its reserves stood at $90 million.[104] By that time, also, about thirty-five thousand GM employees were living in company-owned housing.[105]

Raskob's most famous contribution to the "soft" side of business philosophy, and to what Merle Curti has called the cult of prosperity during the 1920s, came in his 1929 *Ladies' Home Journal* article entitled "Everybody Ought to Be Rich."[106] Here Raskob approached the problem of the unequal distribution of wealth in American society. Instead of blaming the economic system, he argued that it was at least partly caused by a "lack of systematic investment and also the lack of even moderately sensible investment" on the part of American workers.[107] Too many employees squirreled their funds away in low-yield savings accounts and were hesitant to enter the lucrative stock market. He suggested the creation of a "Working Man's Investment Trust" which would invest workers' savings in gilt-edged securities. By agglomerating individual workers' small savings, the trust would be able to buy large quantities of stocks and reinvest the dividends. If workers deposited $15 per month in such a scheme, he predicted, they could expect to have accumulated a retirement fund of $80,000 at the end of twenty years. Any worker could save $15 per month, he told the *Journal*, "and because anyone can do that I am firm in my belief that anyone not only can be rich but ought to be rich."[108] His proposal therefore envisaged a gigantic retirement scheme without need for the government to participate through an expensive social welfare program. By encouraging employees to buy stocks, he hoped that industrial unrest would be minimized. Workers would realize that strikes threatened their nest eggs as well as their wages.[109]

Employee stock-ownership was not a new concept in 1929; Raskob himself had benefited handsomely from the Du Pont Company's stock purchase and bonus plan created by Pierre and Coleman du Pont in 1904.[110] Raskob's scheme, however, envisaged workers from all industries participating in stock purchase. By this means, his vision of a classless society in which the interests of capital and labor would be seen to be identical could be painlessly achieved. "If all workers became participating owners of our industries by means of stockholders [*sic*]," he wrote in 1929, "we shall become in fact a true industrial democracy; that is to say, we shall be one vast national partnership in the business of getting the most good and the most value out of life. We shall arrive, if you please, at something like the goal of the Socialists, with this difference: that instead of an impossible and disastrous levelling of human beings with their infinite variety of capacities which fight against levelling, we shall preserve and utilize the advantages of exceptional ability, the qualities of leadership, to organize and guide the common industrial machine to the benefit of all."[111]

"At every stage of progress," Raskob noted in 1929, "there have been neolithic minds which could see only disaster in any change." Such a view, he thought, had caused "that heritage of class-conflict and class-hatred which has culminated in communism."[112] Displaying a mind that was anything but monolithic, Raskob called for a five-day working week. Although there were still employers "whose sole economic idea is that the workers must be driven as hard, as long and for as little as they will stand," he believed that the idea of a shorter working week was perfectly suited to the New Era. He did not advocate it "in any sentimental spirit, but from the standpoint of good business."[113]

America's industrial machine constantly threatened to outproduce consumer demand. A five-day week would allow workers "additional time and opportunity to function as consumers of what they produce." If Saturday and Sunday were holidays, employees would buy more cars (including those produced by Raskob's GM), tires, gasoline, sporting goods, gardening equipment, home improvement products, and a myriad of other leisure-orientated commodities. Hotels, campgrounds, professional sports, and railroads would all benefit immensely from such a change.[114]

Little came of either of Raskob's proposals. The "workingman's trust" assumed that stock prices would continue their 1928 and early 1929 rates of climb, an assumption that was disproved only two months after the *Ladies' Home Journal* article appeared. Raskob himself recognized that stock prices in 1929 were unrealistically high, and he refused to countenance the creation of the trust until they stabilized.[115] The idea of a five-day week was strongly opposed by the "neolithic minds" of the NAM; a poll of the members of that association in 1926 had revealed overwhelming opposition to the concept, seeing it as a license for radicalism; anarchists and Communists evidently worked better on weekends.[116]

Raskob had shown himself to have a foot in both camps; his political thought conformed to the NAM mold, but his vision of the future of American business stamped him as a business progressive. Yet his thought was not bifurcated. Inherent in all his utterances were several consistent themes. America had to remain an open and free society so as to ensure the survival and prosperity of the self-made man; business was capable of achieving a greater measure of social justice without recourse to government action; social progress was best made through private institutions; the consumer economy, nurtured by a sympathetic government and an enlightened business community, was in itself the best guarantee of continued prosperity. Underlying all of Raskob's political thought, from his most conservative dismissal of an activist government to his most visionary conception of a "workingman's trust," was the premise that there was no inherent class conflict in a modern and effective consumer economy; the key to social progress lay in ensuring that all workers became capitalists.

RASKOB'S INCREASING POLITICAL INVOLVEMENT

Raskob had conformed closely to the antiparty feeling common among business groups for the first quarter of the twentieth century.[117] He and his colleagues saw political parties as vehicles of demagogues wishing to incite the shiftless to action against the accumulations of the worthy. He distrusted Theodore Roosevelt and most likely shared Pierre du Pont's disgust at the "meddling" of the Wilson administration.[118] He did, however, agree to participate in the National Industrial Conference convened by the president in 1919 in the hope of improving relations between labor and management in postwar America.[119] That year he joined the ultra-Republican Union League of Philadelphia, and he voted for Warren Harding in 1920. His financial contributions were, however, slight in proportion to his enormous financial resources: $1,000 to the Republican National Committee in 1922, $5,000 to the Delaware State Republican Financial Committee in 1924 and 1927, and $5,000 to assist Republican James Wadsworth in his campaign against Robert Wagner for one of New York's U.S. Senate seats in 1926. He had also contributed to Al Smith's gubernatorial campaign of the same year.[120]

Despite his occasional contributions, Raskob was by no means enamored of the GOP during the early 1920s. In 1924 Andrew Mellon's tax proposals were modified by pressure from maverick Republican and progressive Democratic senators, and the resulting compromise displeased Raskob. The program as it emerged, he thought, left taxes excessively high and was "not at all designed to encourage business." The Senate, once the bulwark of conservatism and good business sense, had degenerated into "a political bolshevist camp." Both parties, he wrote Charles Warner in 1924, were in a corrupt and dangerous state and threatened to debase the entire political system. Unwittingly foreshadowing his own activities four years later, Raskob concluded that "if there are two knaves—the Republican and Democratic parties—I am unwilling to support either and it will do no good to plead for my support based on the fact that the Democratic knave is blacker than the Republican, even though this might be true. My notion is that one of the knaves should be reformed or we should go out and find a clean man (in this case organize a clean organization) to whip them both."[121]

A variety of considerations pushed John Raskob into partisan politics. The most important was his opposition to prohibition. Nothing offended his conception of the proper role of the federal government more than the Eighteenth Amendment, which he saw as a gross intrusion of governmental power into both the economic and the social life of the nation.[122] Prohibition not only had outlawed an entire industry without compensation but had created an army of enforcement agents which harassed citizens into conformity in their private behavior.[123] He joined the Association Against the Prohibition Amendment in 1921 but did not make any substantial contributions until 1926. From that time on, however, he and Pierre du Pont became the financial stalwarts of the organization, and both became officeholders in it.[124] On the eve of the 1928 conventions Raskob was quoted in the press as being worried that both parties would avoid the question of prohibition in their platforms by adopting innocuous enforcement planks. Those who wished to change the Eighteenth Amendment so as to return the whole matter of liquor control to the states were, he argued, "engaged in a noble effort to restore to our people a feeling of independence and liberty . . . so earnestly sought and finally secured after the great Revolutionary War."[125]

Increasing interest in prohibition reform led Raskob to further involvement in party politics. This was reinforced by the growing political prominence of Al Smith after 1924. The two men were first introduced in 1926 by Broadway producer Eddie Dowling. Dowling later recalled that Raskob had offered Smith a personal check for $50,000 during that first meeting to help defray the costs of his reelection campaign for governor of New York. They began a personal and political friendship that would last until Smith's death in 1944.[126] They had much in common; both were devout Catholics and keen antiprohibitionists, and both considered themselves to be self-made men. They shared a commitment to the maintenance of the open economic system under which they had greatly prospered. This was especially true regarding the acceptable limits of governmental interference with business. Raskob, conservative as he was on such issues, saw little conflict between his opinions and Governor Smith's record in New York. "No man could have higher, finer ideals with respect to the relations which should exist between government and business," he told the press during the 1928 campaign. "He is a strong advocate of less government in business and more business in government."[127]

John Raskob took his position as a prominent businessman in a business decade seriously, and his entry into public life was partly due to a sense of noblesse oblige. "A man who has been fortunate enough to make money," he told *Collier's Magazine* in 1932, "should be willing to give anything asked of him by the country under whose protection he made it." The times seemed especially propitious for businessmen to reconsider their earlier disdain for the sordid business of party politics. "This is very distinctly an economic age, hence an age when business is most fascinating," he thought, "but it is also an age in when business and government are more closely allied than ever before. The transition, therefore, from business to government is natural."[128]

Quite apart from his friendship with Smith, his opposition to prohibition, and his affinity with conservative Jeffersonianism, Raskob may well have had other reasons for renouncing his Republicanism and joining the Democratic party. Raskob's political career lends persuasive evidence to the "investment theory" of political parties put forward in recent years by Samuel Popkin and Thomas Ferguson.[129] Investment theory holds that political parties do not primarily compete for votes but rather for funds, and that the most influential actors in partisan politics are not large voter blocs but large investor groups. The enormous costs involved in mounting national political campaigns make it imperative for political parties to attract large investors. This makes party platforms and candidates inherently susceptible to capture by large corporate interests, who alone have the capacity to finance campaigns in the age of mass media.[130] Minority parties, shut out from national power, are especially vulnerable to capture. Large investors can exercise enormous influence in determining economic and social policy because the party is simply too poor to resist.[131]

As a financier, Raskob could not have been unaware of the Democrats' penniless condition during the 1920s. Acting on William Seward's dictum that a political party was "a joint stock association, in which those who contribute most direct the action and management of the concern,"

Raskob saw great opportunities within the party.[132] As a minority party chronically short of funds, it was ripe for a takeover in 1928. Raskob could finally make good his 1924 resolve that "one of the knaves should be reformed." He could use his fortune to influence the Democratic party far more than he could within the GOP, which was not short of wealthy supporters. He could be Mark Hanna to Smith's McKinley. Together they could complete the process of turning the national party away from its Bryanite and Wilsonian past and toward a new acceptance of business-orientated conservatism and protectionism.[133]

8

"WALL STREET LIKES AL SMITH"

THE ELECTION OF 1928

The 1928 presidential campaign has been minutely studied by political historians, and for good reason. Al Smith, as a Catholic, a wet, and an out-and-out urbanite, was a different type of candidate from those who had come before him. He was the first of his faith ever to have been accorded a major party nomination, and his candidacy was seen by many of his contemporaries as a litmus test of American toleration. Was there a religious bar to the presidency? Could a lower East Side boy who left school at fourteen realistically aspire to the White House? The 1928 election, in short, has generally been viewed as much as a contest between two cultures as a purely political struggle between two parties, candidates, and platforms.[1]

Historians have approached the 1928 election in three ways. The first has been to assess the role of bigotry in Smith's defeat.[2] The second line of inquiry has led to a debate as to whether 1928 was a "realigning" election, presaging Franklin Roosevelt's New Deal coalition by mobilizing previously inactive members of the electorate to vote for the Democratic party.[3] Other historians have stressed the overriding influence of prosperity upon electoral behavior in 1928, playing down bigotry as a decisive factor in the contest of 1928.[4] Little attention has been paid to the platforms of the two candidates or to the tenor of the campaigns which they ran. Yet such questions are important, and answering them can reveal much about the state of the Democratic party in 1928. The 1928 campaign was an important milestone along the path taken by the conservative northeastern group in their quest for control of the national party.

THE DEMOCRATIC PLATFORM

Unlike that of 1924, the platform of 1928 was a product of the candidate's wishes and convictions.[5] The Smith forces dominated the platform committee's deliberations and modified their proposals only when faced with particularly difficult issues such as prohibition. On issues such as the tariff, labor, agriculture, and foreign policy, however, they had their way. This was inevitable, given the clear lead in delegate support that the governor enjoyed before the convention opened. By conceding the nomination before the convention opened, southern and western progressives also relinquished control of the platform-drafting process.

The Houston platform represented a rethinking of traditional Democratic doctrine. It announced that the party was now led by a candidate who had turned his back on much of the received wisdom of the Wilsonian and Bryanite Democracy. For the first time in at least three generations, the platform contained no explicit attack upon the GOP theory of a high protective tariff as the best guarantee of high wages and prosperity.[6] Although the tariff plank contained an offhand criticism of "log-rolling" in the setting of tariff rates, its substance promised that tariffs under a Smith administration would "permit effective competition, insure against monopoly and at the same time produce a fair revenue for the support of the government." What was most controversial, however, was the platform's definition of an acceptable level of protection. Tariffs would be set on the "actual difference between the cost of production at home and abroad, with adequate safeguard for the wage of the American laborer."[7] This was generally taken to imply that little or no change would be made to the Republican Fordney-McCumber tariff of 1922, which had removed the cuts in protection instituted by the Underwood-Simmons Tariff of 1913.[8] The Democratic party, which for over a century had upheld the principle of tariffs for revenue only as the chief distinguishing factor between it and the GOP, had now committed itself to the principle of a protective tariff.

The contrast between the Houston tariff plank and that adopted in New York four years before demonstrates the magnitude of this change. The earlier platform condemned the Fordney-McCumber Tariff of 1922 as a piece of "class legislation which defrauds the people for the benefit of the few." Republican tariff laws, the 1924 platform declared, were written to aid monopolies, and rates were high in order to raise revenue without the need to levy high income taxes upon the rich. The New York platform promised to redistribute the burden of the cost of government from consumers to the wealthy by means of a more sharply progressive income tax.[9] The Houston tariff policy of 1928 was closer to that which the Republicans adopted at their 1928 convention than to its own immediate predecessor.[10] The GOP promised that a Hoover administration would reexamine tariff schedules to ensure that American industries could compete with foreign producers who enjoyed an unfair advantage "because of lower foreign wages and a lower cost of living abroad."[11]

The reason for this change in tariff policy went to the root of the conservative agenda devised by the Smith forces. As befitted representatives of the Northeast—the home of big business and as such the chief beneficiary of Republican economic and fiscal policy—the Smith group forswore any policies that were disapproved of by the business groups that had invested so heavily in the party.[12] Raskob was an ardent proponent of the new policies. "Smith's ideas of protecting big businesses are quite in accord with yours and mine," the new chairman wrote to Irénée du Pont soon after the convention. "He believes in a tariff of honesty, that is, to give all the tariff protection that industry that is honestly and efficiently managed needs in order to enable it to pay high wages. . . . I happen to know that the Governor believes that there is too much interference by the Government in business. For example, the powers of the Interstate Commerce Commission are getting beyond reason and interfere too much with the management and best operation of the railroads."[13]

In other ways, too, Smith's platform seemed to go out of its way to soothe business sensibilities at the expense of the progressives' agenda. Its agriculture plank was one of the longest in the platform, yet provided little of substance. Overproduction and low crop prices had become chronic economic problems, and the rural sector as a whole had lagged behind urban economic growth during the 1920s. Average annual per capita income of farm dwellers in 1929 was $273, little more than one-third of the national average of $750.[14] The Houston platform made no direct mention of the McNary-Haugen scheme for farm relief but pledged instead to adjust tariff policy to ensure that agricultural products were as protected as industrial goods.[15] The creation of a Federal Farm Board to assist farmers to market their crop surpluses and the fostering of cooperative marketing associations were also promised. A veiled reference to the travails of the McNary-Haugen scheme over its controversial "equalization fee" came in the platform's promise of an "earnest endeavor" to devise a scheme by which the cost of surplus marketing at a loss was shared among all producers of the crop. Such a scheme, however, would not involve a "government subsidy."[16]

The Houston platform disappointed progressives on other issues. Water-power development, long a western preoccupation, was disposed of in the vaguest terms. Although the platform committed the party to the principle that the "sovereign title" to water-power sites should always remain under state or federal control, development of sites and transmission of the generated electric current seemed to be reserved to private utilities, albeit "under such regulations as will insure to the people reasonable rates and equitable distribution."[17] This fell considerably short of the demands of western and southern progressives but was consistent with Smith's policy as governor of New York.[18] The question of what to do with the idle Muscle Shoals development was ignored at Houston.

On taxation the platform was content to criticize Republican delays in securing the passage of tax relief for most taxpayers and to declare that the party favored "further reduction of the internal taxes of the people." Gone was the ringing statement in the 1924 platform that the income tax "was intended as a tax on wealth" and the commitment of the party to a graduated income tax, "so adjusted as to lay the burdens of government upon the taxpayers in proportion to the benefits they enjoy and their ability to pay." As if to complete the platform's reversal of Wilsonian progressivism, no mention of the League of Nations was made at all. "The Houston Convention was a great disappointment to me," Newton Baker wrote a friend; "McKinley could have run on our tariff plank and Lodge on our plank on international relations."[19]

The labor plank adopted at Houston was also deliberately vague. Although it recognized that there had been "grave injustice" in the use of injunctions during strikes, the platform suggested no remedies other than the institution of a notice period before they were issued and the calling of a conference of lawyers and representatives of labor and employers to devise means of eliminating abuses of this legal procedure.[20] No attack was made, however, upon the actual use of this bête noire of organized labor.[21] William Green, president of the American Federation of Labor, described the Democratic plank as a "meaningless patchwork, highly disappointing and entirely unsatisfactory to labor."[22] Over six hundred injunctions had been issued against strikers in 1927 alone, and the removal of this powerful legal weapon from the hands of employers had become labor's chief priority. Neither the Democrats nor the Republicans, however, were willing to grasp this nettle in 1928.[23]

All in all, Louise B. Hill of New York wrote FDR at the close of the campaign, it would take an "acrobatic stunt" for Wilsonians to support Smith as a protector of the great president's reformist vision.[24] George Fort Milton was similarly blunt. "A Democratic party nominating Al Smith," he complained to McAdoo soon after the convention, "wants to forget everything Woodrow Wilson ever thought worthwhile!"[25]

THE SIMILARITY BETWEEN SMITH AND HOOVER

Smith's campaign between July and November can best be described as embodying a me-too strategy, in which, to quote a contributor to the *Outlook*, "the Democratic party must . . . be made to look as nearly identical to the G.O.P. as possible."[26] Much to the chagrin of progressives, that is exactly what Smith did. Al Smith on the stump was at times very difficult to distinguish from Herbert Hoover.

Given the degree to which the two candidates shared philosophical assumptions, this sameness was to some extent natural. The investment theory of political parties, discussed in chapter 7, accounts for the me-too syndrome by noting that if all major investor groups oppose the discussion of certain issues, the parties are likely to acquiesce, no matter how many small investors (or voters) might benefit from such discussion.[27] Certainly Smith's wealthy backers like Raskob had no interest in seeing their candidate espouse economic policies that varied significantly from those of the GOP. In his acceptance speech on the steps of the Albany capitol, Smith declared that "it is a fallacy that there is inconsistency between progressive measures protecting the rights of the poor and weak, and a just regard for the rights of legitimate business." Both objectives could be achieved by extirpating "the forces of corruption and favoritism" and substituting those of "equal opportunity."[28]

Hoover, for his part, had declared as early as 1923 that the basic questions to be asked of any government initiative were, "Does this act safeguard an equality of opportunity? Does it maintain the initiative of our people?"[29] Both men considered equality of opportunity, personal freedom, voluntarism, the overlapping of the interests of labor and capital, and the rejection of abstract philosophies of government as the cornerstones of their credos.[30] Hoover opened his campaign with an image that could have come from Smith's own conception of government. "It is as if we set a race," Hoover intoned from his childhood home in Iowa. "We . . . provide the training of the runners; we give to them an equal start. . . . The winner is he who shows the most conscientious training, the greatest ability, and the greatest character."[31] The farm boy turned millionaire and the East Side boy turned governor were in basic agreement over the former's belief that "with impressive proof on all sides of magnificent progress, no one can rightly deny the fundamental soundness of our economic system."[32]

It was on this basis that the two candidates set out to do battle. Smith, as the underdog, struggled to find issues upon which to take the initiative. The governor was quickly put on the defensive over the tariff, with Republicans taunting him for copying their traditional policy on the one hand, and progressive Democrats berating him for his betrayal of Democratic orthodoxy on the other.[33] On farm relief, too, the distinctions between the two men were hazy. Both Hoover and Smith declared themselves in favor of fostering cooperative marketing schemes, improving water transportation, and calling a farm conference of experts to devise ways to reduce the surpluses that were depressing crop prices—all with the avowed intention of ensuring that farmers' incomes were equal to those of their industrial brethren.[34] The most important issue concerning agriculture in 1928, however, was not cooperative marketing schemes but rather the McNary-Haugen proposal. At first, Smith seemed to disregard the vague language of his platform and to cast his lot with the supporters of the bill. When George N. Peek consulted with John Raskob at the end of July 1928, he was delighted. Smith and Raskob had led him to believe that they supported the principle of dumping surpluses overseas with the costs so incurred to be borne by producers of the crop. Peek promptly announced his support for Smith and began work on his behalf in Chicago.[35] Hoover, in contrast, had long opposed McNary-Haugen as an unwarranted tampering with the operation of the free market and as a source of international friction because of its dumping provisions. Never popular with farmers, he preferred voluntary production control to coercive state measures.[36] Smith seemed to have a golden opportunity in his grasp to wean disgruntled farmers from the GOP.

Two days after his conversion of Peek, however, Smith backed away from his commitment to the McNary-Haugen proposal. The equalization fee as found in the bills of 1924, 1927, and 1928 was, he declared, "not acceptable."[37] He did not bother to suggest alternatives but promised to create a board of experts after his election to devise a more satisfactory means of implementing farm relief.[38] Although Peek remained loyal, other McNary-Haugenites were angered at this straddle.[39] Without a clear agricultural policy with which to differentiate himself from Hoover, Smith made little headway against the traditional loyalty of the corn and wheat belts' to the GOP or their suspicion of an eastern, urban candidate. Republican hegemony in the midwest and West had reduced Democratic local organizations to little more than empty shells, making Smith's job even harder. He failed to win a single western or midwestern state, although he did improve upon Cox's abysmal showing in these regions in 1920.[40]

As Smith failed to distinguish himself from Hoover on agriculture, so too did he fail to provide a clear alternative on other issues. The two candidates did not differ markedly in their promises to improve the structure of federal government. Hoover's declarations in favor of a reorganization of the federal governmental structure so as to reduce "the multitude of unnecessary contacts with government bureaus . . . and the duplication of governmental activities" were echoed by the governor, who could point to his own achievements along these lines in New York.[41]

Smith did venture beyond his platform on two issues. He replaced his platform's silence on the Muscle Shoals issue with a promise that it would be developed under federal government ownership and control. At the same time, he rejected the possibility of public distribution of electric power generated by the Muscle Shoals complex. At Denver he aired the possibility that a quasi-public corporation empowered to issue bonds would undertake this work.[42] Hoover was vague on this issue, although he hinted that public operation of Muscle Shoals would be acceptable to him. Although Senator George Norris, the nation's foremost advocate of public power generation and distribution, crossed party lines to support Smith, there was no significant difference between the two candidates. Hoover attacked Smith's proposals for Muscle Shoals as "state socialism," but this was meaningless in light of the similarities in the two positions.[43]

On labor, too, Smith ventured beyond the confines of his platform by making a definite pledge to introduce legislation to limit the use of injunctions to break strikes.[44] Hoover, too, criticized the abuse of injunctions and declared that it was imperative that they be curtailed. His proposals, however, were less specific than those of his opponent. Until that time little had separated the two candidates on labor issues; both Smith and Hoover were popular with labor leaders and their constituents.[45] Smith had long championed the right of labor to organize and had initiated legislation in New York to improve working conditions. Hoover, as secretary of commerce, had played a prominent part in persuading U.S. Steel to abolish its twelve hour day in 1922, and he had cooperated well with Samuel Gompers.[46] Both men pledged themselves to maintain restrictions upon immigration, a big issue for organized labor, and Smith's new tariff stand brought his party in line with the GOP as protectors of industrial wage-earners. Although many union leaders privately supported Smith, the AFL endorsed neither candidate. With both nominees at least sympathetic to labor, little seemed at stake in the election.[47]

These deviations from the Houston platform and from the strategy of me-tooism were scarcely sufficient to turn Smith's campaign into a progressive crusade. Although the similarities between the messages of the two men cast some doubt upon David Burner's and Donald Lisio's assessments of Hoover as the more progressive candidate, it is undeniable that Hoover's campaign revealed the broader vision.[48] It was Hoover, and not Smith, who uttered the much-quoted hope that "we shall soon with the help of God be in sight of the day when poverty will be banished from this nation."[49] Too busy reassuring business that he was as safe as any Republican, the Happy Warrior had no time for such flights of reformist fancy.

Within the campaign headquarters in the General Motors Building in New York City, a special emphasis was placed upon winning converts among small and large businessmen.[50] The *Campaign Handbook*, issued to speakers in the field to alert them to the dominant themes of the campaign, refuted the idea that Democratic administrations brought hard times. The business cycle, speakers were told, operated independently of party fortunes; in fact business failures during the 1920s were increasing, despite the much-vaunted "Republican prosperity."[51]

One of the great ironies of the 1928 campaign saw Franklin Roosevelt leading this part of the publicity effort. Although he would later recall that he was treated by Raskob and Moskowitz "as though I was one of those pieces of window-dressing that had to be borne with because of a certain political value in non–New York City areas," in fact FDR spent his time writing letters to businessmen all over the country extolling Smith's virtues as a guardian of business interests.[52] Hoover had by his nature an intrusive and meddling bent, Roosevelt wrote a New York shoe manufacturer, and "he has also shown in his own Department a most alarming desire to issue regulations and to tell business men generally how to run their affairs."[53] "The whole tendency of his mind," Roosevelt told a Toledo manufacturer, "is to expand the paternal relations of the government to industry and trade." This was "a very dangerous tendency, for the whole history of government interference is that, starting first with a well meant attempt to be merely advisory and helpful, it invariably ends by becoming regulatory and dictatorial." Smith, however, aimed to "simplify the government's function" and to limit the functions of bureaus "to where they legitimately belong."[54]

THE PROGRESSIVES' VIEW OF SMITH

While Raskob and Roosevelt worked behind the scenes to woo business support for Smith, independent progressives remained lukewarm about the Smith-Hoover contest. The salient issues of their agenda —an end to the open shop, government ownership of railroads, the ratification of the Child Labor Amendment, an end to intervention in Latin America, the overhaul of the taxation system to tax the wealthy more heavily, and government transmission of electrical power—had received little support in the Houston platform.[55] Many of these reformers were wary of Smith and doubted his commitment to their cause.[56] The appearance of John Raskob deepened these doubts, as did Smith's ambivalent stance on water power. Yet independent progressives had little time for Hoover, who in their eyes had sold out to the forces of privilege. The whispering campaign based on bigotry and class prejudice against Smith struck them as offensive. Smith eventually won their support, but it was never enthusiastic. Mercer Johnston, the national chairman of the Progressive National Committee, summed up this feeling in his assessment that the governor was "the best we could do, in bad progressive weather, for the cause of human rights."[57]

The progressive community as a whole shared this sense of caution over Smith and his platform. The *Nation* was by no means impressed with the Houston platform, nor with Smith's interpretation of it. "His platform everywhere stops short of firing the blood of a true progressive," an editorial at the end of September 1928 stated. "He does not go the whole distance on water power; he does not use the words 'government operation' which are the crux of the problem; he does not say that he will take corrupt big business by the throat as Wilson promised to do. The millionaires who are flocking to him ostensibly because he is an honest Wet would not do so did they not feel sure that he is satisfactorily safe and sane." The *Nation* found itself in a quandary as the campaign wore on. Although horrified by the prejudices that Smith seemed to attract, it could not completely forget his close links to business and to Tammany Hall, or the disappointing platform. In the end, the editors left it to "the individual conscience of each progressive voter" as to whether to support Smith or the Socialist Norman Thomas.[58]

At the *New Republic* a more positive attitude to Smith eventually emerged, but not before some soul-searching on the part of its editors and contributors. Both Hoover and Smith, Herbert Croly argued in July 1928, "are unprogressive in their political concepts. They consider that the fulfillment of American life depends upon the preservation of an inheritance rather than . . . its re-adaption to changing conditions."[59] A month later the magazine ran an editorial warning its readers that they "should fully understand that Governor Smith is no crusader in the progressive cause. He does not propose to distribute among less enfranchised groups . . . some of the power which is now exercised by organized business."[60] In early September, however, the magazine reported that, after "patient and watchful hesitation," it had decided to endorse Smith, who had conducted a forthright campaign in the face of disgraceful prejudice. He had at least made an effort to face the issues of water-power control, prohibition, and farm relief. Hoover, on his part, had conceded nothing to the progressive cause.[61]

Smith may have won over the *New Republic* and secured a reluctant neutrality from the *Nation*, but he continued to have difficulties with other progressives. The only major newspaper chain to consider itself progressive, the Scripps-Howard organization, endorsed Hoover.[62] Thomas Gammack, writing in the *Outlook* at the outset of the campaign, was also unconvinced. "Governor Smith," he noted sourly, "is, from Wall Street's point of view, the most acceptable Presidential candidate offered by the Democratic Party since Grover Cleveland." All in all, Gammack concluded, "Wall Street likes Al Smith."[63]

Wall Street may have liked Smith, but would it vote for him? The attitude of the *Wall Street Journal* to the campaign revealed the futility of me-tooism. Noting with approval that "both platforms fought shy of radicalism," the *Journal* advised its readers in the first week of July that "business has little or nothing to fear in the 1928 presidential campaign. Both candidates are men with constructive records. It is not a case of choosing between good and bad but a case of choosing which is better."[64] The editors approved of Raskob's appointment, for it showed that "as never before, the Democratic party is now equipped with organization power, capital power and head power."[65] But if the *Journal* was pleased that the platform and candidate were eminently safe, it still endorsed Hoover as "the soundest business proposition for those with a financial stake in the country."[66] Me-tooism had won business confidence but few votes. It carried within itself seeds of its own failure, for it provided no incentive for a prosperous business sector to change its political allegiance.

The Democrats may have been overoptimistic in their hope that they could reassure business interests of their trustworthiness simply by drafting a sympathetic platform and running an acceptable candidate. In an article published in September 1929, Professor Arthur Burns of Rutgers University noted that the leading businessmen of the nation still believed that "Democratic rule is invariably accompanied by depressed business conditions." Although Burns's research showed that there was little basis for this belief, businessmen remained wedded to this "shibboleth."[67] Their reservations about the Democrats involved three main themes: the tariff, the "tradition that the Democrats are the party of the masses," and the memories of William Jennings Bryan and his free silver crusades. Even in 1928, although the tariff had essentially disappeared as an issue between the two parties, although thirty-two years had passed since 1896, and although the Democrats were now openly solicitous of business interests, businessmen remained suspicious.[68] Newton D. Baker encapsulated the futility of me-tooism in a letter to James Cox soon after the election. "Protected industries are never going to look to us for protection, and why should they?" Baker asked. "The Republicans are experts in that sort of thing and we would be half-hearted amateurs."[69]

SMITH AND THE SOUTHERN DEMOCRATS

If Smith's strategy failed to win the votes of the corporate sector of the Northeast, the reaction to his candidacy and platform among those who considered themselves to be the guardians of Democratic principles was even more damaging. Nowhere was the hostility to the Houston platform more marked than in the South, where Smith's personal liabilities—his religion, his stand on prohibition, and his Tammany origins—had already made many Democrats reconsider their previously unshakable loyalty to the party. The selection of John Raskob, with his much-quoted view of prohibition as a "damnable affliction" and his affiliations with big business, was for many the last straw. At Asheville, North Carolina, a convention of "self-labeled anti-Smith Democrats" met on July 19, 1928, from all over the South to issue a declaration of principles. Citing Smith's opposition to prohibition and his Tammany affiliations, the convention went on to attack the Houston platform in forthright terms before endorsing Hoover.[70] In Texas, a large group of anti-Smith Democrats met in Dallas on July 17, 1928. Objecting to Raskob's appointment and the probusiness tone of the platform, the group resolved to vote the national GOP ticket and the state Democratic ticket. The "Hoovercrats" were funded by the southern Republican organizations, already scenting the breakup of the solid South.[71]

Other southerners were concerned at the direction in which their party seemed to be going. In Mississippi and Alabama, normally Democratic newspapers reacted with horror at the choice before the voters in November. Smith's religion, wetness, and urbanism were such pressing issues that policy issues such as farm relief, water power, and the tariff received scant attention.[72] Yet these Democrats were more sensitive to racial issues than they were to the other cultural threats that Smith seemed to pose, and as the campaign wore on, the need to preserve white supremacy became uppermost.[73]

Hoover, readers were reminded, had desegregated office workers in Washington while he was secretary of commerce; there was no knowing what he might do from the White House.[74] No "red-blooded white Democrat," Governor Theodore Bilbo of Mississippi declared, "can vote for Hoover after his action in making white women work with negroes, using the same basins, towels and temporary housing." [75] The *Jackson* (Tennessee) *Sun* raised the same point. Hoover, the paper claimed, had forced "all white and colored employees to use the same lavatories." [76] Religious prejudice was fought with racial bigotry in what many observers found to be the most racist presidential campaign since Reconstruction.[77] Many listened; across the old Confederacy, Smith won 184 of the 191 counties with majority black populations, while he carried only 79 of the 266 counties with fewer than 5 percent blacks.[78] In Alabama, for instance, he won every county which had a black population of more than 50 percent; he won less than a quarter of those counties with fewer than 20 percent black populations.[79] In Texas only 1 of the 22 counties with more than 35 percent black population went to Hoover, but 113 of the 150 counties with less than 5 percent black population deserted the national Democratic ticket.[80]

In those areas of the South with fewer blacks and a less secure one-party system, the issues were more complex. An examination of the varying reactions of prominent Democrats in Tennessee, North Carolina, and Virginia to the campaign of 1928 reveals much about the ideological turmoil that lay below the surface of the more spectacular cultural reaction against Smith. In Tennessee, Cordell Hull looked in dismay at the changes wrought upon the party that he had tried so hard to rehabilitate. Although he had acquiesced in Smith's nomination after the stillbirth of his own candidacy, the appointment of Raskob and the Houston platform alarmed him. He had struggled at the convention to have the platform include more explicit policies on international matters and prohibition, but he had been outvoted by the governor's supporters. What offended him most, however, was the tariff plank, which he later described as "the unconditional surrender of the Democratic party to the forces of high-tariff greed and privilege."[81] Hull, however, had strong reasons to remain loyal to the ticket; not only had he invested much of his time and money into the national party organization, but he was also facing a reelection campaign for his House seat in 1928. By staying loyal, he hoped, he would be in a better position to influence the party's return to traditional principles after Smith's defeat. This, after all, was the thinking that underlay his acceptance of Smith's nomination in the first place.

In neighboring North Carolina, two Democratic leaders were coming to opposite conclusions as to how to respond to Smith's platform. Senator Furnifold Simmons was the leader of the state organization and had long served as North Carolina's national committeeman.[82] Elected to the U.S. Senate in 1900, he had risen to the chairmanship of the Senate Finance Committee during Wilson's administrations, achieving fame as the co-author of the Underwood-Simmons tariff of 1913.[83] In 1924 he was a strong supporter of McAdoo's presidential ambitions.[84] Although he was not enthusiastic about Smith's nomination, Simmons showed no sign that his loyalty was at stake until Raskob burst upon the political scene. Simmons took great exception to the new chairman as "the head of two of the biggest monopolies in the nation." By this action Smith had denied the Democrats any chance of attacking Republican favoritism toward big business and its unfair taxation policies.[85] Simmons resigned from the DNC at the end of July, and three weeks later declared that he would vote for neither presidential candidate. By the end of October, however, he had taken a more explicitly anti-Smith stance. "In God's name," he implored a radio audience, "do not place upon the tarnished brow of the Democratic Party the brand of Liquor, Alienism and Plutocracy."[86] Enough North Carolinians heeded his call to take their state into Hoover's camp; he carried North Carolina by sixty-two thousand votes, winning sixty-three of the state's one hundred counties and in the process elected two GOP congressmen and seven state legislators on his coattails.[87] Simmons's defection was to cost him the Democratic nomination for his own Senate seat in 1930.

From his vantage point in Durham, Josephus Daniels reacted to the campaign in a very different way. Although he had swallowed his objections to Smith's nomination, Daniels did not shed his deep faith in prohibition and in the Democrats' obligation to battle with economic privilege. He was convinced that the party could remain a viable force only if it waged the campaign on "the big issue" of "privilege and its twin brother, corruption."[88] Not surprisingly, he was deeply alarmed at the tenor and the personnel of Smith's campaign. A visit to Birmingham, Alabama, strengthened these reservations. He noted that "all the big iron, steel, utilities captains" of that city were supporting Smith in 1928, and remembered, "What I saw in Birmingham troubled me. Was Smith the bold warrior against monopoly as I had supposed? If so, why were the agents of monopoly . . . giving him support? And why did the DuPonts [*sic*] and Raskobs pour out their money to elect him? . . . I began to fear that Smith's association with the Rascobs [*sic*] and the DuPonts and others who crossed party lines to support him on the ground of antagonism to prohibition, had behind it a willingness to put Big Business and Monopoly in places of power."[89] Like Hull in Tennessee, however, Daniels supported the ticket in the name of party regularity—and in the hope of purging his party of its unwelcome ideological baggage after November.

Further North, in Virginia, the state's two most powerful Democrats were pondering their options. Harry Flood Byrd, Democratic national committeeman and the undisputed ruler of the "Byrd Machine," saw a threat to his control of state politics in Smith's campaign.[90] As a conservative, Byrd found little in Smith's economic policies that worried him. As governor of Virginia, in fact, he was engaged in many of the same reforms that Smith had implemented in New York between 1918 and 1928. Like his northern colleague, he interpreted his election as a mandate for structural reform along "business principles" rather than for sweeping social change. Although he did push through the first antilynching bill enacted in the old

Confederacy, Byrd concentrated upon rationalizing the Old Dominion's rambling government edifice, building roads, improving education, and reducing taxes.[91] Smith's prohibition policy, however, was profoundly disturbing to Byrd. Himself a dry, he considered that Virginia's Democrats would not stand for a wet candidate for the Presidency.

As the consummate machine politician, however, Byrd understood the need for loyalty to the ticket, and his own ambitions for higher office gave him an additional interest in supporting Smith. Accordingly, he worked hard for the ticket in the name of party unity and survival.[92] He explained his stance to his fellow Virginians in realpolitik terms. "If Smith be defeated by the electoral votes of the Southern States," he warned in a campaign speech, "the co-operation of the Northern and Eastern Democrats with the Southern Democracy may be made impossible for years." The result of this breach would be that "the Republican party may need no longer consider the Democratic party a serious contender for the Presidency."[93]

Byrd's fellow Virginian Carter Glass reacted more strongly to Smith's campaign. In June 1928 he reported to his fellow Virginian senator Claude Swanson that Cordell Hull had heard a rumor that Smith would insist upon including in the platform a "protective tariff plank that will not be distasteful to Massachusetts and New Jersey." If the party was to surrender in such manner to "Republican doctrines, and permit certain Republican States to nominate its candidate," Glass thought, "it had as well disband and go over to the enemy."[94] The selection of Raskob infuriated Glass as much as it had Simmons. "I think no more deliberate or greater insult was ever offered a national party," he wrote Josephus Daniels of the appointment. Raskob was a "rank Union League Republican" who was interested in the Democratic party only because he wished to end prohibition.[95] The irascible senator declared to Robert Ailsworth that Raskob's appointment was supposed "to identify the Democratic party with big business," but it seemed to Glass that "stock gambling, altogether responsible for Raskob's fortune, is not the sort of big business that the Democratic party has been accustomed to endorse."[96]

Perhaps because of what he termed the "moral constraints of party regularity," Glass remained loyal.[97] A more likely explanation, however, is that he had been repelled by the intolerance and political meddling of Bishop Cannon, a fellow Methodist, whom he considered to be a disgrace to his church. Cannon's bitter opposition to Smith on religious grounds guaranteed that Glass would swallow his own distaste for the platform and support the governor.[98] In keeping with many of his fellow southern leaders, however, this support was given in the expectation that the damage done by the Houston platform and Raskob would be quickly undone after the election.

William Gibbs McAdoo, who still considered himself to be the leader of both progressive and southern Democracy, needed time to consider his loyalty to the ticket. The Houston platform, he thought, "abandoned . . . every principle for which Woodrow Wilson stood"; furthermore, Smith himself repudiated its liquor plank. "This," McAdoo concluded to his former secretary Brice Claggett, "absolves every Democrat from any obligation to follow him so far as party regularity is concerned." Yet he professed a desire to remain loyal. "Apart from anything else," he wrote to Claggett, "my attitude is likely to have a very great effect with a large number of people who will follow my lead." Smith had not made it easy for him, McAdoo complained, by his deference to big business in both his platform and the choice of his chairman. This was simply "giving point . . . to the prevailing notion that there is practically no difference between the two political parties and that each is controlled by privilege and big business." McAdoo eventually decided to wait and see how Smith conducted the early part of his campaign before he committed himself.[99] Dan Roper and George Fort Milton, his closest allies, temporarily deserted their party and campaigned for Hoover.[100]

McAdoo vacillated through most of the campaign.[101] In the middle of October he privately declared that to support Smith would be to stultify himself, and so he resolved to take no part in the campaign.[102] In the end, however, his ambition to remain a force in the party made him decide to appear loyal once Smith's defeat seemed certain. Not wishing to be on the sidelines when the party regrouped, he announced his support of the ticket on November 3—the very eve of the election. This was so late as to be useless, yet McAdoo was unrepentant. "I doubt very much," he wrote to his old friend Homer Cummings, "if the Tammany outfit would have done as much for me if the conditions had been reversed."[103]

ANALYSIS OF SMITH'S DEFEAT

Why, in the face of so much resistance from the core constituency of the party, did the Smith forces persist in their strategy? The answer lies in the dictates of the electoral strategy which underpinned their campaign. "It is in the East that we must win," a Washington attorney wrote FDR just before the convention. "The Bryan illusion that the Democratic party can win in the West is the most false idea that we can chase after. The Western farmer with a grouch may *talk* anti-Republican but he always comes in, when the dinnerbell rings on election day, to the Republican kitchen." There was therefore no need to emphasize such western concerns as McNary-Haugen or water power if to do so would be to jeopardize votes in more promising areas.[104]

Despite the continuing rural depression the Democrats targeted the industrial Northeast and hoped that victory would come by adding those votes to the solid South.[105] "This whole campaign is predicated," George Fort Milton wrote to McAdoo, "on the political theory that Smith can be elected by adding the wet, alien, negro votes of the East to the stupid, somnolent yellow-dog votes of the South. In other words, that nothing Smith can do or say can alter the traditional party regularity of the Southern states."[106] Although the Smith strategists were too tactful to make this plain, it is clear that they took the South for granted.

The Smith forces therefore made only token efforts toward the South. As noted earlier, assurances were made that the candidate was "reliable" on racial issues. Eleanor Roosevelt told an Alabama correspondent during the campaign that "he does not believe in intermarriage. . . . He has a full understanding of conditions as they are in the South and would never try to do violence to the feelings of the Southern people."[107] When the Ku Klux Klan accused Smith of having a "negro wench" as his private stenographer, the candidate went to the trouble of releasing a press statement denying the truth of this rumor. "Employment of Negroes by the State of New York under his administration," the statement declared, "has been done only to fill such jobs as they are given in the South, to wit: porters, janitors, charwomen, etc."[108] Confirmation of Smith's alleged racism came from W. E. B. Du Bois, who noted angrily that "he has sedulously avoided recognizing Negroes in any way."[109] Campaign speakers were also directed to remind southern audiences that Tammany Hall had come to the rescue of the "beleaguered South" and white supremacy in 1875 and 1890, when it instructed its congressmen to vote against the Force bills of those years.[110]

Whatever comfort such protestations afforded white southerners was largely negated by Smith's attitude toward prohibition. Me-tooism served a purpose other than that of soothing the financial markets of the East. By eliminating or reducing the areas of conflict between the two parties on economic issues, Smith and his advisers hoped that the issue of prohibition would assume greater importance. This, they considered, was essential to the wooing of the North, which they saw as ready for a wet campaign. "Personally," John Raskob wrote to Irénée du Pont, "I can see no big difference between the two parties except the wet and dry question," a sentiment echoed by Pierre du Pont in his decision to support Smith so handsomely.[111]

Accordingly Smith went out of his way to stress his opposition to the Eighteenth Amendment and the Volstead Act. The Houston platform, in a concession to southern and western pressure, limited itself to an innocuous plank which pledged the party to "an honest effort to enforce the eighteenth amendment and all other provisions of the federal Constitution and all laws enacted pursuant thereto."[112] The candidate, however, upset this delicate compromise by cabling the convention that he would, indeed, enforce the prohibition laws but that he would use his influence as president to urge "fundamental changes in the present provisions of national prohibition."[113] During the campaign, he argued for a modification of the Volstead Act to allow for the sale of beer and light wines, and for the ultimate resubmission of the Eighteenth Amendment itself to the voters to decide whether the whole issue of liquor control should be returned to the states.[114] "I ask that the prohibition question be treated in accordance with the Jeffersonian theory of states' rights," he told a Nashville audience, "This great section . . . during all of its history has been devoted to the Jeffersonian principle of states' rights. Why not apply it to this question?"[115]

Southern and western dries were enraged by Smith's disregard of the Houston platform's prohibition plank, which had been their only victory in the convention.[116] Josephus Daniels travelled to Albany in August and put his case directly to the governor, then engaged in writing his acceptance speech. "No argument . . . availed anything," Daniels reported to Harry Flood Byrd; "he is obviously acting on the theory that the South is obliged to vote for him regardless of anything or everything, and that his sole effort in the campaign must be directed to getting the vote of certain wringing wet Eastern states." Daniels tried in vain to convince Smith that his ideas regarding the modification and resubmission of the Volstead Act and the Eighteenth Amendment were "impossible of accomplishment" because the South would never vote for such a scheme. To the governor's argument that this would be possible under "courageous leadership," Daniels replied that "he was confusing courage with recklessness by proposing to cast away certain electoral votes for a desperate adventure to get uncertain electoral votes."[117]

Although Smith's electoral strategy was offensive to southerners, it had beneficial effects on fund-raising. The combination of a conservative platform, the efforts of John Raskob, and Smith's own popularity ensured the Democrats of an ample war chest with which to do battle. Estimates of campaign funds are notoriously vague, but it appears that the DNC outspent the Republican National Committee for the first time since the Civil War. When the outlays of the various state committees are included, however, the Republicans retained their customary lead in campaign spending.[118] Yet the total of over $6 million raised by Raskob's organization in 1928 made Davis's 1924 fund of $1.3 million, and Cox's $900,000 four years earlier, seem paltry indeed.[119] Such business titans as Pierre du Pont, William H. Woodin, Thomas G. Condon, and Spruille Braden all contributed large amounts, and Raskob himself donated $230,000 to the campaign and underwrote a loan to the DNC of $150,000 more.[120] It seems clear that Raskob's presence at the head of the Smith campaign was a vital factor in the giving of such large sums. Pierre du Pont, who donated $50,000, declared that such generosity was mainly due to his faith in his old friend and protégé. "Personally I thought the injection of business heads into politics might work some good," he wrote a fellow Delawarian after the campaign. "I should not have subscribed so liberally to the Democratic campaign had not the business management existed."[121]

As Smith's strategy and ideology were weighted toward the East, so too were the fund-raising activities of his campaign. The receipts of the DNC reveal that over 80 percent of its campaign funds came from the Northeast, with New Yorkers alone contributing over 74 percent.[122] Smith's financial support was strongly class-specific as well as geographically localized; nearly 19 percent of the total amount of contributions came from donations of more than $50,000, and nearly 30 percent came in gifts of more than $25,000.[123] For the first time since 1860 the total number of Republican contributors (145,000) was greater than that of Democratic benefactors (90,000). By contrast, 170,000 people had contributed to Wilson's campaign in 1916.[124] Of the five largest single contributions to either party in 1928, the first four went to the Democrats.[125] It was Smith, not Hoover, who could lay claim to being the rich man's candidate in 1928.

Despite the insights into the workings of political institutions that have been afforded by investment theory, votes are still vital to any electoral strategy. Here the Smith electoral strategy looked sound on paper. A coalition of New England (with 44 electoral votes), the eastern states of New York, New Jersey, Pennsylvania, Maryland, and Delaware (with 108 votes), and the old Confederacy (114 votes) would yield a total of 266 electoral votes—exactly half of the Electoral College. Surely, the Smith forces reasoned, enough votes could be garnered from the border states (with 43 electors) or the West (with 65) to make up for any defections in the East and create a majority in the college. In this way a victory could be won with little or no reliance on the radically minded agrarian West.[126]

This strategy, however, was only as strong as its assumptions. Only political ingénues such as Raskob could believe that Pennsylvania would vote Democratic, and Smith's own New York was decidedly unsafe even before the first campaign speech was made. In 1920 and 1924 Pennsylvania had delivered over 65 percent of its votes to the GOP, and New York had given the Republicans 64 and 55 percent respectively. New Jersey's figures were 67 and 62 percent. The Northeast as a whole, from West Virginia to Maine, had given Harding 64.8 percent and Coolidge 60.1 percent of its votes.[127] To expect these states to turn Democratic on the strength of the Houston platform and Smith's statements on prohibition was tantamount to expecting a political realignment during a time of prosperity and political apathy. This was nothing short of political fantasy.

The second major assumption of Smith's strategists, that the South would vote solidly Democratic, may well have been better founded in fact. Here, at least, the Democrats had tradition on their side. Yet the fears of Harry Byrd, Carter Glass, Josephus Daniels, Cordell Hull, and Furnifold Simmons were not imaginary. With a member of the eastern "plutocracy" as his chairman, and arguing the need to change the prohibition laws radically, Smith pushed the South—already concerned by his religion and Tammany origins—too far. His candidacy and platform made possible a Republican "southern strategy," masterminded by former secretary of interior Hubert Work. Dixie's Republican parties moved quickly to incorporate "Hoovercrats" into a general anti-Smith movement led by a coalition of white Republicans and disaffected Democrats.[128] The results of Smith's confrontation and Hoover's wooing were evident in November. Florida, North Carolina, Virginia, Tennessee, and Texas all returned majorities for Hoover.[129] Whereas Davis had won the Confederacy and Kentucky and Oklahoma with a vote of 66.8 percent in 1924, these states gave Smith only 53.9 percent of their votes.[130]

Despite the northeastern strategy, Smith failed to win any nonsouthern states other than Massachusetts and Rhode Island. When the Electoral College met, Smith had only 87 electors to his name. "Well," he reflected sadly, "the time just hasn't come when a man can say his beads in the White House."[131] Even the hapless Davis, who did not carry a state outside of the South, had 136 votes in 1924. The northeastern strategy, mooted in 1920, developed in 1924, and perfected in 1928, had not only been largely responsible for the third successive Democratic defeat, but it had split the party along regional and ideological lines as well.

Much has been made of Smith's electoral strategy and performance in 1928 as an important prelude to Roosevelt's New Deal coalition. Smith's candidacy, this argument has it, mobilized immigrant and first-generation immigrant voters, and especially immigrant women, to vote for the first time. This election therefore opened up previously untapped electoral resources for the Democratic party which, when combined with western and southern Democrats, would create national Democratic victories between 1932 and 1952.[132] While it is true that Smith won 76 percent more votes than Davis and 64 percent more than Cox and that voter turnout jumped from 51 percent in 1924 to 67.5 per cent in 1928, some caution is necessary in discussing the "mobilization" of 1928.[133]

Smith won nearly 15 million votes, which was 6.6 million more than Davis won in 1924, and 5.8 million more than Cox in 1920.[134] In the cities, especially, Smith did well, although his poor performance in rural areas lent a deceptively urban character to the Democratic coalition of 1928. Smith won approximately 50 percent of the urban vote nationwide, but his gains were heavily biased toward the Northeast. He won New York

City by a huge majority, but when that is taken out of the calculation, his share of the urban vote dropped from 50 percent to 46 percent.[135] In the western cities he trailed Hoover by 30 percent, and he even lost the southern urban vote.[136] The narrow base of Smith's mobilization should not, furthermore, obscure the impressive electoral achievement of the GOP in 1928. Hoover achieved a mobilization of his own; his ticket gained 5.7 million votes over 1924. In 1924 the Republicans' lead over the Democrats was 7.33 million votes. In 1928, in spite of the disappearance of La Follette's Progressives and the impact of Smith's mobilization, their lead was still 6.38 million.[137] The northeastern strategy and me-tooism had achieved a relative nationwide gain of only 910,000 votes, at the cost of the solid South and what remained of the party's ideological coherence.

David Burner has argued that Smith was an essentially limited politician who failed to present himself as a truly national figure. He and his supporters were culturally provincial, insensitive to the cultural values and expectations of the hinterland. The brash urbanite, fond of a drink, unashamed of his Tammany background, and proud of his Catholicism, refused to modify his image to appear less threatening to audiences west of the Hudson River.[138] This is undeniable, yet the 1928 campaign also revealed Smith to be ideologically provincial in that he did not realize that his probusiness, antistatist platform was peculiarly a creature of his own section and that members of the party beyond New York City were not pleased at the prospect of their party being taken over by those who saw no need to adjust economic relationships in the name of social justice. Accordingly, Smith failed to take advantage of what progressive sentiment still existed around the country; he won only 43 of the 409 counties that had given La Follette majorities in 1924.[139]

The progressive strategy that had muted opposition to the nomination of Smith had therefore proved only a partial success. The assumption that 1928 was not to be a Democratic year had been vindicated, yet events during and after the Houston convention were profoundly alarming to progressive and southern leaders who had awaited Smith's nomination and defeat. The Houston platform signaled a new philosophical direction for the party which was unwelcome to them, and Raskob's appointment suggested that control of the party machinery for the next four years would be in distinctly unfriendly hands. "If the Democrats lose in November," a

Georgia newspaperman wrote to McAdoo in September 1928, "we of the South will have a chance to run the Democratic Party in the future, and that is one of the impelling reasons for my sticking to it."[140] By November, however, such a happy ending from a progressive and southern point of view seemed increasingly unlikely.

THE POLITICS OF MONEY

JOHN RASKOB AND THE DNC, 1929–1932

Less than six months after Smith's defeat, John Raskob took an important step in his campaign to apply "business principles" of organization to the Democratic party. Although the election had left the national committee deeply in debt, the chairman refused to allow it to subside into its customary inactivity. He announced the creation of a permanent headquarters in Washington that would function as a clearinghouse for publicity and for the management of campaigns.[1]

Although the new permanent organization would soon be embroiled in the Democrats' internecine disputes, its announcement was a clear peace offering to a divided party. The need for a permanent organization was one of the few areas of agreement within the party; when FDR sent another circular letter to Democrats around the country after the 1928 elections, he found that "at least 98%" of the party's county leaders favored such a step.[2] For once, it seemed, the controversial chairman was concentrating on issues upon which all the party agreed, instead of driving wedges between its antagonistic groups. This feeling was reinforced by Raskob's choice of Jouett Shouse of Kansas as the head of the new permanent organization.

Shouse was an ideal choice because he had successfully straddled the divisions within the party. Born in Kentucky in 1880, he attended the University of Missouri before embarking upon a varied career. After beginning working life as a reporter, he tried horsebreeding and banking before settling down as a lawyer. In the process, he moved from Missouri to Kansas and then represented his new state in the House of Representatives between 1914 and 1918. Following his defeat in the 1918 elections, he joined the Wilson administration as assistant secretary of the treasury. In this capacity he supervised the enforcement of prohibition during the short period between the adoption of the Eighteenth Amendment and Warren Harding's inauguration.[3]

Shouse supported McAdoo for the presidential nomination in 1920 and 1924 and was especially active in corralling Kansas delegates for the secretary.[4] Although he supported Smith's nomination in 1928, he had not been part of the conservative northeastern business group which had so offended southern, western, and progressive Democrats after 1920. He had succeeded in keeping private his increasing doubts about the efficacy of the Eighteenth Amendment after 1926. Consequently he remained acceptable to both sides of the liquor question. "Personally," Shouse wrote McAdoo in 1926, "I can herd with a wet Democrat just as well as I can herd with a dry Democrat, if thereby I can prove of benefit to the Democratic party."[5] Prohibitionists welcomed his appointment. Shouse was, the *Macon* (Georgia) *Telegraph and News* declared, "so ardently dry as to be comparable only to a parched tongue."[6] However, his service in Smith's cause in 1928 and his privately expressed doubts about prohibition indicated to the governor's group that he was a sympathetic colleague.[7]

Shouse was not about to waste his good standing through inactivity. Amid much fanfare, he appointed Charles Michelson, a respected Washington correspondent for the *New York World*, as the head of the new publicity bureau.[8] Michelson remained as the Democrats' chief publicist until 1940, becoming something of a legend in the process.[9] Frank R. Kent, a columnist who ordinarily found little to commend in Raskob and Shouse's activities, described Michelson's appointment as "the smartest thing that has been done in national politics for a long time." The DNC's publicity bureau, Kent argued in 1930, was the agency that "more than any other has helped to mould the public mind in regard to Mr. Hoover." Michelson's expertise and Raskob's funds created "the most elaborate, expensive, efficient and effective political propaganda machine ever operated in the country by any party, organization, association, or league."[10]

The publicity bureau under Michelson issued nearly five hundred press releases between June 1929 and September 1930, chiefly on Republican failures in farm relief, Hoover's "inactivity" after the Wall Street crash, and the Smoot-Hawley Tariff. The new tariff law had passed in 1930, despite the opposition of economists who feared retaliation from America's trading partners.[11] Press releases were distributed to the Washington correspondents of the major newspapers, to each member of the DNC and the Democratic congressional contingent, and to the burgeoning number of radio stations around the nation.[12] Michelson brought to his work a conviction that effective political publicity needed more than a reactive approach to problems; instead he sought out and then publicized the administration's mistakes.[13] He also made specific attacks on Herbert Hoover's performance. This provided Democrats with a single and highly visible target for criticism, making the blunders of a faceless administration the failures of the president himself. The Smoot-Hawley Tariff thus became the "Hoover Tariff," and the depression the "Hoover panic."[14]

So effective was Michelson's work after the Wall Street Crash that the Republicans claimed it represented a Raskob plot to discredit the president during a time of national crisis. In this they were correct, although Michelson only encouraged the public disaffection with the Great Engineer that stemmed from forces far greater than those mustered by the DNC. Yet the publicity division was a sufficiently new phenomenon to cause some commentators to declare that a new age had dawned in political life.[15] The advent of a full-time and professional publicity machine under the control of Democrats meant that national partisan competition was now on a year-round basis and that the president could no longer hide behind the dignity of his office to escape criticism and responsibility for the actions of his administration. Will Irwin found this development alarming; in his

1936 book *Propaganda and the News* he blamed Raskob and Michelson for transferring the propaganda methods used in World War I to domestic political debate. The DNC, Irwin argued, had revived the wartime phenomenon of "the propaganda of hate" and applied it against the hapless president.[16]

Whatever its longer-term implications, the publicity bureau performed an important bonding function for a divided party. Michelson's press releases leaned heavily upon the utterances of Democratic congressmen and senators on the floors of their respective chambers. This provided a valuable source of publicity for them and won for the new permanent organization the loyalty of this important group of Democrats. By giving the impression of neutrality in the internal struggles of the party and by concentrating instead upon the common enemy, Michelson and Shouse made their organization useful to all factions. In public Shouse tried to steer a neutral and mediating course between the hostile forces around him; he remained uncommitted about the future of prohibition until 1931, and in 1930 argued that the Democratic primaries should be open to those southerners who had voted for Hoover in 1928.[17] Shouse's politics of inclusion and mediation worked until 1931, when even his tact could not bridge the deepening divisions within the party.

Although the onset of the depression made Charles Michelson's job easier, it made fund-raising harder than ever for the party. The 1928 campaign had left the DNC $1.5 million in debt, and funds were slow to come in as the economic situation deteriorated. Even in August 1932, the debt still stood at $400,000.[18] Only large contributions from Raskob enabled the national, senatorial and congressional campaign committees to assist Democratic candidates in the 1930 elections.[19] Shouse was anxious to improve this precarious financial condition before the 1932 campaign, and in October 1931 he announced the creation of a "Victory Fund." Under the chairmanship of John W. Davis, the fund aimed to raise $1.5 million by encouraging prominent Democrats to donate $2,000 each to the party. This they could do individually or by pooling smaller donations from party stalwarts in their areas.[20] These "Minute Men" were both prominent and wealthy; Shouse described the group as "a rather select organization, in no sense a snobbish organization, but nevertheless select enough to make people want to join to be members of it." Anyone could be a Minute Man, John Raskob told the DNC in 1932, simply by donating $2,000 or by persuading one's friends to raise that sum on one's behalf.[21] The realities of the depression, however, seemed to have escaped him; $2,000 proved to be an unachievable amount for either single or collective contributors.

Only three states—Raskob's Delaware, Davis's West Virginia, and Maryland—managed to fill their allotted quotas by June 1932. More typical were the experiences of Alabama, which raised 16 percent of its quota, Florida (36 percent), Illinois (43 percent), Louisiana (27 percent), Nebraska (20 percent), and California (1 percent). Arkansas raised $296 of its quota of $15,000, while Nevada could manage only $10 toward its $5,000 target. Overall, only $538,000 was raised by the time of the Chicago convention, a little more than a third of the goal of $1.5 million. New York alone contributed 48 percent of collected funds, and the five states of New York, New Jersey, Maryland, Illinois, and Indiana accounted for nearly 72 percent.[22]

The Victory Fund attracted criticism from some Democrats concerned about its elitist implications. It seemed insensitive to set the membership fee for the Minute Men as high as $2,000 in a time of acute economic distress. Mary Staples Porter wrote John Davis in November 1931 to warn him against applying business principles too closely to political organizations. "We must prevent an organization of the Democratic National Committee that imitates a Corporation with Boards of Directors and Advisers and Investors," she wrote. This would mean that influence within the party would "depend upon ability to pay and that is totally undemocratic."[23]

Porter's forebodings were shared by many of her fellow Democrats. The failure of the Victory Fund to achieve its target highlighted the fact that the party was increasingly dependent upon John Raskob for its financial support. The new permanent organization was paid for almost entirely from the chairman's personal funds, as were Shouse's salary of $50,000 per year and Michelson's of $25,000.[24] Raskob was the party's largest creditor between 1928 and 1932, lending it well over $200,000 and jointly underwriting loans to the DNC of $375,000 more.[25] Raskob lent the DNC $10,000 every month between January 1928 and June 1932 to cover its salary and administrative costs. The party's financial dependence upon him can be gauged from the DNC's monthly financial statements. That of August 1931, for example, shows Raskob's usual loan of $10,000. Total contributions from all other sources amounted to $4.00. The September statement shows Raskob's $10,000 and contributions from other sources to be $5.50. The DNC's running costs were $10,200 per month, of which the chairman provided 98 percent.[26]

Although Raskob's organizational reforms won praise, they had also maintained his strong influence within the party structure until 1932, and many Democrats were not pleased. The dominant sentiment of progressives, westerners, and southerners, the *New York Times* reported in January 1929, was that Raskob and his friends were responsible for the 1928 debt and therefore should pay it. That view did not, however, include the notion that Democrats should "feel obligated to that wing of the party for future leadership."[27] Most Democratic leaders wanted a permanent organization, but they did not want Raskob, the paper noted two years later, so their hope was to use his money while rebuffing his attempts to influence the party's platform.[28]

Many of the Democratic rank and file were less willing to make such a compromise for the sake of the party's finances. This was especially true in the South, where the chairman was unpopular among the "Hoovercrats" who had defected to the GOP in 1928. In June 1929 anti-Smith Democrats met at Roanoke, Virginia, to organize themselves for the Virginia elections of that year. It had been the hope of many southerners, delegate Frank Lyon declared, "that the Tammany influence of Governor Smith would be thrown out of the house of the Democratic Party . . . and there was the hope of many that the occasion would be used to eliminate Mr. Raskob from the Democratic Party."[29] Instead, Raskobism seemed further entrenched than ever, James Cannon told the convention, and the "real outstanding issue in the Democratic Party today is Rascobism [*sic*] versus Southern democracy. They are as wide apart as the poles."[30]

The reaction of more moderate southerners to developments within the DNC during 1929 showed how distant Raskob's goal of achieving a conservative East-South alliance was. Cordell Hull reacted to Smith's defeat by arguing that the party must avoid "crimination" in order to "maintain at least the appearance of a cohesive national party." To this end, he believed, a "tactful and diplomatic" way should be found to persuade Raskob to pay off the debt and then to disappear as soon as possible. "We should then," Hull concluded, "seek a unanimous consent agreement for some two-fisted person not especially objectionable to any large group of Democrats to take charge of the national committee."[31] For his part, Harry Flood Byrd of Virginia had more parochial interests in mind. Mindful of the anti-Smith Democrats organizing their Roanoke convention, he wrote Hull at the beginning of 1929 that "it is very important that we do something in regard to Raskob. . . . If Raskob resigns the backbone of the anti-Smith movement in Virginia . . . will be dissipated."[32]

Democrats from the West were also alarmed by Raskob's seeming permanence as chairman of the DNC. The *Lincoln* (Nebraska) *Star* editorialized in 1931 that he had "made himself very obnoxious to a major portion of the democrats of the country" by his attitude on prohibition, his "persistent courting of Big Business," and his tariff views. The party did not place him in the chairmanship, the *Star* concluded, and "it did not want him in that capacity. . . . It was all a sorry mistake from the start and the quicker it is forgotten the better it will be for the organization."[33]

Raskob survived as chairman because of his great wealth. The party wanted a permanent organization, but the failure of the Victory Fund and the monthly financial statements of the DNC attested to their unwillingness to pay for it. The chairman's support of the party during a time of straitened economic circumstances proved too generous to refuse.[34] In an open letter to the chairman published at the beginning of 1931, Frank Kent revealed this conflict between principle and expediency. "You are just a breast-beating amateur in politics," he told Raskob. His sharpest attacks, however, were directed against the party as a whole for allowing Raskob to dominate it. The thought of Raskob holding the party's purse strings "gives a Democrat an unpleasant and uncomfortable feeling," Kent wrote, it "ought not let any rich man so completely finance its activities and pay its bills. It isn't self-respecting, and it isn't Democratic, and it isn't good."[35]

RASKOB'S INITIATIVES IN PROHIBITION

Fears that Raskob would attempt to translate the power of his checkbook into control over the party's platform were soon justified. In keeping with the tenets of his political and social beliefs, his efforts were directed toward the party's policies on prohibition and the economy.

In both areas his forays started a pitched battle between the members of his conservative northeastern group and their progressive, southern, and western opponents.

"There is one thing that I shall insist and demand, with all the force of the office of the Chairman," Raskob wrote FDR in March 1932, "and that is that the Democratic platform treat honestly, fairly and squarely with the prohibition question."[36] By that time the chairman had made a political hobby horse out of the need for prohibition reform. He was encouraged in this by several signs that pointed to a change in public opinion toward modification or repeal of prohibition. The 1930 elections saw the Democrats mount a strong recovery from the defeats of the 1920s, and those who ran on wet platforms did well in the Midwest and North.[37] Although the Republicans emerged from the elections with nominal majorities of one in the Senate and three in the House, the Democrats were able to organize the House because of deaths of some GOP representatives during the thirteen months between the polls and the meeting of the new Congress in December 1931.[38] This success emboldened the chairman to attempt to clarify the party's attitude on liquor control. George Fort Milton feared as much, writing to Harry Byrd that "the danger of the situation is that our Raskobs will interpret the result as naught but a prohibition defeat," with damaging effects upon the party so soon after its triumph at the polls.[39]

Two *Literary Digest* polls also encouraged Raskob. The first, taken during the first half of 1930, revealed that 30.4 percent of the 4,806,464 respondents favored no change and strict enforcement of the Eighteenth Amendment and the Volstead Act, 29.1 percent favored modification of the Volstead Act so as to allow the sale of beer and wine, while 40.4 percent supported the repeal of national prohibition altogether. This meant that over 69 percent of the population were in favor of some change to prohibition.[40] Two years later another poll revealed that over 73 percent were now in favor of repeal, with only 26 percent in favor of the continuation of prohibition.[41]

In order to ascertain Democratic feeling on the subject, Raskob sent a questionnaire in November 1931 to the ninety thousand people who had contributed funds to Al Smith's campaign in 1928. He made clear his belief that the Eighteenth Amendment represented an unwarranted addition to federal power and that it was "an outstanding example of paternalism." He then asked the contributors to respond to seven questions, six of which referred directly to prohibition.[42] He announced the results of this poll on January 5, 1932. Of all respondents, 93 percent favored the submission of the whole issue of prohibition to the people in the form of a referendum, 95 percent supported Raskob's proposal to make all future constitutional amendments come under the scrutiny of the electorate by means of referenda, 80 percent agreed with his proposal for a referendum on the alteration of the Eighteenth Amendment to allow each state to devise its own liquor policy, 79 percent favored his proposal to conduct a referendum on the outright repeal of the amendment, and only 22 percent believed that the economic issues arising from the depression were so pressing that the party could safely ignore the liquor issue altogether.[43]

Reactions from other sections of the party were swift. Many of the dries accused Raskob of stacking the deck; Smith had run in 1928 on a personal platform of prohibition reform, making it likely that his financial supporters shared such views. Josephus Daniels's *Raleigh News and Observer* described the exercise as tantamount to "stuffing the ballot box before the voting begins."[44] The survey group was also geographically unrepresentative, in that nearly half of the contributors lived in New York, New Jersey, Illinois, or Massachusetts.[45] Raskob's canvass also attracted criticism on a conceptual level. Underlying the chairman's action seemed to be the assumption that those who paid for campaigns had a special right to influence party policy, as if they were stockholders in a corporation.[46] The *Omaha World-Herald* pointed to the danger of "carrying business practices too literally into the political field." The rank and file of the party would resent the implication that financial contributors were more important than those less fortunate Democrats who could contribute only their time, effort and votes.[47]

This criticism may have been well founded; although the chairman declared that the opinions of all contributors, regardless of the size of their gift, counted equally, the replies that are preserved in his papers are generally annotated with the size of the respondent's contribution. Although nearly ninety thousand questionnaires were sent out, only about a thousand are preserved, most from congressmen, local party leaders, and members of the DNC. The vast majority of the replies that Raskob preserved are typewritten, suggesting that this was hardly a poll of the grass roots of the party.[48] Even Raskob conceded that there was "a great deal of truth" in the claim that his poll was strongly weighted toward the wet side of the argument.[49]

Unabashed, the chairman undertook a long campaign to change the party's position on prohibition in advance of the 1932 convention. To this end he proposed a "home rule" plan for liquor control and called a meeting of the DNC for March 5, 1931, to discuss it. The plan envisaged a modification to the Eighteenth Amendment to allow each state to take "complete control" over its own liquor industry. Raskob's scheme also envisaged that a state might rescind its action and come back under the jurisdiction of the Eighteenth Amendment and the Volstead Act. The amendment would therefore remain in force, although it would no longer automatically cover every state.[50]

At the DNC meeting on March 5, 1931, the chairman found his proposal opposed by a phalanx of southern and western committee members, who had been organized by Franklin Roosevelt. Led by Cordell Hull, Harry Byrd, and Joseph Robinson, the opponents of the home rule plan within the DNC succeeded in forcing him to defer any vote or resolution to a later meeting.[51] The party's dries had no wish to commit their party to a dismembering of national prohibition, and Roosevelt did not want to see the conservative group succeed on this crucial policy issue.[52] Roosevelt's coalition was strong enough to rebuff Raskob in 1931, and the chairman's defeat was cemented ten months later when another DNC meeting decided to refer the entire matter without debate to the national convention.[53]

Why did Raskob persist in his efforts to commit the DNC to a policy of modification of national prohibition? Historians have generally taken his statements at face value and have portrayed him as obsessed with the dangers inherent in the Eighteenth Amendment.[54] It is certainly clear that prohibition offended his conception of the limited powers given to the federal government and that he saw his plan as the first step toward prohibition's eventual removal.[55] Yet the chairman also had other concerns in mind. The first revolved around the creation of a North-South coalition within the party. He realized that the growing sentiment for prohibition reform in the northern states had to be addressed by the party if it was to cement the electoral gains made in these areas in 1928 and 1930. The party's traditional strength, however, was in the South, which remained wedded to the Eighteenth Amendment. Given the decline of the western wing, the Democrats had to devise a way to unite the South and the northeast if they were to create a winning coalition for 1932. Yet these sections were divided over the future of prohibition; they were, as the *New York Times* put it at the end of 1928, "like two unfriendly battalions of a regiment, cut off and entirely surrounded by the enemy, unable to make a junction and—were they able—more inclined to start internecine war than to turn bayonets to the enemy."[56] The chairman hoped that his home rule plan would make that junction.[57]

Raskob believed that his plan achieved this purpose by allowing each state to choose its own form of liquor control. This gave the North the opportunity to dispose of prohibition, while at the same time permitting the South to maintain the status quo.[58] This appeal to states' rights arguments was a clever one, for not only did it root the home rule proposal in traditional Democratic rhetoric, but it also carried a subtle message to the South. James Truslow Adams made this explicit in his 1929 work *Our Business Civilization*. Southerners who fought for strict enforcement of the Eighteenth Amendment, Adams observed, were skating on thin ice. These ardent dries were unthinkingly bringing "the crisis of racial hostility nearer to us than it could ever have been brought in any other way." It was true that the Eighteenth Amendment was widely ignored; but so too was the Fifteenth. "The time is rapidly coming," Adams prophesied, "if the . . . Prohibition forces insist upon the sanctity of the Eighteenth Amendment, when the fifteen million negroes . . . will insist upon the sanctity of the Fifteenth."[59]

James Cox alluded to this argument in a less direct way in a letter to Joe Tumulty soon after the March 5, 1931, meeting of the DNC. Raskob's proposal was an ideal one around which to forge an alliance between the North and South, he wrote Tumulty, if only the South could be made to see reason. "Have you thought of this," he continued, "we are being oppressed in the North now by a super government precisely as the South was terrorized during reconstruction days." Northern Democrats came to their southern brethren's assistance then by using their power in Congress to end carpetbag rule. What Cox suggested, in genteel terms, was a deal: if the South would allow the nonenforcement of the prohibition amendment, northern Democrats would continue to support the nonenforcement of the Fifteenth.[60]

Raskob's interest in the home rule plan was also based upon his desire to steer the party along a conservative economic course. This had become even more pressing after 1929, as the deepening economic crisis led to calls for federal intervention. Modification of prohibition to allow the sale of liquor in states which desired it would provide an economically painless way of combating the depression, providing jobs for the unemployed and excise revenues for empty treasuries.[61]

If southern and northern conservatives could bury the hatchet over prohibition, Raskob and his allies reasoned, they then could combine to prevent the party from becoming a vehicle of economic radicalism in 1932. This strategy can best be described as "booze before bread," since it was an inversion of the progressives' cry in 1932. Arthur Holcombe, a prominent political scientist, drew attention to this in an article published at the end of 1931. By stressing the liquor issue, Holcombe observed, conservatives hoped to divert voters from the fact that "the business depression compels attention to relief measures," and so muzzle "far sighted politicians [who] will look beyond the immediate emergency and seek for measures which will help to prevent the recurrence of such crises in the capitalistic world."[62]

Raskob's progressive and dry opponents were well aware of the hidden agenda behind the prohibition fights of 1931 and 1932. "I wonder where the Raskob and Smith leadership is trying to land us in 1932?" McAdoo asked Carter Glass in April of 1931. "I can think of nothing more stupid and fatuous than to impinge the next campaign on the liquor issue. . . . If that can be negatived and we can force the battle on economic and social issues . . . we may win."[63] Josephus Daniels thought that he knew the answer to McAdoo's question, writing Claude Bowers that "of course, Raskob is against prohibition, but he would like to paramount that to prevent the discussion of any economic issues and old-time Democratic principles. . . . Evidently his only idea is to put Smith in the White House astride a whiskey barrel, and with himself as Secretary of the Treasury. And then Mellonism would go on."[64] This view was best summed up by Thomas Walsh in a long letter to a Californian Democrat soon after the March 1931 DNC meeting. "I am firmly convinced," the dry Montana Senator wrote, "that the policies advocated by Chairman Raskob will, if adopted, bring certain and disasterous [sic] defeat to the Democratic party in 1932. To impinge the next national campaign, as he proposes, upon the restoration of the liquor traffic, to the subordination of the grave economic and social problems now tearing at the vitals of Democracy and imperilling the welfare of the people . . . would be fatuous in the extreme. Relegalizing liquor will not put food into a single hungry mouth nor provide employment for the great army of jobless men and women in the United States. Is liquor the Democratic answer to this vital problem? If it is, then the party is too impoverished in ideas to enter even a snail's race." [65]

RASKOB AND VIRGINIA'S HARRY BYRD

An examination of Raskob's relationship with Harry Flood Byrd suggests that the chairman's opponents were premature in claiming in 1931 that they had saved the party from running on a me-too platform in 1932. Harry Flood Byrd was the political master of the Virginia Democratic party and therefore of the commonwealth itself. Although Virginia's constitution forbade him a second term as governor in 1930, he was still very much in control of his "Byrd Machine." In addition, he was a vice-chairman of the DNC and an acknowledged leader of southern Democrats and dries within the national organization. [66] A fiscal conservative hostile to any federal initiative which lessened the power of the states, he represented the very type of southern leader whom Raskob needed to convert if his hopes for a North-South alliance were to come to fruition.

When Raskob announced the purpose of the March 5, 1931, meeting of the DNC, Byrd unhesitatingly opposed his home rule plan. He had no wish to see the prohibition issue raised at all, having seen the backlash against Smith in Virginia during the 1928 campaign. "Another fight like 1928 will just rip the guts out of our state organization," his close friend A. Willis Robertson wrote in the middle of January. [67] Byrd, who had remained loyal in 1928, heartily agreed. Less than two weeks later he wrote to Franklin Roosevelt to ask his assistance in blocking Raskob's plan. "I am told," he wrote FDR, "that unquestionably it is the present intention of Mr. Raskob and Mr. Shouse to force through a resolution . . . not only against prohibition but in favor of a moderately high tariff, thereby having only one issue between the two parties." This was most dangerous, Byrd thought, because if the GOP adopted a "moist or wet plank," there would be no differences to fight over in 1932. [68]

Byrd was delighted at the outcome of the March 5 meeting. The dries, he wrote Josephus Daniels, had won "a distinct victory."[69] However, other thoughts were beginning to influence him. One of his closest political advisers, Roy Flannagan, wrote him in April 1931 to advise that it would be best if Raskob were *pulled* along at this particular time rather than lambasted over the head." The chairman had powerful publicity machinery at his disposal, Flannagan warned, and his position on prohibition was winning support among northeastern Democrats. Although the chairman had "an ulterior motive, i.e. that of obscuring economic liberalism with anti-prohibition preachments," Flannagan advised Byrd that he "should be patted on the back as though he were a good little warrior" until his opponents could come up with a scheme of their own with which to combat the chairman's suggestions.[70]

The following day Byrd wrote to Edwin A. Alderman, president of the University of Virginia. The party was in grave danger of splitting along regional lines, he told Alderman, with the northern wing of the party favoring changes to prohibition against southern and western opposition. If the party adopted a wet plank, southern dry Democrats might defect to the GOP, destroying any chance of victory in 1932; if, however, the party assumed a strongly dry position, it would lose the North and suffer similar consequences. Action was clearly necessary, Byrd told Alderman, and he was coming to the conclusion that "the only possible solution of the . . . situation is to submit this question in some legal way to the voters themselves." He also displayed a new appreciation of the difficult task that faced Raskob. "I enjoyed greatly meeting Mr. Raskob," he reported to Alderman, "and was greatly impressed by the clarity of his vision and his understanding. I sincerely hope that he and I will not be placed in a position of hostility, but if we are I know it will only be because each of us follows his own conscientious convictions."[71]

Byrd had made a crucial concession in the battle over the party's prohibition policy. By agreeing to the concept of a plebiscite on the future of prohibition, he had agreed to reopen the matter to public scrutiny, something that he had refused to do in March. Although he objected to Raskob's home rule plan as too biased in favor of the wet states and as insufficiently protective of those which wished to remain dry, he had opened the door to a future compromise. This development created a warming of relations between the two men. They took to exchanging long and frank letters in which they explored the issues that separated them. On April 9, 1931, for example, Raskob sent a letter explaining his motives for the March 5 meeting and the home rule plan that prompted it. Although he conceded that the DNC had no power to *create* party platforms, Raskob maintained that it was vitally necessary that such a contentious issue as prohibition should be aired as much as possible before the convention.[72] Like a committee of shareholders in a large corporation, it was essential that the DNC act as a clearinghouse for new ideas and policies during the four years between conventions. Turning to his home rule plan, Raskob pointed out its strong basis in the doctrine of states' rights. Southerners, he thought, should respond favorably to the essential justice and fairness of the home rule plan's stress on the right of individual states to determine their own policies.[73]

Byrd replied nine days later. Although he noted that they were in agreement that the DNC could not "legally adopt a platform," Byrd took the chairman to task for equating the committee to a group of shareholders. This was not the case, for "a business corporation is a continuing thing, while the Democratic party adopts new policies every four years." Conventions had to set party policy because the DNC was too removed from the rank and file to represent it properly. If the Committee were to recommend a new party policy, this would create confusion because "it would stand in the public mind as the party's platform until and unless vetoed by the national convention." Therefore, Byrd concluded, it was inappropriate for the DNC to recommend policies, although it "may discuss with profit" any important political issue. He had again narrowed the differences between himself and the chairman to a procedural point as to the advisability of the DNC's recommending a change of policy as opposed to simply discussing it and reaching an informal consensus.[74]

Correspondence between the two men and their allies during the middle of 1931 also brought them together on a crucial area of economic policy. In mid-April, Byrd wrote to Flannagan that he and Raskob were moving closer together with respect to prohibition, but that "as a matter of fact I am more opposed to his tariff provision than I am to his liquor provision." Raskob, he complained, was so intent on reducing the differences between the two parties to the liquor issue alone that he was prepared to accept the Smoot-Hawley Tariff rates. Byrd found this thought intolerable; the chairman's tariff stance was too Republican for his comfort.[75]

Raskob wrote Byrd eight days later in an attempt to resolve this difference. The Smoot-Hawley Tariff was "the most atrocious law ever put on our statute books." "The impression seems to have gone abroad that I am in favor of high tariffs," the chairman continued; "such is not the case at all." He was concerned only to define the party's policy so as to reassure the industrial East that the party aimed not to "destroy industry" but rather to be "in favor of the lowest tariffs that will adequately protect and restore prosperity to American industry."[76]

Raskob's assurance seems to have had the desired effect, for Byrd ceased to criticize the chairman on his tariff views. It was an important change, because the two men differed little on other areas of economic policy. "In my judgement we should touch lightly upon the new 'fads and isms' and avoid radicalism," Byrd wrote Governor Josiah Bailey of North Carolina in June 1931, "but adopt a platform of broad vision and in harmony with our traditional principles."[77]

The fruits of this blossoming understanding between Byrd and Raskob were evident at the second DNC meeting over prohibition, held on January 9, 1932. Roosevelt and his allies had assumed that Byrd's hostility to Raskob and his schemes was unchanged, for Louis Howe sent him a detailed battle plan for defeating the chairman at the end of 1931.[78] Byrd, however, was in close contact with Raskob during the same month, and he reported to Colonel Henry Breckinridge on December 31 that the chairman had proved himself to be "cooperative, and anxious and willing" to adopt the proposals that Byrd made to him.[79] At the meeting itself, Byrd acted as a mediator between Raskob and Roosevelt; his proposal not to discuss prohibition at all but to refer the matter to the convention was clearly the same one that he had referred to in his letter to Breckinridge. By avoiding another defeat for Raskob, Byrd had in effect been on his side, and therefore against FDR.

When Byrd finally unveiled his own plan regarding the Eighteenth Amendment, he attempted to incorporate aspects of Raskob's scheme. Byrd proposed a two-step process by which the electorate would first vote on another constitutional amendment which would allow a direct vote by the people on prohibition. If that amendment passed, the referendum on prohibition could be held and its future determined.[80] This scheme, he thought, was more favorable to the dries because it would necessarily take more time than Raskob's home rule plan, thus allowing prohibition a longer period in which to show its usefulness.[81]

By May 1932, therefore, Byrd and Raskob had developed a much closer understanding and agreement over prohibition and economic policy than had been the case when the chairman first mooted his home rule plan. Byrd had conceded the need to test popular opinion on prohibition, and Raskob had agreed to drop the idea of having the DNC endorse his plan. The meeting of their minds was by no means perfect, but it was a hopeful sign of the eventual creation of a political alliance. If Byrd could be won over, it would seem that the whole concept of a North-South conservative alliance was a workable one. Raskob's experiences with Harry Flood Byrd were to provide a valuable lesson as the 1932 convention neared. He had weaned the Virginian away from FDR and toward his own conception of the party's proper ideological and policy direction.

RASKOB'S TARIFF POLICY

Raskob's economic platform for 1932 was based upon the premise that government should be taken out of business and that trade should be liberated from "unnecessary and unreasonable governmental restriction, interference and manipulation."[82] Tariff policy should be formulated to reassure large corporations that the Democrats had outgrown their earlier free-trade ideas, and a scheme of farm relief that "will redound to the benefit of our whole country" should be devised. A scheme of unemployment insurance should be instituted "based on cooperative effort between capital and labor," and the party should commit itself to Raskob's earlier proposal of a five-day working week "without diminution of weekly wage." After this brief reference to workers, the chairman returned to the issue of relieving business from "unnecessary restriction." The Sherman Antitrust Act should be modified so as to protect from subsequent criminal prosecution mergers and agreements that had been certified to be in the public interest. Finally, the party should resist calls to advocate "federal curbs" on public utilities. It was up to state and local governments to ensure that their citizens did not pay inflated costs in order that "overcapitalized" utility-holding companies could pay dividends on their watered stock. Federal control, however, "is another of the regrettable tendencies to extend the powers of the central government" and should be rejected as an affront to the party's Jeffersonian principles.[83]

The tariff had become a pressing political issue with the passage of the

Smoot-Hawley Act of 1930, which raised tariff rates to their highest level in history. Rates on raw materials jumped between 50 and 100 percent over the 1922 Fordney-McCumber levels, and the average levy rose from 33 percent to 40 percent.[84] As his dealings with Byrd had shown, Raskob was in a delicate position on this issue. The Smoot-Hawley Tariff had created a resurgence of Democratic antitariff feeling, and the chairman had to tread carefully between the desire of his party to see a large downward revision of rates on one hand, and the strongly protectionist sentiments of business interests on the other. His solution was to advocate "fair," rather than free, trade and to urge the party to support the creation of a nonpartisan tariff commission.[85]

Jouett Shouse supported his chief's economic platform loyally, in the process revealing his increasing identification with the northeastern conservative group. As the primary spokesman of the permanent organization, Shouse used his many speeches and press releases to urge that the chairman's suggestions be followed in 1932. He attacked the Smoot-Hawley Tariff as "the most reprehensible tariff bill in the history of the country" and lent his support to Raskob's tariff commission proposal.[86] The Democrats, he promised, had realized that "the vast majority of the people . . . have come to accept a protective tariff as an American institution."[87] Shouse also attacked Hoover for interfering with free enterprise. The president, he claimed, had "gone into business with both feet, and with the support of half a billion dollars of the taxpayers' money through the Federal Farm Bureau, thereby retarding recovery."[88] The Democratic party would not interfere with business in such an un-American way. When asked by the editors of the *Democratic Bulletin* in October 1931 to outline his suggestions for the Democratic platform for 1932, Shouse made plain his sympathy with Raskob's philosophy and platform by incorporating the chairman's views in toto into his article.[89]

The Raskob-Shouse economic platform struck many Democrats as too conservative for the times. Claude Bowers mocked the conservatives' "silly notion that the way to win is to make love to the enemy."[90] Roy Flannagan, for his part, was worried that the chairman's tariff policy was too close to that of the GOP to excite the electorate. Raskob's "fair trade" seemed a mere quibble over tariff rates compared to the traditional difference between the parties over protection. High-tariff Democrats, he told Harry Flood Byrd, were "betwixt and between people" who were "most embarrassing."[91] George Fort Milton found me-tooism equally frustrating. "There are real issues which the Democratic party must impress [*sic*] if . . . it is either to be successful or to have any real right to be continued in existence. It is bread, not booze, that the people need and want. Any party platform or commitment which declares an armistice in the battle against unemployment and seeks to direct our Democratic forces in a battle over a bottle, is in my view, a real betrayal of party duty and principle." It was far better, Milton thought, for the party to address squarely the protection issue, farm relief, Muscle Shoals, and the regulation of banking and credit rather than simply ape the GOP economic platform.[92]

Other progressives shared Milton's sentiments. Cordell Hull led the battle against the Smoot-Hawley Bill in the Senate and was dismayed at Raskob's ambivalent attitude toward it. "There must be more than mere hair-splitting differences between the two political parties on tariff and commercial policy," he declared in a public statement of opposition to Raskob's platform. "If the two old political parties are to be merged with respect to this, the major and most powerful special-privilege group, then they should be merged as to all the minor forces of special privilege." High tariffs meant "economic isolation," which to Hull was pure folly. Considerations such as these led him to give early support to FDR's presidential aspirations, seeing his nomination as the best hope of defeating "Raskobism."[93]

Thomas Walsh, Hull's Senate colleague from Montana, was equally damning of Raskob's platform. Walsh argued that the party should use its opportunity for victory in 1932 wisely, presenting a platform which promised a complete overhaul of the nation's banking, credit, and social welfare systems. Only then, he declared in 1931, could "a more equitable diffusion of the benefits of Democracy . . . be secured for the eighty percent of the people who have been reduced, under the Republican system of privilege, to the ownership of a trifling percentage of the wealth of the United States."[94] It seemed obvious to the chairman's critics that such goals were precisely those that Raskob hoped to forestall by me-tooism. They saw Raskob as obstructing Democracy's great chance to define a new ideological identity. Alfred E. Cohn of New York replied to the Raskob's questionnaire in terms that had become almost a chant among the party's progressives. "The world is bristling with interests and problems; and you offer for discussion only the 18th Amendment. To find no other issues . . . is to be politically bankrupt. If the Democratic Party is merely 'just as good' as the Republican Party, it has, I think, little further excuse for existence. It cannot be true that everything that is desirable in political life is comprised in the objects of the Republican party. Is it not time then that the Democratic Party rediscover its excuse of being and time also to galvanize into life the legitimate objects of liberal sentiment?" [95]

THE DEMOCRATIC "COOPERATION STATEMENT"

The complaints of Democrats such as Alfred Cohn were even louder in the aftermath of the "Cooperation Statement" of November 1930. The leaders of the conservative northeastern group—Cox, Davis, Smith, Raskob, and Shouse—joined with minority leaders Senator Joseph Robinson and Representative John Garner in a statement released soon after the 1930 elections. The seven Democratic leaders, however, seemed to apologize for their triumph. "To the extent of [the party's] ability, it will steer the legislation of the nation in a straight line towards the goal of prosperity, nor permit itself to be diverted either by political expediency, or a desire to show that it now dominates the enacting branch of the government. It has in mind no rash policies, but will seek as carefully as possible to remedy the evils that are afflicting the nation. . . . [The party] will not seek to embarrass the President of the United States, but will be glad to cooperate with him and with the members of the opposite party in House and Senate in every measure that conduces to the welfare of the country." [96]

The statement appears to have been the idea of Raskob and Shouse, who were concerned that business might be unsettled by the prospect of a Democratic House. [97] Joe Tumulty had suggested to Raskob in October that victory in the coming polls was certain and that "in the present critical business situation it would be a striking thing if in some dramatic way the leaders of the party in the campaign could quickly convey to the country a word of assurance." [98] Raskob was inclined to take this advice. He was anxious to calm business fears about Democratic "radicalism," and cooperation seemed to him to make good political sense. If, as he believed, economic recovery was imminent, the GOP would reap the benefits and would be in a strong position for 1932. In that case, the Democrats might be able to salvage something by pointing to the help that they had given. If, however, recovery did not come before November 1932, the Democrats were in an even stronger position, since they could say that the Republicans failed even with their help.[99]

Jouett Shouse defended the statement against its many Democratic critics. It was necessary, he wrote in 1931, because of the "wide speculation" that the Democratic victory would cause a new business slump. "It was a situation almost as serious as the crisis of war. It seemed an hour for necessary action."[100] He denied that the statement was an apology for the party's victory, insisting that it was a pledge to the American people that the party "would strive to make itself a constructive, not an obstructive or destructive force." Shouse and Raskob seem to have been unaware of the embarrassing implication behind their statement that the party was considered to be a "destructive force," nor did they consider the point that a more logical time to release such a statement would have been before the election. The people had decided, so why question that decision with an ex post facto qualification on the meaning of that victory? The idea of an angry electorate rebuffing an incumbent president's party halfway through his term was hardly a new one in American politics. Shouse failed, however, to see the point. "No suggestion here of abdication," he wrote, "only the assurance to the country that in a crisis of extreme moment it might depend upon the Democrats to chart and follow a constructive and a patriotic course."[101]

As its signatories had hoped, the Cooperation Statement was well received among business and conservative circles. The *New York Times* and the *Wall Street Journal* both lauded it, the former noting that it would do much to lay to rest the Democrats' image as irresponsible populists.[102] The latter described it as a patriotic effort. Its only fault, the *Journal* editorialized, was that it did not go far enough; the Democratic leaders should have abandoned partisanship altogether for the duration of the economic crisis.[103] The Illinois Manufacturers Association expressed its hearty approval and the wish that politics could be adjourned until recovery came.[104] Prominent businessmen rushed to congratulate the chairman and his friends; Bernard Baruch thought it was exactly the right remedy for the "highly excited condition" of the country, while Melvin

Traylor, a prominent Chicago banker who would later become a dark horse candidate for the 1932 nomination, hailed the statement as an example of "sound Americanism." [105]

Others were not impressed. Their criticisms tended to fall into two categories. The first concerned the right of the seven leaders, of whom only two held elected office, to commit the party's congressmen and senators to a policy of cooperation. This seemed to be a particularly galling example of the control which Raskob's conservatives considered that they exercised over the party. Carter Glass was especially annoyed; the signatories had no right to pledge him and the 263 other congressional Democrats to any course of action because they were "undelegated gentlemen." [106] Democratic senators and representatives had been given no opportunity to vote on the policy of cooperation. [107] Shouse replied that "in our form of government there is no leader of the minority," which begged the question as to why he and his colleagues felt justified in assuming such a role. [108]

The second main criticism of the statement concerned its me-too implications. "I voted the Democratic ticket because I was *opposed* to the Hoover administration," Professor Sumner Slichter of Harvard wrote Raskob. "Is it not a betrayal of public confidence for the men who were elected on a platform of opposition immediately to announce that they propose to cooperate with that administration?" [109] Josephus Daniels disliked the whole tone of the statement, which suggested that "it is more important to defend than change." [110] Bainbridge Colby thought that the statement's goal to "allay the justified apprehensions of the privileged and exploiting interests" was an affront to the party's reformist past, and he predicted that "the poultice will prove to be dry and worthless" once the Congress actually went into session. [111] McAdoo described the whole affair as an exercise in "pink-tea politics," and he told his new protégé John Nance Garner that "I don't believe the country wants the Democrats to cooperate with the Republicans in their economic measures because the country isn't satisfied with what the Republicans have thus far done." [112]

Garner seems not to have listened to his friend, for the new Speaker of the House proved to be an enthusiastic supporter of the document which he had signed. Democrats in the House, he told the press, would cooperate "so far as the prosperity and good faith of the country warranted." [113] When Secretary of the Treasury Mills conferred with him in

February 1932 about the $1.3 billion budget deficit, Garner formed a Democratic Economy Committee which recommended deep cuts in government spending. Prodded by the speaker's determination to cooperate, the Democratic House approved such administration measures as the Reconstruction Finance Corporation, the debt moratorium, and the Glass-Steagall Banking Act with minimal debate. "This isn't a session of Congress," Congressman Fiorello LaGuardia grumbled, "this is a kissing bee."[114] Progressive resentment finally triumphed over cooperation when a sales tax was proposed to balance the budget. This was proposed by Mills and the GOP, with the support of Raskob and Shouse.[115] With the help of conservative southern congressmen, who objected to further federal taxation, the Democratic insurgents defeated the proposal 223-153 in the House.[116]

Progressives outside Congress shared the frustration of their colleagues in Washington. Josephus Daniels was so concerned about the conservative drift of his party after the Cooperation Statement that he wrote to Garner in February 1932 saying that "unless our party does something more than give first aid and takes steps that will bring about plans for permanently better living conditions, how can we go before the country?" The congressional Democrats were being "generous" in helping the president, yet the danger was that "next Fall when we go out and criticize Mr. Hoover everybody is going to ask what did the Democratic Congress do to prevent a return of old conditions?"[117] Paul Anderson, writing in the *Nation*, was more direct. Citing the Democrats' lack of constructive action in the Congress, Anderson concluded that the two parties were "simply two wings of the same bird of prey." "As long as the elephant and jackass work in double harness it matters little to the rest of us who is in the driver's seat. We shall walk in either case."[118]

"You leaders of the Democratic party are up against a tremendous decision," Amos Pinchot wrote Raskob at the end of 1931. "You must decide whether you are going to run it as a party representing wealth, privilege, and industro-financial cream-skimming, or on the other hand, as a party honestly standing for the interests of the people and the Jeffersonian philosophy. . . . Query: Is there room in this country for a Democratic party which will virtually amount to a wet Republican party? In the long run, the Democratic party—being a minority party—can only hold its own against the Republican party by standing on definite and popular issues."[119]

Raskob and his allies had clearly made their decision; they would try to run the 1932 campaign on a platform that stressed "booze before bread" and which differed from that of the GOP only in its attitude toward the Eighteenth Amendment. The party's progressives and dries, in contrast, were equally determined to steer the party toward a "bread before booze" platform which provided more activist and far-reaching solutions to and relief from the economic distress that promised to sweep the party into power. This much had been made clear by the debate engendered by Raskob's activities as chairman. Yet these were policy matters, and policies amounted to little without effective leadership. From the liberal Democrats' perspective, William McAdoo had performed this function throughout the 1920s, but his day had passed. A new leader for the fight against Raskob and the conservatives had to be found.

10

IN McADOO'S STEPS

FRANKLIN D. ROOSEVELT, 1928–1932

In November 1928 Jesse Grantham, an attorney in Fort Lauderdale, Florida, saw only one hope for his divided and defeated party. The Democrats had just suffered their third landslide defeat in as many elections, and even the South had shown that its loyalty to the party was not unshakable. Only by achieving unity could the party hope to win public confidence. "You are a real, civilized man, forceful, intelligent, liberal, diplomatic, serene and calm," Grantham wrote Franklin Roosevelt; "of all the outstanding men of the party, you are the one man who possesses the necessary qualities to restore harmony in our ranks."[1]

Grantham's opinion has since become historical orthodoxy. Historians of the party and biographers of FDR have all portrayed him as the great unifier of the party. Around Roosevelt wets and dries, westerners and southerners, Wilsonians and Bryanites, workers and farmers could join together and create a new coalition that would ensure Democratic dominance in national politics for a generation.[2] Roosevelt succeeded where McAdoo had failed; he united the South and West upon a progressive platform to defeat the conservative northeastern wing of the party. In so doing, he not only inherited the secretary's constituencies but also followed his strategy; Roosevelt, too, decided that the best way to develop his power was to act as a champion for those Democrats who felt threatened and pushed aside by the conservative group.

FDR's credentials, however, as the savior of the western, southern, and progressive Democrats were at best dubious by 1928. Although he had served with vigor in the Wilson administration, his activities during the 1920s were disquieting to the opponents of the conservative coalition. He had run with Cox in the ill-fated campaign of 1920; he had been one of Smith's convention managers in the bitter fight with McAdoo at the 1924 convention, and he had placed the Happy Warrior's name before the convention in 1924 and again in 1928. He seemed to many progressives to be at one with the conservative northeasterners who had taken the party over; he was a New Yorker, a Manhattan lawyer, and to all appearances a close ally of Al Smith.

Following his election to the Governorship of New York in 1928, Roosevelt performed a delicate and skillful political feat: he established himself as the leading opponent of the northeastern strategy and its economic philosophy at the same time as occupying New York's highest office. He was not completely successful. He alienated the very conservatives who had persuaded him to run for the governorship in the first place, and even his famous charm could not woo the jealous McAdoo until the last minute. By the Chicago convention of 1932, however, FDR had succeeded in being governor of New York and also the candidate of the southern, western, and progressive wings of the national party. Al Smith had once argued that FDR's paralysis did not disqualify him from being governor of New York because the people wanted a governor, not an acrobat. Roosevelt, however, had shown that he could perform some delicate balancing acts of his own.

ROOSEVELT AS NEW YORK GOVERNOR

As governor of New York, FDR played to a national as well as a state audience; his actions became inextricably linked with the broader battle for the 1932 presidential nomination. In his first term he aimed to cement his power base within the state so as to ensure reelection, and his second revolved around the need to establish his credentials as a leader of the anti-Raskob groups in the national party.

The new governor's first task was to build upon Smith's achievements while simultaneously placing his own stamp upon the office. He had won office largely on the basis of promises to continue and extend his predecessor's policies, yet he had no wish to be seen as a Smith clone. His first step was to assemble his own staff of advisers. Smith had gathered together an intensely loyal coterie which was led by Robert Moses, the recently appointed secretary of state, and Belle Moskowitz. The latter was eased out of the new administration altogether and became a publicity consultant in New York City. Roosevelt had strong personal reasons for disliking Moses and refused to reappoint him secretary of state. Moses remained, however, as parks commissioner because his term was fixed by statute.[3] Although FDR kept sixteen of Smith's eighteen department heads, the departure of Moskowitz and the demotion of Moses made it plain that he would seek advice from sources different from those of his predecessor.

The second major area in which FDR eased away from Smith's shadow was in the policy priorities of his administration. Smith had been a frankly urban governor; the focus of his park, labor, and social policies had always been directed toward metropolitan constituencies, with a resulting neglect of the more rural upstate concerns.[4] These regions, which had long been Republican, reacted with electoral hostility. Even at the height of his popularity Smith had never carried upstate areas, and he owed his victories to his ability to win New York City with a majority sufficient to outweigh his losses north of the Bronx.

Roosevelt, in contrast, took great pains to woo hinterland voters away from their strong Republican allegiance. Many of the new governor's policies were aimed squarely at upstate issues. The most important concerned agriculture, a largely forgotten industry during the Smith years. Roosevelt established the Agricultural Advisory Committee under his friend Henry Morgenthau. The committee's investigations pointed to the heavy burden of taxation as an impediment to rural communities' attempts to weather the nationwide farm crisis of the 1920s. Relief was soon forthcoming; a new system of road funding was established which rested upon a gasoline tax and state appropriations. The land tax, long a bone of contention among asset-rich but cash-poor farmers, was abolished.[5] Roosevelt even sponsored a rudimentary acreage-reduction scheme, in the form of a Reforestation Amendment to the Constitution, adopted in 1931. The state was empowered under this amendment to reforest marginal farming land in the hope of raising farm prices and increasing New York's lumber resources.[6]

On the issue of water power Roosevelt at first seemed content to continue Smith's policy that the state should retain ownership of water-power sites while leaving the distribution of hydroelectric current to private utilities. In 1929, however, the new governor unveiled an extension of Smith's policy designed not only to appeal to rural and metropolitan voters but also to impress progressives outside New York. He was well aware that cheap electrical power was a vote winner among all New Yorkers. In March 1929, he asked the state legislature for a bill empowering the state to *distribute* electric power, should private utilities be found to have artificially inflated their prices. He suggested that a return of 8 percent on invested capital would be the measure of fairness.[7] Although little came of this suggestion, Roosevelt had discovered a potent weapon for his 1930 reelection campaign. He had also established his credentials with western progressive Democrats and Republicans, to whom water power and public transmission had long been vital issues.

Roosevelt's farm and water-power policies did much to improve Democracy's standing in rural New York. The coming of the depression allowed him to complement these gains with a social welfare program addressed to the plight of the urban worker. He secured a forty-eight hour working week for women and an end to the granting of temporary injunctions without a hearing in labor disputes. He publicly endorsed proposals for old-age pensions and unemployment insurance, much to the delight of progressives.[8] These issues, however, faded in importance as unemployment worsened after 1929. Roosevelt moved cautiously at first; he waited until 1931 before calling a special session of the legislature to create the Temporary Employment Relief Agency (TERA) to provide relief for the army of New York's jobless. TERA was the first of its kind in the industrial states, and FDR justified it in sweeping terms that clearly distinguished him from his conservative opponents. "In broad terms," he declared, "I assert that modern society, through its government, owes the definite obligation to prevent the starvation or dire want of any of its fellow men and women who try to maintain themselves but cannot."[9]

The third way in which FDR attempted to adjust his message to suit both his local and national audience was in his attitude toward Tammany Hall. In this he was less successful. Roosevelt found himself in a political dilemma almost impossible to resolve. He needed at least the acquiescence of the Hall to ensure that he could win New York City, and yet upstaters, westerners, southerners, and progressives insisted that he make good his claim to be independent of Tammany's corruption and vice. The issue was brought to a head by new allegations of corruption on the part of Tammany Hall and New York City mayor James Walker in 1930 and 1931.[10]

Roosevelt's troubles with Tammany began in earnest in the summer of 1930, when allegations of malfeasance and bribery in New York's magistrates courts were made public. Moving quickly to forestall an upstate backlash against his reelection campaign, Roosevelt appointed Samuel Seabury, a prominent Democratic foe of the Hall, as the head of an investigative commission.[11] There the matter rested until after FDR's victory in 1930, but the following year Seabury's investigations revealed a web of corruption within New York City's judicial system. As Seabury's investigations widened, he uncovered evidence that Mayor Walker himself was involved in the graft and bribery, including the receipt of a huge payment for giving a bus transportation franchise to a firm that possessed no buses.[12]

Fearful of losing any hope he might have for Tammany's support at the 1932 national convention, Roosevelt sat on his hands. "For every Tammany vote [Walker's] acquittal brings you," he was warned, "you will lose a dozen in the West."[13] FDR therefore used a variety of legal ploys to postpone Walker's day of reckoning.[14] Seabury persisted, however, and in May 1932 he presented a report which outlined numerous charges against Walker, detailed the evidence supporting those charges, and concluded that the governor should remove him forthwith. Roosevelt, with the convention less than two months away, played for time. He forwarded the report to his legal counsel, where it stayed until the end of June. He then sent it to Walker, who announced that he would respond to its charges *after* the convention. Roosevelt had thus achieved his goal of avoiding a hostile act against Tammany such as removing its mayor until after the votes had been cast at Chicago.

The whole episode had revealed FDR at his worst. His willful vacillation had cost him much of the respect he had won from reformers and progressives across the nation and fueled earlier doubts as to the genuineness of his separation from the Hall and its wrongdoings. Furthermore, Tammany Hall, which was enraged at the appointment of Seabury in the first place, remained implacably opposed to his nomination. Roosevelt had impaled himself on both horns of his Tammany dilemma.[15]

FDR'S RISING POLITICAL FORTUNES

Against this backdrop Roosevelt began his campaign for the 1932 nomination. To westerners, southerners, and progressives, he could point to his achievements in agricultural policy, water power, and unemployment relief. He could also point to hard statistics; he had won reelection in 1930 by a plurality of 725,001 votes, more than twice Al Smith's largest margin of victory. For the first time in the century, the Democratic gubernatorial ticket had won a plurality in upstate districts, and even his New York City plurality exceeded Smith's in 1926.[16]

Roosevelt's strong performance in the 1930 campaign made him the clear front-runner for the 1932 nomination. A poll of delegates to the 1928 convention taken by Jesse Strauss in March 1931 showed FDR to be the first preference of well over half of those who replied.[17] After three losing candidates, the party was eager for a proven winner. This was especially true in the West and South, regions in which Democrats had suffered under the candidacies of Cox, Davis, and Smith. It was here that Roosevelt concentrated his preconvention campaign in the hope of inheriting McAdoo's constituency.[18]

As McAdoo had done, Roosevelt put forward a philosophy of an active state to provide an ideological rallying point against Smith, Raskob, and the other conservatives. Even in 1928, FDR had quietly disagreed with Smith's reiteration of Jefferson's dictum that the best government was the least government. This was a "sound phrase," Roosevelt wrote, "but it applies only to the simplification of governmental machinery and to the prevention of improper interference with the legitimate activities of the citizens. But the nation or state which is unwilling by governmental action to tackle new problems caused by immense increase of population and the astounding strides of modern science is headed for a decline and ultimate death from inaction."[19]

Roosevelt's best-known preconvention speeches served to sharpen the ideological differences between himself and the conservatives, as well as to strengthen his claim to McAdoo's mantle. The "forgotten man" speech of April 1932 and that at Oglethorpe University in the following month outlined a challenge to the economic message presented by Smith, Raskob, and Shouse. At Oglethorpe, Roosevelt questioned the conservative view of economic downturns as natural and unavoidable. This attitude represented, he told his audience, a "greater faith in immutable economic law and less faith in the ability of man to control what he has created than I, for one, have." In the face of the "awful paradox" of a nation blessed with a superabundance of natural resources yet with its people hungry and unemployed, FDR declared himself unwilling to accept the conservatives' "invitation to sit back and do nothing."[20]

Instead, Roosevelt argued the advanced progressive line that the federal government owed a duty to its citizens to step in to solve this "paradox." What was required was "a more equitable distribution of income" and "a larger measure of social planning." How this was to be achieved the governor did not say, other than to advocate "bold, persistent experimentation." A critical *New York Times*, attacking the speech as "indefinite, abstract and irresolute," noted that FDR had "decided to cast his lot with the West and the South," for his speech only inflamed eastern conservatives' distrust of him.[21]

Roosevelt combined this economic philosophy with his policy record as governor to portray himself to the South and West as a candidate in complete sympathy with the concerns of progressive Democrats. His water power policy was especially effective, for this was of great moment to westerners long concerned with water rights and to southerners eager to see the development of the Muscle Shoals project.[22] For his part, FDR refused to accede to requests by more conservative Democrats that he modify his position to avoid the impression that he was conducting an antiutilities campaign.[23] He saw the political dividends of his pronouncements when James Farley reported to him after his tour of the West in the summer of 1931.[24] Farley returned in a buoyant mood; the whole West was enthusiastic for Roosevelt, with the exception of the "Power crowd."[25]

Many Democrats who considered themselves to be opponents of the Raskob-Smith faction of the party were fully satisfied that FDR had succeeded in his attempts to prove to the party as a whole that he was not part of the conservative northeastern group. In Connecticut, Homer Cummings, a former McAdoo supporter, wrote a correspondent in 1932 that he was "beginning to feel again the stirring of Democratic hope." If Roosevelt was nominated, he felt, the party could go forward and win in November. This prospect dispelled the apathy and gloom which Cummings had felt since 1922 about his party's drift into me-tooism.[26] Roosevelt, Cummings wrote to George Fort Milton in an attempt to win this key McAdoo supporter to FDR's standard, was the best hope for progressive democracy. Of all the possible candidates for the nomination, only FDR would insist that the 1932 campaign be based on economic issues rather than on prohibition.[27]

Democrats in other areas of the nation were coming to similar conclusions. In Nevada, Senator Key Pittman threw in his lot with FDR. To him, the issue was simple. "I want to win," he declared; "I am tired of being in the minority."[28] From North Carolina, Josephus Daniels wrote his former subordinate to congratulate him on his "forgotten man" speech. Roosevelt had clearly distinguished himself ideologically from Raskob, Daniels thought, and he had brought home to Democrats the point that "we cannot win by letting the folks think that the Republican party is 51% bad and we are only 49% bad."[29] Daniel Roper, who like Cummings and Daniels had supported McAdoo strongly during the 1920s, also found himself converted to FDR's cause. Roosevelt had convinced him that he was different from the "New York group" against whom he had fought for twelve years. "There are two major political groups in the Democratic Party," Roper wrote his cousin in March 1932. "One is headed by former Governor Smith, the other by the present Governor of New York. You and I cannot work with the Smith contingent. We can work with the Roosevelt contingent because my close association with the Governor in the past convinces me that he stands for the things we stand for. He is a Woodrow Wilson progressive in National affairs and is a National character rather than a provincial character as Governor Smith proved to be. Furthermore, Roosevelt will never be dominated by or controlled by improper Tammany influences."[30]

Southerners were particularly interested in the relationship between FDR and Al Smith. As rumors that the two men were at odds became increasingly common after 1931, Roosevelt's stocks rose in Dixie. George Fort Milton wrote to Harry Byrd during March 1931 with the news that "the intimation has come to me again and again that there is a real schism between the Roosevelt people and the Smith people, and that the Tammany political hierarchy does not intend to give Roosevelt a chance."[31]

Other southerners, however, were not convinced. Roosevelt's delicate balancing act over Tammany had left many confused as to where his real loyalties lay. Tyre Taylor, secretary to North Carolina governor O. Max Gardner, wrote to Byrd in March 1931 to express his suspicions about FDR. "If the split between Roosevelt and Raskob and Smith is genuine," Taylor wrote, "this is going to make the former a formidable candidate indeed in North Carolina. I have thought, however, that this breach might be more apparent than real and designed for the very purpose of delivering the South to Governor Roosevelt."[32] There was a widespread feeling even after Smith's entry into the race for the nomination that the two men were working in tandem. Smith, it was thought, would capture northeastern delegations and deliver them to FDR during the convention. This misconception arose from the long collaboration between the two men during the 1920s.[33]

If many of McAdoo's followers were confused as to the precise relationship between FDR and Smith during 1930 and 1931, they were also profoundly disappointed by Roosevelt's position on prohibition and the League of Nations. Although he had long avoided committing himself on prohibition for fear of alienating McAdoo's dry supporters, Roosevelt's position as governor of a wet state forced his hand.[34] In September 1930 he came out in favor of repeal of the Eighteenth Amendment and ran for reelection on this platform in 1930. Dries were horrified; Max Gardner wrote Byrd that the immediate reaction to FDR's statement was that he had eliminated himself as a candidate for 1932 "as far as the South is concerned." If Roosevelt was wet and was seen by southern voters as somehow connected with Tammany, Gardner was worried that he had accumulated all of Smith's liabilities except Catholicism.[35] William T. Reed, one of Byrd's most loyal supporters in Virginia, shared Gardner's reaction and thought that Roosevelt's support in the South would evaporate as soon as Smith took himself out of the nomination contest.[36]

Just as dries were dismayed at Roosevelt's concession to local New York sentiment on prohibition, internationalists were disgusted at his change of heart on the League of Nations. Roosevelt had campaigned hard for the League in 1920, and he had given Democrats no reason to believe that he had changed his mind during the 1920s. In 1928 he advocated not only that America cooperate with the league but also that the United States take an "official part" in its proceedings.[37] On February 2, 1932, however, he declared that the league was no longer the body that Woodrow Wilson had created. It was now a "mere meeting place for the political discussion of strictly European political national difficulties," in which America had no interest. "Because of these facts," FDR concluded, "I do not favor American participation."[38] This about-face was designed to win the support of William Randolph Hearst, who was now in alliance with McAdoo in boosting John Nance Garner for the nomination. It was not successful. Internationalists were angered by this opportunism, and Roosevelt's reputation for political expediency and dissimulation was strengthened. His new position on the league seemed as self-serving and cynical as his legal justifications for avoiding a showdown with Tammany Hall and Mayor Walker. On both issues Roosevelt's balancing act failed.

Sensing that his nomination prospects were at stake, Roosevelt set about a less subtle policy of distancing himself from Raskobism and the northeastern wing. He made a point of directly attacking the chairman from the end of 1928 until the Chicago convention in 1932. By that time he could point to two distinct victories, first over Raskob and then over Shouse. In so doing, he sharpened the differences separating him and the conservatives in charge of the national organization. Progressives, southerners, and westerners could not fail to be impressed with the enemies that he had made.

FDR'S MOVES AGAINST RASKOB

Almost immediately after his victory in 1928, FDR sent another circular letter to Democratic leaders around the nation. These letters were drafted by Louis Howe and were ostensibly designed to gauge reaction to the idea of creating a full-time national publicity organization in Washington. Howe's draft contained a sentence aimed directly at Ras-

He Sails Through the Air With the Greatest of Ease,
Does This Daring Young Man on the Flying Trapeze.

William Gibbs McAdoo: the world's greatest son-in-law.

The cartoon, by McCutcheon, is entitled "The Chauffeur Gives a Demonstration."

The cartoon, entitled "Both Eating Out of His Hands," is an illustration of me-tooism, 1924 style.
New York American, July 10, 1924 (courtesy of the Herbert Hoover Presidential Library)

The cartoon, entitled "Different Times, Different Manners," is an illustration of me-tooism, 1928 style.
New York American, October 15, 1928 (courtesy of the Herbert Hoover Presidential Library)

The cartoon, by James North, is entitled "'Tis a Wise Father Who Knows His Own Son."

Raskob, Shouse (and Michelson) at work, 1931.

The cartoon, by Ireland, is entitled "The Innocent Bystander" and illustrates the Democratic convention of 1932.

The cartoon, by Sykes, is entitled "A Tardy Response."

From the *New York Evening Post*, October 26, 1932, reprinted with permission

The cartoon, by Berryman, is entitled "The Break-up of the Old Gang!"
Baltimore *Evening Sun*, October 15, 1935 (courtesy of the Herbert Hoover Presidential Library)

kobism and the chairman's investment theory of political parties. "The amount of money needed [for the] national organization," Howe wrote, "is surprisingly small. It should be obtained in small sums from a great number of people." Although FDR cut this sentence from the final versions of the letter, the circular letters did become an informal poll on Raskob's popularity.[39]

The results of this poll were extremely significant for FDR's strategy against Raskob over the next four years. Of the 1,029 replies that Roosevelt preserved, practically all were in favor of the creation of a permanent national organization. Yet this agreement did not extend to the person in charge of it, as 116 respondents, or 11 percent, took the trouble to write in an objection to John Raskob. Only 38, or 3.7 percent, gave the chairman an endorsement.[40] These were by definition write-in votes, since FDR's letter did not ask for an opinion on the chairman. Of the preserved replies, 457, or 44 percent, expressed a preference for Roosevelt as the 1932 nominee. This was again a write in vote, which must have been encouraging for the new governor. Of these votes, 164, or 36 percent, came from the states of the old Confederacy and Kentucky, while 116, or 25 percent, came from states west of the Mississippi. Neither FDR nor Howe could have missed the clear correlation between the geographic distribution of pro-FDR and anti-Raskob sentiment; nearly 60 percent of those expressing a negative opinion of the chairman wrote from southern addresses, while 25 percent came from the West. These two sections therefore accounted for approximately 60 percent of FDR's support and 85 percent of Raskob's opposition. Anti-Raskobism, therefore, was clearly a potent issue in the areas in which FDR was targeting his appeal.[41]

The early skirmishes of FDR's battle against Raskob consisted of quiet objections to the chairman's policy agenda for the party after 1928. Roosevelt used his correspondence with Democrats in the South and West to reiterate his opposition to the adoption of prohibition reform as a Democratic party platform. "I have always insisted," he wrote a Mississippi correspondent, "that prohibition was not a party issue in the right sense of the word, in either party. It seems to me that we should not label anything a party principle unless it is a principle of the great majority of our party."[42] He also lent support to those Democrats who objected to Raskob's high-tariff ideas and wished to see the Houston tariff plank reversed in 1932.[43] When Raskob, Shouse, and the other leaders released their Cooperation

Statement in November 1930, FDR was not forthcoming with praise. He
maintained instead a "discreet silence," he told Charles McCarthy, because
"the great majority of Democrats were displeased at the method and text
of that joint statement."[44]

Roosevelt's gloves came off, however, when Raskob announced the
March 5, 1931, meeting of the DNC to discuss and recommend his home
rule plan for prohibition. The chairman had presented FDR with a golden
opportunity to act as the unifier of the South and West against Raskob's
proposal.[45] He became a champion of Raskob's opponents by leading the
argument that the DNC had no power to set party policy.[46] Pressing political concerns lay behind this technical argument. Although Roosevelt had
publicly advocated the repeal of national prohibition six months previous
to the DNC meeting and had run for reelection on a similar platform,
Raskob's proposal presented him with a politically dangerous dilemma.
To support the proposal would not only contribute to a victory for the
chairman but would also alienate much of the support he had cultivated
in the West and South, where sentiment for prohibition remained powerful. By opposing Raskob's scheme, however, he would have repudiated his
own state platform. By using the legal argument that the DNC was not
empowered to decide the issue, however, he avoided this trap by opposing
Raskob on technical grounds rather than on the merits of the proposal
itself. Accordingly, FDR had his New York State Democratic Committee pass a resolution on March 2 denying the DNC's right to pronounce
judgment on the home rule plan.

As FDR had hoped, his actions reinforced his western and southern
support and established him as the most prominent of Raskob's opponents. The chairman had been beaten at the March 5 meeting, and he
held Roosevelt to be primarily responsible. He wrote a hurt letter to the
governor, criticizing him for opposing the proposal and thus giving the
GOP much-needed ammunition. He also referred to the fact that FDR
had not given him a copy of the New York State committee resolution,
even though it had been distributed to all other members of the DNC.[47]
Harry Flood Byrd met Raskob soon after the meeting and reported to
Tyre Taylor that the chairman was "very indignant" over FDR's use of the
New York State committee to embarrass him.[48]

Roosevelt made little attempt to improve his relations with the chairman. Instead, he sought to consolidate the political gains he had made

among southerners and westerners. The prohibition fight won, he widened the scope of his criticisms against the chairman to include Raskob's economic and me-too policies as well.[49] A sharper note crept into Roosevelt's correspondence about the chairman. To one supporter in Montana, for example, FDR not only took primary responsibility and credit for the outcome of the DNC meeting but also implicitly questioned Raskob's commitment to party success in 1932. "If you have followed closely the recent meeting . . . I think you will feel that the Democratic Party is still the party of progress and that there is no danger of it being made over into a poor imitation of the conservative Republican group which has only the interests of big industry at heart. I hope you also noticed that the State of New York . . . took a firm stand against permitting the National Committee to attempt to bind the party to any conservative or backward-looking doctrines."[50]

The final skirmish between FDR and the Raskob group involved Jouett Shouse. During a meeting of the DNC Committee on Arrangements for the convention held in Chicago on April 4, 1932, the question of the temporary chairmanship came up. This was a largely ceremonial position, involving a keynote speech and conduct of the convention until the permanent chairman was elected. Shouse considered that this honor should be his in recognition of services to the party since 1929, a view that was heartily endorsed by Chairman Raskob. FDR's supporters on the Committee on Arrangements demurred; Shouse had been so much in the public eye that a fresher face would be more desirable to open the convention.[51] To Josephus Daniels, Roosevelt was more frank, writing, "I am doing everything possible to prevent Jouett Shouse from being made Temporary Chairman of the Convention." Although Shouse had done good publicity work, "he is generally regarded as an ultra-conservative" and as a "mere attacker on the Hoover administration."[52] A compromise eventually emerged, by which Senator Alben Barkley of Kentucky would be temporary chairman, and Shouse would be "commended" to the delegates for consideration as permanent chairman, a more powerful and long-lived office.[53]

Roosevelt and his allies, however, began to edge away from this agreement almost as soon as it was made. Key senatorial supporters—notably Cordell Hull of Tennessee, Clarence Dill of Washington, and Burton Wheeler of Montana—were well aware of the significance of the permanent chairmanship, especially in a closely contested convention. A ruling by the chairman against the interests of one of the contestants for the nomination could be overturned only by a two-thirds vote, and FDR did not possess such a margin of delegate support.[54] "I gather . . . that nothing occurred in Chicago which commits us to support Mr. Shouse," Homer Cummings wrote Hull a week after the meeting. "If this is your view of it, I shall feel very much relieved."[55] Hull replied in the affirmative and then began to pressure FDR to disown the agreement.

On June 6, less than three weeks before the convention opened, the Roosevelt group announced that it did not favor Shouse's appointment as permanent chairman and that it would support Thomas Walsh instead.[56] A furor of criticism erupted from Shouse and his supporters, who claimed with some justification that good faith had been broken. Newton Baker wrote to Shouse that Roosevelt's betrayal was "a portent of what we may have to face for four years."[57] Given FDR's own sentiments before the April 4 meeting and the care with which the word "commend" rather than the stronger "recommend" was used, it appears that the compromise was designed to avoid a fight within the Committee on Arrangements— on which Shouse had majority support—rather than to create a genuine agreement.

The argument against Shouse was put in increasingly ideological terms as the convention neared. Josephus Daniels thought that Shouse's election to the either the temporary or the permanent chairmanship would be "almost as fatal an error as to have made [Alton B.] Parker Chairman of the Convention in 1912, starting us off with a man who wanted to have the party . . . committed to high tariff, pro-trust and paramounting of the liquor question."[58] George Fort Milton believed that what lay behind the Shouse-Walsh contest was no less than an ideological battle for control of the party. "The contest which is looming between Senator Walsh and Jouett Shouse . . . seems to me not an unhealthy one. Walsh is such a splendid Democrat, and Shouse's alignments with the Raskob element have been so intimate, that it seems to me that all delegations with a progressive purpose and candidate might very properly join with the Roosevelt delegates in the election of Senator Walsh. . . . [T]he election of Senator Walsh will be a real challenge to the big business–Tammany control of the party."[59]

McADOO'S PRESIDENTIAL ASPIRATIONS

The fight over both the home rule plan and Shouse's chair-manship revealed Roosevelt's increasing determination to challenge the Raskob group and its agenda for the national party. The South and West had responded; although confused by FDR's machinations within New York, they could not mistake the growing separation between Roosevelt and the Raskob group once their struggles took place in the national party's organization. By 1932 FDR had taken McAdoo's earlier role as the most visible critic of the northeastern conservatives' group.

But what of McAdoo? He and Roosevelt had never been intimate friends, although they had collaborated after 1913 to attempt to establish a progressive Democratic organization in New York State.[60] After 1920, however, their paths diverged. FDR became closer to Tammany through his association with Smith; McAdoo remained adamantly opposed to the Hall and left for California. When they met again in the national arena, they did so as opponents during the 1924 convention.

For his part, Roosevelt attempted to improve his relations with the secretary after 1924. After the campaign of 1928 he wrote to McAdoo to apologize for the failure of the Smith's inner circle to extend the olive branch. McAdoo was not included in the campaign, FDR wrote, because of a "stupid piece of bungling" on the part of John Raskob and his friends. Combining criticism with flattery, he explained that Raskob did not have the political acumen to recognize McAdoo's influence in national affairs.[61] Mutual friends also attempted to bring the two men together. FDR was very angry at the way McAdoo was treated during the campaign, Byron Newton explained, and he was "very desirous of holding or regaining your friendly attitude to him personally. I am firmly . . . of the belief," he concluded, "that Franklin is planning to draw away from those factors and personalities which were shown to be so obnoxious to the people of the country, by what happened on election day."[62] McAdoo, however, was slow to forget a grudge and replied in a noncommittal way.[63] He did, however, pass on some not-so-oblique warnings to Roosevelt. The party, he declared, would "never dare again to nominate a Governor of New York who, like Smith, maintains the non-enforcement policy of that state with respect to federal prohibition."[64]

FDR's second circular letter did little to change the secretary's attitude. "I don't think anybody much takes seriously the leadership of Franklin D. Roosevelt," he wrote the editor of the *Augusta* (Georgia) *Chronicle*. FDR was so "thoroughly identified" and "intimately connected" with Tammany that the rest of the party would not tolerate it.[65] Roosevelt was simply Smith with a more acceptable demeanor, he wrote George Fort Milton in 1930. "He is just as much Tammany as Smith and just as wet too."[66]

McAdoo maintained his position until the Chicago convention of 1932. Although he continued to object strongly to Raskob's emphasis on prohibition reform over economic issues, he refused to lend support to FDR's battles with the chairman in 1931 and 1932.[67] This was despite the large areas of agreement between their economic policies and on Democracy's need to distinguish itself from the GOP on issues other than the Eighteenth Amendment. The secretary shared FDR's belief that the DNC had no business in making even a recommendation for the 1932 platform on either prohibition or economic matters.[68] Yet McAdoo by no means considered himself an ally of FDR on this issue, arguing instead that Roosevelt was simply using the DNC fights to rally support to his own candidacy. McAdoo had no illusions that Roosevelt was a genuine supporter of prohibition; the governor's 1930 platform had made that clear.[69] Despite the importunings of some of his friends, the secretary refused to endorse Roosevelt during the rest of 1931.[70]

Events in 1932 did little to improve the situation. FDR's entry into the California primary in May further alienated McAdoo. The Roosevelt forces joined the northern California Democrats under Isidore Dockweiler, from whom McAdoo and his allies in Los Angeles had split with great bitterness in 1926.[71] McAdoo threw his support behind John Nance Garner, and Roosevelt was decisively beaten. The secretary, it seemed, had joined the "block Roosevelt" movement.[72]

Ideological considerations can be largely discounted as explanations for McAdoo's course, for there was little difference between the two men's views on the burning issues within the party. They agreed that Raskob's me-tooism represented a travesty of the party's recent Wilsonian past and that it should be fought at every turn. They agreed that prohibition should not be a partisan issue, and they were both advocates of a "bread before booze" strategy for 1932. Although McAdoo did not have Roosevelt's public standing between 1930 and 1932, he used his voluminous correspondence to urge upon the party an assertive and innovative economic policy which seemed similar to FDR's "forgotten man" and Oglethorpe addresses. To Senator Kenneth McKellar of Tennessee, he wrote in January 1931 that "the Democratic Party is supposed to be the party of humanity, at least we have always claimed that. The Republican Party, on the other hand, is supposed to be the party of property, and I think everybody concedes that. The Democratic Party is not opposed to property but it certainly puts humanity, or at least it is supposed to put humanity above merely material considerations. . . . I am in favor of doing everything that may reasonably be done to enlarge the opportunity for employment, but nothing in that direction can be done quickly enough to relieve destitution and starvation actually existing. . . . The Democrats have a great opportunity to serve the suffering people. Will they prove equal to it?"[73]

In the absence of any real ideological conflict between the two men, it is likely that personal and political factors entered into McAdoo's calculations. His primary motivation seems to have been his long-frustrated ambition to be president. That McAdoo entertained hopes that the lightning might finally strike him in 1932 was an open secret within the party. The secretary himself kept his options open, repeating a line of argument that had become all too familiar to Democrats since 1920. To the Washington publisher W. M. Kiplinger he wrote in June 1930, "It is barely possible that something may happen to force me to say that I would permit my name to be considered . . . although I don't want you to derive, from what I have said, any implication that I am either thinking about returning to politics in 1932, or that I would, for one moment, seek the nomination. Of course, to be perfectly frank, conditions might develop where I might change my mind."[74]

During 1931 McAdoo continued to test the waters regarding his candidacy, asking his correspondents about the strength of his support in their states, inquiring about the attitude of organized labor groups, and declaring to all who inquired that, although he did not want to run again, conditions might force him to do just that.[75] Although he did not specify what those conditions might be, it seems clear that he counted the increasing likelihood of Roosevelt's nomination as one of them. Writing to a North Carolina relative in June 1931, McAdoo was uncharacteristically frank. "What is the sentiment in your part of the country? Do you think there is any real demand for me? There seems to be a good deal of talk about Roosevelt, based, I imagine, on the old and thoroughly discredited theory that a man who carries New York for Governor might carry the state for President. This has been demonstrated to be a mistake so many times that I wonder people don't recognize it." [76]

McAdoo's continued opposition to FDR was part of his strategy for 1932. He hoped to keep his nucleus of supporters from endorsing Roosevelt so as to have them at his call should the political climate appear promising as the convention neared. His public endorsement of Garner may well have been designed to create such conditions by heightening speculation that Roosevelt could not be nominated and that a deadlocked convention would result at Chicago. This suspicion was strengthened by the secretary's surprise announcement on the eve of the convention that, in order to remove prohibition as an issue in the coming campaign, he now favored a referendum on the future of the Eighteenth Amendment. This was a considerable change from his heretofore "bone dry" attitude and was clearly designed to increase his acceptability as a compromise choice in the event of Roosevelt's defeat.[77]

The Roosevelt camp was in little doubt that such was the case. Isidore Dockweiler wrote to Homer Cummings in March 1932 that McAdoo was well aware that "Garner cannot be nominated; but McAdoo still cherishes the delusion that he is . . . presidential material." The secretary hoped that the delegates in Chicago would be so swept off their feet by the mention of his name that he would be "elevated to the presidential nomination à la Bryan in 1896."[78] Roosevelt maintained a tactful silence about McAdoo's grandiose hopes. Privately, however, he could not resist passing on via Cummings a subtle message to the secretary that the torch, whether McAdoo liked it or not, had passed. "In regard to our friend McAdoo, I hope much that Roper and House and you can pour oil on the somewhat troubled waters of his mind. Mac is a fine fellow, but I don't think that he has any perspective about the present situation and that it is only his real friends who can persuade him that a last minute insurgency will get him nowhere and will do harm to the progressive ideals with which all of us were associated in the old days."[79]

UNCERTAINTY AT THE CONVENTION

Despite McAdoo's petulance, it appeared that FDR had succeeded in inheriting the secretary's constituencies. It was now Roosevelt,
and not McAdoo, who carried the liberals' hopes for an assertive and interventionist economic policy substantially different from that of the GOP.
Roosevelt had, in sum, convinced the West and South that although he
was a New Yorker, he was sensitive to the concerns of the nonmetropolitan
areas of the United States.

Delegates arriving in Chicago for the convention were presented with
graphic evidence of this in the form of a large map of the United States
prominently displayed at FDR's headquarters. States that had instructed
their delegations for Roosevelt were shaded in red, while those which were
not were hatched in different colors. The delegates could not fail to be
impressed by three salient features of this presentation. The first was that
FDR's own state of New York was listed as "uninstructed," although most
knew that the strong Tammany delegation from the Empire State was
determined to prevent their own governor from succeeding. The second
feature of the map was the overwhelming preponderance of red shading
in the South and West; Roosevelt had every state of the old Confederacy except Byrd's Virginia and Garner's Texas, and he claimed every state
west of the Mississippi except Missouri and California. The third feature
of interest was that FDR was weakest in his own section; the northeast
was heavily hatched with his opponents' colors. Massachusetts, Rhode
Island, New Jersey, Connecticut, Pennsylvania, New York, Ohio, Illinois,
and Maryland were all either committed to other candidates or divided in
their support for FDR.

No clearer message could have been sent of Roosevelt's preconvention
strategy. He had captured McAdoo's 1924 states almost intact at the cost
of his own geographic section. The northeast had again stayed aloof from
the most overtly liberal candidate for the nomination. Roosevelt was in
the unusual position of being the front-runner for the nomination without the support of the state which he governed or its powerful neighbors.
Instead, he had won the support of the states which had lined up against
New York and its northeastern section within the party since 1920. He had
won McAdoo's constituencies, but he had also inherited McAdoo's great
problem. As the Smith group pointed out, Roosevelt had won more acres

than delegates.[80] Without the northeast, he did not have the necessary two-thirds of the delegates to win the nomination. His most optimistic supporters counted 691 Roosevelt delegates, which was nearly 80 short of the 770 needed to nominate. The northeastern conservatives, with unexpected assistance from their old foe McAdoo, had succeeded in throwing the outcome of the convention into doubt. That they had undertaken to block Roosevelt as they had blocked McAdoo in 1924 made it quite clear to all but the secretary himself that FDR had followed in McAdoo's footsteps all too well.

THE COALITION RESPONDS

NOMINATING A PRESIDENT, 1930–1932

The 1932 nomination was of vital significance to the conservative coalition for two interconnected reasons. The Raskob group was well aware of the political consequences of the depression. By the middle of 1931 it was clear that 1932 would be a Democratic year. The 1930 elections had given an indication of the electorate's mood, and the ensuing two years brought only more bad news for the GOP. The Democratic conservatives therefore knew that the man who won the party's nomination would also win the presidency. The presidency brought with it control of the national party organization and policies; the Raskob group's hopes of molding party policy would be dashed if an unsympathetic nominee emerged from the Chicago convention.

The second factor adding to the significance of the 1932 nomination also revolved around the depression. The worsening economic situation prompted many challenges to the economic doctrine put forward by the conservative northeastern Democrats. Growing unemployment strengthened calls for direct federal relief; bank failures brought demands for stricter regulation; the stock exchange crash led to demands for securities legislation. From all sides came evidence of a widespread feeling that the federal government had to take more responsibility for the economic welfare of its citizens. Raskob, Smith, Davis, and their colleagues had spent a good deal of the 1920s attacking prohibition as a gross federal invasion into their private lives. To have countenanced a far-reaching federal regulatory and relief program in response to the depression would have contradicted all their principles of government. They were therefore determined to keep the party from adopting a platform and nominating a candidate for 1932 committed to economic activism and social reform.

SMITH'S CANDIDACY FOR PRESIDENT

"I would advise," ran Raskob's standard reply to correspondents who sought his opinion during 1930 and 1931 of possible nominees for 1932, "that no one could advise you as to who the next Presidential nominee will be. There are several possible candidates but I have no way of knowing which one will be selected."[1] In fact, the conservatives attempted to block Roosevelt as soon as his boom began. Unobtrusively at first, they began to encourage favorite-son candidacies in order to prevent FDR from accumulating a two-thirds majority before the convention met.

Although the presidential primary elections did not take place until 1932, much was done in 1931 to further this strategy. In November of that year, for example, Jouett Shouse visited Alabama to make a speech. His ostensible purpose was to publicize the work of his permanent organization, yet there was suspicion that the Kansan had other ideas in mind. At that time the anti-Roosevelt forces in Alabama were advocating that no convention or primary should be held and that an uninstructed delegation selected by the legislature should be sent to Chicago. These groups trumpeted Shouse's arrival as a clear encouragement to their efforts. Louis Howe wrote a frosty letter to Shouse urging him to cancel his trip south,

for "the Governor's friends in Alabama feel that your visit under the circumstances could only be construed as a deliberately unfriendly act."[2]
James Farley had reported similar efforts during his trip through the West
in the summer, and the Alabama incident confirmed Roosevelt's suspicions that the conservatives were at work against him.[3] By December he
could stand the charade of neutrality no longer and wrote Shouse that
"very enthusiastic friends of mine in different states have jumped to the
conclusion that while you and John have very properly not come out in
favor of any candidate . . . you are going into different states seeking to
'block Roosevelt' by uninstructed delegations or favorite sons. They feel
that this would be just as unethical as if you and John were to come out
definitely for an individual and, of course, they are right in this point
of view."[4]

Shouse replied to both Howe and FDR in an unrepentant tone. "I
shall go ahead and do my duty as I see it," he replied to Howe, "without
reference to any candidacy."[5] Less than two months later, however, he
announced to the press what had long been an open secret within the
party. Citing the volatility of the economic climate as reason for extreme
caution, he argued that it would be "unwise to attempt to foreclose the
nomination months in advance of the Convention." Shouse declared that
"I have not hesitated to voice the belief that it would be wiser . . . not
to instruct delegates to the convention." At the same time, however, he
claimed that this did not compromise his "absolute neutrality" on who the
nominee should be.[6] The timing of Shouse's announcement cast doubt on
this. Only two days before, on February 7, Smith had announced his own
candidacy, and the first primary election was only four weeks away. As the
New Republic noted, Roosevelt had the most to gain from instructed delegates, since his supporters had been campaigning throughout the South
and West since the beginning of 1931.[7] Roosevelt and his advisers were in
no doubt that this was an overtly hostile act, and it contributed greatly
to their reluctance to see Shouse chosen as temporary chairman of the
convention.

Shouse's statement and Smith's candidacy began a new phase of the
conservatives' strategy for the 1932 nomination. Smith had delighted his
opponents within the party by declaring soon after his 1928 defeat that
he would not run for the presidency again. He had since occupied himself as
president of the Empire State Building, a venture funded by Raskob and

his friends, and had publicly forsworn political activity. Yet during 1931 he had remained ominously silent about speculation that he and Roosevelt were not as close as they once had been, and he made no endorsement of FDR's candidacy for the nomination.[8] Smith finally came into open conflict with Roosevelt over six proposed amendments to the New York State constitution in October 1931.

When Smith announced his opposition to four of those amendments, analysts ascribed his action to personal motives. Smith and FDR had fallen out; this was the first opportunity for the Happy Warrior to make that separation public.[9] Yet Smith's stated reasons for his opposition were in keeping with the thrust of conservative Democratic thought since 1920. His 1931 dissent was closely connected with the two themes of his group's agenda for the national party: opposition to prohibition and minimal government interference in business.

The proposed amendments seemed innocuous enough. They concerned mainly administrative matters: the substitution of the federal census for the state census for apportioning the legislature, the removal of the old constitutional ban upon legislators' receiving civil appointments, the creation of another judicial district in Long Island, a change of name for the state Department of Charities, and the reorganization of Westchester County's local government. The most important proposal imposed a mandate on the legislature to provide $19 million out of current revenues over eleven years to buy marginal farming land for reforestation purposes. Of these six amendments, Smith supported only those concerning the use of the federal census and the Department of Charities.[10]

Although none of the amendments concerned liquor law, it is clear that Smith applied the lessons he had learned in the prohibition fight. "No argument is needed," he declared, "to prove that the Constitution of the State should contain only the barest essentials of fundamental law." In opposing the Long Island judicial district amendment, for example, he argued that "it is wholly undesirable to write local legislation into the fundamental law." This matter could and should be handled by legislation. He opposed the Westchester County amendment on the same grounds.[11] This reasoning was at one with the spirit behind Raskob's home rule plan. Liquor control was a purely local matter, and once a constitution, either of the United States or of an individual state, became used for the imposition of local concerns upon the polity as a whole, it lost its sanctity as a statement of fundamental principles of government. As G. K. Chesterton remarked, the Eighteenth Amendment was analogous to the British Constitution stating that "the government of England shall be a hereditary King, a House of Lords and a House of Commons, and there shall be no dogs on Wimbledon Common."[12]

Smith also applied his principles regarding the proper relationship between government and business in his opposition to the Reforestation Amendment. This, he considered, was the most important amendment of all. The state's right to acquire forest preserves was already enshrined in the Constitution, thus rendering the amendment unnecessary. Furthermore, its mandate on successive legislatures to appropriate funds was "without precedent and wholly undesirable." Each legislature should be free to make its own appropriations as it saw fit, he argued, and "if we keep this up every group in the state with an axe to grind will write a budget for its particular hobby into the constitution."[13]

Smith's most weighty objection to the amendment was that it necessitated the state's entering the lumber industry. Timber on reforested lands would be grown, cut, and sold by the Conservation Department. Like Cox, Davis, and Raskob, he was uncomfortable with the idea of the state taking such a prominent role in industry. His preference for bond funding was also in keeping with his colleagues' thinking and was consistent with his practice as governor.[14]

Smith's opposition to the Reforestation Amendment did not prevent the state's voters from approving it by a margin of over 200,000 votes. The two amendments that he had supported also passed overwhelmingly, while the remaining three that he opposed failed of passage.[15] Given the Happy Warrior's stress upon the Reforestation Amendment, the outcome of the vote seemed a personal defeat for him. Having taken issue with FDR on the grounds of undue interference with business, however, Smith had established himself as Roosevelt's most prominent conservative critic within the party. This was confirmed by his announcement in February 1932 that he would seek the nomination.

Like his opposition to the Reforestation Amendment, Smith's entry into the race for the nomination was widely seen as a personal decision stemming from his estrangement from FDR.[16] Yet his motives were more complex than mere spite or ambition. Worried by Roosevelt's leftward trend, he entered the race in order to fight a holding action. Although he did not consider that he could win the nomination, he hoped to use his popularity in the Northeast to win enough delegates to wield a veto over Roosevelt's nomination.[17] Those delegates could then be delivered to an acceptable candidate once the convention was in session.[18]

The heart of Smith's nomination campaign was his economic policy, and he used this to distinguish himself further from FDR. On May 16, 1932, he delivered a radio address entitled "A Financial Program for the Present Crisis." The overwhelming need of the hour, he told his audience, was to balance the budget. The cost of government must be ruthlessly pared and its bureaus consolidated and streamlined. The increasing demand for early payment of the veterans' bonus was fiscally irresponsible and had to be resolutely denied.[19] Once the cost of government had been cut to the "irreducible minimum," Smith warned, further sources of revenue would still be required to balance the budget. In a clear repudiation of Roosevelt's views, Smith lent his support to the sales tax proposal that had recently failed in Congress.[20] "It is important in the imposition of new taxes," he argued, "that no greater strain be put upon industry or business than is absolutely necessary." The sales tax, by spreading its burden across all members of society, would not single out business profits or capital investment to bear the brunt of the government's budgetary woes.[21]

Smith pressed home his attack in a reference to FDR's "forgotten man" speech of the previous month. Opponents of the sales tax, he argued, wanted wage earners to believe that "in order to make up the deficit [the government must] soak the rich." "It is a false friend," he warned, "who leads the poor man to believe that capital can be unreasonably taxed or soaked without injury to him." He also advocated the amendment of the Volstead Act so as to allow for the immediate relegalization of beer and wine. This would not only create revenue without "soaking capital" but also create new employment.[22]

Having outlined his plans to save and augment the federal government's revenues, Smith went on to discuss ways of assisting the unemployed. In contrast to the proposal made by Raymond Moley to FDR that $2.5 billion should be raised for public works out of current revenues, Smith argued that $5 billion should be set aside for this purpose but that it should be funded by a federal bond issue.[23] This not only would allow the budget to remain in balance but also would prevent the imposition of heavy taxation upon higher incomes. Smith argued that the federal highway-aid programs to the states should be greatly increased to provide jobs and that the federal government should undertake a building program so that its offices around the nation could be housed in federally owned structures. This would create jobs and save the government millions of dollars in rent. On no account, however, should private revenue-producing ventures be assisted to provide jobs. This would be an unjustified intervention into private business life. Aid should be limited to "productive public works."[24]

No better summation of Smith's challenge to Roosevelt can be found than in Hamilton A. Long's pamphlet entitled *Roosevelt or Smith* published in June 1932.[25] Long, a New York attorney, addressed his pamphlet to the businessmen of the Northeast. Proceeding on the assumption that victory in November depended upon a candidate's good standing with the business community, Long criticized FDR as an enemy of honest business. His water-power policy, designed to appeal to "the so-called progressives of the Middle West," was a unjustified attack upon honest utilities. He had bowed to Hearst in his stated belief that war debts should not be canceled, despite the contrary views of "enlightened business leaders," and his "forgotten man" speech was the final straw. Nothing better demonstrated FDR's lamentable tendency to value votes above principles than this speech of demagogic "generalities with no practical suggestions as to how to convert them into realities."[26]

Al Smith, in contrast, enjoyed the confidence of business groups across the nation. New York's corporate sector, Long noted, "always felt safe with him at the helm," because "he always kept his famously progressive social welfare legislation program well within the bounds of established sound principles of business and government." His recent proposals for public works were eminently sensible and friendly to business; he was opposed to the "colossal waste and stupidity of the dole," and his programs envisioned only self-sustaining economic projects. Finally, Long pointed with approval to Smith's proposal to fund his scheme by bonds rather than taxation.[27] All in all, he concluded, only Smith could command the confidence of the business sector and enable it to lead the nation out of the depression.

Behind this bluster, however, lay the reality that Smith was not a genuine candidate for the nomination. That Smith had no real expectation of winning the nomination is suggested by the financial statements kept by Belle Moskowitz. The Smith-for-president campaign cost a total of

$14,630 between April and October 1932.[28] Roosevelt's expenditures, in contrast, totaled more than $86,000 by the end of March.[29] Smith's supporters ran a highly localized campaign, limiting their major efforts to Massachusetts, New York, New Jersey, Pennsylvania, Rhode Island, and Connecticut. Although Smith's name was entered in the California primary, for instance, he did not visit the state, and his campaign committee spent only $250 there.[30]

NEWTON BAKER AND OWEN YOUNG

Agreeing that Smith did not want the nomination himself, historians of the 1932 convention have generally agreed that Newton D. Baker was the conservative coalition's first choice.[31] A West Virginian by birth and an Ohioan by residence, Baker had shared a boardinghouse with Woodrow Wilson while at Johns Hopkins University and had attended Washington and Lee Law School in the company of John W. Davis. After serving in Grover Cleveland's second administration, he was elected mayor of Cleveland in 1911 after an eight-year stint as that city's solicitor. He entered Wilson's cabinet as secretary of war in February 1916.[32]

Despite his Wilsonian background, Baker seemed to many observers to become more conservative during the 1920s. Returning to Cleveland to resume his corporate law practice, he came out in favor of the open shop in 1922, and his most famous briefs argued for a restrictive interpretation of the federal Water Power Act so as to limit the extent of federal control over power generation.[33] He opposed government transmission of power from Muscle Shoals and argued that states' rights should not be abridged by drastic federal regulation of utilities or other industries.[34]

Like Raskob and his group, Baker maintained a profound distrust of government beyond the local level. Throughout his life he tended to accept far more activism on the part of local government than he could tolerate from federal or even state governments. Localism and voluntarism, he thought, were far preferable to federal activism.[35] The conservative coalition was also impressed by his opposition to prohibition. As a member of the Wickersham Commission, created by President Hoover in 1930 to report on the current effectiveness and future prospects of national prohibition, Baker declared himself personally in favor of the repeal of the Eighteenth Amendment. He did, however, also sign the statement of all the commissioners which advocated the continuation of national prohibition.[36]

Baker's greatest political concern during the 1920s, however, was the League of Nations.[37] He remained an ardent internationalist all his life and dedicated most of his political efforts to the hopeless task of persuading Americans that they should join the league. Even in November 1921, a year after a presidential election which was widely perceived as an overwhelming repudiation of Wilsonian internationalism, he wrote Homer Cummings, "It seems to me clear that the popular mind . . . is changing, daily more and more, toward the League."[38] In January 1932, however, he declared that he no longer favored a plank calling for U.S. membership in the league. Contemporary analysts saw this move as an attempt to appease the Smith-Raskob group, who had little interest in the league, and to remove Baker's greatest political handicap.[39] He had earlier improved his electoral viability by renouncing his open shop views.[40] Finally, on April 17, 1932, the ill-kept secret was made public: Baker would not conduct a campaign for the presidential nomination, but he would accept it if it was tendered to him.

Baker's suitability as a anti-Roosevelt candidate was problematic. On the one hand, his attitude toward Roosevelt was cool. At the end of 1931 he refused to criticize FDR publicly, although he confided to Walter Lippmann that he was still "trying to make up my own mind about a man whom I did not see much in Washington and who I have ever since been trying to measure." Roosevelt, he thought, was "too politically minded and selfish."[41] To Raymond Fosdick he argued that "the whole Roosevelt clan" was "intellectually unreliable and emotionally unsound."[42] Baker's chief political adviser, Ralph Hayes, saw FDR as a threat. "It would be a grave misfortune," he wrote in April 1932, "if the party should be handed over to Roosevelt as it would have been to deed it to McAdoo eight years ago—and as it *was* to give it to Bryan at the turn of the century."[43]

On the other hand, Baker was not an ideal candidate for the Raskob-Smith group. Although he was eminently "safe" on economic policy, he had not been especially close to either Smith or Raskob. Although he had supported the Happy Warrior in 1928, he had not approved of Smith's stress on prohibition and his silence on international affairs. Even in August 1928, he wrote that he was going to vote for Smith, but that he was still "trying very hard to find out why." As a strong internationalist, furthermore, Baker had little time for Raskob's high-tariff ideas, and he strongly disapproved of the Houston platform.[44]

Despite his advocacy of the repeal of the Eighteenth Amendment, Baker did not agree with the conservative coalition's "booze before bread" strategy. He never joined the AAPA and remained a moderate wet. He could not, he confessed, share the antiprohibitionists' excitement over an alleged "right to drink."[45] In particular, he did not wish to see the 1932 campaign degenerate into a "conflict between a raging thirst on one side and the Sahara Desert on the other."[46] He insisted that the party could not shrink from the economic challenges of the depression and that it must recognize that "it is more important to get men jobs than drink."[47]

For their part, Smith and Raskob could not have been unaware of Baker's political liabilities. His service as secretary of war had alienated the sizeable German-American vote; his advocacy of the League until 1932 had lost him support among the other ethnic groups who had taught Cox such a painful lesson in 1920; his former support of the open shop made him an enemy of organized labor; and his large corporate clients promised to be even more embarrassing to Baker than they had been to Davis in 1924.[48] Rather than risking their strategy solely upon Baker's political fortunes, the coalition preferred to nurture several dark-horse candidates who shared the coalition's conception of the party's proper ideological direction.

Several other candidates were therefore mentioned as possible beneficiaries of the coalition's strategy.[49] Owen D. Young, the chairman of General Electric, was generally considered to be a strong contender. By any standard, Young was the outstanding business leader of the time. He had served on the Dawes Committee on Reparations in 1924 and had chaired the Young Committee when that issue was again investigated in 1930. A frequent speaker on public issues, Young had developed a reputation as an enlightened spokesman for welfare capitalism during the 1920s.[50] Relishing his role as the gadfly of big business, he supported high inheritance taxes and the partial payment of the soldiers' bonus in 1931.[51] Like Raskob, however, he believed that business corporations should be allowed to reform themselves without government intervention. His achievements within General Electric were the equal of Raskob's within Du Pont and GM; he had instituted higher piecework rates, a pension plan, and a

stock investment plan during the prosperous 1920s.[52] Young's connections with the coalition's leaders were strengthened when he, Raskob, and
Pierre du Pont served together on the board of General Motors in the
early 1920s.[53]

Although he was on good terms with FDR, Young did not approve
of the governor's water-power policies, and he considered him to be too
opportunistic and vacillating.[54] He was reported ready to cooperate with
Raskob on the chairman's home rule plan for prohibition, and in return
Raskob had promised Young his full support.[55] Young seemed to confirm
this when he wrote to his doctor in July 1931 to seek advice regarding his
wife's health. "I have been asked to accept nomination as the Democratic
candidate," he wrote Dr. Chace; "I have reasonable assurance from the key
leaders of the party that I could be nominated."[56]

Young's boom ended on May 16, 1932, when he declared that he would
not accept the nomination. His wife's health was such that Dr. Chace
could not be sure whether she would survive a campaign, and Young was
not prepared to take the risk. Only two days before Young's announcement, FDR had written to Daniels to report that Young was the first
choice of the "Smith-Shouse-Raskob crowd," but in the event that he declined to run, "they will turn with a deep sigh" to Baker.[57] The *New York
Times* agreed; Young's withdrawal, it argued, had removed the "strongest prop" from the stop-Roosevelt movement, leaving the conservative
coalition with only Baker as a nationally acceptable candidate.[58]

Other names were rumored to be favored by the coalition.[59] Melvyn
Traylor, a Chicago banker, was put forward as a dark horse by his backers
in Illinois. Traylor would have been acceptable to Raskob, but he was too
old to withstand a campaign.[60] Governor's Albert Ritchie of Maryland and
Harry Flood Byrd of Virginia were also considered to be favorites of Raskob and his allies. The sheer number of possible conservative candidates
created confusion among Democrats as they pondered the Raskob-Smith
strategy. In 1965 Jouett Shouse wrote to the historian Elliot Rosen with
the opinion that Smith had favored John Garner above Baker or Young.[61]
Ralph Hayes wrote to Newton Baker in March 1932 that Baker and Ritchie
were the favored candidates behind Young with "the group about the
A.E.S. headquarters."[62] John Raskob told Harry Flood Byrd that he was
the coalition's first choice, while Belle Moskowitz encouraged Ritchie in
the belief that he was the great hope of the conservatives at Chicago.[63] In

August 1931, Byrd wrote Governor Gardner of North Carolina that he had heard that Raskob and Shouse favored Young but that "a little while later" the favorite was said to be Baker. James Cox had persuaded Shouse that Baker could not win Ohio because of "antagonism from the labor people" and that the current favorite was Traylor.[64]

The booms and candidacies of Newton Baker and Owen Young have been thoroughly analyzed by their biographers and historians of the party, but those of Ritchie and Byrd have received less attention.[65] Yet these candidatures encompassed the two main thrusts of the conservatives' strategy for the party in 1932. Ritchie, as a northeastern figure who had built his reputation on states' rights and antiprohibition, fitted the strategy of "booze before bread" perfectly. Byrd, on his part, promised to fulfill the coalition's goal of forming a North-South alliance along conservative economic policy lines. Examination of the political thought of the two men therefore provides an opportunity for delineating both strategies to block Roosevelt.

ALBERT RITCHIE AND HARRY BYRD

Albert Cabell Ritchie's upbringing was as close to aristocratic as American conditions allowed. Related on his mother's side to the Virginia Cabells, he attended private schools and was taught by home tutors before embarking upon an undistinguished university career at Johns Hopkins and then the University of Maryland Law School. After some years in legal practice, he ran for governor of Maryland in 1918, at the age of 43.[66] Although his winning margin was a mere 165 votes, he became a fixture in Maryland politics throughout the 1920s. Before Ritchie, no Maryland governor had even been reelected. Yet he occupied the governor's mansion for sixteen uninterrupted years until his defeat in 1934, a record tenure for any governor in America up to that time.[67]

Despite the dissimilarity of their backgrounds, Albert Ritchie and Al Smith were uncannily alike in their political careers. Both men became governors of their states in 1919, both opposed the Nineteenth Amendment, and both were to stake their political fortunes on opposition to national prohibition. Ritchie's gubernatorial policies were also very similar to Smith's; he improved Maryland's roads, schools, factory laws, and workman's compensation legislation; he won a bond issue to remove grade crossings, and he opposed sumptuary laws as infringements upon personal liberty.[68] Like Smith, he stressed the need for economical government, and he oversaw the reorganization of Maryland's state governmental structure. Both men relied upon an ethnic urban constituency for their electoral successes; Ritchie invariably ran most strongly in Baltimore.[69]

In keeping with his conservative colleagues in Delaware and New York, Ritchie described himself as a liberal. He defined his political principles in distinctly nineteenth-century terms, providing a definition of "liberalism" that owed more to Grover Cleveland than to the subsequent positive-state implications of the term.[70] He objected to government interference in the private lives of citizens and maintained a deep hostility to almost every form of business regulation. He shared John Raskob's distrust of government and its tendency to aggrandize its power. "Never before," he declared in 1924, "has the tendency to control the individual, his actions, and his liberty been as strong as it is now."[71] He characterized the largely somnolent federal government of the Coolidge years as the most restrictive in the world, save only those of Russia and Italy.[72]

States' rights were a sacred creed for Maryland's governor. When Warren Harding asked him to use state troopers to open the mines during the coal strike of 1922, Ritchie indignantly refused. He had no sympathy for the strikers, but he considered Harding's request to be an affront to Maryland's right to deploy its own law enforcement authorities as it saw fit.[73] In 1928 he urged the repeal of the Sixteenth Amendment because it incorporated no limit upon the federal government's power to tax its citizens.[74] He was also conscious of more tangible disadvantages of an activist federal government; in 1928 he calculated that Maryland was one of eleven states—mainly from the Northeast—which received back less than 4 percent of their taxation contributions to Washington in the form of federal appropriations. The South and West, he thought, were milking the East dry.[75]

Nothing offended Ritchie's concern for states' rights and limited government more than the Eighteenth Amendment. In keeping with all the members of the conservative coalition, he saw prohibition as an extension of federal power that threatened the delicate balance between governmental authority and individual liberty. "I summon again the memory of Grover Cleveland," Ritchie declared in an antiprohibition speech of 1928, "who believed in a maximum of self government and held that the true ideals of liberty and democracy can be attained only under a Government which grants the utmost autonomy to local political units."[76]

Ritchie's solution to the problem of national prohibition was simple. "The 18th Amendment should never have been put in the Constitution," he declared in 1932, "and . . . therefore, it should be repealed and taken out of the Constitution."[77] The whole matter should be returned to the states.[78] The Constitution, furthermore, should be protected from future experiments in social control. In 1922 he suggested changing the constitutional amendment process so as to make it more difficult. Under the existing situation, he told a bankers' convention, it was possible for 32 percent of the population to force an amendment upon the nation. Instead, he urged, future amendments must be essential, and they must not affect the existing powers of the states. In addition, proposed amendments should be ratified by state legislatures elected after the amendment was proposed, and then passed by a referendum.[79]

Ritchie's standing with the Raskob group was enhanced by the tenor of his preconvention campaign in 1932.[80] In his own state, he was conspicuously slow in recommending emergency legislation to relieve economic distress after 1929. In 1931, in his annual message to the Maryland legislature, he asked the lawmakers to leave the problems of the depression to correct themselves through the processes of "natural" economic laws, and he waited until July 1932 before he appointed a commission to investigate the need for unemployment relief.[81] His great obsession throughout the period between 1929 and 1934 was to keep the state budget in balance and to avoid unnecessary tax increases.[82] At the same time, he attacked Hoover's unemployment relief proposals as a "rush headlong and unseeing into . . . radical, if not socialistic, panaceas." The Farm Board and the Reconstruction Finance Corporation struck him as futile and extravagant attempts to interfere with normal economic processes of depression and retrenchment.[83]

Ritchie's own program for the depression corresponded closely to those proposed by Smith and Raskob. The three most pressing issues of the day, he declared in a radio speech in April 1932, were unemployment, taxation, and prohibition. Although unemployment was "disasterous [sic] in its effects and . . . baffling in its cure," Americans had to remember that "one great danger of bad times is that they produce bad remedies." No "new and unsound panaceas" or ventures into "Communism" or "un-American practices" like the British system of unemployment insurance should be countenanced.[84] Public works were permissible, but always within the constraints of a balanced budget. Such projects should be "self-liquidating" and funded by bond issues.[85]

Ritchie made clear his affinity with the Raskob-Smith group by explicitly endorsing Raskob's proposal to shorten hours of work so as to spread employment as widely as possible.[86] On taxation, too, he positioned himself squarely in the conservatives' camp. Government expenditure had to be cut ruthlessly in order to facilitate recovery. "Every dollar cut from the expense of government means not only increased efficiency," he held, "but also a dollar less in taxes imposed upon American railroads and banks and industry and labor and agriculture, all of which are being taxed to the limit already."[87] What was needed was "retrenchment without stint," because the government was no different from its citizens; each group had to spend less.[88]

Even with retrenchment, new taxes would have to be raised in order to balance the budget. Like Smith and Raskob, Ritchie supported the imposition of a general sales tax as "the fairest and least burdensome way to balance the budget in this emergency."[89] The removal of national prohibition therefore represented a major solution to the depression itself; Ritchie had clearly subscribed to the "booze before bread" strategy. He also distinguished himself from FDR on the issue of utility regulation, coming out against government ownership of public utilities in September 1931. This, he warned, would lead to "economic and political slavery." The power question, he declared in an implicit attack upon Roosevelt's stand, would become a "political football." "I am for the irreducible minimum of legislative interference in every field of human effort, including the public utilities. Our detours from this principle are already too many. There should be no more." Although there is no evidence to suggest that Ritchie and the Raskob group came to any firm agreements or alliances before the convention, there was certainly informal contact between them.[90] Belle Moskowitz kept in close contact with Norman W. Baxter, Ritchie's publicity director, and the two shared information and mailing lists.[91]

Less than two hundred miles to the south, Harry Flood Byrd was also considering his options for 1932. While Ritchie hoped to win the nomination on the strength of his long-held antiprohibition views and "booze before bread" doctrine, Byrd had a very different strategy in mind. During his dealings with John Raskob during the DNC fights over prohibition in 1931, he had developed his own plan for deciding the future of the Eighteenth Amendment. This, he hoped, would remove the most important issue dividing southern and northern Democrats and facilitate an alliance between the two groups so as to ensure victory in 1932. Gradually, Byrd came to consider the possibility that he might use such an alliance to win nomination to national office. At first he thought that his best chance was for the vice-presidential nomination, but by the summer of 1932 he was persuaded that the presidency itself was within his reach. His new friend John Raskob encouraged him to come to this conclusion.

Byrd at first discouraged attempts to put his name forward for the nomination. He saw himself as a mediator between Roosevelt and Raskob and had no wish to compromise that position by an early candidacy.[92] As indications that Raskob and Smith had decided to block Roosevelt became more apparent during 1931, however, his attitude began to change. Henry Breckinridge, one of his most enthusiastic supporters, wrote from New York at the beginning of October 1931 that he had heard that Jouett Shouse was "extremely friendly to you and, confidentially, would be strong in your favor as opposed to Frank Roosevelt."[93] Although Byrd still refused to make a public statement of availability for the nomination, he did agree to a discreet campaign on his behalf.[94] It was also an inexpensive effort; the Virginia for Byrd Committee spent only $9,125 between January and June 1932, 80 percent of which was contributed by William Reed.[95]

Byrd's backers stressed his suitability for the nomination to their fellow southerners. They argued that the time had long passed when the former Confederate states were barred from providing presidents. Woodrow Wilson had been born in Virginia from Confederate ancestry, and that had not been an issue in 1912. Democrats all over the nation had witnessed the South's loyalty to the party for over a century; now was the time for Dixie to see one of its sons claim its just reward.[96] Roy Flannagan reported to Byrd in April 1932 that he had heard no objections to his southern heritage. "There has been opposition because you were a dry," Flannagan wrote, "but not because you were a Southerner. This is remarkable in view of past political history."[97]

His boosters did not, however, make much of their candidate's increasingly friendly contacts with John Raskob and his group. Yet this was an essential part of Byrd's strategy. He continued to move away from Roosevelt's circle, consulting instead with Shouse and the chairman. He even came to repent of his earlier opposition to Raskob's home rule plan, because it was this fight that had given FDR "his first start" towards the nomination.[98] The governor's drift toward Raskob was not lost upon Roosevelt's advisers, although they did not perceive the scope of Byrd's ambitions. Robert Woolley warned FDR at the end of January 1932 that Byrd was no longer to be considered an ally. He should not "rely on the Virginian delegation until it is all over except the shouting. . . . Byrd wants the vice-presidential nomination and thinks his best chance to land it is by tying up with Newton D. Baker."[99]

Raskob and Byrd continued to correspond about their prohibition plans and the prospects for the 1932 nomination. In January 1932, the chairman wrote Byrd expressing the belief that southerners were the great hope for Democratic success because they were "a much more temperate and conservative people than the average in this country." They were "a much older people in experience and in American traditions and . . . understand American government, principles and doctrines better than the average, and particularly better than the younger sections of our country." The South was an essential bulwark against the progressives of the West, whom Roosevelt was assiduously courting.[100] By thinking aloud to Byrd, Raskob was intimating that the Virginian could play a prominent role in this North-South alliance.

For their part, Byrd's southern friends were privately confident that he would benefit from Raskob and Smith's opposition to Roosevelt. When Smith announced his candidacy in February 1932, Roy Flannagan was delighted. Smith had "seriously impaired Governor Roosevelt's chance of securing the nomination," he wrote Breckinridge, and "the way is wide open for a man like Byrd." Baker, in Flannagan's opinion, could not win the nomination because of his long identification with the League of Nations.[101] Two months later, he was even more optimistic. "I have believed for some time," he wrote Byrd, "that the stop movement will be successful, and that you have the next best chance at the nomination. . . . Things are looking brighter every day."[102] Byrd received similar encouragement from a more significant source in June 1932. "I had a very satisfactory talk with Mr. Raskob," he told his friend John Hanes. "Confidentially, he told me that I am his first choice, Ritchie second and Baker third."[103]

Harry Byrd's platform for 1932 amply justified Raskob's growing admiration and support. As Ritchie defined himself as a liberal, Byrd and his friends called themselves progressives, but they defined the term in similar terms. William Reed addressed this point in a long letter to Byrd just before the Chicago convention. Distinguishing Byrd from other self-professed progressives like Roosevelt, Reed defined "progressivism" in a way that would echo closely Raskob's and Smith's criticisms of FDR's "demagoguery." "If your record as Governor of Virginia was a progressive one, and I think it was, then we are both progressives, which to me means abolishing needless offices, reducing taxation, balancing the budget, changing a deficit into a surplus, and last but not least, not making any promises to the electorate which you do not feel fairly sure you can and desire to make effective. . . . If putting the government into all public business, passing laws in an effort to regulate people's morals, . . . and promising the masses day after day some new legislation that is going to give them some easy money, or distributing wealth, accumulated by the brains of the nation, in the shape of taxation . . . is progressiveism [*sic*]; then I am a 'stand-patter' on the other side of the fence, or whatever you choose to call it."[104]

Byrd carried this limited definition of progressivism to his platform for 1932. Speaking to Democrats at a 1932 Jefferson Day rally, he outlined his conception of the priorities facing the party as it contemplated the coming elections. The cost of government was the most pressing problem that Byrd could see ahead; although the task of retrenchment would be painful, it was no less essential for that. Hoover's extravagance had led to the federal government's becoming an incubus upon the economic life of the nation. "The Democratic party should declare for lowering our governmental costs," he argued, "to the ability of the citizens to pay. This can only be accomplished by less government in business and more business in government."[105] The plight of agriculture, too, loomed large in his analysis of the nation's ills. Farm income had dropped precipitously because farmers could not sell their surpluses abroad. The Smoot-Hawley Tariff was responsible for this situation, and its revision should be the first goal of a Byrd administration.[106] The centerpiece of his program for 1932, however, concerned his prohibition proposal.[107]

Byrd's platform was most interesting for its omissions. For the depression he proposed only the most traditional remedies: tariff reform and governmental economy. He made no reference at all to unemployment and put forward no proposals for expanded public works or other relief programs. He was equally silent on utility regulation and banking reform. Although his prohibition plank was not completely to Raskob's liking, the chairman could not have failed to approve of Byrd's economic program. His assurance that Byrd was his group's first choice was hardly a binding promise, since both Baker and Ritchie had been led to believe that they, too, were the favored candidates. With a number of acceptable candidates in the field, the chairman awaited the hoped-for deadlock at Chicago.

ROOSEVELT'S SUCCESS AT THE CONVENTION

From the point of view of the conservative coalition, the convention itself incorporated three main struggles, of which they won only one. The first was the unfinished business regarding Jouett Shouse. Despite intensive lobbying on Shouse's behalf, the Roosevelt forces managed to defeat his bid for the permanent chairmanship by a margin of 826 votes to 626.[108] As an indication of the relative strengths of the two groups, however, this vote was deceptive. Shouse received many votes from delegates who had little sympathy with his or his friends' views but who were dismayed at FDR's breach of faith in putting Walsh forward.

The second major test of strength was over the platform, and its outcome gave Raskob's group profound satisfaction. The draft platform accepted by the Platform Committee was written chiefly by A. Mitchell Palmer and Daniel Roper, who were on the right wing of FDR's coalition.[109] In its economic planks the platform gave little concern to the conservatives. Although its preamble promised a "drastic change in economic governmental policies," the platform's substance was by no means radical. The most drastic change promised was a reorganization and retrenchment of the federal government to "eliminate extravagance" and to reduce public expenditures by "not less than twenty-five percent."[110] The party committed itself to a balanced budget, to "a sound currency to be preserved at all hazards," and to the collection of America's foreign debts.

Raskob and his allies had no objection to any of these planks, and they were also pleased at the absence of what the chairman described in his opening address as "barnacles and isms." Instead of a promise of direct

federal unemployment relief, the platform limited itself to advocating federal loans to those states which could no longer afford to provide for their
needy citizens, and for an expanded federal public works program. Raskob's proposals for a shorter working week were included, and no radical
farm relief proposal appeared.[111] No definite pledge on federal control of
water power appeared other than a promise that the nation's power resources would be managed "in the public interest." Banking reform and
securities legislation were promised, but only in the vaguest terms.[112]

The draft platform recommended that the Eighteenth Amendment be
referred to the states for resubmission to the people, a stance that mirrored
the GOP's prohibition plank.[113] Senator David I. Walsh of Massachusetts,
a strong supporter of Smith, proposed instead a plank which called for the
outright repeal of the amendment. When Walsh's proposal was accepted
by the delegates by a vote of 934¾ votes to 213¾, the Raskob group won
its most signal victory of the convention.[114] Overall, the *New York Times*
noted approvingly, "There was not one wild nostrum or disturbing proposal in the whole list. In the matter of economic and financial policy, the
Democratic platform was fully as sound as the Republican." [115]

The draft platform displeased the Raskob group in only two areas.
Cordell Hull won his fight to reverse the Houston tariff plank, and the
Chicago platform reverted to the traditional Democratic stance of supporting "a competitive tariff for revenue." Hull also succeeded in including
endorsements of reciprocal trade treaties and an international economic
conference.[116]

The main prize to be won at Chicago was the presidential nomination, and in this crucial struggle the conservative coalition met defeat. Its
strategy of encouraging a pool of suitable candidates showed its limitations as soon as the nomination process began. Roosevelt's forces arrived
in Chicago more than a hundred votes short of a two-thirds majority, while
Smith, Baker, Byrd, and Ritchie could muster only 214 votes between
them. Both sides needed to reach out to other favorite-son candidacies in
order to achieve victory. "The main point is now to persuade Garner to
take no part in any mere 'block movement,'" Roosevelt wrote Daniels six
weeks before the convention met; "I think Garner is big enough to see
this." [117] For his part, Garner was determined not to deadlock the convention against Roosevelt if to do so would create another 1924.[118]

On the conservatives' side, overtures were made to the Texas and

California delegations through, of all people, William Gibbs McAdoo. McAdoo was known to be adamantly opposed to Roosevelt's nomination, and so a marriage of convenience was proposed which completely ignored the profound ideological and personal differences dividing the secretary and Raskob's group. Although it is clear that Smith and McAdoo met in Bernard Baruch's hotel room in Chicago, the outcome of that meeting is shrouded in controversy. On the one hand, Smith later claimed that the two men decided to eliminate FDR and then to decide on an acceptable compromise. In return, Smith agreed to visit California to make speeches on behalf of McAdoo's anticipated campaign for a U.S. Senate seat.[119] McAdoo, on the other hand, always denied that any such agreement existed.[120]

Although the weight of evidence favors Smith's side of the argument, it seems unlikely that any such alliance could have achieved its purpose of agreeing upon a compromise candidate.[121] McAdoo had strong objections to all of the coalition's candidates. Smith was unthinkable; Ritchie's obsession with antiprohibition was equally unacceptable; Byrd was too conservative; and William Randolph Hearst would not hear of Baker.[122] In addition, Hearst was adamant that no candidate even remotely connected with Al Smith should be nominated. Smith and Hearst had been sworn enemies since the early 1920s, and neither man was prepared to bury the hatchet.[123]

Quite apart from the individual liabilities of the coalition's favored candidates, the strategy of not settling upon a single candidate hampered the Raskob group's activities. Without a single figure to put forward as the inheritor of Smith's delegates, the coalition failed to agree upon a cohesive strategy for broadening the base of its support. Accordingly, each of the candidates' supporters went their own way, attempting to negotiate individually for their own benefit. Ritchie was offered the vice-presidency by the Roosevelt camp but declined the honor.[124] Baker's supporters concentrated upon building up support among southern delegations for a possible fifth-ballot swing.[125] Byrd's friends, meanwhile, were waiting for Smith to withdraw before contesting Baker's claims to southern support.[126]

Al Smith bore much of the responsibility for the failure of the coalition to establish a coordinated strategy at Chicago. By not withdrawing, he unwittingly helped Roosevelt maintain his strength between the vital third and fourth ballots. Had he withdrawn then, William Allen White wrote Ralph Hayes soon after the convention, FDR's support would have evaporated quickly. "So long as Smith was in, Roosevelt was fairly safe," White argued. "You cannot imagine the fear and dread of the South and West, which even the possibility of Smith's nomination produced."[127] In the final analysis, however, the ideological lines dividing the party held firm.

McAdoo, having been assured that he would be consulted on key cabinet appointments and California patronage and that Garner would win the vice-presidential nomination, finally threw in his lot with FDR.[128] In so doing, he belatedly acknowledged what most of his supporters had known since 1928: that FDR was his rightful heir. To have allied with Raskob, Smith, Baker, Ritchie, and Byrd would have made a mockery of his long battles against me-tooism and the northeastern wing of the party. McAdoo had nowhere else to go other than to join Roosevelt's bandwagon. By his action the national party finally achieved the goal he had set for it since 1920: it had freed itself of northeastern conservative control and had delivered itself into the hands of a candidate who had consciously set out to complete McAdoo's failed crusade. "The people of this country want a genuine choice this year," Roosevelt declared in his acceptance speech, "not a choice between two names for the same reactionary doctrine. Ours must be a party of liberal thought, of planned action."[129] "Not since 1912," the *New York Times* observed after the nomination was decided, "have the West and South as effectively and completely established their ascendancy in the Democratic party."[130]

Roosevelt's opponents were deeply disappointed by the outcome of the convention. Joe Tumulty wrote James Cox that he had given himself over to "brooding and regretting." "The mountain moved and brought forth a mouse," he complained, "and the tragedy of the whole thing is that even he will win."[131] Cox, who had taken a quiet role in the block-FDR movement, agreed. He wrote to Newton Baker with the opinion that the party had missed a great opportunity by nominating Roosevelt. "There was a certain class of business Republican [*sic*] who do not want to vote for Hoover and who would have supported any Democrat except Roosevelt," he told Baker. "So far as I am able to observe, this vote will be lost to us."[132]

Former chairman Raskob had very mixed feelings as he looked back on the Chicago convention. The nomination fight had been a terrible disappointment. "It is too bad that we did not have a general in charge of our forces," he wrote Byrd, "and thus had someone in command to make a quick decision and save our party from the radical element, which is now in control."[133] That he had lost the struggle for control of the party weighed heavily upon him. Roosevelt's nomination had shattered his hopes for a North-South conservative coalition based upon conservative economic policy. Raskob expressed his despair to Byrd. "When the Democratic Party, born and bred in the fine, old aristocracy of the South, and always fostered and nourished by a conservative people, is turned over to a radical group such as Roosevelt, Hearst, McAdoo, Senators [Huey P.] Long, Wheeler and [Clarence C.] Dill, and is taken out of the hands of such men as you, Governor Ritchie, Carter Glass, Mr. Reed, Colonel Breckinridge, Governor Smith, John W. Davis, Pierre S. du Pont, Governor Cox . . . etc, one cannot help losing faith in the ability of that Party, under such leadership, to command that confidence necessary to elect."[134]

Yet all was not lost. "I think we accomplished a great deal that cannot be destroyed," Raskob wrote Colonel Arthur O'Brien only days after the convention. "We did get a short, concise platform and a strong liquor plank, even though the Party's choice resulted in a nominee not as strong as we would like to have seen."[135] By pledging himself to the platform, Roosevelt had tried to reassure his conservative foes in order to win their loyalty during the campaign. The coalition responded, and all its members lent their support and funds to the cause.[136] This loyalty, however, reflected the dictates of party discipline and admiration for the platform rather than enthusiasm for the candidate. As long as FDR honored the platform, he could count on at least the acquiescence of those who had tried so hard to defeat him. As the events of the 1930s showed, however, this truce would shatter almost as soon as Roosevelt strayed from the promises made in Chicago.

12

THE IDEOLOGY OF ANTIPROHIBITION

FROM THE AAPA TO THE AMERICAN LIBERTY LEAGUE

Franklin Roosevelt's nomination and the Chicago platform's promise to repeal the Eighteenth Amendment were milestones in the history of both the Democratic conservative coalition and the antiprohibition movement. The events at the Chicago convention of 1932 highlighted the close links between the two groups. James Cox, John Davis, Al Smith, and John Raskob were all opponents of the Eighteenth Amendment, and their group led the impetus toward a new party policy on prohibition. Antiprohibition was a by-product of their political ideologies, which stressed the limits of federal power, the sanctity of state prerogatives, and the value of self-government. It was also a product of the political mood of their region; the urban Northeast had long resented the Eighteenth

Amendment, and men like Smith, Cox, and Ritchie had built successful political careers by appealing to the wet vote.

Antiprohibitionists moved steadily closer to the Democrats throughout the decade, lured by the party's slow drift toward repeal and repelled by the GOP's increasing identification with the Eighteenth Amendment.[1] This process was best illustrated by the experiences of John Raskob and Pierre du Pont, who combined leadership and support of the AAPA with a deep involvement with the national Democratic organization. The connections between the AAPA and the Democratic conservative coalition extended beyond the 1920s and the fight against prohibition. Antiprohibitionism seemed peculiarly susceptible to transmutation into opposition to the New Deal. Within nine months of the repeal of the Eighteenth Amendment, the AAPA had been transformed into the American Liberty League by the same men who had organized, supported, and funded the AAPA. Of the seven members of the Liberty League's executive committee in 1934, three had served in the same position with the AAPA, and three more—Al Smith, John Davis, and Pauline Sabin—had also been prominent in the fight against prohibition.[2]

The leaders of the conservative coalition—Raskob, Davis, Smith, and Shouse—also became publicly identified as the New Deal's most prominent critics. Antiprohibition, the conservative coalition, and the American Liberty League were thus funded by the same sources, led by the same men, and united by the same philosophy of government.[3] An examination of antiprohibitionism is important to an understanding of the development of the conservative revolt against FDR after 1932.

Antiprohibitionism has only recently shed its unsavory reputation as a movement behind which America's wealthiest men concealed their desire to lower income taxes. Early historians of the campaign against the Eighteenth Amendment characterized the AAPA as a hypocritical "wrecking crew" which preached traditional American principles of government but practiced gross economic selfishness.[4] If the liquor trade was relegalized, the antiprohibitionists were supposed to have thought, then excise taxes would largely replace income taxes as the major source of federal revenue.[5] More recent historians, and most notably David E. Kyvig, have restored ideological credibility to the AAPA.[6] The movement was not a sham; it gathered, in Kyvig's phrase, the "mass public response" needed to repeal a constitutional amendment for the first and only time in American history because its concerns went to the heart of national values.[7] How far should the federal government intrude into the private habits of its citizens? Was prohibition's unpopularity endangering respect for *all* laws? Was it appropriate to use the Constitution to entrench sumptuary laws in the fundamental plan of government? Genuine social concern and deeply held ideological considerations, rather than economic self-interest, underpinned the movement to repeal national prohibition.[8]

Kyvig's argument is sustained by the example of the conservatives who were loosely termed the "Raskob group." Their papers do not substantiate the claim that taxation was their primary motive. Economic and fiscal arguments came to the fore only after the onset of the depression, in response to widespread concerns about the budgetary deficit and unemployment.[9] When Irénée du Pont detailed his objections to national prohibition to his cousin Coleman in 1926, he referred to taxation only tangentially. "To my mind the Volstead Act and the 18th Amendment have resulted in untold corruption of Governmental employees, demoralization of a considerable part of the young people, the poisoning of or blinding of hundreds, if not thousands, of citizens, the sacrifice of hundreds of millions of governmental income and is the opening wedge to tyranny which will become intolerable. It is only because the average man is rather stupid and rapidly becomes used to his surroundings that has prevented the people rising up against the iniquitous action of legislators acting through fear of the Anti-Saloon League."[10]

Nor were the AAPA's arguments simply elaborate justifications for a legal drink, for that purpose would have been served by a campaign for modification of the Volstead Act to allow for the legalization of beer and wine. By 1926 the cry of the wets had focused upon eventual repeal of the amendment; mere modification would not have resolved the challenge to political traditions and institutions presented by any form of national prohibition.[11] To James W. Wadsworth, a conservative Republican who had long been associated with the wet cause, prohibition "bedevilled our politics, multiplied corruption, and made hypocrites of millions."[12] Antiprohibition was as much a reform movement as that conducted by the dries since the early nineteenth century; it too was based upon a body of ideas concerning the acceptable limits of governmental power to correct social problems.[13]

Men like Pierre and Irénée du Pont expressed almost identical concern over the implications of the Eighteenth Amendment as did the leaders of the Democratic conservative coalition. The amendment had outlawed a major industry without compensation. Brewers and distillers, as well as their stockholders, had been stripped of their livelihoods and assets by a legislative coup. In 1916 there were 1,332 breweries operating in the United States, representing at least $800 million worth of fixed assets. In 1932 only 221 remained operational, making "near beer."[14] This was almost unprecedented in American constitutional law, comparable only to the effect of the Thirteenth Amendment.[15] Even the slave traders in 1787 had been allowed twenty years to rearrange their affairs. Thomas Gilmore, a leader of the Model License League, which had been created by the liquor industry to try to prevent the ratification of the Eighteenth Amendment, expressed this fear in a letter to Woodrow Wilson in 1918. "It has become a sort of fad for businessmen to look with more or less complacency on the goring of the liquor man's ox, but the time has arrived when every businessman must look for the gore of his own ox. The . . . amendment bids fair to start a landslide that will grow into an avalanche carrying private ownership of property over the brink of socialism and thence into the gulf of anarchy."[16]

To the antiprohibitionists, national prohibition had made the federal government into a policeman, regulating matters that had traditionally fallen within the jurisdiction of local government. If the federal government could outlaw the liquor industry by means of constitutional amendment, it could also ban other industries that fell into public disfavor. The du Ponts owed their wealth to the manufacture of explosives during World War I. Would the armaments and munitions industry be the next to be prohibited?[17]

Although the ideological connections between antiprohibition and political conservatism are clear, the actual process of transition from antiprohibitionism to anti–New Dealism remains largely unexplored.[18] With the prominent exception of David Kyvig, historians have generally taken this for granted after noting the organizational and ideological continuities between the AAPA and the American Liberty League.[19] Yet the transition from a campaign against a single target—the Eighteenth Amendment—to a campaign against a whole gamut of governmental policies and philosophy merits further inquiry.[20] The conservative attack upon the New Deal was as far-reaching as the New Deal itself, and it imposed new demands upon the leaders of the old antiprohibition movement. How did they apply the lessons of their fight against prohibition to political conditions after repeal? What organizational changes were necessary to broaden the single focus of the AAPA into a multifaceted defense of traditional political values? These questions are of great importance to the understanding of the conservative reaction to the New Deal, and they are also vital to a comprehension of the continuities between the Democratic conservative coalition, the AAPA, and the Liberty League. Examination of the experiences of two prominent antiprohibitionists, Pierre du Pont and William Stayton, illustrates these issues.

PIERRE DU PONT

Pierre du Pont had, in his own estimation, suffered greatly from federal intrusion. Like John Raskob, du Pont ended his corporatism at the factory door. As early as 1906 his recently reorganized powder company came under the scrutiny of antitrust investigators. Although Pierre's cousin Coleman was a generous supporter and a prominent member of the Republican party, his influence was not sufficient to prevent an antitrust suit against the Du Pont Company from coming to trial in 1908. Three years later, the company and its executives were held to have violated the Sherman Act, and its powder operations were broken up into independent units. Pierre and his brothers were infuriated by this interference by the Roosevelt and Taft administrations into the conduct of their firm.[21]

This anger was redirected against the Wilson administration after 1912. Progressivism, whether in the form of Theodore Roosevelt's trust-busting or Woodrow Wilson's New Freedom, met with little sympathy from Pierre du Pont. By 1916 relations with the administration were extremely strained; Wilson and his colleagues considered that the Du Pont Company was making too much money from the war, and for his part Pierre objected strenuously to the taxes imposed upon munitions makers in that year.[22] Du Pont made his displeasure clear by his donation of $92,500 to Charles Evans Hughes's presidential campaign of 1916, the largest single donation to the Republican cause.[23]

After the United States entered the war in April 1917, Secretary of War Newton D. Baker began negotiations with the company to construct a huge powder plant in Tennessee. Baker, who shared his president's distaste of the du Ponts' huge war profits, insisted upon a fixed profit of $1 million for the company instead of the 15 percent and a yearly commission proposed by the du Ponts. The du Pont proposal would have netted the company a profit of $13.5 million for the construction of the plant, and at least $22.5 million for the production of the gunpowder. Although a compromise was reached, whereby the company would build the plant for the fixed profit of $500,000 and then manufacture half of the powder requirements of the army for a profit of three and a half cents per pound, du Pont privately questioned why the company could not make an "appropriate" profit from the war effort.[24] This contract was replaced by a later agreement, whereby the company agreed to double its powder production capacity for a total profit of one dollar.[25]

Although relations between the administration and the company improved somewhat after 1917, Pierre du Pont's distrust of federal activism remained. He became apathetic or even hostile to both parties. Both, it seemed to him, interfered with individuals' conduct of their business and private life. He considered himself neither a Republican nor a Democrat, although it is likely that he moved even further away from the Democrats during the 1920 campaign. In October 1920 James Cox attacked Coleman du Pont, who was the GOP's chief fund-raiser, as "the Krupp of America." The du Pont family, according to Cox, were selfish munitions magnates who would stop at nothing to prevent the success of the League of Nations and the establishment of world peace.[26] In a sharp letter to Cox, Pierre described his charge as a malicious lie. The Du Pont Company, he argued, had made only small profits from the U.S. government. The really big profits had come from foreigners.[27]

The coming of national prohibition in 1920 was not sufficient to move du Pont from his apolitical position. Like many industrialists, he was even mildly in favor of the Eighteenth Amendment in the hope that sober workers would be more productive, healthier, and less combative.[28] By 1925, however, he had reassessed his position. Prohibition was not working; bootlegging was rampant, substandard beverages were causing health problems, and disrespect for liquor laws was endangering respect for the Constitution itself.[29] Still suspicious of the two major political parties, he and his brothers Irénée and Lammot joined the nonpartisan AAPA and soon became the association's most prominent and generous leaders.[30]

There is little evidence to suggest that du Pont was primarily motivated during the 1920s by the argument that modification or repeal of
national prohibition would reduce income and corporation taxes. This is
not to say, however, that he was uninterested in the taxation issue. In a
series of letters to Senator Smith Brookhart of Pennsylvania at the end
of 1923 and during 1924, du Pont made plain his belief that high income
taxes were not only economically self-defeating but also socially unjust.
High taxes on the very wealthy encouraged tax evasion and decreased investment. The poor always outnumbered the rich, he told Brookhart in
January 1924, and the imposition of high tax rates upon the wealthy was a
fearful weapon from which the democratic system gave the victims no redress.[31] There were, however, more important considerations at stake, he
told his kinsman Francis I. du Pont in August 1928, for the taxation argument was "nothing compared to the jeopardy to which our Constitution
is submitted by this Prohibition Amendment."[32]

The onset of the depression changed both the AAPA's and du Pont's
attitudes toward taxation and prohibition. Economic distress was an increasingly powerful political issue, and the AAPA could muster strong
arguments to take advantage of public concern about the cost of government. Captain William Stayton, the AAPA's founder, made this clear in
1932. "While Repeal is and ought to be primarily a question of whether or
not our government can endure if we ignore the fundamental difference
between the proper functions of Federal and State governments respectively," Stayton told the AAPA, "present conditions require us to give
serious thought to the prevailing economic situation." Stayton argued
that repeal might reduce personal and corporate taxes by as much as half.[33]
This new emphasis became even stronger after FDR's victory in 1932. As
part of the new economy measures instituted at the beginning of 1933, tax
increases, including a 5 percent surtax on dividends and a one-half-cent
increase in the gasoline tax, were due to come into effect in 1934 if the
Eighteenth Amendment remained effective at that time.[34] Du Pont and
his colleagues therefore had even stronger reasons for pushing for quick
passage of the Twenty-First Amendment, for the dividend tax increase in
particular struck at the basis of their enormous wealth.[35]

In the 1920s, however, such considerations were unforeseeable, and income and corporate taxation rates were already low. Prohibition offended
du Pont's conception of the proper extent of federal interference. The

"fundamental wrong" of the Eighteenth Amendment, he declared in 1926, was that it imposed odious restrictions upon the majority of Americans in the name of protecting the very small proportion of the population prone to alcoholism.[36] The amendment also "rendered useless" the property invested in the liquor industry, "and there was no thought of recompense to the innocents who suffered." Businessmen, he wrote a Florida nurseryman in 1928, had pressing reasons for opposing national prohibition. "If the XVIIIth Amendment is justified, so would an amendment to establish a national religion, to do away with trial by jury, to confinscate [sic] property, or to do any of the things forbidden by the Bill of Rights, which heretofore have been considered sacred against legislation. I am sure that you yourself would not relish an amendment . . . by which all of your profits save a bare living for yourself were confinscated to the public, and you would think such an amendment quite out of line with American tradition; but if you believe in the XVIIIth Amendment you must submit to the other one if it is proposed."[37]

"The whole prohibition effort, as conducted," he complained in 1925, "has been an outrage to American institutions," including the Constitution itself.[38] Like Albert Ritchie in 1922, du Pont was worried that it was too easy to change the Constitution. He was convinced, furthermore, that the Eighteenth Amendment was unconstitutional. He came to this conclusion early in 1928 and spent much of the next three years devising arguments to support it. The prohibition amendment, he argued, assumed that any change to the Constitution, legally adopted, was permissible. "The fallacy of such an assumption," he declared in a 1929 memorandum, "may be shown very easily by reduction to an absurdity. Let us suppose," he continued, "an Amendment was proposed abolishing private property in the States of Massachusetts, Pennsylvania, Ohio, Michigan, Connecticut, New Jersey, Indiana, West Virginia, New York, Virginia, Illinois and California." Such an amendment would be theoretically passable if it received two-thirds of a quorum in each House and if all the other 36 states assented to it, despite the fact that the twelve affected states contained 50.7 per cent of the total population of the United States. If the Eighteenth Amendment was legal, du Pont warned, then this amendment would be as well.[39]

Rather than accept such an unpalatable conclusion, he argued that the Constitution was not subject to unlimited change. The Bill of Rights, he thought, was essential to the republican form of government guaranteed to the states by article 4 of the Constitution. No subsequent amendment could annul the protections afforded by the first ten amendments.[40] The Eighteenth Amendment contravened the Fourth Amendment because searches for and seizures of alcohol were not "reasonable." "If the moderate use of alcohol is admitted to constitutional prohibition," he concluded, "we must prepare ourselves for a life of restriction and regulation far narrower than the confines of the most absolute monarchy ever known and with no semblance to freedom in the conduct of our lives."[41]

Du Pont returned to his constitutional reflections in a 1931 letter to John Raskob. There were, he thought, two classes of rights "more or less distinct one from the other." The first group were "inalienable" rights, referred to by the Declaration of Independence, codified in the Bill of Rights, and repeated in almost all of the state constitutions. These rights stemmed from God and nature, and they could not be abridged or surrendered. The second class of rights were those which were creatures of law, either delegated by the people to representative bodies or created by those bodies themselves in the process of governance.[42] National prohibition offended Americans' inalienable rights. To support this contention, he turned to the experience of prohibition enforcement. If the people had genuinely surrendered their right to drink, he told Raskob, they would have supported prohibition in practice. Instead, they had reacted to the Eighteenth Amendment's abrogation of "the universal right of centuries to possess and use intoxicating liquor" by refusing to obey it. The amendment was therefore "subject to the fate [of all laws] referred to in the Declaration of Independence; if they do not meet with popular approval, they are ignored."[43]

These arguments were scarcely unassailable. Du Pont appears to have argued that the Eighteenth Amendment was ultra vires the Constitution; sumptuary laws could not be inserted into the fundamental plan of government and were therefore invalid regardless of the ratification process. This argument had been put forward in the *National Prohibition Cases* of 1920 and had been clearly rejected by the Supreme Court. The Constitution, the Court held, was capable of embracing any subject that had been duly ratified in accordance with article 5.[44]

Du Pont's personal conception of the right to drink as "inalienable" was without legal foundation. The fact that he considered such a right to exist implied an extremely broad view of the extent of "inalienable rights" which extended far beyond those listed by the Declaration of Independence. In 1928 he had made this clear to Professor Hugh Willis of Indiana University Law School. "Such rights as can be pursued without any injury to others or to society in general," he told Willis, "should be held inalienable and not subject to change at the whim of a few people, or even a majority."[45] He therefore proposed a subjective test on the basis of social welfare to decide which rights were protected from constitutional abridgement. His antimajoritarian conception of legal change casts grave doubt over whether he considered that any rights could be altered by the democratic process. This contradicted his view of two classes of rights that he expounded to Raskob in 1931. Who would decide if a given "right" was injurious to "society in general" if the majority of citizens could not?

Du Pont had come to conclusions which denied the right of the majority to alter their form of government, a right which underpinned the Constitution itself. The experience of national prohibition had led him to intimate that the agenda of constitutional change was effectively closed; any more accretions of federal power would contravene either his broad definition of "inalienable rights" or his unrealistic test of complete popular approval of any change to the "rights" of the people. Antiprohibition, in short, had conditioned him to regard any increase in the power of the federal government as a travesty of the Constitution. As subsequent events would show, the implications of his antiprohibitionism quickly molded his attitude toward the New Deal.

The antimajoritarian bent of du Pont's constitutional theories was also reflected in his social thinking during the 1920s. The Eighteenth Amendment, he thought, graphically illustrated the dangers inherent in majority rule. The great challenge before American statecraft was therefore to find ways to limit the political power of the ignorant, the indigent, and the weak so that it could not be turned against those who had succeeded in life. In 1931 he and Raskob vehemently opposed the establishment of a Delaware old-age pension program funded from taxation revenue. Care of the elderly, they argued, was best left to "interested relatives and friends" rather than the state and its taxpayers.[46] When Ella Cordray, chairwoman of the Delaware branch of the WCTU, wrote to du Pont in 1925 with the opinion that prohibition had saved millions of former drunkards' children from lives of penury and abuse, he disagreed. "A much more humane and effective plan," he replied, "would be the sterilization of individuals who through excessive use of alcohol, or in fact any other reason, have made themselves unfit to have children."[47] Two years later, his views had progressed from medical sterilization to political disenfranchisement. "Our endeavor," he wrote his friend Arthur Little, "should be to discourage the unintelligent vote" by refusing to support "any party that tries to promote indiscriminate voting." His rationale for this point of view demonstrated the dark side of "business principles" in political life. "If we let the mass of voters alone," he told Little, "they would not vote, and there would be some chance for intelligent capable people to operate governmental affairs the same way that they are permitted to operate corporation affairs."[48]

The directions in which du Pont's antiprohibitionism pushed his political thinking can be seen in his changing ideas on the most appropriate ways in which the liquor business should be conducted in a postrepeal America. He faced a delicate task in formulating plans for the resumption of legal liquor sales, for he had to balance the demands of public opinion with those of his own philosophy. During the 1920s dry sentiment was still strong, and great care was needed to reassure undecided voters that the evils of untrammeled liquor sales, the old saloons, and public drunkenness would not return. How much state interference in the revived liquor industry was permissible to satisfy public opinion on the one hand and the arguments of the antiprohibitionists on the other? In addressing this question, du Pont undertook a philosophical journey which had profound implications for what he saw as the proper role of government in society at large and in business in particular. The lessons he learned during his fight against the Eighteenth Amendment were of clear relevance to his later battles against FDR in the 1930s.

When he first came to consider postrepeal plans in 1925, du Pont supported the adoption of the "Quebec plan" for liquor control, established in that province in 1921. It created a government monopoly over the sale of all distilled liquor. The Quebec system was managed by a powerful Liquor Commission which had complete control over the marketing of spirituous liquors and regulatory powers over the sale of beer and wine.[49] Initially this scheme seemed to him to be the most likely means by which Americans could wean themselves from national prohibition. In a *Current History* article published in October 1926, he argued that the "liquor problem" would remain for many years, and perhaps forever. "Therefore," he concluded, "the only question before us is:—What means of distribution of alcohol that must be consumed will cause the least harm?" His reply contradicted his whole political philosophy. "There can be but one answer," he wrote: "State control of sale and distribution of all intoxicating drinks." The Quebec system ensured that the quality of liquors was guaranteed by the state and that the saloon would not reappear. Quebec's rates of drunkenness, he noted approvingly, had dropped dramatically since the establishment of its government dispensary system, and bootlegging had almost disappeared.[50]

As du Pont's opposition to national prohibition hardened, he began to reassess his support of the Quebec system. The logic of antiprohibitionism scarcely permitted the replacement of one form of state control with another. Even while he was publicly singing its praises, he was privately qualifying Quebec's reliance upon state control and monopoly. In a letter to the economist William Z. Ripley at the end of 1925, he reaffirmed his general opposition "to government rule and regulation of any kind for the reason that the Government in its administration is no stronger than the individuals who fill the governmental positions."[51] However in 1926 the process of reconciling these views with his postprohibition plans led him to argue that the federal government was not the appropriate agency for liquor control and that the dispensary system would have to be conducted by the individual states.[52]

Although this change was in keeping with du Pont's emphasis upon states' rights, the Quebec plan still did not sit well with his philosophy of the proper role of government in business. It is likely that he saw little alternative to this plan in 1926, when antiprohibition sentiment in the country at large was still fragile and localized. Between 1926 and 1930, however, the increasing discontent with prohibition emboldened him to apply his philosophy of government more fully. He began to edge away from his earlier support of a state monopoly of the liquor industry. By 1928 he was privately expressing the belief that the same logic which disqualified the federal government from control of the liquor industry also applied to the state governments. These, too, were made up of officious bureaucrats who were more adept at wastage and corruption than at applying "business principles."[53] "Personally," he told a correspondent in 1928, "I advocate turning the whole liquor business over to a corporation organized by substantial people, to be operated at a reasonably small profit, the Government to obtain all profits above the agreed amount."[54]

Du Pont's retreat to privatism and ideological consistency again manifested itself in his advocacy of a second postrepeal plan in 1930. This was based upon the system prevailing in Sweden and closely paralleled his revised opinion concerning the proper role of the government in the liquor trade. Instead of Quebec's state dispensaries, Sweden had created a private monopoly which had complete control of the sale of all beverages containing more than 3.6 percent alcohol. The liquor corporation was allowed a maximum profit of 5 percent.[55] In an article prepared for the *Chicago Tribune* in March 1930, du Pont extolled the virtues of this arrangement. "A majority of the American people," he argued, "will agree that State governments are not capable of conducting business operations." This was especially true regarding a business as intricate and sensitive as the sale of liquor.[56] If the liquor trade was entrusted to a corporation, the twin evils of governmental corruption and bootlegging would disappear.

This new plan involved a considerable retraction of state power from that envisaged by the Quebec system he had advocated four years previously. The federal government's influence would extend only to the protection of dry states from the interstate transportation of liquor.[57] The state governments would supervise the conduct of their liquor corporations, and they would retain all excess profits. At this stage he also envisaged that the states would set statutory prohibitions upon the sale of liquor to alcoholics and minors. To this end he suggested the adoption of the Swedish *motbok*, a purchaser's license card upon which all transactions were entered. Motboks were issued by the states only to people more than twenty-one years of age who could show sufficient economic means to afford to buy alcoholic beverages. Only one *motbok* could be issued to a family, and only four liters of distilled spirits could be bought per month. Motboks could be forfeited upon proof of chronic drunkenness.[58] Beyond these "restrictions of undoubted propriety," he warned, excessive regulation should be avoided at all costs. The key to effective liquor control was not state coercion but rather individual responsibility.[59]

He retreated even further from the concept of state control of the liquor industry in the years between 1930 and 1933. He disavowed the *motbok* system of purchasers' licenses at the end of 1930 as an encouragement to bootleggers, and he also reconsidered his earlier denial of the "right" to drink to habitual drunkards.[60] In 1933 he was influential in the formulation of Delaware's liquor policy after the repeal of the Eighteenth Amendment. The Delaware system, of which he became the sole commissioner, reduced the state's involvement in the dispensing of liquor to a bare minimum. Delaware chose a simple licensing system which authorized properly qualified individuals to sell both beer and spirits. License fees were deliberately high to discourage undesirable licensees. The sale of drinks by the glass in taverns was allowed, and the state's primary function was one of supervision of its licensees.[61] This licensing system, with local variations, was adopted by twenty-five states and territories after 1933. Eighteen states either retained prohibition or adopted variations of the Quebec system, with state or county public monopolies to control the sale of distilled or fermented beverages.[62]

Du Pont justified the minimal state intervention of the Delaware scheme in terms of the benefits to producers rather than to the consumers of alcoholic beverages. In language that foreshadowed the New Left analysis of the usefulness of regulation to businessmen, he told Stayton, "I agree with you that paternalism is to be avoided and that the maintenance of standards should not be too far subject to Government inspection. On the other hand, it seems wise and necessary that standards should exist so that those who do seek standard quality may avail themselves of the fact to advertize their wares. Without standard, the purveyor of food and drink is quite at the mercy of unscrupulous competitors."[63]

By 1933, therefore, du Pont had followed the implications of his antiprohibition to its logical philosophical destination of antistatism and "individual responsibility." In the process he had unconsciously laid the foundations for his later opposition to the New Deal as an unprecedented expansion of federal power into the business life of the nation. His obsession with the legitimate extent of statism in modern society, first aroused by his troubles with antitrust legislation and then strengthened by his experience under national prohibition, would become the basis of his political philosophy during the 1930s. Antiprohibition had been the catalyst for breaking his political apathy, but its philosophical implications had created in him a more rigid conservatism and a more definite determination to combat any growth of federal activism. Antiprohibition had been du Pont's rehearsal for his revolt against the New Deal.

WILLIAM STAYTON

As Pierre du Pont's philosophical journey through the ramifications of antiprohibition was guided by his objection to state interference in the lives and businesses of its citizens, that of William H. Stayton followed his single-minded adherence to states' rights. Examination of his antiprohibitionism reveals not an evolution of thought, for the basic assumptions of his political philosophy remained unchanged throughout the 1920s, but rather a clear illustration of the ease with which the tenets of antiprohibition could be transferred to a challenge to the New Deal. It was Stayton who provided the ideological and organizational transition between the two movements, and an analysis of the ways in which he brought it about provides an insight into the transmutation of the AAPA into the American Liberty League.

William Stayton was the undisputed hero of antiprohibition. Born in Delaware in 1861, he graduated from Annapolis and served two tours of duty in the navy. He graduated from Columbian (later George Washington) University Law School in 1889 and practiced admiralty law in New York, taking time off to return to the navy during the Spanish-American War. He entered political life as a bitter opponent of William Jennings Bryan and his "free-silver heresies" in 1896.[64] His primary concern, however, was for the maintenance of states' rights against a federal government that had greatly expanded its powers under the influence of progressive activism. The original nature of the Constitution, he thought, had been perverted by centralism and bureaucracy. The Sixteenth Amendment had crippled the states as financial entities, and it had tipped the balance of power toward Washington. Further encroachments of federal power had to be opposed if the genius of the Founding Fathers' creation was to be preserved. The Eighteenth Amendment was an egregious example of federal intrusion, and he resolved to devote all his energies to opposing its adoption and then lobbying for its repeal. To these ends he created the AAPA in 1919.[65]

Stayton founded his association not on promises of lowered taxes but rather on the principle of states' rights.[66] Federal dictation of what citizens from Alaska to Louisiana could drink created disrespect for the Constitution, and it served to "start crops of dissensions and perhaps of future civil war."[67] In 1922 he described the Eighteenth Amendment as a "rotten insult to the American people," and a "mutilation of the Constitution." "This prohibition business," he told a New York City audience, "is only a symptom of a disease, the desire of fanatics to meddle in the other man's affairs and to regulate the details of your lives and mine."[68]

Stayton raised other arguments against national prohibition that found a sympathetic response from within the Democratic conservative coalition. The Eighteenth Amendment, he declared in 1923, was nothing more than legal theft of an entire industry's assets. As such it was a worrying precedent of state confiscation. Stayton's language and imagery must have added to the du Ponts' own fears of losing their enormous wealth by similar acts of public appropriation.

> A few years ago a barrel of whisky was private property; objectionable property if you will, but property none-the-less, manufactured under Government supervision, gauged, stamped and taxed by Federal officers. So, breweries and distilleries and their contained machinery were private property, duly recognized and taxed. Then came forward people saying, "We do not approve that kind of property; we think it works harm to the people; and because we do not approve it, we demand that it be confiscated," and in effect, confiscated it was.
>
> But there are many people in this country who do not approve accumulated or inherited fortunes, believing them to be harmful to the people; indeed, some of those among us do not approve of any kind of private ownership. When the time comes that these classes demand confiscations to suit their beliefs, the employers will be in no position to turn to the working man for help in sustaining property rights; for the poor man may well reply, "No, it was *you* who made this precedent, and you made it for no good purpose, but with the intent to rob me of my hours of relaxation, so that you might get more work and more profit out of me.[69]

Despite Stayton's best efforts, the AAPA's early years were not easy ones. Although the association claimed to have 100,000 members by the spring of 1921, this was most probably an exaggeration.[70] Its chief financier was Stayton himself, who contributed $12,000 per year to support his organization between 1919 and 1924.[71] His attempts to find wealthy supporters brought him into close contact with the du Ponts, and then with the Democratic conservative coalition itself. By the beginning of 1924, he had been mentioned in William Gibbs McAdoo's correspondence as being part of the enemy's camp. Stayton, one Californian wrote to the secretary, was "a former Delawarian of malodorous memory. He is resourceful, unscrupulous, influential with the itching palm crowd and thoroughly untrustworthy."[72] The Anti Saloon League, too, was becoming concerned at the AAPA's increasingly sophisticated and well-funded campaign against prohibition.[73]

The du Ponts did not agree, for their support of the AAPA became so great as to relieve Stayton of all his financial burdens. Pierre and Irénée du Pont, along with John Raskob, contributed generously to the AAPA from 1926 onward. In 1929 they gave $130,000; two years later the total had risen to over $200,000.[74] Their largesse did not come without strings. By 1928 Stayton's methods were thought too old-fashioned and his attitude toward his organization too possessive. In that year Pierre and Irénée du Pont, Raskob, and Senator James Wadsworth of New York masterminded a reconstruction of the AAPA's leadership. Stayton's power was greatly diminished after the appointment of an executive committee led by Henry H. Curran.[75] A new publicity campaign was entrusted to Bruce Barton—the best-known American publicist of the time—and Stayton was given the largely titular job of chairman of the national board of directors. Curran's performance was disappointing, and in 1932 he was replaced by Jouett Shouse. Stayton remained, however, as the philosophical conscience of the movement that he had pioneered.[76]

The story of the antiprohibition movement and its eventual triumph has already been comprehensively described by David Kyvig. Although the AAPA claimed much credit for the repeal of the Eighteenth Amendment in 1933, it seems clear that it was the depression, rather than the AAPA's publicity, that gave the wets their triumph. Suddenly in 1929 prohibition became not only an annoyance but also an incubus upon American life; with repeal came the hope of new revenues and—most important of all—the precious hope of jobs.[77] Another significant factor in the demise of national prohibition was the Anti Saloon League's failure to sustain and defend its great triumph of 1920.[78] Nevertheless it is difficult to dispute Kyvig's claim that the AAPA's work since 1919 had done much to prepare the way for the Twenty-First Amendment. Americans everywhere had been made painfully aware of the widespread corruption, organized crime, and hypocrisy that national prohibition had foisted upon the nation. When the depression struck, Americans were already well aware of prohibition's shortcomings, and for that the AAPA could claim much responsibility.[79]

Once repeal was achieved, however, the AAPA was forced to consider its future. It was decided to disband the organization in December 1933, immediately following the ratification of the Twenty-First Amendment. A new group called the Repeal Associates emerged in its place. By May 1934, ninety-seven of the former directors of the AAPA, including the du Ponts, Raskob, and Shouse, had joined the new organization. Stayton served as its leader, and Pierre du Pont provided most of its small budget.[80] The Repeal Associates were to play a crucial intermediary role between the AAPA and the American Liberty League.

The Repeal Associates' charter was publicly announced in April 1934. Two of its four stated purposes related directly to its antiprohibition antecedents; its function was to "hold together that splendid group of men and women" who had worked so hard to remove the Eighteenth Amendment, so as to "act as a clearing house for information concerning developments in liquor control in the various States."[81] Repeal Associates was to be much more, however, than a watchdog over postrepeal liquor laws. The associates would keep state authorities abreast of developments in Washington that affected their powers and prerogatives, and they would monitor federal legislation so as to safeguard the constitutional balance of powers between the central government and the states.[82] From its inception, Repeal Associates concentrated upon broad political issues rather than the supervision of state liquor legislation.[83]

To this end Stayton began to formulate plans and policies to guide the associates. He produced seven long memoranda during the first three weeks of August 1934, laying out a blueprint for both the Repeal Associates and the newly formed Liberty League. They represented a conservative manifesto that made clear the lessons and implications of the antiprohibition campaign in the new political context of the depression and the New Deal. Stayton devoted the first three of his memoranda to a discussion of what he saw as the single greatest threat to the American system of government: the "usurpation of power by officials." "I do not mean," Stayton declared at the outset of his disquisitions, "to place special emphasis on the policies developed under the present [Roosevelt] administration—much as I fear and deplore them." The trends which worried him so much predated 1933.[84] Although the Constitution had clearly limited federal power to a defined list of specified items and had divided that power between three independent departments, these impediments had proven insufficient to restrain "that lust of power inherent in official breasts."[85]

This usurpation of power had taken many forms, and it had affected each of the three departments of the federal government. Subsequent memoranda gave examples of this encroachment. The federal legislative department had ignored the limits of the constitutional grant of power to the Congress. Stayton praised Grover Cleveland's veto of the Texas Seeds Bill in 1887, which denied Congress any power to relieve individual suffering. Yet the Congress had subsequently usurped this power, recently passing direct-relief legislation in defiance of traditional constitutional principles. This represented an illegal reinterpretation of the General Welfare Clause of the Constitution.[86] The executive department, too, had assumed power by vesting its bureaus not only with executive power but also with judicial functions, in clear contravention of the separation of powers institutionalized by the Constitution. Unelected bureaucrats now exercised enormous power over every citizen in the United States; taxation tribunals and investigators conducted quasi-judicial and executive functions that were seemingly beyond judicial review.[87]

The federal judiciary, too, had been guilty of usurpation. The Supreme Court had shown its willingness to alter constitutional interpretation "on the casual assumption that changes in public sentiment justify such reversal without constitutional amendment."[88] Only months before the Supreme Court's 1935 assaults upon the New Deal, Stayton concluded sadly that "the court has not been an effective instrument in combating legislative and executive usurpations." During World War I it had allowed the broadest possible reading of Congress's constitutional power to declare war, to the detriment of private business and individual rights; it had decided that it would no longer hear taxpayers' suits questioning the right of the Congress to appropriate funds for unconstitutional purposes, and it had acquiesced in the illegal delegation of judicial and executive powers to the burgeoning federal bureaucracy.[89]

Having outlined the problem in general terms, Stayton went on to provide two specific examples. The first of these concerned federal taxation. In keeping with his colleagues in the AAPA, his attention had been forcibly drawn by the depression to the taxation issue. Demands for sharply progressive income taxation worried him greatly, and these concerns led him to reexamine the Sixteenth Amendment as a whole.[90] He was disturbed by what he found. The federal taxation system, he thought, had been perverted by reformers to serve ends that were far from those originally intended by the framers of the amendment. The elements of an ideal taxation system, in his view, were equality, uniformity, and universality. The Supreme Court had allowed each of these ideals to be severely compromised. "Uniformity" now applied only in the geographic sense; now the wealthy paid tax at a higher rate than their less fortunate fellow citizens. The requirements of "equality" and "universality," too, had been removed by the Congress and a compliant Court. Year by year, Stayton complained, legislators "strive to exclude ever greater numbers from the tax lists and to increase the burdens of the few."[91]

The federal inheritance tax, "under a fair interpretation of the Constitution," was unconstitutional. The right of bequest was a sacred and ancient one, and it qualified as one of Pierre du Pont's "inalienable" rights which could not be tampered with. The Supreme Court, however, had upheld this usurpation as permissible. Stayton reserved his most damning criticism for the Sixteenth Amendment's income tax. This, he considered, was "the gravest danger of all the many that confront us. [S]o long as the Income Tax is interpreted as at present, it offers an irresistable [*sic*] temptation to the demagogue to confiscate accumulated property and to apply it as a slush fund to buy his election through doles to the venal."[92] Pierre du Pont, too, came to regret that his political energies during the 1920s had not been directed toward the repeal of the Sixteenth rather than the Eighteenth Amendment. National prohibition, he came to see, was merely the "younger brother" of the federal income tax power.[93]

Stayton, however, fell short of advocating the repeal of the amendment in 1934. This, he thought, would be irresponsible during a time of acute budgetary imbalance, and it would also leave the wealthy leaders of Repeal Associates vulnerable to the charge that their motives were "selfish and unworthy." A campaign to repeal the amendment, in contrast to that against national prohibition, "would carry no emotional appeal to the mass of the people and would be devoid of the necessary "moral issue." Far better, he thought, that the amendment be reinterpreted so as to free it from the usurpations of the reformers and income redistributors.[94]

Stayton's second example of usurpation at work concerned the "squandering" of public monies for unconstitutional purposes.[95] He estimated that nearly 75 percent of the current federal budget of $12 billion was appropriated for unconstitutional ends. He also quoted with approval James M. Beck's gloomy prediction concerning the effect of swollen federal appropriations. "Unless the tide of increasing public expenditures begins to ebb," Beck declared, "this Nation, originally dedicated to individualism, will increasingly become a socialist State. Indeed, few States are more socialistic. . . . Russia is not more bureaucratic than America."[96]

Stayton agreed with this startling conclusion. The Congress had, he maintained, no enumerated power to appropriate money for relief purposes. Cleveland had established this principle in 1887, and Stayton refused to countenance the theory that changing times and contexts lent constitutional legitimacy to the provision of direct federal relief. The bulk of the budget, he noted, was devoted to "welfare and relief work and for going into business ventures, buying up commodities, lending money, guaranteeing debts and securities, etc., in defiance of the Constitution." In the face of the distress arising from the depression, Stayton argued, it "would have been easy, and it would have taken but a very few months" to amend the Constitution so as to allow such appropriations. No emergency and no suffering, he implied, was so great as to justify constitutional "change by usurpation."[97]

There were now 600,000 "federal job-holders" on the public payroll, and this army was being swelled by the millions who now received direct federal relief. These enormous numbers meant votes, and votes meant power. In order to satisfy this constituency, the Roosevelt administration was creating bureau after bureau, and relief project after relief project. Many of these were patently useless, inefficient, or extravagant, yet they were apparently safe from judicial disqualification or organized political opposition.[98] What was needed was a well-organized movement of taxpayers, property holders, and states' rights advocates to mount a determined assault upon this edifice of unconstitutional greed before it entrenched itself permanently.

It was to this problem that Stayton devoted the final two memoranda of his series. He turned first to discuss the remedies that were necessary to return America to its constitutional bearings. Drawing upon his naval training, Stayton laid out an "Estimate of the Situation" for the coming campaign.[99] The "enemy" was composed of federal officeholders and "those receiving some form of federal aid," including farmers and the unemployed. These groups, and their dependents, were perhaps fifteen million strong. "Our own forces," those citizens "willing to make sacrifices for liberty, individualism, and personal and property rights," potentially numbered forty million. How many of this huge group would actually join the crusade depended on the quality of the Repeal Associates' message and publicity.[100] The final memorandum dealt with tactics. The people had to be persuaded to take back the power that they had lost through usurpation. Those men and women who had led the AAPA had the necessary financial resources, leadership, organizational ability, and publicity skills to save the Constitution from its enemies.[101] The fight against prohibition had been merely a successful prelude to the struggle that lay ahead.

William Stayton's journey from the AAPA to the Liberty League showed the ease with which antiprohibitionism transformed itself into anti–New Dealism. These changes were organizational in nature; the philosophical foundations for the conservative revolt of the 1930s had already been laid. Pierre du Pont took five years to follow the implications of his own antiprohibitionism to its logical conclusion of opposition to all forms of federal expansion and activism; William Stayton made the transition in three weeks and within the space of seven memoranda.

INCREASING OPPOSITION TO THE NEW DEAL

Although Stayton had been in little doubt of the implications of antiprohibition for the New Deal, his fellow antiprohibition leaders still had one more step to take. In the case of Pierre du Pont, this took the form of a political lesson learned during the first months of FDR's administration. Although the Democratic platform's planks on prohibition and government economy had won his approval during the 1932 campaign, he was only a hesitant supporter of Roosevelt himself. The Oglethorpe and "forgotten man" speeches worried him greatly, and the tenor of FDR's postnomination campaign had done little to assuage these fears.[102] Yet for him the overwhelming issue in 1932 was the repeal of prohibition, and Roosevelt's platform was unequivocal on that point.

Swallowing his fears about FDR's character, philosophy, and associates, du Pont not only voted for the Democratic ticket but also contributed over $27,000 to the campaign.[103]

Franklin Roosevelt gave du Pont an opportunity to observe the New Deal at first hand by appointing him chairman of the Industrial Advisory Board and member of the National Labor Board in November 1933. These bodies were creatures of the National Industrial Recovery Act (NIRA), and they were designed to hear disputes over labor matters arising out of the various industrial codes.[104] General Hugh Johnson had devised a program whereby prominent industrialists and labor leaders served on these boards for rotating terms of three months.[105] When du Pont's invitation came, he accepted with alacrity. Like many of his peers, he was initially impressed by the National Recovery Administration (NRA) in action. Although he had at first shuddered at the extent of the president's powers under the NIRA, he told reporters in February 1934, he had since become "completely converted." The code-making and review processes were beneficial to businessmen because industrywide problems could be resolved without fears of infringing antitrust legislation. He also noted with approval that labor disputes were on the wane.[106]

By the second half of 1934, however, his attitude had changed markedly. His experiences in Washington convinced him that Stayton's charge that bureaucrats were inherently inefficient and megalomaniac was correct. Extravagance, he recalled to a cousin at the end of 1935, seemed "part of the program," and FDR's demand for "unlimited funds to be placed at his disposal" without proper constitutional authorization seemed to him to be "a dangerous experiment which should not be tolerated."[107] In August 1934, while Stayton was writing his seven memoranda, du Pont was noting with increasing concern the seeming permanence of such "emergency" New Deal measures as the NRA. He, too, became convinced of a conspiracy on the part of the New Dealers to change permanently the traditional balance between federal power, state prerogatives, and private business.[108]

Du Pont resigned from the National Labor Board at the end of June 1934. In his letter of resignation to the president, he suggested various changes to the code-review process which pointed to his other concerns about the NRA as a whole. Minorities, he told Roosevelt, should be given a place in the process and protected from exploitation. By this he meant those workers who chose not to join trade unions. His concern that the

NRA was too favorable to unions led him to suggest new limitations upon their freedom of action. Employees should be "protected from the professional agitator," and there should be a legal requirement that employees exhaust all remedies provided by NIRA before resorting to a strike.[109] Within six months, therefore, du Pont had gone from praising the NRA as a savior of industrial employers to criticizing it as an unwelcome boost to trade unions and industrial disputation.

While Pierre du Pont battled the bureaucracy in Washington, the AAPA was already coming to blows with the New Deal. At the beginning of 1933 Jouett Shouse, the AAPA's president, publicly criticized a proposal that the Twenty-First Amendment (which repealed the Eighteenth) should provide that the federal government retain residual control over liquor sales in the states. This, Shouse complained, was contrary to the spirit of states' rights that was inherent in the antiprohibition movement. The federal authorities, he argued, should vacate the field of liquor control.[110]

The AAPA's concern for states' rights also led it to oppose the NRA code devised for the newly legalized liquor industry at the end of 1933. The Federal Alcohol Control Administration (FACA) was established on December 4, 1933, the day before the Twenty-First Amendment was ratified. FACA was charged with formulating and enforcing codes to promote fair trade and labor practices within the liquor industry. Answerable only to the president, FACA exercised enormous power over the industry, including the right to grant and revoke permits to engage in liquor manufacture and the authority to control production.[111] At a victory dinner held to celebrate the ratification of the Twenty-First Amendment, Shouse warned his fellow AAPA members that "the code forced upon the distilling industry" threatened to undermine the whole ideological thrust of antiprohibition. The NRA code promised a recrudescence of government control "by the Federal Government which gives the industry no opportunity to speak for itself or to act for itself."[112]

Three days later, on December 8, 1933, Shouse sharpened his attack upon the NRA in a speech delivered to the New England Society of Pennsylvania. The great lesson of prohibition, he argued, was that the federal government was incapable of regulating the private affairs of its citizens. Its only useful function was the protection of dry states by such legislation as the Webb-Kenyon Act. This legislation, passed in 1913, had divested intoxicating liquor of its interstate character, thus allowing dry states to prevent it from crossing their borders.[113] The NRA code, however, flew in the face of states' rights by creating "a super-power of the Federal Government known as the Federal Alcohol Control Administration."[114] This was empowered to enforce the code's production and price provisions as it saw fit. The federal government was therefore attempting to "exercise a power over the industry that might prove as unwise and as undesirable as methods employed in the attempt to enforce the unenforceable Eighteenth Amendment." If this unfortunate situation came to pass, Shouse predicted, "it may well be that the people of America will once more be compelled to register their protest against Federal control of the liquor industry."[115]

Shouse went on to make some suggestions concerning more appropriate solutions to the problems posed by the relegalization of the liquor industry. The significance of these comments extended far beyond their primary focus of liquor legislation, because they reflected an increased hostility to all forms of government regulation of industry. His observations therefore closely paralleled those of Pierre du Pont and William Stayton. He began by criticizing the various state liquor schemes for being "too severe." Governments across the United States had been too eager to place high license fees and taxation rates upon distilled liquor. This, he warned, only perpetuated the evil of bootlegging.[116] He even advocated the return of the saloon, albeit in a sanitized form. This was a clear contradiction of the whole thrust of the AAPA's publicity effort during the 1920s, which had stressed that the saloon would never reappear in any form.[117] With repeal now achieved, he expressed a different point of view. Human nature, he thought, demanded public places for drinking liquor, and this could not be ignored. Unless provision was made for sales of drink by the glass, the speakeasy would never disappear.[118] Shouse's views were therefore in keeping with the changing nature of the antiprohibition argument. His emphasis was now upon the minimum of state interference with the liquor industry; with repeal achieved, the earlier concessions to dry opinion could be considerably modified. The antiprohibitionists were beginning to show their true colors.

By August 1934 the transformation from antiprohibitionism to anti–New Dealism was complete. The economic conservatives who had organized and funded the AAPA were now intent upon putting their experience to use against the New Deal. They approached that task with some confidence, for they were in no doubt that the two crusades were philosophically consistent and that the logic of antiprohibition demanded that the New Deal be opposed. Armed with these comforting certainties, the American Liberty League set out to convince the electorate at large of the necessity for ideological consistency during a time of acute economic distress.

13

THE POLITICS OF CONSISTENCY

THE AMERICAN LIBERTY LEAGUE, 1934–1940

The American Liberty League has not fared well at the hands of historians. Like the AAPA, it has generally been dismissed as an elaborate front for the greed and spite of millionaires and their corporations disgruntled at the high cost of reform.[1] "The fundamental danger that the du Ponts increasingly perceived in the New Deal," Robert F. Burk argued in 1990, "was its threat to the economic prerogatives that the family had built up over the decades."[2] For their part, the New Dealers claimed that the league, while preaching the sanctity of the Constitution, acted as if "the Revolution was fought to make Long Island safe for polo players."[3] Historians have, by and large, agreed that its views were scarcely worthy of analysis. Despite the flood of monographs, articles, and essays on the New Deal, the activities of its best-organized, best-funded, and most ideologically coherent opposition have received little attention in their own right.[4] This chapter explores the origins, views, and activities of this important organization from the perspective of the Democratic conservative coalition, who formed its leadership nucleus and provided the bulk of its funds.

The existing interpretation of the concerns of the Liberty League can be described as a "spite and ignorance" argument. Although the league is conceded to have expressed a coherent political ideology, other factors are accorded greater importance in its creation and activities.[5] It has long been seen as primarily a vehicle for spiteful attacks upon Roosevelt. "Not a few" of its leaders, George Wolfskill argued in 1950, "had reason to dislike Roosevelt because of some personal unpleasantness with the President." Shouse had been slighted over the permanent chairmanship affair; John Raskob felt that FDR had betrayed his confidence by opposing the home rule plan in 1931, and Al Smith still smarted from his defeat at the Chicago convention.[6] Such personal animosities made the League as much an anti–Roosevelt organization as an anti-New Deal one.

Wolfskill argued that the league was also fatally flawed by ignorance. Its leaders were so enraged by FDR and so fearful for their personal fortunes that they overlooked the true nature of the New Deal. Their charges that Roosevelt was leading the nation to Communism and that he was riding roughshod over the Constitution in order to entrench himself in power reflected an "appalling misunderstanding" of the philosophy of the New Deal. They missed the point that FDR's programs were aimed not to destroy American liberties and prosperity but to save them. The New Deal gave Americans time to collect themselves and to reassert their faith in a system that had seemed dangerously close to collapse in 1932. Roosevelt was in fact the savior of businessmen and the system under which they had risen to affluence, for otherwise the people may well have "defaulted to madmen and lunatics and their wicked dreams."[7]

This interpretation leaves major questions unanswered, but only recently has it been questioned. Thomas Ferguson, in particular, has argued that the key to understanding the emergence of the Liberty League lies in the changing perceptions of the New Deal by the huge labor-intensive and protectionist corporations. So long as Roosevelt maintained the strongly nationalist policies of the early New Deal, corporations such as the Du Pont Company and General Motors were prepared to support him. By 1935, however, as the New Deal focused upon labor reform, reciprocal tariff arrangements, and social welfare, these large employers defected to organizations such as the Liberty League.[8]

Other questions, however, remain to be answered. Why did the league, despite its lavish funding and expert direction, fail so badly in comparison to the successes of the AAPA and the DNC between 1929 and 1932? The same men were responsible for all three campaigns, and the basic themes of the league's message were similar to those of its successful antecedents. If selfishness was the primary motivation of the Liberty Leaguers and their corporations, why did the du Ponts take such an active role in it at a time when their company's profits were increasing by leaps and bounds? The New Deal was very good for the Du Pont and General Motors organizations; in 1932 the Du Pont Company declared a profit of $1.82 per share, which had risen to $3.00 at the end of the first year of the Roosevelt administration. Two years later, the company's profit was $5.04 per share.[9] The company's 1936 earnings increased 72 percent over its performance in the first half of 1935, and those of General Motors showed a 70 percent increase.[10] In his recent study of the political activities of the du Pont family (as opposed to the Du Pont Company) between 1920 and 1940, Robert F. Burk argued that the family's support of the Liberty League represented its last line of resistance against the emerging "broker state" of the New Deal. Despite the rising profitability of their companies after 1932, the du Ponts recognized that the New Deal, and especially its recognition of labor, consumer, and special-interest groups, incorporated a profound threat to the industrial and political hegemony that they had enjoyed during the 1920s. The du Ponts had been major beneficiaries of the "corporate state" of the 1920s, and the Liberty League became the vehicle through which they hoped to reassert the position they had enjoyed during the palmy days of normalcy.[11]

Other answers to these questions can be found by exploring the ideological consistency with which the leaders of the AAPA and the Democratic Conservative coalition approached political affairs after 1920. The Liberty League represented the confluence of both groups in terms of personnel, tactics, and ideology. The AAPA was much more than a taxpayers' revolt, and the Raskob wing of the Democratic party was much more than an Al Smith booster club. Both organizations embraced far-reaching political agendas which looked toward common goals: the reduction of federal power in the social and business life of the nation, the return of powers lost to the states by two decades of Progressive reform, and the reassertion of individual liberties in the face of an increasingly intrusive state. The Liberty League was the chosen agent of both the conservative Democrats and the antiprohibitionists to continue this agenda into the 1930s. Reexamination of the league in a way that changes its context from the partisan battles of the 1930s to its organizational and ideological antecedents of the 1920s frees it from the debilitating and obscuring imagery of "spite and ignorance."

This approach strikes at the heart of the "ignorance" argument. The members of the Liberty League did not mistake the New Deal at all. From their perspective it offended every conception of the proper role of the government that they had developed during their interrelated struggles during the preceding decade. The league continued the thrust of the "hard" business ideology of men like Julius Barnes, Pierre du Pont, and John Raskob into the 1930s. Business should be freed from regulation, government should not meddle with the private affairs of businessmen, and individuals should be allowed to rise and fall according to their own abilities. As Raskob and his colleagues had opposed the McNary-Haugen Bill in the 1920s, so too did they oppose the AAA; as they had fought against government distribution of electric power during the Muscle Shoals controversy, so too did they fight the TVA; as they condemned the Child Labor Amendment, so too did they condemn its revival in the 1930s, and as they fought against measures to curb labor injunctions, so too did they fight against the Wagner Act.[12] Antiprohibitionists had based their campaign upon opposition to excessive governmental supervision of personal affairs and private business practice; the New Deal, with its legions of bureaucrats, inspectors, boards, and tribunals, represented an even graver threat to the individual's freedom to live life and to conduct business as he or she chose.

To ascribe the Liberty League's continuation of the conservatives' fight during the 1920s to personal animosity and ignorance is to overlook its historical context and philosophical concerns. Not coincidentally, such an approach also distorts the New Deal into a moderate, nonintrusive attempt to defuse radicalism. From its opponents' perspective, the New Deal represented radicalism itself, incorporating a vision of American social, economic, and governmental development which differed fundamentally from that which preceded it. A fuller analysis of the philosophy of the Liberty League not only places it in its proper perspective and context, but also serves as a reminder of the scope and the importance of the changes to American life engendered by the New Deal.

RESISTANCE TO THE NEW DEAL

While prominent members of the AAPA moved toward a position of outright hostility to the New Deal, the leaders of the conservative coalition undertook the same journey. Their experiences were generally similar to those of Al Smith, which have been described above.[13] All the leaders of the Raskob wing gave lukewarm support to FDR and the Democratic ticket in 1932, but during 1933 increasing doubts made them reconsider their position.

Albert Ritchie strongly disapproved of Roosevelt's federal activism almost from the beginning, but the political demands of his position as governor of Maryland required his public acquiescence so that Maryland's share of New Deal largesse would not be endangered. After his defeat in 1934, however, he became an outspoken critic of Roosevelt's policies. "American self-government is being destroyed before our eyes," he declared in 1935, and the "spirit of individual American freedom is being imperiled by a counter spirit of bureaucratic centralization and by a regimented and nationalized economy."[14] Although his health declined rapidly after 1934, Ritchie supported the Liberty League until his death in February 1936.[15]

John W. Davis was even more hesitant in his support of Roosevelt's candidacy and early presidency. He had found Hoover's antidepression policies too radical in their assumption that the federal government was now responsible for the economic welfare of its citizens. Admitting that his economic views were "rather primitive," Davis wrote his friend Lord Midleton in England at the beginning of 1930, "I more and more resent the idea so prevalent today that prosperity lies in the gift of governments, and that whenever the patient's pulse is weak they must administer some sort of artificial stimulant. I sympathize with the antiquated maxim: 'The world is governed too much, let the man alone.'"[16]

Davis had a chance to discuss his own solutions to the depression at a Jackson Day dinner in Washington at the beginning of 1932. His suggestions were even more conservative than those put forward by Al Smith. The government, Davis warned, had no "magic ointments" with which to achieve economic recovery; only the "inexorable laws" of supply and demand could do that.[17] Washington should live within its means and eliminate the federal deficit without excessive tax increases upon the wealthy. Tariffs should be reduced, and states' rights respected. Davis was unwilling to see the federal government go beyond these limited and essentially negative steps.[18] Roosevelt's first year in the White House only confirmed Davis in his "primitive" philosophy. The Agricultural Adjustment Act (AAA), the NRA, and the relief effort quickly dissipated his approval of the Economy Bill and the repeal of prohibition. By August 1933, he was ready to declare himself at odds with the administration. "I still believe that too much government is far worse than too little," he wrote a Washington correspondent. "If this be treason, make the most of it."[19]

John Raskob's journey from doubtful Roosevelt supporter to New Deal critic was a longer and more complicated one. He was deeply concerned that the existing American economic system was on trial and that Roosevelt's presidency would prove to be crucial in the history of the free-enterprise system. In November 1932 he wrote an old family friend that conditions in America were "at a point where there is little difference between conditions here, as far as capital is concerned, and those in Russia" before 1917. "Russia brought its condition around by revolution, but we are rapidly drifting into the same state by evolution."[20] Despite the gravity of his fears, Raskob did remain loyal to the new administration for most of 1933. Like Pierre du Pont, he was impressed by the NRA as a welcome aid to businessmen beleaguered by antitrust legislation. Roosevelt's bold and decisive leadership during the Hundred Days elicited effusive congratulations from his old adversary, who was gracious enough to concede in May 1933 that "never in my whole life have I been so mistaken about a man and his ability as I was about Franklin Roosevelt."[21]

This unlikely reconciliation was based upon Raskob's assumption that the emergency legislation of 1933 was simply a short-term response to an immediate crisis.[22] He had not forgotten the platform upon which FDR was elected, and once the immediate crisis had run its course, he began to press for its promises to be fulfilled. By the end of 1933 he had become restive. Although the banking crisis had eased and the dark days of the winter of 1932–33 had passed, government expenditures were increasing, the NRA seemed to be helping trade unions as much as businessmen, and taxes were not being reduced. "Under our present income tax laws," he complained, "it is practically impossible for any young man to get out, and through hard and continuous work and service, build up a fortune for himself as his parents and grandparents had the opportunity of doing. To destroy initiative is to destroy progress." [23] The New Deal was threatening the rise of future John Raskobs.

Raskob's business friends shared his growing doubts. R. R. M. (Ruly) Carpenter, Pierre du Pont's brother-in-law and a member of the Du Pont Company Executive Committee, wrote to him in March 1934 to express his fear that the administration was using its relief programs for sinister purposes. "Unless the Administration is embarked on a campaign to buy the popular vote" through the New Deal, Carpenter enquired, why was it competing with industry for labor and raising the prevailing rate of wages in depressed areas? He went on to give specific examples of this. "Five negroes on my place in South Carolina refused work this Spring, after I had taken care of them and given them house [sic] rent free and work for three years during bad times, saying they had easy jobs with the Government. A cook on my houseboat at Fort Myers quit because the Government was paying him a dollar an hour as a painter when he never knew a thing about painting before." Seemingly oblivious to the irony of a leisured multimillionaire complaining during the depths of a depression about his cook earning a dollar an hour, Carpenter went on to ask Raskob's advice. Why was FDR conducting "a campaign of labor against capital, and a campaign to eliminate wealth? Who can possibly give employment to labor if wealthy men and capital are eliminated?" [24]

Raskob replied in terms that showed that his honeymoon with the New Deal was over. Because Carpenter had time and money to spare, Raskob suggested, he should form an organization "to protect society from the suffering which it is bound to endure if we allow communistic elements to lead the people to believe that all businessmen are crooks, not to be trusted and that no one should be allowed to get rich." [25] Such work was not to Carpenter's taste, but Raskob took steps to carry out his own advice. During the summer of 1934 he drew up a charter for an organization with the awkward title of the "Union Asserting the Rights in Property" or the "Union Asserting the Integrity of Persons and Property." He sent this to his former Democratic colleagues John Davis, Al Smith, Jouett Shouse, and Pierre du Pont, as well as to senior executives of Du Pont and General Motors.[26]

Raskob's charter came at the same time as Stayton, Shouse, and Pierre du Pont were moving the Repeal Associates into a position of outright opposition to the New Deal, and only weeks before Stayton began his seven memoranda outlining the basis for an attack upon Roosevelt's policies. It seemed wise to merge the two groups into a single organization. A third group, organized by Walter Chrysler and Edward Hutton, also dedicated to the protection of property rights against the New Deal, remained separate from, but sympathetic to, the new organization.[27] From this confluence of conservative fears about the New Deal the American Liberty League was born.[28]

Jouett Shouse, who had agreed to serve as president, did Roosevelt the courtesy of alerting him that a new "nonpartisan" organization was about to be created.[29] After receiving FDR's affable approval, the American Liberty League was announced to the world on August 22, 1934. It began life amid great publicity and flourish, although its organizational beginnings were shaky. By the end of 1934 the league had raised only $94,000, despite its professed hope of raising $1 million.[30] Eventually, however, the league's office staff numbered fifty, and its Washington headquarters occupied thirty-one rooms. The Republican National Committee, which employed seventeen people in twelve rooms, seemed modest in comparison.[31]

Of the conservative coalition's leaders, only James Cox and Harry Byrd were missing from the Liberty League's roster. Cox conformed to the pattern of behavior established by the other members of the coalition until Roosevelt's election. At the Jackson Day dinner in January 1932, for example, he echoed many of John Davis's limited conceptions of the government's proper role during the depression. He told his audience that it was imperative that states' rights be scrupulously respected. The experience of national prohibition had shown the "plain truth" that "when Uncle Sam became a local common constable he ceased to be a statesman." It was up to the states to be the primary economic regulators and "supervisors" during the crisis; the most constructive action the federal government could take would be to balance its budget. The Democrats must abjure economic radicalism at all costs, for "if we run with the Russian hares, we will neither deserve nor receive support." Instead, the party's platform and campaign should aim to bring labor and capital together so as to create the atmosphere of trust and cooperation necessary for recovery.[32]

Despite the economic orthodoxy of these views, Cox did not become a prominent critic of the New Deal. Aware of the depth of the economic crisis, he supported Roosevelt throughout his first term. The New Deal saved the nation from radicalism, he believed, and its measures were a good deal less sweeping than those enacted elsewhere. "We hear a good deal about regimentation," he noted in his autobiography "If the control of products and of acreage is regimentation, then we have had a very mild dose of it as compared to England." He allowed himself to criticize only Roosevelt's labor policies, which struck him as being too weighted toward support of trade unions.[33] Overall, however, he ranked FDR along with Jefferson, Jackson, Lincoln, and Wilson as the nation's greatest leaders.[34]

Cox's refusal to follow the logic of his economic views into the anti–New Deal camp was most probably because of his close friendship with Roosevelt, who had shared Cox's ticket in 1920. The two men had remained in contact during the intervening years, and FDR showered Cox with invitations to join his new administration. Cox, heavily involved with his extensive newspaper interests in Ohio and Florida, regretfully declined the president's offer of the chairmanship of the Federal Reserve Board and the ambassadorship to Germany.[35] He did, however, accept appointment to the London Economic Conference in 1933, where he served as chairman of the Monetary Commission. Although he was disappointed at the failure of the conference to achieve its goal of international economic stabilization, he did not share the internationalists' anger at FDR's famous telegram to the delegates declaring that the United States would pursue domestic solutions to its economic crisis.[36] Cox remained aloof from the Liberty League throughout the decade, limiting himself to occasional friendly reminders to the White House that businessmen deserved good will and cooperation as well as regulation.[37]

Harry Flood Byrd had very different reasons for not joining the American Liberty League. Although he had disliked FDR's 1932 campaign because of its economic unorthodoxy, he had supported the ticket loyally.[38] When Virginia's Senator Claude Swanson became secretary of the navy,

Byrd was appointed to take his place in the U.S. Senate. From that vantage point Byrd looked with increasing disfavor upon the recovery program that the president rushed through Congress during 1933. The NRA and AAA struck him as particularly objectionable, and by the end of 1933 he had joined his fellow Virginian Carter Glass, Thomas P. Gore of Oklahoma, Millard F. Tydings of Maryland, and Josiah Bailey of North Carolina in an informal Democratic opposition bloc against the New Deal that would develop into the bipartisan congressional conservative coalition in 1935.[39]

Raskob was very keen for Byrd to join the Liberty League as a member of its Executive Committee in August 1934. "His plan," Henry Breckinridge wrote Byrd, "is to get sixty men to give $25,000 apiece and then set forth to save the country." Byrd was sympathetic to the league, but he decided not to join it. He considered that he could best serve the cause of "constitutional liberty" by remaining in the Senate and by avoiding overt affiliation with the league. He remained, however, as a supportive spectator of and occasional adviser to Raskob's organization.[40]

Newton Baker remained independent from the conservative coalition throughout the 1930s. As he had done in the preceding decade, he expressed sympathy with the thrust of the conservative revolt against the Democratic liberals without identifying himself with it completely. Like Raskob, du Pont, and Shouse, he lauded the Hundred Days as a brave attempt to take control of the chaotic situation facing FDR on Inauguration Day, and he gave the new president his full support during 1933.[41] Yet he found it impossible to suspend his disbelief that the depression could be legislated away. "It never would have occurred to me to do many of the things that [the President] has done," he wrote Edward A. Filene in March 1934, because the New Deal struck him as being "at variance with what I have always regarded as the lessons of human experience and the teachings of sound theory."[42]

Baker grew increasingly concerned about the recovery program in 1934. He worried that the New Deal was unduly centralist; local government, he thought, was "the very essence of our theory of government."[43] The NRA struck him as especially intrusive into the prerogatives of local and individual self-government, and as antithetical to the American tradition of "individual opportunity, individual initiative and individual freedom."[44] Federal relief, he thought, was "frankly in the interest of the portion of our population which has been least thrifty and industrious and will prove a sad discouragement to those who have worked hard."[45] The great danger of relief, he told the *New York Times* at the end of 1934, was that "we are coming more and more to regard the State as a legitimate and responsible carrier of all individual, group and class burdens."[46]

Baker declined to turn his theoretical objections into political action by joining the Liberty League. He had not been consulted about the league's formation, and even at the end of 1934 he noted to a friend that he had not been sent any of its literature. "For some reason, like the little old gentleman who sat in the corner in one of Dickens' novels," he wrote a friend, "I have been quite overlooked."[47] After Raskob and Davis urged him to join the league and to help lead the legal fight against the New Deal, however, he declined to join the organization.[48] The Liberty Leaguers, it seemed to him, were too one-sided in their attacks upon the administration. He disliked the New Deal, but at the same time he could not forget the injustices of the "old deal" which had done so much to bring on the depression. As the election of 1936 neared, he found himself in a quandary. "It has been very difficult for me to reach any conclusion about my relation to the present political situation," he wrote. "My party has left me completely and the only thing I am sure about is that my boat has not stranded on Republican shores."[49] "Governor Smith's formula of taking a walk means nothing since we have nowhere to go," he wrote Walter Lippmann in 1936; "my situation is that I find it difficult to be a Democrat and impossible to be a Republican."[50] He did, however, lend his talents to the legal fight against the TVA on behalf of the Edison Electrical Institute.[51]

With the exceptions of Cox, Byrd, and Baker, however, the Raskob group and their admirers rallied to the American Liberty League.[52] Like the AAPA and Raskob's DNC, the league's largest financial contributors were members or intimate friends of the du Pont family, who together provided nearly 30 percent of the organization's funds between 1934 and 1940.[53] As the 1930s wore on and as enthusiasm for the league waned, the du Ponts' contributions became steadily more important. Of the $483,000 donated to the League during 1935, for example, nearly 50 percent came from du Pont or associated sources.[54] By the end of 1936, Irénée du Pont had donated or lent a total of $119,500 to its coffers, an amount matched by Pierre.[55] By 1938 the costs of the league were being borne almost entirely by the two men. When the league was finally wound up in 1940, they were left holding notes to the value of over $200,000 each, which they wrote off for taxation purposes.[56]

This degree of financial dependence did not escape the attention of the league's foes. Although it claimed to have 36,000 members in July 1935, some 75,000 in January 1936, and nearly 125,000 in the summer of 1936, the embarrassing fact was that most of the league's funds came from the du Pont family.[57] This weakened the league's claim to be a grass-roots movement of concerned Americans.[58] The American Liberty League should be called "the American Cellophane League," Jim Farley joked in 1936, because "first, its a du Pont product and second, you can see right through it."[59] Frank R. Kent, although sympathetic to the aims of the league, cited the number of du Ponts among the league's list of sponsors as evidence of its political ineptitude. The family, he thought, should have pooled its contributions and made them all through one person.[60]

Just as the league inherited its financial support from the AAPA and the conservative coalition, so it used the same tactics in its political activities. Like the AAPA, it stubbornly clung to a professed policy of nonpartisanship in order to encourage both Democrats and Republicans into its ranks. In fact, the league was so patently anti–New Deal that no one was deceived by its leaders' public protestations that the league was above party politics. Smith, Raskob, Shouse, and the du Ponts all announced their intention to vote for Alf Landon in 1936, and the league supported only two administration actions in its six years of existence.[61] During the presidential campaign of 1936 it functioned as an unofficial research organization and publicity agent for the Republican National Committee.[62] The Democrats were so successful in portraying the league during the 1936 campaign as nothing more than the plutocratic wing of the GOP that the league was forced to vacate the field. On September 30 its Executive Committee, responding to pressure from the league's erstwhile Republican allies, decided to cease formal campaigning for the rest of the presidential campaign.[63] Although Landon publicly denied any association between the GOP and the league, in fact he continued to consult regularly with members of its executive, and his 1936 platform bore marked resemblance to the league's Document No. 83, *A Plan for Congress*. One-third of the members of the Republican Finance Committee were associated with the league.[64]

After FDR's massive victory in 1936, Jouett Shouse wrote privately that the only hope for conservatives was to amalgamate the league with the Republican party. This, however, proved impossible. The league's southern supporters, Shouse told an Oregon correspondent soon after the election, "are bound by old fetishes to the point that they cannot bring themselves to cooperate within the Republican Party."[65] For its part, the GOP became increasingly hesitant to become closely identified with the league and its plutocratic image.[66] The fiction of nonpartisanship was therefore maintained, fooling nobody and exposing the league to charges of hypocrisy and deviousness.

The Liberty League also took advantage of the lessons in the dissemination of publicity that its leaders had learned within the AAPA and the DNC. The league's campaigns were lavishly funded and cleverly devised, with heavy reliance upon radio speeches and pamphlet distribution. It produced an average of one pamphlet per week, and its bulletins were mailed to all parts of the nation and sent to more than 1600 newspapers and every major radio station.[67] By the end of 1935 there were seventy-five thousand members on the league books, and by early in the following year college chapters had been created on 151 campuses across the nation.[68]

Charles Michelson had directed the thrust of DNC publicity between 1929 and 1932 against Herbert Hoover, and now the league's publicists focussed their attacks upon Franklin Roosevelt. In the same way that Michelson's campaign had made the depression into the "Hoover panic," the league's efforts were directed toward portraying the New Deal as Roosevelt's personal quest for dictatorial power and unlimited tenure in the White House. If Michelson could make Herbert Hoover a national villain within two years, the league reasoned, it could do the same to FDR.

The most important link between the Liberty League and its antecedent organizations, however, was the similarity between the conceptions of government held by the AAPA, the old conservative coalition, and the campaign against the New Deal. This similarity encompassed both the utterances of its leaders in their correspondence and the more public declarations of the league itself. The league borrowed heavily from Raskob's and Smith's cult of the self-made man. Raskob himself attacked the New Deal as a betrayal of Horatio Alger's vision in a 1936 letter to fifteen thousand prospective members of the league. "Beginning life as a poor boy blessed with splendid health," he recalled, "I have been successful . . . in retaining good health and, through hard work and saving, in acquiring a competence for old age and the care of dependents." This was possible only under the liberties guaranteed by the Declaration of Independence and the Constitution, and only by protecting those liberties could "the children of future generations enjoy the same opportunities to be happy and succeed through working, earning and saving."[69]

The Liberty Leaguers also inherited and refined the strict constructionism which the conservative coalition and the AAPA had emphasized during the 1920s. This was clear not only in its frequent defense of states' rights against an expanding federal government but also in its view of the meaning of the Constitution for modern life in general and the depression in particular. Economic slumps, they argued, were cyclic phenomena, which were to be endured in the expectation of the prosperity that would follow. There was no need to alter radically the traditional roles of the federal or the state governments in order to combat the depression. On the contrary, such acts were dangerous, for they endangered the fluid and open economic system which functioned so well during good times. Depressions, the league thought, were no times for experiments in reform. Governments should retrench, individuals should recoup, and recovery would inevitably come. Irénée du Pont summed up this attitude in February 1935: "We should bear in mind that under the government described by the Constitution, the United States became the wealthiest and most free country in the world's history. We are ready to throw that over on the grounds of emergency. To be sure, we have unemployment and compared with 1928, perhaps we have something which might be stretched to be considered an emergency, but still today the United States is more prosperous than any country in the world's history. The people of this country are willing to throw this overboard and follow what is called the 'new deal,' but which is really as old as history, i.e., government by men who will usurp power and tyrranize [sic] over their fellow men."[70]

Du Pont's colleagues agreed with this assessment. Pierre du Pont noted in 1944 that the recent depression was by no means a unique event. He could remember the slump of 1893–96, as well as those of 1910–13 and 1920–23. "We recovered from all of them promptly," he observed to a relation in Massachusetts, "without the prolonged period of 'pump-priming' and other operations which we indulged in in the years 1933–1939, nor did we require a war to bring us back to normal employment."[71] John W. Davis also preferred to trust the forces of the free market above those of governmental activism to produce recovery. Human needs "must be supplied, and men live by struggling each to serve another," he declared at the end of 1932. "When shelves are empty merchants must buy; when trousers wear out men must work to buy another pair. In this simple faith I still hope for an issue out of all our troubles."[72] Just as "human nature has not changed at all during the period covered by recorded history," Davis believed, so "the axioms of free society do not change from age to age."[73]

In its defense of traditional American liberties, the league and its leaders leaned heavily upon Captain Stayton's seven Repeal Associates memoranda of 1934. Stayton's conspiracy theory of usurpation of power was particularly useful and provided the unifying theme of much of the league's criticism of the New Deal. FDR and his advisers were conspiring to subvert the federal system of checks and balances. The president was centralizing power not only to Washington but also to his executive department; the states and the Congress had largely abdicated their constitutional roles as independent political entities and constitutional watchdogs. Even the people had traded many of their individual freedoms for the material security of federal relief schemes and government extravagance.

Although Stayton had argued that this tendency to usurp power was as old as government itself, the Liberty League claimed that the New Deal represented a new twist in the age-old struggle between the megalomania of government and the liberties of the people. The usurpations of the New Deal, it argued, were consciously planned to entrench the administration in power. It was therefore morally as well as legally wrong. FDR had set class against class by using taxation to redistribute wealth, relief schemes to buy votes, and the power of the federal government to turn public opinion against the "economic royalists," whose only crime was to have succeeded in the race for success.[74]

The Liberty League also inherited the antiprohibitionists' fear of expanded state action in any form. Jouett Shouse lent his organization's support at the end of 1934 to a proposal to transfer all relief distribution from state and federal governments to the Red Cross. "Distribution of largesse from the public treasury," he warned, "is one of the most ancient devices by which bureaucracies and other undemocratic governments have sought to maintain themselves in power." The massive relief programs were being used for political purposes, to the detriment of states' rights and individual freedoms.[75] The league's conflation of property and human rights led it to perceive sinister motives behind economic legislation. It maintained Stayton's view that inheritance taxes and redistributive income taxes were unconstitutional, since they were in effect confiscatory measures which discriminated against the wealthy.[76]

Although the repeal of national prohibition had not created the general climate of hostility to federal expansion hoped for by the AAPA, the Liberty League did not tire of reminding its audience of the lessons of the prohibition experiment. Pierre du Pont, for example, strenuously opposed the perennial Child Labor Amendment proposal throughout the 1930s as a revival of the spirit of the Eighteenth Amendment. "I cannot refrain from doing everything possible," he wrote the director of the National Committee for the Protection of Children in 1935, "to prevent another federal prohibition amendment of *any* kind."[77] Irénée du Pont followed the ramifications of the fight against prohibition even further. He based his opposition to the National Securities Exchange Act upon the lessons he had learned in the 1920s. It was pointless to try to eradicate speculation in stocks, he wrote Senator Daniel Hastings of Maryland in 1934, because men "are by nature speculators . . . and that human craving is going to be satisfied by one route or another, just as Prohibition did not take away the appetite for liquor."[78]

The strong strain of antimajoritarianism inherent in the AAPA's fight against prohibition also carried through into the struggle against the New Deal. Although the Liberty Leaguers considered the New Deal to be an affront to American political and social institutions and traditions, they were well aware of its popularity among less privileged Americans. To save America, they mused, it would be necessary to muzzle the political power of those voters who had allowed themselves to be bought by federal relief programs or to be seduced by FDR's personality cult. The league's traditional view of the Constitution strengthened this opinion, for the original Constitution had been careful to limit the people's power by such means as indirect election of the president and U.S. senators. Irénée du Pont began to distinguish the Constitution's definition of "republicanism" from the modern meaning of "democracy." "This country has gradually gotten away from the form of a Republic to a Democracy," he wrote Senator James Hughes of Delaware in 1937; "democracy ends in dictatorship. I fear we are nearing the end."[79] Captain Stayton agreed with his benefactor. In 1937 he argued that the Sixteenth Amendment could not be repealed because "we have been breeding stupid and anti-social people faster than we have good citizens." The democratic process encouraged demagoguery and envy, and the average voter of the 1930s was "certainly not going to object to 'lawful' confiscation of funds from the very wealthy."[80] Pierre du Pont, as Robert Burk has pointed out, hoped that the Liberty League might purify the American political system by en-couraging a new party alignment along ideological lines. Reverting to his earlier distrust of the existing two-party system, du Pont in 1936 argued that "instead of the old-time relation, which for years has been based on contentions between protectionists and their adversaries or fighting over the Civil War, we must have a new line-up which needs a conservative party based on defense of the Constitution . . . and perhaps a communistic party based upon radicalism and abandonment of the Constitution and also of our economic system."[81]

Both Pierre du Pont and John Raskob continued to contemplate re-strictions on suffrage so as to prevent the majority from asserting itself to the detriment of constitutional tradition or economic privilege. They agreed that "any practical way of excluding a very large and undesirable population from voting" would solve many of the problems posed by the New Deal's excesses.[82] Raskob suggested that the right to vote should be treated in the same way as the right to drive an automobile. Voters should be issued "licenses" to vote after they had passed an examination of the "simple fundamentals" of government, "such as describing the powers and the duties of the various offices to be filled." Such licenses could be revoked for infringements of the law or for a failure to vote in two consecutive elections.[83]

The Liberty Leaguers' doubts about the efficacy of popularly elected institutions to protect traditional American liberties were reflected in their hope that the judiciary would stem the tide of federal activism. The league's most prominent offshoot was its National Lawyers Committee, chaired by Raoul Desvernine and staffed by fifty prominent lawyers, in-cluding James M. Beck, John W. Davis, and George W. Wickersham.[84] The committee issued a critique of each major piece of New Deal legislation passed after 1934, invariably finding them to be not only unsound but also unconstitutional. Four examples illustrate the Lawyers Committee's ac-tivities. In September 1935 it released an indictment of the National Labor Relations Act. This, it argued, was unconstitutional because it attempted to apply to all firms, regardless of whether or not they were engaged in interstate commerce. Furthermore, by infringing employers' and employees' freedom of contract, the act abrogated the protections against government interference that were enshrined in the Constitution. It is clear, however, that the committee was more concerned with the rights of employers than for those of employees; most of its criticisms revolved around the act's limitations upon employers' rights to hire and fire labor as they saw fit.[85]

The Bituminous Coal Conservation Act of 1935 came under the committee's scrutiny three months later. This legislation, it noted with alarm, represented the first attempt by the federal government to single out one industry for detailed regulation. The Bituminous Coal Board was to set prices, determine production levels, and supervise working conditions. The act levied a "tax" of 15 percent upon producers, 90 percent of which would be waived if the Bituminous Coal Code was followed. The committee found the act to be unconstitutional; it attempted to regulate activities that had no real interstate character, it arbitrarily infringed the individual liberties of coal producers and their employees, and its taxation provision was not a tax at all but rather a "coercive penalty," designed to hide the act's usurpation behind the taxing power of the Constitution.[86] A majority of the Supreme Court agreed; on May 18 1936 the act was struck down.[87]

The committee also expressed its disapproval of the Potato Act of 1935, which again used a removable tax in order to encourage compliance with a federal scheme of production allotment. The Potato Act was, in the committee's estimation, "flagrantly unconstitutional" because of its ruse of using the taxing power to circumvent the commerce power's distinction between inter- and intrastate commerce. If this act was allowed, the committee warned, no industry would be safe from federal control.[88] The Supreme Court's willingness to strike New Deal legislation down delighted the committee. The 1936 decision *United States v. William M. Butler*, which invalidated the Agricultural Adjustment Act, prompted the Liberty League's lawyers to issue a disquisition on the meaning of the General Welfare Clause of the Constitution.[89] Citing with approval Grover Cleveland's veto of the Texas Seeds Bill, the committee argued that the *Butler* decision had confirmed that the clause was not a separate power but rather a qualification upon the taxing power. The New Dealers could not legally increase the scope of federal law by relying on the General Welfare clause; the Constitution remained one of specific and enumerated powers, against which all federal legislation had to be measured.[90]

Parallels between the activities and philosophies of the conservative coalition, the AAPA, and the Liberty League were also drawn in the league's more public statements throughout its existence. Its pamphlets and transcripted speeches blanketed the country between 1934 and 1937. Over 51 million pamphlets were mailed from the league's headquarters over this period, as well as weekly bulletins and membership recruitment letters.[91] In keeping with the new publicity techniques pioneered during World War I and implemented by the AAPA and the DNC, the league's publicity centered upon a few key themes and then reiterated them for maximum effect.

In approximately 135 pamphlets and speeches distributed by the league between 1934 and 1936, nine major points were driven home.[92] The New Deal was unconstitutional; its centralization of power to Washington threatened to create a dictatorship; its economic planning was dangerous to the liberties of the people; FDR's policies were patently self-serving and politically motivated; they were dividing Americans along class lines, pitting the poor against the rich; the New Deal represented an abrogation of the Democratic platform of 1932; its governmental activism and reforming spirit prevented the market's natural process of recovery; most of its measures were either Communist or fascist; and its taxation policies unduly penalized the rich and discouraged investment into the weakened economy.[93]

Three examples of this publicity demonstrate the close ideological links between the anti–New Deal movement, the conservative coalition, and the AAPA. On June 13, 1935, Jouett Shouse gave a speech entitled "You Are the Government" at Battle Creek, Michigan.[94] "It is no overstatement," Shouse began, "to say that the basic issue now confronting our country is a choice between absolutism and self-government." By absolutism, he explained, he did not mean that form of government associated with ancien régime France, but rather "a philosophy of government under which a few men temporarily vested with official power are deemed omniscient enough to direct the lives and destinies of more than one hundred and twenty-five millions of citizens." FDR and his underlings seemed determined to destroy the states as political entities, taking the view that "all economic and social problems should be controlled by the Federal

Government." The Eighteenth Amendment had tried to impose central-ization upon Americans, and in so doing had left "a trail of bloodshed and corruption probably unparalleled in history."[95]

One of John Raskob's goals as chairman of the DNC had been to forge a North-South conservative alliance, and it was to this issue that the league addressed a pamphlet at the end of October 1935. Entitled *The Economic Necessity in the Southern States for a Return to the Constitution*, the pamphlet was written by Forney Johnston, an Alabamian member of the League's Lawyers Committee.[96] Johnston appealed to white southerners' economic self-interest and racial prejudice. The New Deal threatened to return the South to the dark days of Reconstruction by imposing upon it economic and social reform which paid no heed to Dixie's "special circumstances." "The proposed constitutional revolution," he warned, "would rend the South into armed economic camps, with agricultural labor organized against the farm proprietor, with suffrage qualifications overturned in the struggle for class advantage, with town against country." The imposition of national wage scales upon southern agriculture and industry would rob the South of any hope for economic progress. "The South, by reason of its relative weakness in industry, the limits on its markets, the peculiar nature of its local problems," Johnston concluded, "is of all sections most in need of the protection of the Constitution and most certain to suffer stagnation if standardized by political control in Washington."[97]

As the 1936 elections approached, the Liberty League's pamphlets grew increasingly acerbic in their criticism of the administration. On the eve of the Democratic convention of that year, Jouett Shouse delivered a radio address which severely criticized the "betrayal" of the 1932 platform and of those Democrats who had invested so much money to ensure the party's victory over Herbert Hoover.[98] Despite the admirable nature of the plat-form, however, the Roosevelt administration had wasted little time in introducing measures that were "wholly alien to the American concept of government." Every industry and every farm in the nation was subject to "regimentation," and control of the people in their private affairs "became the apparent objective behind much of the proposed legislation." The platform's promises of economy were "summarily scrapped," and instead the president undertook an "orgy of spending" which had "no counter-part in all history." All in all, Shouse charged, "the New Deal represents the attempt in America to set up a totalitarian government, one which

recognizes no sphere of individual or business life as immune from governmental authority and which submerges the welfare of the individual to
that of the government."[99]

Shouse concluded his address by unwittingly expressing a political epi-
taph not only for himself but for the entire conservative Democratic group
which had fought national prohibition, revived the Democratic party, and
finally opposed the New Deal. The imminent convention, he declared, was
only "masking under the name of the Democratic Party." The meeting
that was to convene in Philadelphia was a New Deal convention, which
would write a platform radically different from "the basic principles upon
which the Democratic Party was founded and for which it has consistently stood. Those who have seized the party machinery have changed
the whole picture of the party." Democrats who remained loyal to the old
party of Jefferson, Jackson, and Cleveland were now "without a Party,"
for they "owe no duty of loyalty to the New Deal."[100] With these ringing
phrases Shouse led his Liberty League, his old conservative coalition, and
his former antiprohibitionists out of the party and into political oblivion.

THE FAILURE OF THE LEAGUE

"The perfect example of a political pouter pigeon," Frank R.
Kent observed in August 1936, "the League has set an all time record for
ineptitude." It had spent over a million dollars in the hope of discrediting the New Deal, but in fact it had actually aided Roosevelt by allowing
him to "capitalize the silly and fallacious idea that all his opponents were
multi-millionaires."[101] Much can be said in favor of this view. Despite the
successes of the AAPA and the DNC during the 1920s, the league's leaders
did prove themselves to be incompetent at publicizing their cause; it was
insensitive in parading its millionaire sponsors too prominently; it did
allow its message to be too dominated by antitaxation arguments and self-
interest; and it did show lack of judgment in the allies it courted in the
fight against the New Deal.[102]

It is important, however, not to exaggerate these failings. David Kyvig
has argued that the league did exercise a significant moderating influence
upon New Deal policies between 1934 and 1936. Roosevelt remained wary
of a conservative backlash throughout his first term, limiting the scope

of banking reform and ensuring that the NRA kept on good terms with business groups. Even in 1935, FDR insisted on a conservative approach to the funding of the Social Security Act and only reluctantly lent his support to the National Labor Relations Board Act. These concessions, Kyvig maintains, were at least partly due to the Liberty League's efforts.[103] Nor should the league's failures be allowed to obscure the concerns about the direction of American statecraft which its message encapsulated. The men who had helped to defeat prohibition and then revived the Democratic party measured the New Deal against their political philosophy and found it wanting. They therefore set out to repeat their crusades of the previous decade, using the same arguments, publicity methods, and organizational structures that had proved so successful only a few years previously. The league was correct in seeing the philosophical consistency between the fight against prohibition, the policy concerns of the conservative Democrats in the 1920s, and the struggle against the New Deal. It was wrong, however, in its assumption that public opinion would allow ideological consistency to prevent effective national action in the face of the economic crisis after 1929. Its members, Professor James Hart of Johns Hopkins declared in 1935, were "honorable gentlemen, and many of them have brilliant nineteenth-century minds."[104] The Liberty League was a victim of its own philosophical consistency; America had changed, but it had not.[105]

CONCLUSION

A fierce struggle for control of the Democratic party's national organization and philosophical direction took place between 1920 and 1932. Its most spectacular aspects centered upon cultural issues such as Catholicism, urbanism, and prohibition. Other disputes, however, revolving around states' rights, the proper extent of federal activism, the relationship between business and government, and tariff policy also divided Democrats. Instead of setting Catholic against Protestant and urbanite against farmer, these disputes divided Democrats along ideological lines as they struggled for influence over party platforms and candidacies.

As the minority party during the 1920s, the Democrats were forced to reassess their philosophical direction to regain electoral viability at the national level. The crushing defeat of 1920 was generally seen as a rejection of their recent reformist record. Party leaders were faced with the urgent need to develop a new message for the changed times. Their victory in 1912 had been a political fluke, made possible by the divisions within Republican ranks, and that of 1916 had been atypical in its emphasis upon the antiwar issue. The hard fact was that the party had not won a normal two-party presidential election on domestic issues since Grover Cleveland's victory in 1892. After that election the electorate had realigned to give the GOP majority status. The great question facing Democrats in the years after 1920 had been whether to maintain the Wilsonian heritage of activist federal policy in the hope of persuading the electorate that its acceptance of the Republicans' business-oriented conservatism was misguided, or whether to deliver a new message more in tune with the noninterventionist spirit of the times.

Conservative Democrats like James Cox, John Davis, Al Smith, and John Raskob attempted to lead their party on the latter course. The 1920s were, they thought, a Republican decade. The only way that the Democrats could hope to win national victories was by recognizing that the GOP had captured the national consensus on business policy, federal activism, and the proper role of government in citizens' everyday lives. Rather than attempt to educate the electorate toward further economic reform, conservative Democrats argued that it was better to renounce the

Wilsonian past and espouse policies that echoed the Republicans' acquiescence to business control of the national economy. By becoming more like the Republicans, they hoped, the Democrats could share the GOP's electoral success.

Arrayed against this conservative group was a loose collection of Democrats who had drawn very different conclusions from the party's electoral experience after 1892. Men like McAdoo and FDR had been closely identified with Woodrow Wilson and his reformist agenda and were determined that the party maintain Wilson's willingness to use and expand federal power in the fields of business regulation and social reform. To these liberals, me-tooism was a doomed policy, for it provided no incentive for a contented electorate to change its political allegiance. Although aware that reform at the federal level was out of fashion in the 1920s, followers of McAdoo and then FDR were convinced that the political pendulum would eventually swing back toward an acceptance of an active and reformist policy agenda. If the Democrats surrendered their progressive heritage, they would lose their reason for being, and their place in the political system would be preempted by a new organization that would benefit from the inevitable reaction against the Republicans.

The 1920s were a time of intense conflict between these points of view. Until 1930 the initiative had lain with the conservatives, who had largely replaced the Wilsonian progressives within the national party organization after 1920. Demoralized and disorganized by the defeat of 1920, liberals within the party found themselves unable to mount an effective challenge to the conservatives and their new agenda for the party until the depression revived their hopes of a new political alignment. Not only were the conservatives able to nominate men of their persuasion to the presidency throughout the 1920's, but their control of the party's national organization had enabled them to attempt to change party policy in areas such as the tariff, prohibition, and business regulation. Well funded and well organized, the conservatives dominated the national party.

The conservatives attempted to use their control of the national party to direct it upon a new course. Instead of following the old West-South electoral strategy used by William Jennings Bryan and Woodrow Wilson, the conservative coalition based its three presidential campaigns upon a North-South alliance. The South, it was assumed, would vote Democratic regardless of the platform to protect its racial policies against Republican interference. In order to win the large northern states, the new Democratic leadership attempted to get rid of the remnants of Bryan's agrarian reformism and to persuade northern voters that their industrialized, corporate economy would be safe in Democratic hands. The protective tariff would be maintained to protect wage levels; business regulation would not be allowed to impinge upon either profitability or the "right" of businessmen to conduct their affairs as they saw fit; and national prohibition would be substantially changed or repealed. Western concerns, such as government control of water-power resources and farm relief, were consequently ignored by the conservative wing as politically dangerous threats to northeastern business interests.

The conservative Democrats thus sought to use their influence within the party to create a new political alignment during the 1920s. They correctly recognized that the East, with its powerful business interests and rapidly increasing population, could not be ignored if the party hoped to win national elections. Instead of integrating the Northeast into the western-southern strategy, they abandoned the West and concentrated upon winning the Northeast. Traditionally, American electoral realignments have occurred during periods of economic depression such as 1892–96 and 1930–36. The conservative coalition, however, attempted to create a realignment during the 1920s by appealing to the most prosperous section of the country. This "prosperity strategy" was inherently conservative because it was aimed at portraying the Democrats as trustworthy guardians of the economic status quo.

Accordingly, the conservatives downplayed Wilsonian concepts of reform in favor of a policy strongly for states' rights and economic nonintervention. Business would be left alone to continue its upward trend; citizens would be given the maximum liberty to make their own economic decisions free from federal paternalism. With the exception of the conservatives' espousal of the protective tariff, this was the same philosophy as that implemented by Grover Cleveland, the last Democrat to win a normal presidential election. Senator William Cabell Bruce of Maryland encapsulated this spirit of neo-Clevelandism in his reply to Franklin Roosevelt's circular letter of December 1924, as noted above in chapter 4. Appealing to Cleveland and Jefferson, Bruce argued that "conservatism with a whiff of national liberalism should be the leading trait of the party."[1]

Antiprohibition provided this "whiff of national liberalism" for the

Democratic conservatives. They considered their campaign against the Eighteenth Amendment to be in keeping with the old liberal spirit. As we have seen, this definition of liberalism, with which Grover Cleveland would have identified, had been superseded by a new vision of an active and interfering state regulating individual behavior in the name of social and economic justice. Consequently prohibition became the focus of not only the cultural divisions within the party but also its ideological conflicts.

The campaign to modify or repeal national prohibition was therefore an important part of the conservatives' attempt to redefine the Democratic party's philosophical direction. Antiprohibition was an increasingly popular issue throughout the industrialized Northeast, and the Raskob wing hoped to use it to serve their purposes of redefining Democratic ideology and creating a partisan realignment in the East. By attracting the votes of the industrial rank and file thirsty for a legal drink, the conservatives hoped that the rest of their agenda—which was considerably less attractive to the average voter—would also be implemented. If a realignment could be created over prohibition, then the Democrats could win majority status in the North. When these votes were added to those of the solid South, the party would win national power. By such means it could portray itself as the champion of the rank and file's liberty to drink as well as the defender of businessmen's right to be free from reformist meddling.

Although this strategy was well in place by 1930, the depression added new urgency to the Raskob group's plans for the party. By attempting to separate the party's policies from the concerns of the agrarian West, the conservatives prevented the party from addressing the farm crisis of the 1920s. This had allowed them to frame platforms and run campaigns which paid little heed to rural economic distress or to schemes such as the McNary-Haugen Bill which were designed to alleviate it. The party could avoid far-reaching federally funded or organized farm relief programs and preach instead to the prosperous industrial North. The depression, however, threatened this strategy by creating demands within the North for activist economic policy and federal relief. After 1930, the cry for positive government action became popular in all sections of the nation, preventing the conservatives from playing the economic contentment of the North off against the West's interest in economic reform. The depression became a potent national issue which threatened to swamp all others in electoral importance in 1932. It seemed increasingly unlikely that the conservative Democrats could succeed in using prohibition reform as the vote-winning smoke screen for an economic policy favorable to the interests of the corporate sector.

The conservatives responded to the challenge of the depression by modifying their earlier reliance upon prohibition reform. Whereas in the 1920s they had argued that the repeal of national prohibition would return usurped liberties and powers to individuals and their states, after 1930 they argued that the end of national prohibition was, in itself, a vital step toward economic recovery. By drawing revenue in the form of excise taxes and by creating hundreds of thousands of jobs, the relegalization of the liquor trade would hasten recovery. Privately, the conservative coalition hoped that these arguments would be sufficiently persuasive to the rank and file of the party that other, more fundamental economic reforms would be forgotten. "Booze before bread" therefore was an attempt to harness the electoral attractiveness of antiprohibitionism to the coalition's wider political concern to prevent the party from being tainted with economic radicalism as it had been during Bryan's campaigns.

Just as the depression challenged the conservatives' strategy both within and without the Democratic party, so it also reinvigorated their opponents. It also offered hope that the electoral system which had created Republican majorities since 1896 could be realigned so as to leave the Democrats as the majority party. In these circumstances, liberals believed, it was essential that the party define itself as ideologically distinct from the GOP to take advantage of the political ramifications of the depression. Me-tooism threatened to rob the Democratic party of the political benefits of popular discontent with Republican rule. New policies were needed to signal to the electorate that the Democrats were prepared to take more aggressive steps toward economic recovery than those of the Hoover administration.

Liberals within the party also wished to revive the old Bryanite and Wilsonian alliance of southern and western states while simultaneously exploiting the economic anxieties of the Northeast. The depression provided an opportunity for the party to build a truly national coalition. This could be achieved in a party platform which incorporated both farm-relief programs and employment projects such as public works. In keeping with their desire to appeal to all sections of the nation, liberals opposed the

Raskob wing's emphasis upon prohibition reform. Prohibition was still popular in large sections of the West and South, and Democratic insistence upon repeal would endanger the party's success in these sections. In addition, liberals like McAdoo and Josephus Daniels correctly recognized the conservatives' strategy of emphasizing repeal as an attempt to sidetrack the growing popular demand for economic reform and tighter business regulation.

This liberal agenda needed a nationally prominent leader as its champion. After his election as governor of New York in 1928, Franklin Roosevelt replaced William McAdoo in this role. FDR rallied the nation's liberal Democrats to his cause by leading the fight against the Raskob wing and its attempts to impose me-tooism and the "bread before booze" strategy upon the party. By remaining neutral in the bitter cultural conflicts of the party and by stressing instead his ideological objections to the conservatives, Roosevelt became the chief spokesman for the liberal cause and consequently their leading candidate for the presidential nomination in 1932. The Raskob wing recognized FDR's candidacy as a direct ideological challenge to their control of the party organization and opposed his nomination with all the resources of the national organization and their personal prestige. Roosevelt's victory at the Chicago convention of 1932 represented not only a victory for liberal Democrats but also a return to the South-West alliance created by Bryan and then Wilson.

When Franklin Roosevelt accepted the Democratic party's presidential nomination in 1932, he began a new era of party history. In stymying the conservatives' campaign against his nomination, Roosevelt had also denied them a place in the party's policy-making process. The platform, to be sure, was economically conservative and incorporated the conservatives' wishes on prohibition. Yet few doubted that FDR would win the election, and then it would be he—and not the DNC or Raskob or Smith—who would create policy. Roosevelt knew this, and in his famous acceptance speech to the delegates at Chicago he continued to distinguish his views from those of his recent opponents. Although he declared the platform to be an "admirable document," he also gave notice to Raskob and his colleagues that their era had passed. "I warn those nominal Democrats who squint at the future with their faces turned toward the past, and who feel no responsibility to the demands of the new time," the new nominee told the cheering delegates, "that they are out of step with their Party."[2]

The northeastern wing had, indeed, been out of step with the majority of its party between 1920 and 1932. Despite the efforts of Cox, Davis, Smith, Raskob, and Shouse, the party as a whole had proved to be unresponsive and even hostile to their ideological agenda. Barring repeal, the conservative coalition failed to alter permanently the party's policy direction. Their views on federal activism, business regulation, and tariff policy had polarized the party along ideological lines. At the same time, the party had been ripped apart by cultural division, making it doubly difficult for it to present a coherent ideological message to the electorate. Although the conservative coalition made lasting *structural* contributions to the party, by creating a permanent extracongressional party organization that functioned year-round to disseminate publicity and organize campaigns, its *ideological* contributions were neither significant nor lasting.

The chief cause of the Raskob wing's failure to unify the party around its ideology lay in the limitations of that ideology itself. During the 1920s the conservatives' stress upon prohibition reform, antistatism, and pro-business policies deepened divisions within the party. Those Democrats who had been Wilsonian progressives protested at the renunciation of the party's recent reformist past, while western agrarian Democrats resented the exclusion of their concerns from the party's agenda. Southerners were, by and large, unmoved by Raskob's and his colleagues' attempts to create a North-South alliance, since the conservatives' economic policy seemed to cater more to established northern industrial interests than to the economic demands of the industrializing South. The conservatives' attempt to make the Democratic party a vehicle of business ideology and antiprohibitionism had alienated those Democrats who hungered for a genuine alternative to Republican normalcy and its passive economic management. Like the Democrats of the 1980s, the party during the 1920s left itself vulnerable to "values" issues because it failed to enunciate alternative economic policies to those presented by the Republicans.

With the onset of the depression the conservatives' ideology became even more contentious, as other sections of the party called for constructive and innovative responses to the economic decline of 1930–32. Other party leaders, and especially Franklin Roosevelt, sensed that voters in 1932 would demand a more positive economic policy than that of Raskob and his colleagues. The message of the Raskob wing, which championed the ability of the unfettered business sector to satisfy the material needs of

Americans and to ensure rising living standards in the most efficient manner possible, appeared increasingly insensitive to the realities of the deepening depression. FDR had succeeded in gathering around him a loose
coalition of anti-Raskob southern and western liberals by expressing ideas
which, although vague, promised new policy directions better suited to
the times. Roosevelt, therefore, responded to the new political conditions
of the depression more effectively than had his conservative opponents. By
underestimating the political consequences of the crash, the Raskob wing
failed to adapt its policy agenda sufficiently to ride the wave of popular
discontent that swept the Republicans from power in 1930 and 1932.

The conservative coalition's failure to impose its philosophy upon the
party at large was also due to strategic and tactical mistakes. Their goal of
uniting the North and South on an economically conservative platform
was not reached. In 1920 and 1924, the Northeast failed to respond to
Cox and then Davis, and the West returned to its pre-Wilson Republican
ways. Only the solid South remained electorally loyal. In 1928 the damage
caused by the Cox and Davis campaigns was made worse by Smith's loss
of the upper South to the Republicans. Me-tooism had not impressed a
northern electorate already satisfied with Republican policies; instead it
had cost the Democrats support in their key constituencies to the South
and West. By 1929 the conservatives had compiled a record of three successive landslide presidential defeats, making the party as a whole even less
prepared to follow them in the future.

The conservatives also failed to extend their influence outside the national headquarters into local and state party organizations. Their power
within the party lay in their control of the national headquarters, achieved
through the nominations of Cox, Davis, and Smith and through the large
amounts of money that they were prepared to invest in the party. Their
opponents were prepared to use the conservatives' money to build up
the party's organizational structure at the national level, and even to concede the 1928 nomination to Smith, but they did not allow the coalition
to develop significant influence within local organizations. The conservatives therefore remained merely as a clique of leaders ensconced in New
York and Washington. Their failure to develop a strong grass-roots organization was also caused by the unattractiveness of their ideology to the
rank and file of the West and South, who had little interest in policies designed to assist big business or to emphasize prohibition reform. Finally,

none of the coalition's candidates could be properly described as nationally accepted party leaders. Both Cox and Davis owed their nominations to brokered conventions, and neither developed a mass popular following during or after his campaign for the presidency. Al Smith, on the other hand, did enjoy grass-roots support in his own section. Yet Smith was not, as David Burner pointed out, a truly national leader in that he was unacceptable to large numbers of Democrats outside the northeastern states.[3]

The conservatives' organizational weakness compounded the ideological limitations and the tactical errors of their message. These factors proved to be fatal handicaps in their attempt to remold the party, making it easier for the conservatives' opponents to organize against them. When John Raskob attempted to have the DNC pass judgment on his plan for the modification of prohibition in 1931 and again in 1932, for example, Roosevelt quickly mobilized a majority of the national committee to oppose him by using his contacts with state leaders across the nation. At the Chicago convention, too, the conservatives missed their opportunity to deny FDR the nomination because they lacked a nationally acceptable candidate with strong links to the party outside the national organization. The coalition therefore remained largely isolated from the rest of the party, with their power based upon defeated presidential candidates and unelected office-holders like John Raskob and Jouett Shouse. They attempted to change the party's ideological direction from the top down through their large financial resources and control of the national organization instead of developing grass-roots support for their initiatives. The limitations of this approach quickly became apparent when the coalition was faced with the necessity of assembling votes at DNC meetings and the convention of 1932.

The conservative coalition performed a paradoxical function within the party during both the 1920s and the 1930s. Instead of uniting the Democrats around a new policy agenda, it helped to keep Democratic progressivism alive by providing men like McAdoo and Roosevelt with a clearly identifiable enemy against which to rally their supporters. The unpopularity of the northeastern conservatives assisted FDR's drive for the nomination, and then the American Liberty League enabled him to portray the New Deal as a righteous battle against economic royalism. By attempting to make the Democrats more like the Republicans, the coalition unwittingly strengthened the progressives' determination to sharpen the issues separating the two parties.

Although Franklin Roosevelt healed the party's cultural divisions of the 1920s, he was less successful in reconciling the ideological differences that also separated Democrats. Conservatives were not assimilated easily into the new party that FDR forged between 1932 and 1936. Some formed the congressional conservative coalition that developed in 1935 to block further social and economic reform; others left the party altogether and took their stand within the American Liberty League. The close connections between the conservative coalition of the 1920s, the AAPA, and the Liberty League lent continuity to the conservative cause between 1920 and 1940. The activities of both the antiprohibitionists and the Democratic conservatives during the 1920s were rehearsals for what George Wolfskill described as the "revolt of the conservatives" against the New Deal. Despite the false dawn of its triumph over national prohibition, the conservative revolt failed to achieve its objectives. Although it killed prohibition, the depression also destroyed the Raskob wing's hopes of translating that victory into a popular movement against federal activism. Transformed into a majority by the depression, the Democratic party turned away from John Davis, Al Smith, John Raskob, and their conservative colleagues, dismissing them as relics of a discredited past.

NOTES

INTRODUCTION

1. Burner, *The Politics of Provincialism*, p. 3.
2. Petersen, "Stopping Al Smith," p. 439.
3. See Lichtman, *Prejudice and the Old Politics*; Eagles, "Congressional Voting."
4. See Eagles, "Urban-Rural Conflict in the 1920s," pp. 26–48.
5. See Noggle, "The Twenties"; Eagles, "Urban-Rural Conflict in the 1920s"; Wiebe, *The Search for Order*; Hawley, *The Great War*.
6. See Kleppner, *Continuity and Change*, p. xiv; McCormick, *The Party Period and Public Policy*, p. 13; Sarasohn, *The Party of Reform*.
7. McCormick, *The Party Period and Public Policy*, p. 11.
8. Ibid., p. 13.
9. See Merrill, *Bourbon Leader*; Kelley, *The Transatlantic Persuasion*; Tugwell, *Grover Cleveland*; Hollingsworth, *The Whirligig of Politics*.
10. See, for example, Link, *Woodrow Wilson and the Progressive Era*; Wiebe, *Businessmen and Reform*; Wesser, *A Response to Progressivism*; Sarasohn, *The Party of Reform*; Tindall, "Business Progressivism."
11. See Schlesinger, Jr., *The Age of Roosevelt* 3; Wolfskill, *Revolt of the Conservatives*; Wolfskill and Hudson, *All But the People*.
12. Rosen, *Hoover, Roosevelt, and the Brains Trust*, pp. 28, 266; Kyvig, *Repealing National Prohibition*. See also Kyvig, "Objection Sustained."
13. See Eagles, "Urban-Rural Conflict in the 1920s," p. 46.
14. Wiebe, *The Search for Order, 1877–1920*, pp. 111–163.
15. Hawley, *The Great War*, pp. 66–79, 100–110. For a more recent discussion of the significance of Hawley's work, see Gerber, *The Limits of Liberalism*, pp. 184–189.
16. Quoted in Gerber, *The Limits of Liberalism*, p. 190.
17. See ibid., p. 238.
18. Burk, *The Corporate State and the Broker State*, p. vii.
19. See ibid., p. viii.
20. Ibid.
21. Ibid., p. ix.
22. See ibid., p. ix. See chapter 2 below for a discussion of the divergence between liberals' and conservatives' interpretation of the Jeffersonian legacy during the 1920s.
23. Burk, *The Corporate State and the Broker State*, p. ix. The emphasis is Burk's.
24. See Kelley, *The Transatlantic Persuasion*, p. xxxi.
25. Popkin et al., "What Have You Done for Me Lately?"; Ferguson, "Party Realignment"; Ferguson, "From Normalcy to New Deal."
26. Ferguson, "Party Realignment," p. 6.

27. Quoted in Steel, *Walter Lippmann*, p. 257.
28. Lynd and Lynd, *Middletown*, p. 417. See also McGerr, *The Decline of Popular Politics*.
29. Geertz, "Ideology as a Cultural System," p. 47.
30. See Apter, "Introduction," p. 18. In 1971 Mostafa Rejai described ideology as "an emotion-laden, myth saturated, action-related system of beliefs and values about man and society, legitimacy and authority acquired as a matter of routine and habitual reinforcement. . . . Ideologies have a high potential for mass mobilization, manipulation and control; in that sense, they are mobilized belief systems" ("Political Ideology," p. 10).
31. Bendix, "The Age of Ideology," p. 294.
32. See Rejai, "Political Ideology," p. 17; Bell, "The Passing of Fanaticism"; Lane, "The United States."
33. Lipsett, "The End of Ideology?," in ibid., p. 47–66, p. 50.
34. Burns, "Political Ideology," p. 212. See also Burns's approving quotation of Arthur M. Schlesinger's definition of ideology as "a body of systematic and rigid dogma by which people seek to understand the world—and to preserve or transform it" (ibid., p. 211). This is similar to the definition put forward by Joseph La Palombera: "a set of values that are more or less coherent" and that link "given patterns of action to the achievement or maintenance of a future, or existing, state of affairs" ("A Dissenting View," p. 246).
35. Bell, "The Passing of Fanaticism," p. 38. See also H. Mark Roelofs's definition of ideology as a "framework of political consciousness . . . [which] gives patterns for political action" (*Ideology and Myth in American Politics*, p. 4).
36. Rossiter, *Conservatism in America*, pp. 6ff.
37. Ibid., p. 71. See also McCloskey, *American Conservatism in the Age of Enterprise*. In 1970 Frank S. Meyer defined conservatism as "a movement of consciousness and action directed to recovering the tradition of civilization" ("The Recrudescent American Conservatism," p. 76).
38. Rossiter, *Conservatism in America*, p. 58.
39. See Meyer, "The Recrudescent American Conservatism," pp. 75–92.
40. See Rossiter, *Conservatism in America*, p. 191; Bernard Baruch, quoted in Gerber, *The Limits of Liberalism*, p. 42.
41. Quoted in McCloskey, *American Conservatism*, p. 48.
42. Quoted in Stone, "Calvin Coolidge," p. 139.
43. Rossiter, *Conservatism in America*, p. 12. Robert Kelley notes that liberalism, like conservatism, has almost lost any particular use as a description because "so many divergent meanings have been stuffed into it" (*The Transatlantic Persuasion*, p. xxxii).
44. See Rossiter, *Conservatism in America*, p. 71; Gerber, *The Limits of Liberalism*, pp. 44–46; Almond, "The Political Attitudes of Wealth," p. 244.
45. Peterson, *The Jefferson Image*.
46. Ibid., p. 263. See also Rossiter, *Conservatism in America*, p. 130.

47. Fine, *Laissez Faire and the General Welfare State*, p. 30; Kelley, *The Transatlantic Persuasion*, p. 406. See Kelley's general discussion on the similarities between the English and the American "liberal democratic mind" during the period 1828–96 (pp. 347, 408).
48. See Fine, *Laissez Faire and the General Welfare State*, pp. 30–31.
49. See Meyer, "The Recrudescent American Conservatism," p. 79.
50. Spencer, "The New Toryism," in *The Man versus the State*, p. 10. For a discussion of Spencer's enormous influence upon American social thought in the late nineteenth century, see Fine, *Laissez Faire and the General Welfare State*, p. 41.
51. Holcombe, *The Political Parties of Today*, p. 366.
52. Davis to Frank L. McKinney, October 8, 1934, Davis Papers, Reel 1.
53. See Dabney, *Liberalism in the South*, p. xiii; Spencer, "The New Toryism," p. 10.
54. See Fine, *Laissez-Faire and the General Welfare State*, p. vii.
55. Quoted in Rossiter, *Conservatism in America*, p. 59.
56. See McCormick, *The Party Period and Public Policy*, pp. 264ff.; Buenker, "Essay," pp. 31–69.
57. Link, *Woodrow Wilson and the Progressive Era*, pp. 21, 224.
58. See Burnham, "Essay," p. 15; Buenker, "Essay," pp. 47ff.
59. Glad, "Progressives and Business Culture," p. 81.
60. See Tobin, *Organize or Perish*, p. 8.

CHAPTER ONE

1. See Newton Baker to A. S. Burleson, April 23, 1926, Baker Papers, Container 48. See also Blum, *Joe Tumulty*, p. 242; Baruch, *The Public Years*, pp. 145, 173; Ferrell, *Woodrow Wilson and World War I*, p. 223.
2. See Burleson to Wilson, July 3, 1920, Cummings Papers, Box 68; Joe Tumulty to Edith Bolling Wilson, July 4, 1920, Tumulty Papers, Box 46.
3. See Homer Cummings, "Memoranda and Correspondence of Homer Cummings re Woodrow Wilson," January 18, 1929, Cummings Papers, Box 68; Bainbridge Colby to Wilson, July 4, 1920, Cummings Papers, Box 68; Ferrell, *Woodrow Wilson and World War I*, p. 223.
4. Sullivan, *Our Times* 6, p. 126.
5. Stratton, "Splattered with Oil," p. 65.
6. See McAdoo to Wilson, May 14, 1920, McAdoo Papers, Container 526; Baruch, *The Public Years*, p. 173; Burner, *The Politics of Provincialism*, p. 61. Little evidence exists as to Wilson's attitude toward McAdoo. David Burner suggests that the president was annoyed at the timing of McAdoo's resignation and by his son-in-law's accommodating attitude toward Elihu Root's proposed amendments to the League of Nations Covenant (*Politics of Provincialism*, p. 60). The suspicion that Wilson was not enamored of McAdoo was prevalent at the time (see, for example, Lane and Wall, *Letters of Franklin K. Lane*, p. 240) and is seemingly confirmed by

the president's consistent failure to support publicly McAdoo's political ambitions after 1918. See also Broesamle, *William Gibbs McAdoo*, p. 140.

7. *Literary Digest*, June 12, 1920, p. 20.

8. Bagby, *The Road to Normalcy*, p. 68; Blum, *Joe Tumulty*, p. 244.

9. Baruch, *The Public Years*, p. 13; Blum, *Joe Tumulty*, pp. 78–80; Lane and Wall, *Letters of Franklin K. Lane*, p. 99.

10. Baruch, *The Public Years*, p. 68.

11. Bowers, *My Life*, p. 113. For McAdoo and Tammany, see Broesamle, *William Gibbs McAdoo*, pp. 84–93.

12. See chapter 2 below.

13. Lane and Wall, *Letters of Franklin K. Lane*, p. 115; Blum, *Joe Tumulty*, p. 157.

14. See Gould, *Progressives and Prohibitionists*, pp. 257–63.

15. See Coben, *A. Mitchell Palmer*, pp. 53–89, 246–62; Coben, "A Study in Nativism," pp. 52–75.

16. For apportionment rules and the geographic distribution of convention votes, see David, Goldman, and Bain, *Politics of National Conventions*, pp. 166–67; Editorial Research Reports, *Presidential Politics, 1928*.

17. Quoted in Bagby, *Road to Normalcy*, p. 75.

18. Perrett, *America in the Twenties*, p. 111.

19. Cox, *Journey through My Years*, p. 117.

20. Mayer, *The Republican Party*, p. 373.

21. Cox, *Journey through My Years*, p. 117.

22. See ibid., p. 150; Morris, *Progressive Democracy of James M. Cox*, p. 82.

23. Kenkel, *Progressives and Protection*, p. 101.

24. Quoted in ibid., pp. 25, 92.

25. Burner, *The Politics of Provincialism*, p. 62. See also Steuart, *Wayne Wheeler, Dry Boss*, p. 162; Gould, *Progressives and Prohibitionists*, p. 269; Kerr, *Organized for Prohibition*, p. 169.

26. Walsh to Dan Tracy, May 29, 1920, Walsh Papers, Box 372.

27. Quoted in Bagby, *The Road to Normalcy*, p. 62.

28. Quoted in Schriftgiesser, *This Was Normalcy*, p. 49.

29. Perrett, *America in the Twenties*, p. 111.

30. Mencken, *Carnival of Buncombe*, p. 15.

31. Davis, *FDR: The Beckoning of Destiny*, p. 608.

32. Levine, *Defender of the Faith*, p. 151.

33. "The Democratic Platform of 1920," p. 2388.

34. Ibid., p. 2391. By February 1919, the demands of wartime government financing had pushed income tax rates up to a maximum of 77 percent, corporation tax rates to a maximum of 12 percent, excess-profits tax rates to a top rate of 40 percent, and inheritance tax rates to a maximum of 15 percent. See Paul, *Taxation in the United States*, p. 114; Ratner, *American Taxation*, pp. 321–99, Witte, *The Politics and Development of the Federal Income Tax*, p. 86.

35. "The Democratic Platform of 1920," p. 2395.

36. Blum, *Joe Tumulty*, pp. 250, 251. For the impact of labor issues in the campaign, see Bornet, *Labor Politics in a Democratic Republic*, p. 41; Zieger, *Republicans and Labor*, p. 36.
37. See Hines, *War History of American Railroads*, pp. 220–23; Sullivan, *Our Times* 6, p. 537.
38. Cebula, *James M. Cox*, p. 108.
39. Quoted in Fecher, *Mencken*, p. 160.
40. Bryan to Pat Harrison, August 7, 1920, Bryan Papers, Container 33.
41. Quoted in Levine, *Defender of the Faith*, p. 169.
42. Tumulty to Edith Bolling Wilson, July 4, 1920, Tumulty Papers, Container 46.
43. See Cook, *Torchlight Parade*, p. 243; Hanks, "The Democratic Party in 1920," p. 440.
44. McCoy, "Election of 1920," p. 2371.
45. See Burner, *The Politics of Provincialism*, p. 65.
46. Cox to Tumulty, April 24, 1928, Cox Papers, Box 40.
47. See Sarasohn, *The Party of Reform*, p. 218; Schlesinger, *The Age of Roosevelt* 3, p. 409.
48. Chadbourne to Cox, September 12, 1920, Bryan Papers, Box 33.
49. Woolley to Cox, August 17, 1920, Woolley Papers, Box 3.
50. Bagby, *The Road to Normalcy*, p. 147.
51. Early to FDR, August 18, 1920, FDR Papers, Campaign of 1920—Personal Correspondence, Container 2.
52. Hanks, "The Democratic Party in 1920," p. 361.
53. Cashman, *America in the Twenties and Thirties*, p. 87.
54. McCarthy to FDR, October 8, 1920, FDR Papers, Papers as Vice-Presidential Candidate, Container 7.
55. McCarthy to Roosevelt, October 16, 1920, FDR Papers, Papers as Vice-Presidential Candidate, Container 3.
56. Howe to John K. Sague, September 20, 1920, FDR Papers, Papers as Vice-Presidential Candidate, Container 10.
57. Burner, *The Politics of Provincialism*, p. 65.
58. See Cummings Papers, Box 68, "Correspondence with Woodrow Wilson re Democratic Party Politics."
59. Louis Antisdale to Roosevelt, June 21, 1920, FDR Papers, Papers as Vice-Presidential Candidate, Container 4.
60. Blum, *Joe Tumulty*, p. 248.
61. Woolley to Cox, September 14, 1920, Woolley Papers, Box 3.
62. *New York Times*, July 23, 1928, p. 4; McCoy, "Election of 1920," p. 2371.
63. McCarthy to FDR, October 8, 1920, FDR Papers, Papers as Vice-Presidential Candidate, Container 7.
64. Pittman to White, September 25, 1920, Cox Papers, Box 41, File 41.
65. Israel, *Nevada's Key Pittman*, p. 44.
66. Pittman to White, September 25, 1920, Cox Papers, Box 41, File 41.

67. *New York Times*, November 3, 1920, p. 6.

68. Daniels to M. A. Matthews, November 20, 1920, Daniels Papers, Container 673.

69. Sarasohn, *The Party of Reform*, pp. 207, 231.

70. Cox, *Journey through My Years*, p. 273.

71. Quoted in Fenton, *Politics in the Border States*, p. 163.

72. Huthmacher, *Massachusetts People and Politics*, p. 42. See also Lichtman, *Prejudice and the Old Politics*, pp. 98–104.

73. Burner, "The Breakup of the Wilson Coalition of 1916," p. 33.

74. Allswang, *A House for All Peoples*, p. 42.

75. Lane and Wall, *Letters of Franklin K. Lane*, p. 372. Lane also blamed Wilson's unpopularity for Cox's defeat. "Cox will be defeated not by those who dislike him," he declared during the campaign, "but by those who dislike Wilson" (quoted in Cashman, *America in the Twenties and Thirties*, p. 87).

76. See Lane and Wall, *Letters of Franklin K. Lane*, p. 229.

77. Sarasohn, *The Party of Reform*, p. 232.

78. See McCoy, "Election of 1920," pp. 2349–2456; Burner, "The Breakup of the Wilsonian Coalition"; Hanks "The Democratic Party in 1920," p. 361.

79. Lane and Wall, *Letters of Franklin K. Lane*, p. 301.

80. Fite, *George N. Peek*, p. 126.

81. Kleppner, *Change and Continuity in Electoral Politics*, pp. 146–54; Burner, "Breakup of the Wilson Coalition," p. 19.

82. Ferrell, *Woodrow Wilson and World War I*, p. 193.

83. In the month following the Armistice, the Department of War canceled $2.5 billion worth of contracts (see ibid., p. 197). See also Coben, *A. Mitchell Palmer*, p. 157; Cebula, *James M. Cox*, p. 116; Burner, "The Breakup of the Wilson Coalition," p. 27; Burner, "1919: Prelude to Normalcy," p. 11; Lane and Wall, *Letters of Franklin K. Lane*, p. 307.

84. Coben, *A. Mitchell Palmer*, p. 173; Sullivan, *Our Times* 6, pp. 154–67. In 1926, by contrast, 1,035 strikes occurred, involving 330,000 workers (see Slichter, "Current Labor Policies of American Industries," p. 428).

85. Zieger, *Republicans and Labor*, pp. 21ff; Sullivan, *Our Times* 6, pp. 160–63; Taft, *The AFL in the Time of Gompers*, pp. 385–94; Brody, *Steelworkers in America*, pp. 231–62.

86. Ewing, *Congressional Elections*, p. 91.

87. David, *Party Strength in the United States*.

88. Ibid, pp. 302–3.

89. Kleppner, *Continuity and Change*, p. 141; David, *Party Strength in the United States*, pp. 302–3.

90. Quoted in Levine, *Defender of the Faith*, p. 81. The capitalization is Bryan's.

91. See Burner, "The Democratic Party in the Election of 1924," p. 96.

CHAPTER TWO

1. Blum, *Joe Tumulty*, p. 257. See also Burner, *The Politics of Provincialism*, p. 51; Murray, *The 103rd Ballot*, p. 87; Perrett, *America in the Twenties*, p. 110; Link, *Woodrow Wilson and the Progressive Era*, p. 27; Harbaugh, *Lawyer's Lawyer*, p. 170. Arthur Schlesinger described McAdoo as "facile and plastic," one who could simultaneously assail Wall Street and the monopolies while earning his living as a corporate lawyer (*The Age of Roosevelt* 1, p. 95).
2. See Baker to John W. Davis, July 6, 1932, Davis Papers, Series 4, Box 83.
3. For McAdoo's early years see Broesamle, *William Gibbs McAdoo*, pp. 3–8.
4. Quoted in Burner, *The Politics of Provincialism*, p. 114.
5. Broesamle, *William Gibbs McAdoo*, pp. 14–24.
6. For a fuller account of McAdoo's early years, see McAdoo, *Crowded Years*; Synon, *McAdoo*.
7. Broesamle, *William Gibbs McAdoo*, p. 36.
8. Schlesinger, *The Age of Roosevelt* 1, p. 29.
9. McAdoo, *Crowded Years*, p. 121.
10. Synon, *McAdoo*, p. 46; Blum, *Joe Tumulty*, p. 45.
11. Synon, *McAdoo*, p. 9.
12. See ibid., p. 103.
13. Broesamle, *William Gibbs McAdoo*, p. 109. For a description of the travails of the Federal Reserve Act, see ibid., pp. 94–137; Link, *Woodrow Wilson and the Progressive Era*, pp. 44–52.
14. Quoted in Broesamle, *William Gibbs McAdoo*, p. 125. See also Blum, *Joe Tumulty*, p. 70.
15. Sullivan, *Our Times* 5, p. 462.
16. Broesamle, *William Gibbs McAdoo*, pp. 155–58.
17. See Paul, *Taxation in the United States*, pp. 113–14. In fiscal years 1918 and 1919, the total cost of the war was approximately $24 billion. Of this amount, $8.8 billion was raised through taxes and $15.5 billion through Liberty and Victory loans. In 1917 the federal income tax threshold was lowered to $1,000, but the average wage was $830, ensuring that only the middle- and higher-income earners were affected (see Ferrell, *Woodrow Wilson and World War I*, p. 88).
18. Broesamle, *William Gibbs McAdoo*, pp. 217–33.
19. Ibid., p. 233.
20. Ferrell, *Woodrow Wilson and World War I*, p. 104.
21. Kerr, "Decision for Federal Control," pp. 550–60.
22. Ibid., p. 557.
23. Hines, *War History of American Railroads*, p. 155.
24. Lippmann, "Two Leading Democratic Candidates," p. 11.
25. See Newton D. Baker to McAdoo, July 3, 1923, McAdoo Papers, Container 152; McAdoo to Baker, July 10, 1923, ibid., Container 151.

26. Hennings, "California Democratic Politics," p. 268; Brown, *Hood, Bonnet, and Little Brown Jug*, p. 173.
27. See Maurice F. Lyons to Robert Woolley, November 8, 1920, Woolley Papers, Container 12.
28. See Schwarz, *The Speculator*, p. 180.
29. McAdoo to Doheny, March 1, 1922, McAdoo Papers, Container 261.
30. Steuart, *Wayne Wheeler, Dry Boss*, p. 218.
31. *Literary Digest*, June 30, 1923, p. 5.
32. See the *New York Times*, June 27, 1923, p. 22; Brown, *Hood, Bonnet, and Little Brown Jug*, p. 177.
33. Noggle, *Teapot Dome*, p. 60.
34. In March 1924 Daniel Roper reported that over $21,000 had been raised, with Chadbourne donating $10,000 and Baruch $7,500. See Roper to McAdoo, March 15, 1924, McAdoo Papers, Container 297. Baruch's contributions may well have been much larger; in March 1924 one of McAdoo's supporters claimed that the financier had donated at least $15,000 to the McAdoo cause. See Frank A. Thompson to Breckinridge Long, March 17, 1924, Long Papers, Container 172.
35. See McAdoo Papers, Container 287, December 5, 1923; Noggle, *Teapot Dome*, p. 99.
36. McAdoo to Bowers, January 11, 1924, McAdoo Papers, Container 291.
37. Rockwell to McAdoo, January 11, 1924, McAdoo Papers, Container 291.
38. McAdoo to James D. Phelan, January 22, 1924, McAdoo Papers, Container 293. Although McAdoo and his advisers were displeased at the selection of New York, this did not represent a defeat for their cause. The Smith forces, too, would have preferred a different site. (See chapter 3, below.) New York was selected not because of a factional victory or defeat but rather because it offered the most money to the financially embarrassed DNC.
39. See Burner, *The Politics of Provincialism*, p. 111.
40. For an account of the Teapot Dome scandal, see Noggle, *Teapot Dome*; Noggle, "Oil and Politics." See also Sullivan, *Our Times* 6, pp. 272–349.
41. Doheny also revealed that three other prominent members of Wilson's administration had accepted retainers: Franklin K. Lane (secretary of interior), Lindley Garrison (secretary of war), and Thomas W. Gregory (attorney general). See Bates, "The Teapot Dome Scandal and the Election of 1924," p. 305; Margulies, *Senator Lenroot of Wisconsin*, pp. 371–76.
42. Over twenty states had some type of presidential primary election, electing over 600 delegates to the national convention. A total of 1094 delegates assembled at New York. The remaining states' delegates were chosen by state conventions. See Merriam and Gosnell, *The American Party System*, p. 291.
43. See McAdoo Papers, Container 295; Noggle, "Oil and Politics," p. 60; Stratton, "Splattered with Oil," p. 65.
44. See McAdoo to Senator Irving L. Lenroot, Chairman of the Senate Public Lands Committee, February 7, 1924, McAdoo Papers, Container 295.

45. See Thomas L. Chadbourne to McAdoo, February 15, 1924, McAdoo Papers, Container 296; Stratton, "Splattered with Oil," p. 68.

46. See Hicks, *Republican Ascendancy*, p. 84. Between 1922 and 1928, the index of industrial production climbed by over 70 percent, the gross national product rose by 40 percent in real terms, per capita income increased by almost 30 per cent, real earnings by 22 percent, and industrial productivity by 75 percent. See Hawley, *The Great War*, p. 81.

47. Bates, "Teapot Dome," p. 306.

48. Stratton, "Splattered with Oil," p. 69.

49. Walsh to McAdoo, December 18, 1924, Walsh Papers, Container 375.

50. Walsh to McAdoo, April 3, 1924, McAdoo Papers, Container 300. See also Stratton, "Splattered with Oil," p. 70.

51. Dodd to Daniels, April 7, 1925, Daniels Papers, Reel 49.

52. Lippmann, "Two Leading Democratic Candidates," p. 11.

53. Quoted in Perrett, *America in the Twenties*, p. 110.

54. Creel to Daniels, February 10, 1931, Daniels Papers, Reel 47. See also Felix Frankfurter to S. K. Ratcliffe, 20 June, 1924, Frankfurter Papers, Reel 56; Robert Lansing to John W. Davis, January 18, 1924, Davis Papers.

55. Sarasohn, *The Party of Reform*, p. 218.

56. See McAdoo, Radio Address, January 8, 1924, McAdoo Papers, Container 291.

57. McAdoo, "Address Delivered by William G. McAdoo at the Convention of the Co-operative Club International, Des Moines, Iowa, May 25, 1926," p. 3, McAdoo Papers, Container 326.

58. Ibid., pp. 13-14. For the growth of private bureaucracies during the 1920s, see Hawley, *The Great War*, p. 91.

59. McAdoo, "Address Delivered by William G. McAdoo at the Convention of the Co-operative Club International, Des Moines, Iowa, May 25, 1926," pp. 14-16, McAdoo Papers, Container 326.

60. See Kenkel, *Progressives and Protection*, pp. 94-95 and 151-59 for the Underwood and Fordney-McCumber tariffs; McAdoo to William L. O'Connell, March 21, 1924, McAdoo Papers, Container 298.

61. See the *New York Times*, June 19, 1924.

62. Chadbourne to McAdoo, November 30, 1923, McAdoo Papers, Container 287.

63. McAdoo to Chadbourne, December 10, 1923, McAdoo Papers, Container 287.

64. See Brice Claggett to George M. Kendall, March 31, 1920, McAdoo Papers, Container 232.

65. See Chadbourne to McAdoo, November 30, 1923, McAdoo Papers, Container 287.

66. The excess-profits tax was imposed in 1917, eventually reaching a maximum of 80 percent at the end of 1918. It was repealed in 1921. See Paul, *Taxation in the United States*, pp. 112, 128.

67. See Baruch to McAdoo, December 21, 1923, McAdoo Papers, Container 289.

68. McAdoo to Roper, January 2, 1924, McAdoo Papers, Container 290.

69. McAdoo to Roper, January 7, 1924, McAdoo Papers, Container 291.

70. See McAdoo to Roper, January 11, 1924, McAdoo Papers, Container 291.

71. McAdoo, "Jackson Day Address," January 8, 1924, p. 3, McAdoo Papers, Container 291.

72. Ibid., p. 5. McAdoo's argument that tariff reduction would reduce the cost of farm implements was specious. Domestic manufacturers produced such goods more cheaply than did foreign firms, which meant that almost no farm implements entered the United States from overseas. It was for this reason that farm implements had been placed on the free list by the Fordney-McCumber Tariff of 1922. See Saloutos and Hicks, *Agricultural Discontent*, p. 374; Ratner, *The Tariff in American History*, pp. 47–49.

73. Chadbourne to McAdoo, November 30, 1923, McAdoo Papers, Container 287.

74. Carter to Walters, March 20, 1924, Davis Papers, Series 4, Box 26.

75. House to Long, January 15, 1924, Long Papers, Container 172.

76. R. M. Barton to McAdoo, June 18, 1924, McAdoo Papers, Container 306.

77. *Portland Press Herald*, July 8, 1924, FDR Papers, Papers Pertaining to the Campaign of 1924, Container 3.

78. McAdoo to Lea, April 17, 1924, McAdoo Papers, Container 301.

79. McAdoo to David Ladd Rockwell, February 12, 1924, McAdoo Papers, Container 295.

80. See correspondence for February 18 and 19, 1924, McAdoo Papers, Container 296.

81. Davis to Polk, February 18, 1924, Davis Papers, Series 4, Box 26.

82. See Noggle, *Teapot Dome*, p. 137.

83. See Allen, "The McAdoo Campaign," p. 221.

84. Schwarz, *The Speculator*, p. 180; Noggle, *Teapot Dome*, p. 159.

85. Brown, *Hood, Bonnet, and Little Brown Jug*, p. 188.

86. Editorial Research Reports, *Presidential Politics, 1928*, unpaged.

87. Long to Missouri Delegates, May 24, 1924, Long Papers, Subject File "Political Campaign 1924 XXI," Container 173.

88. See McAdoo to William Hard, July 17, 1924, McAdoo Papers, Container 306. See also McAdoo to George Creel, March 1, 1927, ibid., Container 333.

89. See Hennings, "California Democratic Politics," p. 278.

90. McAdoo to Thomas Love, January 12, 1925, McAdoo Papers, Container 312. See also McAdoo to Lewis C. Humphrey, December 23, 1925, ibid., Container 321.

91. See McAdoo, Speech to WCTU, September 26, 1926, McAdoo Papers, Container 565.

92. See chapter 3 below.

CHAPTER THREE

1. Bowers, *My Life*, p. 121.

2. White, *Politics*, p. 104.

3. Burner, *The Politics of Provincialism*, p. 140. See also Murray, *The 103rd Ballot*, pp. 215ff.; Mayer, *The Republican Party*, p. 397; Hawley, *The Great War*, p. 78.
4. James M. Cox to Newton D. Baker, July 15, 1924, Cox Papers, Box 8. Baker was a keen supporter of Cox's candidacy; see Baker to James E. Campbell, April 15, 1924, Baker Papers, Container 50.
5. Cox, *Journey through My Years*, p. 324. See also James E. Campbell to James M. Cox, May 7, 1924, Cox Papers, Box 11.
6. For a detailed biography of Underwood, see Johnson, *Oscar W. Underwood.*
7. Underwood, *The Drifting Sands of Party Politics*, p. xxi.
8. Dabney, *Liberalism in the South*, p. 276.
9. Johnson, *Oscar W. Underwood*, pp. 385–88.
10. Underwood, *The Drifting Sands of Party Politics*, pp. 158, 340.
11. Ibid., p. 383.
12. Ibid., p. 45.
13. See Murray, *The 103rd Ballot*, p. 50.
14. Johnson, *Oscar W. Underwood*, pp. 393–404; Brown, *Hood, Bonnet, and Little Brown Jug*, pp. 177–83.
15. See Johnson, *Oscar W. Underwood*, pp. 390–91.
16. See Burner, *The Politics of Provincialism*, p. 123.
17. Howe to FDR, February 25, 1924, Howe Papers, Container 40.
18. Steuart, *Wayne Wheeler, Dry Boss*, p. 221.
19. See Wesser, *A Response to Progressivism*, p. 124; Weiss, *Charles Francis Murphy*, p. 65.
20. See Carter, "The Campaign of 1928 Re-examined," pp. 263–72.
21. See Perkins, "Reminiscences," 2:289, Columbia University Oral History Project, 1955.
22. Creel to Josephus Daniels, February 22, 1927, Daniels Papers, Reel 47.
23. Mack to Smith (henceforth often referred to as AES), January 24, 1924, Graves Papers, Box 44.
24. George Van Kennan to AES, April 15, 1924, Graves Papers, Container 58.
25. G. N. Orcutt to AES, April 5, 1924, Graves Papers, Container 58.
26. Parker to Chester D. Pugsley, February 26, 1924, Parker Papers, Box 9. See also Andrew P. Ronan to James J. Hoey, June 4, 1924, FDR Papers, Papers Pertaining to the Campaign of 1924, Container 16.
27. Ickes, *Autobiography of a Curmudgeon*, p. 250.
28. Huntley, *The Life of John W. Davis*, p. xiii.
29. Cox to Eugene K. Moulton, January 22, 1951, Cox Papers, Box 8, "Baker, Newton D.—2."
30. Davis, *Party Government in the United States*, p. 40.
31. Ibid., p. 38.
32. See Davis to P. C. Jeffrey, March 23, 1931, Davis Papers, Series 4, Box 72.
33. Davis to Hull, May 25, 1923, Davis Papers, Series 3, Box 16.
34. Quoted in Huntley, *John W. Davis*, p. 262.
35. Ibid., p. 263.

36. Quoted in Burner, "The Election of 1924," p. 2537.

37. See Harbaugh, *Lawyer's Lawyer*, pp. 410ff.

38. Ibid, p. 259. See Davis to Samuel H. Halley, January 30, 1923, Davis Papers, Series 3, Box 18.

39. Frankfurter to Charles C. Burlingham, October 29, 1924, Frankfurter Papers, Reel 19. According to Larry Gerber, Frankfurter "held in contempt" lawyers who pandered to wealthy clients in order to become wealthy themselves. "If it means that you should be that kind of subservient creature to have the most desirable clients, the biggest clients in the country, if that's what it means to be a leader of the bar, I never want to be a leader of the bar. The price of admission is too high" (quoted in Gerber, *The Limits of Liberalism*, p. 109).

40. Davis to J. W. Johnston, September 12, 1923, Davis Papers, Series 3, Box 18.

41. Harbaugh, *Lawyer's Lawyer*, pp. 208ff.

42. Davis to Lansing, December 25, 1923, Davis Papers, Series 3, Box 18. "Hirum J." refers to Hiram Johnson.

43. Homer S. Cummings, Memorandum of Conversation, May 31, 1920, Cummings Papers, Box 68.

44. Johnson, *Diary Letters of Hiram Johnson* 4, June 3, 1924, unpaged.

45. Quoted in Harbaugh, *Lawyer's Lawyer*, p. 212.

46. See Burner, *The Politics of Provincialism*; Burner, "The Election of 1924"; Murray, *The 103rd Ballot*; Neal, *The World beyond the Hudson*; and Harbaugh, *Lawyer's Lawyer*.

47. Editorial Research Reports, *Presidential Politics, 1928*, unpaged.

48. Stratton, "Splattered with Oil," p. 74.

49. Murray, *The 103rd Ballot*, p. 197.

50. Bowers, *My Life*, pp. 115–18.

51. Mencken, *A Carnival of Buncombe*, p. 82.

52. See McAdoo Papers, Container 309.

53. See Arthur F. Mullen to David Ladd Rockwell, May 6, 1924, McAdoo Papers, Container 302.

54. Estimates of the Klan's strength in 1923 and 1924 vary between two and three million members. See Chalmers, *Hooded Americanism*, p. 109; on McAdoo as the Klan's candidate by default, see ibid., p. 203. In Texas, the great issue dividing Democrats for McAdoo and those for Underwood was the Klan. See Brown, *Hood, Bonnet, and Little Brown Jug*, p. 183. During McAdoo's unsuccessful reelection campaign for his U.S. Senate seat in 1938, his opponent's campaign manager produced a tattered KKK membership card made out in McAdoo's name and signed by Hiram Evans. The secretary categorically denied that he had ever been a member of the Klan, and Evans declared that he had never signed such a card. No evidence has subsequently emerged to challenge either denial. See Rice, *The Ku Klux Klan in American Politics*, p. 99; Cato Sells to McAdoo, January 30, 1924, McAdoo Papers, Container 294.

55. Quoted in Chalmers, *Hooded Americanism*, p. 211.
56. See Murray, *The 103rd Ballot*, pp. 168–69; Burner, *The Politics of Provincialism*, p. 119.
57. The vote was 542 3/20 to 541 3/20 (Burner, *The Politics of Provincialism*, p. 118).
58. Cramer, *Newton D. Baker*, pp. 218–21.
59. "The Democratic Platform of 1924," p. 2503.
60. Quoted in Israel, *Nevada's Key Pittman*, p. 53.
61. Fite, *George N. Peek*, pp. 96–130.
62. Ibid., p. 60.
63. Baruch, *The Public Years*, pp. 165–70; Stanley, "Congressional Democrats," p. 266.
64. James W. Wadsworth, the conservative Republican U.S. senator from New York, opposed the McNary-Haugen scheme on the principle that "if the government is to guarantee farmers against all losses due to such causes as over-production or slowing down of demand, it will have to protect other people who produce things and want to be assured of a profit" (quoted in Fausold, *James W. Wadsworth*, p. 178).
65. See Fite, "The Farmer's Dilemma," p. 100; Fite, *George N. Peek*, p. 62.
66. Saloutos and Hicks, *Agricultural Discontent in the Middle West*, pp. 372–403; Fite, *George N. Peek*, pp. 86, 161, 173, 190ff.
67. Hubbard, *Origins of the TVA*. See also Schlesinger, *The Age of Roosevelt* 2, p. 322; Newton Baker to Carter Glass, March 25, 1924, Glass Papers, Box 1. For the attitude of congressional Democrats to the Muscle Shoals issue, see Stanley, "The Congressional Democrats," p. 124.
68. See "The Democratic Platform of 1924," pp. 2491–2523 passim.
69. See Burner, *The Politics of Provincialism*, p. 117.
70. Milton to Walsh, December 15, 1924, Walsh Papers, Box 375. See also Walsh to J. F. T. O'Connor, November 9, 1926, ibid., Box 376.
71. Brown, *Hood, Bonnet and Little Brown Jug*, p. 207.
72. Bowers to Cox, July 18, 1924, Cox Papers, Box 10. See Cox to Bowers, July 21, 1924, ibid.
73. Quoted in Cook, "The Presidential Candidacy of John W. Davis," p. 68.
74. Frankfurter to Charles C. Burlingham, October 29, 1924, Frankfurter Papers, Reel 19.
75. Frankfurter to Walter Lippmann, Undated, Frankfurter Papers, Reel 47.
76. Of the 273 replies to Davis's circular surveyed, 110 made specific reference to the corruption issue, 84 to the need for reductions of tariff rates, 65 to the need for effective farm relief, 56 to the desirability of further reductions in income tax, 44 to the further reduction of the cost of government, 42 to the need to enter the League of Nations, 27 to the issue of denouncing the Klan by name, 23 to social welfare issues such as the ratification of the proposed child labor amendment, and 14 to the issue of prohibition reform. See Davis Papers, Series 4, Box 146.
77. See Davis Papers, Series 4, Box 146, "Individual States" folder. California, Nevada,

Arizona, New Mexico, Oregon, Washington, and Wyoming are treated as western for the purposes of this discussion. Montana, Idaho, Colorado, and Utah are treated as mountain states.

78. Ibid. The states of the old Confederacy, as well as Oklahoma and Kentucky, are treated as southern in this context.

79. Ibid. The midwestern states are Illinois, Indiana, Missouri, Kansas, Nebraska, Minnesota, Iowa, the Dakotas, Michigan, and Wisconsin.

80. Ibid.

81. Ibid. These states are New York, New Jersey, Ohio, Pennsylvania, West Virginia, Delaware, and Maryland.

82. See Murray, *The 103rd Ballot*, p. 248.

83. See Harbaugh, *Lawyer's Lawyer*, p. 237.

84. Noggle, *Teapot Dome*, pp. 167–70; Bates, "The Teapot Dome Scandal," p. 320.

85. Wayne Wheeler complained that Davis made a subtle bid for wet votes by "constant repetition of wet catch phrases like 'personal liberty,' 'illegal search and seizure,' and 'home rule'" (Steuart, *Wayne Wheeler, Dry Boss*, p. 86). The Anti Saloon League had marked Davis as an enemy as early as 1915, when he, as solicitor general, declined to argue for the validity of the Webb-Kenyon Act. See Vose, *Constitutional Change*, p. 79.

86. See Graves Papers, Container 51, "National Convention, 1924."

87. Quoted in Cook, "John W. Davis," p. 87.

88. Pittman to S. M. Pickett, September 27, 1924, Pittman Papers, Box 14.

89. See George Fort Milton to Long, August 12, 1924, Long Papers, Container 79.

90. Breckinridge Long, Diary entry, September 19, 1924, Long Papers, Box 3, "Diaries."

91. Those western delegates who replied to Davis's circular letters were almost unanimous in their belief that La Follette had a strong chance of winning several mountain and western states. See Davis Papers, Series 4, Box 146, "Individual States," especially Nevada, Washington, Wyoming, Montana, Idaho, Colorado, Utah, Minnesota, and Wisconsin.

92. See Cox to Baker, July 15, 1924, Baker Papers, Container 75. See also John Foster Dulles to John W. Davis, July 18, 1924, Davis Papers, Series IV, Box 31; A. Mitchell Palmer to Davis, September 30, 1924, ibid., Box 33.

93. See "Progressive Platform, 1924," p. 2520; Harbaugh, *Lawyer's Lawyer*, pp. 244–45.

94. Davis to Bryan, August 24, 1924, Bryan Papers, Container 40.

95. Cook, "John W. Davis," p. 101; Taft, *The AFL in the Time of Gompers*, p. 483.

96. See Homer Cummings to J. Bruce Kremer, September 3, 1924, Cummings Papers, Box 52.

97. McAdoo to Anna D. Oleson, October 11, 1924, McAdoo Papers, Container 308.

98. McAdoo to Milton, October 1, 1924, McAdoo Papers, Container 308.

99. Harbaugh, *Lawyer's Lawyer*, p. 234.

100. "McAdoo Speech, 1924 Campaign," McAdoo Papers, Container 565.

101. See, for example, David C. Reay to Davis, November 7, 1924, Davis Papers, Series 4, Box 35.
102. See Maurice D. Murphy to AES, November 19, 1924, Graves Papers, Container 51. In Tennessee, Davis received 40,000 fewer votes than Cox. In Kentucky he ran 100,000 behind Cox, and in California the difference was 125,000.
103. Bowers to Thomas J. Walsh, August 21, 1924, Walsh Papers, Container 373. See also Robert Woolley to Davis, October 7, 1924, Davis Papers, Series 4, Box 33.
104. Cook, "John W. Davis," p. 86. See also Israel, *Nevada's Key Pittman*, p. 58.
105. Jesse H. Jones to James M. Cox, October 17, 1924, Cox Papers, Box 4.
106. *New York Times*, July 23, 1928, p. 4; Hicks, *Republican Ascendancy*, p. 100.
107. Quoted in Murray, *The 103rd Ballot*, p. 245.
108. See Zieger, *Republicans and Labor*, p. 181.
109. Mencken, *A Carnival of Buncombe*, p. 97.
110. Jouett Shouse reminiscence to George Wolfskill, June 30, 1959, Shouse Papers, Box 5, "George Wolfskill Correspondence."
111. David, *Party Strength in the United States*, pp. 302–3.
112. Ibid., pp. 288–89.
113. Ibid., pp. 200–203, 164–67, 114–17, 110–13, 236–39, 168–71, 224–27.
114. Ibid, pp. 208–11, 240–43.
115. Ibid., pp. 302–3.
116. Ibid., pp. 294–95.
117. Ibid., pp. 144–47, 140–43, 106–9, 102–5.
118. Harbaugh, *Lawyer's Lawyer*, p. 247.
119. "Why Should the Democratic Party Survive?," *Nation* 119, November 19, 1924, p. 534.
120. These states were Idaho, Montana, Nevada, New Mexico, North Dakota, Utah, Arizona, and Wisconsin. Their combined total of electoral votes was thirty-six, which would not have affected the outcome of the election.
121. "Why Should the Democratic Party Survive?," *Nation* 119, November 19, 1924, p. 534.
122. Quoted in the *Literary Digest*, November 22, 1924, p. 14.
123. In 1912 Wilson won only 42 percent of the total vote. His total of 6,293,019 votes was less than that polled by Bryan in 1908 and was 1,311,444 votes less than the combined totals of Roosevelt and Taft. In 1916 Wilson won by a margin of only 591,385 votes and 23 electoral votes. See Link, *Woodrow Wilson and the Progressive Era*, pp. 24, 249.
124. Cox to Len C. Koplin, December 27, 1924, Cox Papers, Box 4.
125. Claggett to Milton, November 17, 1924, McAdoo Papers, Container 309.
126. Milton to Walsh, December 15, 1924, Walsh Papers, Container 375.
127. Walsh to Milton, December 23, 1924, Walsh Papers, Container 375.
128. See Sam Amidon to McAdoo, November 8, 1924, McAdoo Papers, Container 309.

CHAPTER FOUR

1. Merriam and Gosnell, *The American Party System*, p. 67.
2. Ibid., p. 64.
3. See Bone, *Party Committees and National Politics*, pp. 126–65.
4. Merriam and Gosnell, *The American Party System*, p. 63.
5. See Burner, *The Politics of Provincialism*, p. 147.
6. See Bone, *Party Committees and National Politics*, pp. 4–35.
7. Cotter and Hennessy, *Politics without Power*, p. 20; Ware, *Partner and I*, p. 149.
8. Cotter and Hennessy, *Politics without Power*, p. 25.
9. Ibid., p. 36.
10. Merriam and Gosnell, *The American Party System*, p. 61.
11. Ibid., p. 79.
12. See McGerr, *Decline of Popular Politics*, p. 180. The record of the GOP's attempts to create a permanent publicity organization was little better than that of the Democrats during this period. In 1915 the National Republican Publicity Association was created in Washington, but this organization was largely inactive. The RNC was equally supine until 1918, when Will H. Hays became national chairman. Hays revived his organization, and it played a prominent role during the 1920 campaign. The committee raised and spent over $2 million between 1918 and 1920. After Harding's victory, however, the committee resumed its earlier somnolence, and for the rest of the decade the Republicans relied on their control of the White House and Congress to disseminate its publicity. See Smoger, "Organizing Political Campaigns," p. 99.
13. See Levine, *Defender of the Faith*, p. 183; Brown, *Hood, Bonnet, and Little Brown Jug*, p. 172.
14. See Frank Pace to Homer Cummings, November 3, 1921, Cummings Papers, Box 50.
15. Glass to White, August 23, 1921, Glass Papers, Box 165.
16. See Woolley Papers, Container 11, "Love, Thomas B., 1916–1921."
17. Cebula, *James M. Cox*, p. 119.
18. Baruch to Tumulty, September 2, 1921, Tumulty Papers, Container 55. Baruch later donated $100,000 to the party during the presidential campaign of 1924. See Gerber, *The Limits of Liberalism*, p. 193.
19. See Glass Papers, Box 165; Woolley, "Politics Is Hell," draft autobiography, chapter 43: "Ousting a National Chairman," Woolley Papers, Container 44; Burner, *The Politics of Provincialism*, p. 146.
20. See Paul, *Taxation in the United States*, p. 101; Ratner, *American Taxation*, pp. 326–28.
21. Ratner, *The Tariff in American History*, pp. 44–46; Kenkel, *Progressives and Protection*, pp. 94–95.
22. See Hinton, *Cordell Hull*, pp. 182, 166.
23. Hull to Rufus Doak, January 25, 1924, Hull Papers, Reel 2, Folder 11.

24. Cotter and Hennessy, *Politics without Power*, p. 67; Hinton, *Cordell Hull*, p. 166.
25. During the whole of 1922 Hull could collect only $31,781 (Hull Papers, Reel 2, Folder 17). Detailed financial accounts for Hull's tenure as chairman of the DNC can be found here.
26. Hull to Wilson, February 7, 1923, Hull Papers, Reel 1, Folder 6.
27. Hinton, *Cordell Hull*, p. 169.
28. Hull to Davis, December 8, 1922, Davis Papers, Series 3, Box 16.
29. Hull Papers, Reel 2, Folder 17. New York contributed $16,135; Illinois, $7,800; Indiana, $3,000; Ohio, $2,785; Connecticut, $1,020; and Missouri, $1,575.
30. Ibid.
31. Woolley, "Politics Is Hell," draft autobiography, chapter 45, Woolley Papers, Container 44.
32. *New York Times*, February 2, 1926, p. 6, and October 29, 1926, p. 5. See also Timmons, *Jesse H. Jones*, p. 135.
33. See Davis to Robert Lansing, February 2, 1925, Davis Papers, Series 4, Box 36.
34. John M. Townsend, "Politicians Guessing," *Chicago Manufacturers News*, March 16, 1925, McAdoo Papers, Container 314.
35. Timmons, *Jesse H. Jones*, p. 138.
36. *New York Times*, February 2, 1926, p. 6. See also George Fort Milton to Brice Claggett, November 26, 1924, McAdoo Papers, Container 309.
37. Krock to Cox, November 16, 1925, Cox Papers, Box 25.
38. *New York Times*, April 2, 1925, p. 10.
39. Milton to Claggett, November 26, 1924, McAdoo Papers, Container 309.
40. Milton to Breckinridge Long, August 12, 1924, Long Papers, Container 79.
41. Milton, "Fifty-Fifty and Fight!," pp. 28–31.
42. Ibid., p. 37.
43. Ibid., p. 32. See also Editorial Research Reports, *Presidential Politics, 1928*.
44. Milton, "Fifty-Fifty and Fight!," p. 33.
45. Ibid., p. 36.
46. Randolph to McAdoo, November 10, 1924, McAdoo Papers, Container 309.
47. Randolph to McAdoo, November 12, 1924, McAdoo Papers, Container 309. See also Randolph to Clement E. Dunbar, January 9, 1925, ibid., Container 312. McAdoo himself endorsed this scheme in principle. See McAdoo to George F. Milton, July 3, 1925, ibid., Container 317.
48. *New York Times*, January 20, 1925, p. 20.
49. Dickinson to McAdoo, January 25, 1925, McAdoo Papers, Container 312. See also John Dickinson, "Memorandum on Possible Sources of Future Democratic Majorities" (undated), attached to this letter.
50. See *New York Times*, January 17, 1927, p. 9.
51. *New York Times*, November 25, 1926, p. 29.
52. Editorial Research Reports, *Presidential Politics, 1928*, unpaged.
53. *New York Times*, November 25, 1926, p. 29.
54. FDR to Decourcy W. Thom, July 20, 1925, FDR Papers, General Political Cor-

respondence, 1920–1928, Container 4. Roosevelt evidently changed his mind; in 1944 convention delegate apportionment was changed so as to award two bonus votes for states that had voted Democratic in the previous election. In 1948 the bonus was increased to four votes. See David, *The Politics of National Conventions*, p. 169.

55. Both Hoover and Smith were to play on the growing southern sentiment in favor of protective tariffs to nurture the region's industrial development. See Lisio, *Hoover, Blacks, and Lilywhites*, p. 85.

56. Long to Randolph, January 19, 1925, Long Papers, Container 79.

57. FDR to Mrs. George Bass, November 9, 1920, FDR Papers, Papers as Vice-Presidential Candidate, Container 12.

58. FDR to Hull, November 4, 1921, FDR Papers, General Political Correspondence, 1920–1928, Container 2.

59. It is likely that FDR also wished to improve his standing with those Democrats who had opposed Smith at the 1924 convention. During the fall of 1924, the *Atlanta Journal* reported that Roosevelt took advantage of a trip to Warm Springs to apologize, "as an Al Smith leader, for unfortunate and embarrassing incidents in connection with the Convention." See Freidel, *FDR and the South*, p. 19.

60. "FDR's Circular Letter," FDR Papers, General Political Correspondence, 1920–1928, Container 5.

61. FDR, Undated and Untitled Memorandum, FDR Papers, General Political Correspondence, 1920–1928, Container 5.

62. FDR to Walsh, March ? 1925, FDR Papers, General Political Correspondence, 1920–1928, Container 4.

63. Louis Howe to FDR, February 20, 1925. Howe Papers, Container 40.

64. William Cabell Bruce to FDR, December 18, 1924, FDR Papers, General Political Correspondence, 1920–1928, Container 5.

65. W. A. Ayres to FDR, December 20, 1924, FDR Papers, General Political Correspondence, 1920–1928, Container 5.

66. See, for example, J. H. Gribben to FDR, January 8, 1925, FDR Papers, General Political Correspondence, 1920–1928, Container 5.

67. For FDR's brief summary of the gist of the replies, see FDR to Thomas J. Walsh, February 28, 1925, FDR Papers, General Political Correspondence, Container 5.

68. FDR to Shaver, March 4, 1925, FDR Papers, General Political Correspondence, Container 5.

69. Cummings to FDR, December 12, 1924, FDR Papers, General Political Correspondence, Container 5.

70. Hull to Randolph, December 13, 1924, Hull Papers, Reel 2, Folder 19. To Madge O'Neill, DNC member from Iowa, Hull tactfully remarked, "I cannot believe that it was in the mind of Mr. Roosevelt to offer a criticism of my work as chairman of the national committee. I am constrained, however, to agree . . . that there were, notwithstanding, implications in his letter to that effect" (Hull to Mrs. M. O'Neill, December 29, 1924, ibid.)

71. Howe to FDR, February 25, 1925, Howe Papers, Container 40, File 2.

72. Quoted in Burner, *The Politics of Provincialism*, p. 153.
73. *New York Times*, March 22, 1925, sec. 1, p. 20.
74. Howe to FDR, April 8, 1925, Howe Papers, Container 40, Folder 2.
75. Milton to Cummings, January 1, 1924 (wrongly dated; internal evidence strongly suggests 1925), Cummings Papers, Box 54.
76. George Fort Milton, "No Tammany Conference," Editorial, the *Chattanooga News*, undated. See McAdoo Papers, Container 296.
77. McAdoo to W. W. Howes, December 17, 1924, McAdoo Papers, Container 310.
78. Roosevelt to Charles Hammond, July 20, 1925, FDR Papers, General Political Correspondence, 1920–1928, Container 12.
79. For a detailed examination of later trends in the Democratic party's organization, see Ware, *The Breakdown of Democratic Party Organization*.

CHAPTER FIVE

1. George Fort Milton to Homer Cummings, December 21, 1925, Cummings Papers, Box 54.
2. On the first and only ballot at Houston, Smith (from New York) received 849⅔ votes; George (Georgia), 52 1/2; Reed (Missouri), 52; Hull (Tennessee), 50 5/6; and Jones (Texas), 43. Nine other candidates won a total of 43 votes (Cook, *Torchlight Parade*, p. 282).
3. Burner, *The Politics of Provincialism*, p. 193.
4. See, for example, Handlin, *Al Smith*, p. 125; Murray, *The 103rd Ballot*, p. 272. See also Mayer, *The Republican Party*, p. 406.
5. See Leuchtenburg, *Perils of Prosperity*, p. 232. According to Bernard Baruch, so confident was Tammany Hall of Smith's prospect of reelection to the governorship in 1922 that its leaders bet on the result so as to pay off the campaign deficit. See Baruch, *The Public Years*, p. 17.
6. *New Republic*, July 11, 1928, p. 182.
7. Peter L. Petersen discussed this question in "Stopping Al Smith," pp. 439–54, but only in relation to South Dakota.
8. McAdoo Papers, Container 329.
9. Hollins Randolph to McAdoo, June 1, 1925, McAdoo Papers, Container 316.
10. See Mark Sullivan to Brice Claggett, November 9, 1925, McAdoo Papers, Container 320.
11. See Neal, *The World beyond the Hudson*, p. 237.
12. George F. Milton to McAdoo, March 23, 1927, McAdoo Papers, Container 333.
13. Frank Hampton to McAdoo, April 2, 1927, McAdoo Papers, Container 334.
14. George F. Milton to McAdoo, August 17, 1927, McAdoo Papers, Container 336.
15. McAdoo to George F. Milton, August 27, 1927, McAdoo Papers, Container 336. See also Petersen, "Stopping Al Smith," p. 440.
16. McAdoo to George F. Milton, September 7, 1927, McAdoo Papers, Container 336.
17. McAdoo to Milton, September 15, 1927, McAdoo Papers, Container 336.

18. Louis Howe to FDR, April 22, 1927, Howe Papers, Container 40.

19. George F. Milton to McAdoo, September 17, 1927, McAdoo Papers, Container 336.

20. McAdoo to E. J. Feuling, November 21, 1927, McAdoo Papers, Container 336.

21. Walsh, ironically enough, had been a keen supporter of the leasing of the naval oil leases when this was first mooted (Bates, "Teapot Dome," p. 315; Mayer, *The Republican Party*, p. 392). Louis Howe thought that Governor Ritchie of Maryland was McAdoo's first choice, but this seems unlikely, given Ritchie's outspoken anti-prohibition views. See Howe to FDR, April 2, 1927, Howe Papers, Container 40.

22. See Noggle, *Teapot Dome*, pp. 202ff.; Brown, *Hood, Bonnet, and Little Brown Jug*, p. 382; Petersen, "Stopping Al Smith," pp. 445–46.

23. A brief biography of Walsh can be found in Sullivan, *Our Times* 6, pp. 277–84.

24. Walsh to M. J. Mullen, March 20, 1928, Walsh Papers, Container 181.

25. Walsh to Morgan Axford, November 2, 1927, Walsh Papers, Container 179.

26. Walsh to M. J. Mullen, March 20, 1928, Walsh Papers, Container 181. J. Leonard Bates argues that Walsh had purposely avoided pressing Doheny on his Democratic connections during his Teapot Dome investigations in the hope of protecting McAdoo from public involvement in the scandal ("Teapot Dome," p. 315).

27. Petersen, "Stopping Al Smith," p. 447.

28. Walsh to W. H. Olds, March 15, 1928, Walsh Papers, Container 181.

29. Louis W. Hickey to Walsh, May 24, 1928, Walsh Papers, Container 180.

30. Albert E. Barnett to Walsh, March 5, 1928, Walsh Papers, Container 179.

31. Petersen, "Stopping Al Smith," p. 450.

32. Noggle, *Teapot Dome*, pp. 202ff.; Petersen, "Stopping Al Smith," p. 453.

33. J. T. Carroll to Walsh, May 2, 1928, Walsh Papers, Container 179; see W. J. Pearson to Cummings, May 3, 1928, Cummings Papers, Container 55.

34. See Hull Papers, Reel 5.

35. See Neal, *The World beyond the Hudson*, p. 248.

36. Cordell Hull to H. B. McGinness, February 10, 1928, Hull Papers, Reel 5.

37. Albert C. Ritchie before the U.S. Senate Special Committee Investigating Presidential Campaign Expenditures, May 8, 1928, 70th Cong., 1st sess., S314 O A Part 1, p. 35.

38. *New York Times*, June 19, 1928, p. 1.

39. Bowers, *My Life*, p. 151.

40. Ferrell, *Woodrow Wilson and World War I*, p. 230.

41. Petersen, "Stopping Al Smith," p. 442.

42. Baker to Ralph Hayes, September 22, 1927, Baker Papers, Container 114.

43. Petersen, "Stopping Al Smith," p. 442.

44. Milton, "Progressive Democrats in a Quandary," p. 352.

45. "Memorandum on the Movement to Nominate Alfred E. Smith," p. 27, Moskowitz Papers, Box 1.

46. FDR to Daniels, June 23, 1927, FDR Papers, Family, Business, and Personal Papers, Container 94.

47. Charles O'Neill of Altoona to FDR, January 8, 1925, FDR Papers, General Political Correspondence, 1920–1928, Container 6.

48. *New York Times*, October 20, 1925, p. 1.

49. Neal, *The World beyond the Hudson*, pp. 248ff.

50. Ibid., p. 262. Houston owed its selection to Jesse H. Jones, one of its wealthiest citizens and finance director of the DNC. Jones took it upon himself to put forward his city's bid for the convention, buttressed by his personal check for $200,000 and a promise that a twenty-five-thousand-seat convention hall would be built for the occasion. See Timmons, *Jesse H. Jones*, p. 143.

51. FDR to AES, September 17, 1927, FDR Papers, Family, Business, and Personal Papers, Container 102. Smith, in fact, steadfastly refused to make any comment on matters outside his own realm of New York politics. See George Graves to C. F. Adams, October 14, 1925, Graves Papers, Container 1.

52. Tumulty to Hoey, July 2, 1926, Tumulty Papers, Container 63.

53. Howe to FDR, March 14, 1927, Howe Papers, Container 40. See also Howe to FDR, September 9, 1926, ibid.

54. Claggett to Milton, undated (internal evidence suggests 1924), McAdoo Papers, Container 311.

55. Howe to FDR, April 15, 1925, Howe Papers, Container 40.

56. Howe to FDR, undated (internal evidence suggests 1928), Howe Papers, Container 40.

57. Tumulty to Hoey, February 14, 1927, Tumulty Papers, Container 63.

58. See Burner, *The Politics of Provincialism*, pp. 184ff.

59. McAdoo to E. J. Feuling, November 21, 1927, McAdoo Papers, Container 336.

60. See Howe to FDR, April 18, 1927, Howe Papers, Container 40.

61. George Van Namee before the U.S. Senate Special Committee, May 10, 1928, p. 90.

62. Ibid., p. 85.

63. Theodore B. Nickson before the U.S. Senate Special Committee, December 5, 1928, p. 1,097.

64. Simmons to Santford Martin, January 10, 1927, McAdoo Papers, Container 331.

65. See FDR to Daniels, June 23, 1927, FDR Papers, Family, Business, and Personal Papers, Container 94.

66. Sullivan to Claggett, November 9, 1925, McAdoo Papers, Container 320.

67. FDR to Daniels, June 23, 1927, FDR Papers, Family, Business, and Personal Papers, Container 94. See also Schlesinger, *The Age of Roosevelt* 1, p. 377. For Walter Lippmann's views along these lines, see Hofstadter, "Could a Protestant Have Beaten Hoover?," p. 32.

68. Hull to A. V. Louthan, January 27, 1928, Hull Papers, Reel 5.

69. Baker to Hayes, March 5, 1928, Baker Papers, Container 115.

70. William A. Comstock to R. B. Cassell, May 25, 1928, Hull Papers, Reel 6. The capitalization is Comstock's.

71. Baker to Alexander, January 20, 1928, Baker Papers, Container 16.

72. FDR to Will R. King, March 10, 1927, FDR Papers, General Political Correspondence, 1920–1928, Container 3.

73. See Neal, *The World beyond the Hudson*, p. 234.

74. House to Breckinridge Long, January 13, 1928, Long Papers, Container 89.

75. See Bryan and Baird, *The Memoirs of William Jennings Bryan*, p. 157.

76. Milton to McAdoo, August 17, 1927, McAdoo Papers, Container 336. See also Marshall Stimson to Cummings, October 25, 1928, Cummings Papers, Container 55.

77. Grantham, *The Democratic South*, p. 60; Schlesinger, *The Age of Roosevelt* 1, pp. 344–45.

78. Gerber, *The Limits of Liberalism*, pp. 80, 84–85. As Gerber notes, Daniels's activities in the 1890s corresponded closely to the model put forward by C. Vann Woodward in *The Strange Career of Jim Crow*. See also Daniels, *Editor in Politics*, pp. 283–342.

79. See Gerber, *The Limits of Liberalism*, p. 193.

80. Daniels to FDR, July 19, 1927, FDR Papers, Family, Business, and Personal Papers, Container 94.

81. Daniels to Bowers, October 3, 1927, Daniels Papers, Reel 42.

82. Daniels to FDR, July 19, 1927, FDR Papers, Family, Business, and Personal Papers, Container 94.

83. Daniels to Bowers, October 3, 1927, Daniels Papers, Reel 42.

84. Cummings to Edwin T. Meredith, November 20, 1925, Cummings Papers, Container 58.

85. James Spiller to Cummings, January 12, 1927, Cummings Papers, Container 54.

86. Cummings to Edwin T. Meredith, November 20, 1925, Cummings Papers, Container 58.

87. Cummings to Miles, October 24, 1927, Cummings Papers, Container 54.

88. Cummings to R. T. Jeffrey, January 27, 1928, Cummings Papers, Container 55; Brice Claggett to Mark Sullivan, November 17, 1925, McAdoo Papers, Container 320. For the Smith camp's view, see "Reminiscences on the Movement to Nominate Alfred E. Smith," Moskowitz Papers, Container 1.

89. Milton to Gannett, July 7, 1928, McAdoo Papers, Container 339.

CHAPTER SIX

1. *New York Times*, January 29, 1936, p. 3.

2. See Eldot, *Governor Alfred E. Smith*, O'Connor, *The First Hurrah*; Handlin, *Al Smith*.

3. Perkins, "Reminiscences," 2:469, Columbia University Oral History Project, 1955. Roosevelt is quoted in Perkins, *The Roosevelt I Remember*, p. 157.

4. O'Connor, *The First Hurrah*, p. 137

5. Eldot, *Politician as Reformer*, p. 399.

6. Handlin, *Al Smith*, p. 171. See also Feldman, "An Abstract of the Political Thought of Alfred E. Smith," pp. 239, 171; Eldot, *Governor Alfred E. Smith*, p. 406; Josef Israels, "Memorandum on Book Project," Moskowitz Papers, Miscellaneous Letters; Ickes, *The Secret Diary of Harold L. Ickes* 1, p. 687.

7. Lippmann, *Men of Destiny*, p. 6.

8. Hapgood and Moskowitz, *Up from the City Streets*, p. 6.

9. Robert Moses, "Salute to an East Side Boy Named Smith," *New York Times*, October 8, 1961, p. 118. This view has been persuasively, although briefly, argued by Schwarz, "Al Smith in the Thirties," p. 328; Hand, "Al Smith, Franklin D. Roosevelt, and the New Deal," p. 380; Burner, *The Politics of Provincialism*, p. 187; Leuchtenburg, *The Perils of Prosperity*, p. 232. See also Mayer, *The Republican Party*, p. 406.

10. There is no published full-length biography of Smith from a proponent of the "consistently conservative" school.

11. See Smith, *Up to Now*. For an account of AES's early years, see Feldman, "Political Thought of Smith," pp. 1–25.

12. *New York Times*, August 12, 1914, p. 16

13. Allen, *Al Smith's Tammany Hall*, p. 120.

14. Quoted in Connable and Silberfarb, *Tigers of Tammany*, p. 275.

15. Ibid., p. 250.

16. See Wesser, *A Response to Progressivism*, pp. 70ff.; Buenker, *Urban Liberalism and Progressive Reform*, pp. 42ff.; Huthmacher, *Senator Robert F. Wagner*, p. 42; Huthmacher, "Urban Liberalism and the Age of Reform," pp. 231–41.

17. Wesser, *A Response to Progressivism*, p. 61.

18. Perkins, *The Roosevelt I Knew*, p. 22.

19. Martin, *Madame Secretary*, p. 19.

20. Ibid., p. 108.

21. See State of New York, *The Revised Record of the Constitutional Convention* 4, p. 206.

22. Smith, *Up to Now*, p. 95.

23. See AES, Message to the Legislature, January 1, 1919, *New York Times*, January 2, 1919, p. 3.

24. See O'Connor, *The First Hurrah*, p. 71.

25. Smith, *Up to Now*, p. 94.

26. Villard, *Prophets True and False*, p. 7.

27. Leuchtenburg, *Perils of Prosperity*, p. 232.

28. See Graham, *The Great Campaigns*, p. 133; Grantham, *The Democratic South*, pp. 64–65; Brown, *Hood, Bonnet, and Little Brown Jug*, pp. 11–48, 129–67; Lee, *Tennessee in Turmoil*, pp. 37–75.

29. See Tindall, "Business Progressivism," p. 95.

30. Ibid., p. 103.

31. *New York Times*, January 2, 1919, p. 4.

32. See Ingalls, *Herbert H. Lehman*, p. xviii; Gammack, "Wall Street Likes Al Smith."

33. For a general discussion of AES's housing laws—and of the conservatism under-

lying them—see Hand, "Al Smith." See also Smith, "Housing and Slum Clearance"; AES Papers, PPF 524.

34. Moskowitz, *Progressive Democracy*, p. 332.

35. See Eldot, *Politician as Reformer*, pp. 250ff.

36. Case and Case, *Owen D. Young*, pp. 338–44.

37. State of New York, *The Public Papers of Alfred E. Smith* (1926), p. 757 (henceforth referred to as *Public Papers*). Paula Eldot, however, saw in AES's water-power policies a "repudiation of laissez-faire economics" and an enthusiastic interventionist spirit ("Governor Alfred E. Smith").

38. See Eldot, *Governor Alfred E. Smith*, pp. 268–69.

39. Villard, *Prophets*, p. 14; Eldot, *Governor Alfred E. Smith*, p. 312.

40. AES, *Public Papers* (1923), p. 60.

41. AES, Annual Message to the Legislature, 1924, quoted in *New York Times*, January 3, 1924.

42. See Eldot, *Governor Alfred E. Smith*, p. 338. Eldot argues that the padlock law did not represent a suppression of "free expression" because the law "did not entail censorship in advance" (ibid., p. 341).

43. See Smith, *The Citizen and His Government*, p. 184.

44. Villard, *Prophets*, p. 13.

45. Smith, *The Citizen and His Government*, p. 173.

46. Quoted in Handlin, *Al Smith*, p. 109.

47. *New York Times*, October 5, 1920, p. 4

48. Moskowitz, *Progressive Democracy*, p. 194.

49. See Smith, *Up to Now*, p. 228.

50. Ibid.

51. Smith, *The Citizen and his Government*, p. 68.

52. *New York Times*, November 3, 1924, pp. 1ff.

53. See Flick, *History of the State of New York* 7, pp. 263–64. See also AES, "Status of Workmen's Compensation Administration in New York State," Private Papers, PPF 32; *New York Times*, October 28, 1922, p. 15; AES, Message to Legislature, April 7, 1924, *Public Papers* (1924), p. 294. See also *Public Papers* (1927), p. 170.

54. Handlin, *Al Smith*, pp. 90–112.

55. See AES, Message to the Legislature, quoted in the *New York Times*, January 3, 1924, p. 1.

56. See AES quoted in the *New York Times*, April 8, 1924, p. 9. See also Smith, *The Citizen and His Government*, p. 151.

57. Perry, *Belle Moskowitz*, p. 114.

58. Ware, *Partner and I*, p. 151.

59. Perry, *Belle Moskowitz*, pp. 30–58.

60. Ibid., p. 161–83; Perkins, *The Roosevelt I Remember*, p. 50.

61. Quoted in Carter, *Another Part of the Twenties*, p. 112.

62. See Perry, *Belle Moskowitz*, p. 154.

63. Perkins, *The Roosevelt I Remember*, p. 55.

64. Belle Moskowitz, "Reminiscences on the Movement to Nominate Alfred E. Smith," Moskowitz Papers, MS 8.

65. *New York Times*, January 1, 1919, p. 1.

66. AES, Message to Legislature, January 6, 1926, *Public Papers* (1926), p. 51.

67. *Public Papers* (1923), p. 483.

68. *New York Times*, October 28, 1922, p. 15.

69. Handlin, *Al Smith*, p. 60.

70. Quoted in Ingalls, *Herbert H. Lehman*, p. 117. See also the *New York Times*, March 6, 1934, p. 3.

71. *New York Times*, December 31, 1938, p. 3.

72. *New York Times*, November 5, 1940, p. 21.

73. Quoted in Feldman, "Political Thought of Smith," p. 226. See also the *New York Times*, November 5, 1940, p. 21.

74. New York Times, October 24, 1933, p. 1.

75. See AES, Speech at Carnegie Hall, October 19, 1936, *New York Times*, October 20, 1936, p. 4.

76. *New York Times*, October 25, 1936, p. 34.

77. *New York Times*, January 2, 1919, p. 4.

78. *New York Times*, October 2, 1936, p. 4.

79. See AES, McNaught Syndicate Article, "Real Economy vs. Expediency," Private Papers, PPF 521(c).

80. Smith, *The Citizen and His Government*, p. 30. See also AES, Private Papers, File 531. AES also suggested a similar program of reform for Chicago's city government (ibid., PPF 530).

81. AES, "They're Wasting Your Money," *Red Book Magazine*, 1932, Private Papers, PPF 532.

82. See the *New York Times*, April 2, 1934, p. 19.

83. AES, "Housing," *New Outlook*, February 1934, Private Papers, PPF 528.

84. Feldman, "Political Thought of Smith," p. 192.

85. Smith, *The Citizen and His Government*, p. 145.

86. See Feldman, "Political Thought of Smith," p. 224.

87. Quoted in ibid., p. 193.

88. Quoted in the *New York Times*, July 31, 1940, p. 13. Compare AES's lament to that of Ronald Reagan, explaining his conversion to Republicanism in the 1950s: "I didn't desert my party. It deserted me" (Leuchtenburg, *In the Shadow of FDR*, p. 212).

89. Quoted in Josephson, *Hero of the Cities*, p. 35, and the *New York Times*, October 2, 1939, p. 4.

90. Felix Frankfurter, "Why I Am for Smith."

91. See Meyer, *The Conservative Mainstream*, pp. 20–43.

92. Quoted in Harrison, *Road to the Right*, p. 278.

93. See Kirk, *The Conservative Mind*; Harrison, *Road to the Right*, p. vii.
94. Glazer and Moynihan, *Beyond the Melting Pot*, pp. 232. For contrast, see Cross, *The Emergence of Liberal Catholicism in America*.
95. See Miles, *The Odyssey of the American Right*, pp. 241–57, on the American Catholic conservative tradition.
96. Quoted in Kirk, *The Conservative Mind*, p. 145.
97. Quoted in Eldot, "Governor Alfred E. Smith," p. 3.
98. See Rossiter, *Conservatism in America*, p. 151.
99. See Wyllie, *The Self-Made Man in America*, for a wide-ranging analysis of the meaning and significance of the "self-made man" image in American history.
100. Smith, *Up to Now*, p. 424.
101. See Hawley, *The Great War*, pp. 52–55, 66–71.
102. See Proskauer, *A Segment of My Times*, p. 70.
103. *Public Papers* (1924), p. 544.
104. *New York Times*, November 20, 1923, p. 3.
105. *New York Times*, March 18, 1923, p. 23. In 1925 a survey of millionaires revealed that 88.3 percent had no more than a high school education and that 71.7 percent had either only elementary education or none at all (Wyllie, *The Self-Made Man in America*, p. 95).
106. See Moskowitz, *Progressive Democracy*, pp. 244–45.
107. Ibid., p. 305. See also Caro, *The Power Broker*, pp. 186–205.
108. See Feldman, "The Political Thought of Alfred E. Smith," p. 65; AES, Speech to the American Liberty League, January 25, 1936, *New York Times*, January 26, 1936, p. 36.
109. Quoted in Shannon, *The American Irish*, p. 172. See chapter 11 below.

CHAPTER SEVEN

1. Hoey to Joe Tumulty, July 5, 1928, Tumulty Papers, Container 63.
2. "Washington Notes," *New Republic*, July 25, 1928, p. 249.
3. John Raskob's brief autobiographical notes can be found in the Raskob Papers, File 303.
4. Raskob to Pierre du Pont, July 28, 1900, Pierre S. du Pont (hereafter referred to as PSduP), Longwood Papers, Group 10, File 303.
5. Pringle, "John J. Raskob," p. 342.
6. Dale, *The Great Organizers*, p. 50.
7. Sloan, *My Years with General Motors*, p. 43.
8. See Chandler and Salsbury, *Pierre S. du Pont*; Chandler and Tedlow, *The Coming of Managerial Capitalism*, pp. 372–95.
9. See Hawley, *The Great War*, p. 91.
10. Burk, *The Corporate State and the Broker State*, p. 10.

11. Dale, *The Great Organizers*, pp. 61–62; Chandler and Salsbury, *Pierre S. du Pont*, p. 359.
12. Larry Gerber argues that the excess-profits taxes imposed by the Wilson administration during World War I encouraged corporations to build up large undistributed surpluses, which were not so taxed, rather than distribute large dividends, which would have attracted excess-profits tax (*The Limits of Liberalism*, p. 165).
13. Sloan, *My Years with General Motors*, pp. 12–14. The Du Pont Company had been slowly diversifying from its core gunpowder business since 1910. It had invested in artificial leather and silk manufacturers and in the chemical industry before its large foray into automobiles. See Chandler, *Strategy and Structure*, p. 78.
14. See Perrett, *America in the Twenties*, p. 253; Chandler and Salsbury, *Pierre S. du Pont*, p. 435, 460, 506.
15. See PSduP, Longwood Papers, Group 10, File 303.
16. See Dale, *The Great Organizers*, p. vii; Chandler, *Strategy and Structure*, p. 78.
17. Galambos and Pratt, *The Rise of the Corporate Commonwealth*, pp. 77–80.
18. See Chandler and Salsbury, *Pierre S. du Pont*, pp. 506, 573; Sloan, *My Years with General Motors*, p. 198.
19. See Sloan, *My Years with General Motors*, p. 38.
20. Chandler, *Strategy and Structure*, p. 124. See also Dale, *The Great Organizers*, p. 82.
21. Wiebe, *The Search for Order*, pp. 133–63; Hawley, *The Great War*, pp. 52–55.
22. Sloan, *My Years with General Motors*, p. 204.
23. Chandler and Salsbury, *Pierre S. du Pont*, p. 490.
24. See Chandler, *Strategy and Structure*, p. 124
25. Chandler and Salsbury, *Pierre S. du Pont*, p. 460.
26. See Chandler, *Giant Enterprise*, p. 166; Perrett, *America in the Twenties*, p. 353; Sloan, *My Years with General Motors*, p. 151.
27. See Chandler, *Giant Enterprise*, p. 166.
28. Raskob to PSduP, October 4, 1919, Longwood Papers, Group 10, File 303.
29. Raskob to PSduP, September 6, 1916, Longwood Papers, Group 10, File 303.
30. Sullivan, *Our Times* 5, 489, 370.
31. Quoted in Protho, *Dollar Decade*, p. 200.
32. Mayer, *The Republican Party*, p. 384.
33. Galambos, *The Public Image of Big Business in America*, p. 159; Ferrell, *Woodrow Wilson and World War I*, p. 192; Hawley, *The Great War*, p. 27.
34. The excess-profits tax was repealed in 1921. Three years later, income taxes were reduced by 25 percent, and surtaxes on large incomes were cut from 50 percent to 40 percent. This figure was reduced to 20 percent in 1926, when the federal inheritance tax was also lowered. Corporate taxation rates were also reduced to a maximum of 12 percent in 1928. See Paul, *Taxation in the United States*, pp. 122–67; Ratner, *American Taxation*, pp. 400–450; Witte, *The Politics and Development of the Federal Income Tax*, p. 95.
35. Buenker, "The New Era Business Philosophy of the 1920s," pp. 34–36.

36. For a detailed description of the AFL's role in the war effort, see Taft, *The AFL in the Time of Gompers*, pp. 342–61. See also Brody, *Steelworkers in America*, pp. 180–213; Hawley, *The Great War*, p. 27; Bernstein, *The Lean Years*, pp. 146–66.

37. Zieger, *Republicans and Labor*, p. 72; Galambos, *The Public Image of Big Business in America*, p. 197.

38. Zieger, *Republicans and Labor*, p. 250. In the years between 1914 and 1920, by contrast, AFL membership had jumped from 2.6 million to 5 million (Ferrell, *Woodrow Wilson and World War I*, p. 194). Taft, in *The AFL in the Time of Gompers*, p. 362, gives somewhat lower figures. See Perlman, "Labor in Eclipse," especially pp. 106–8, for a discussion of the variations in historians' estimates of union strength.

39. Lichtman, *Prejudice and the Old Politics*, pp. 188–90. See also Gerber, *The Limits of Liberalism*, p. 213.

40. See Lichtman, *Prejudice and the Old Politics*, pp. 109ff.

41. Ibid., p. 260; Bornet, *Labor Politics*, p. 44.

42. Perlman, "Labor in Eclipse," pp. 118–21.

43. Quoted in Protho, *Dollar Decade*, p. 140.

44. Quoted in Buenker, "The New Era Business Philosophy," p. 34.

45. See Ferguson, "From Normalcy to New Deal," pp. 49–50, 63.

46. Galambos and Pratt, *The Rise of the Corporate Commonwealth*, pp. 71–73.

47. See ibid., pp. 21, 31. Hoover's tenure as secretary of commerce is examined in Hawley, *Herbert Hoover as Secretary of Commerce*; Hawley, *The Great War*, pp. 100–107.

48. Galambos and Pratt, *The Rise of the Corporate Commonwealth*, p. 91.

49. Ibid., pp. 73–80.

50. Ibid., p. 45.

51. Brody, "The Rise and Decline of Welfare Capitalism."

52. See Galambos and Pratt, *The Rise of the Corporate Commonwealth*, pp. 96–99; Heald, "Business Thought in the Twenties," pp. 126–39.

53. Galambos and Pratt, *The Rise of the Corporate Commonwealth*, pp. 93–99.

54. Galambos, *The Public Image of Big Business in America*, p. 220.

55. Ibid., pp. 180–87.

56. See Ferguson, "From Normalcy to New Deal," p. 68. Welfare capitalism was a creature of the very largest firms; smaller concerns were either unable or unwilling to expend large amounts of money in creating group insurance schemes, pension plans, or stock-purchase programs. See Brody, "The Rise and Decline of Welfare Capitalism," p. 161.

57. Immigration rapidly declined after World War I broke out in Europe. In 1913, some 815,000 immigrants arrived in the United States; two years later only 50,000 made the journey, and in 1916 only 19,000 entered the country. See Sclichter, "The Current Labor Policies," p. 395.

58. Ibid., p. 396. See also Brody, *Steelworkers in America*, pp. 214–30.

59. Feis, *Labor Relations*.

60. Brody, "The Rise and Decline of Welfare Capitalism," p. 154.

61. Ferguson, "From Normalcy to New Deal," p. 68.

62. See Wiebe, *Businessmen and Reform*, p. 204; Galambos, *The Public Image of Big Business in America*, p. 200.

63. Quoted in Schwarz, *The Speculator*, p. 165.

64. Filene, *The Way Forward*, p. 32.

65. Ibid., p. 42.

66. Ibid.

67. Ibid., p. 31.

68. In his influential *The Great War and the Search for a Modern Order*, Ellis Hawley argues that welfare capitalism of the 1920s, although largely abandoned under the strains of the Great Depression, nevertheless was "the premature Spring of the kind of modern capitalism that would take shape in the America of the 1940's and 1950's" (p. vi). For a less favorable assessment of welfare capitalism during the 1920s, see Gerber, *The Limits of Liberalism*, p. 213.

69. Feis, *Labor Relations*, pp. 68ff., 165–68.

70. Zwieger, "Herbert Hoover," pp. 97–100; Brody, "The Rise and Decline of Welfare Capitalism," p. 158; Galambos and Pratt, *The Rise of the Corporate Commonwealth*, p. 79.

71. Slichter, "Current Labor Policies," p. 431.

72. See Ferguson, "From Normalcy to New Deal," p. 68.

73. See Wiebe, *Businessmen and Reform*, p. 24, and Fine, *Laissez Faire and the General Welfare State*, pp. 96–125.

74. National Association of Manufacturers, *Platform of American Industry, 1924*, p. 4.

75. Ibid., pp. 5, 6.

76. Ibid., pp. 10, 6, and 7.

77. Quoted in Protho, *Dollar Decade*, p. 40.

78. Quoted in ibid., p. 28.

79. Ibid., p. 171.

80. Ibid., p. 120.

81. Quoted in ibid., p. 118. The emphasis is Fay's.

82. See ibid., p. 197.

83. Barnes, *The Genius of American Business*.

84. Ibid., p. 27.

85. Barnes, *The Genius of American Business*, p. 9. Barnes would not hear of the McNary-Haugen scheme; when called to a meeting to discuss the matter with Secretary of Agriculture Henry Wallace in 1922, he made clear his poor opinion of "a Secretary of Agriculture who would take the time of busy men in considering such a plan." See Saloutos and Hicks, *Agricultural Discontent*, p. 379.

86. Barnes, *The Genius of American Business*, p. 8.

87. Ibid., p. 11.

88. See Darrow, "Democracy," p. 257.

89. See Wiebe, *Businessmen and Reform*, p. 180.

90. Raskob to R. B. Oliver, April 22, 1931, Raskob Papers, File 602.

91. See Raskob to Riley Smith, October 22, 1931, Raskob Papers, File 602.

92. Quoted in the *New York Times*, March 6, 1931, p. 10.

93. *New York Times*, June 12, 1929, p. 28.

94. Quoted in Peterson, *The Jefferson Image in the American Mind*, p. 18.

95. Raskob, Speech to DNC, January 1931, Raskob Papers, File 602.

96. Raskob to H. G. Gaskell, February 23, 1933, Raskob Papers, File 602.

97. See the *New York Times*, February 1, 1936, p. 1. See also Raskob to Glenn Frank, March 30, 1936, Raskob Papers, File 602, Box 13.

98. Raskob to Charles Warner, March 24, 1924, Raskob Papers, File 2393.

99. AES, quoted in the *New York Times*, January 2, 1919, p. 4.

100. Quoted in the *New York Times*, March 16, 1931, p. 16.

101. Raskob to Young, July 29, 1919, Raskob Papers, File 2528.

102. Raskob to Robinson, July 16, 1931, Raskob Papers, File 1978.

103. See Buenker, "New Era Business Philosophy," p. 39.

104. Sloan, *My Years with General Motors*, p. 391.

105. Burk, *Corporate State to Broker State*, p. 13.

106. See Curti, *The Growth of American Thought*, pp. 698–701.

107. Raskob, "Everybody Ought to Be Rich," p. 9.

108. Ibid. Raskob may well have been inspired in this belief by Russell Conwell's famous success lecture *Acres of Diamonds* (1915). "It is your Christian and Godly duty" to make money, Conwell told his audiences; "I say that you ought to get rich, and it is your duty to get rich" (p. 16).

109. See the *New York Times*, June 2, 1929, sec. 2, p. 10. Robert F. Burk argues that Raskob was attracted to stock bonus schemes because they were a cheaper form of employee incentive than wage raises (*Corporate State to Broker State*, p. 13). Given Raskob's willingness to tolerate rising real wages to expand consumption, however, it seems more likely that he saw stock bonus plans primarily as ways to reduce industrial disputation.

110. See Chandler and Salsbury, *Pierre S. du Pont*, p. 135; Sloan, *My Years with General Motors*, pp. 407–28.

111. Raskob, "What Next in America?," p. 517.

112. Ibid., p. 513.

113. Ibid., p. 514.

114. Ibid., p. 516.

115. See Raskob to Calvin Coolidge, May 6, 1929, Raskob Papers, File 479. The average annual wage in 1928 was $1,428, meaning that Raskob's scheme envisaged a savings rate of 12.6 percent. Kenneth S. Davis (*FDR: The New York Years*, p. 116) erroneously computes the required savings rate to be 50 percent. Despite the popular image of the 1920s as a decade in which everyone seemed to be buying shares, the reality was quite different. In 1929, at the height of the stock boom, only 1.5 million Americans (slightly more than 1 percent of the population) owned stock—

and of that number 51,000 large investors received half of the total value of dividends paid by American corporations in 1929 (see Gerber, *The Limits of Liberalism*, p. 222).

116. See Protho, *Dollar Decade*, p. 6.
117. See ibid., p. 188.
118. Lopata, "John J. Raskob," p. 35; chapter 12 below.
119. Baruch, *The Public Years*, p. 150.
120. Lopata, "John J. Raskob," p. 35.
121. Raskob to Warner, March 24, 1924, Raskob Papers, File 2393.
122. See the *New York Times*, September 30, 1928, p. 5.
123. See Raskob to Riley Smith, October 22, 1931, Raskob Papers, File 602.
124. Lopata, "John J. Raskob," pp. 30ff.
125. *New York Times*, June 4, 1928, p. 22.
126. Eddie Dowling, Interview with Ruthanna Hindes, May 1, 1968, p. 10, held on deposit at the Hagley Museum and Library, Greenville, Delaware. Smith refused Raskob's check because it exceeded the legal limit for individual donations to gubernatorial campaigns.
127. *New York Times*, October 7, 1928, p. 4. See also ibid., June 27, 1928, p. 1.
128. Raskob, "Rich Men in Politics," p. 7.
129. See Popkin et al., "What Have You Done for Me Lately?"; Ferguson, "Party Realignment and American Industrial Structure."
130. See Ferguson, "Party Realignment and American Industrial Structure," pp. 8–18.
131. Ibid., p. 18.
132. Quoted in Montgomery, *Beyond Equality*, p. 61.
133. See Raskob, quoted in the *New York Times*, March 6, 1931, p. 16; Ferguson, "From Normalcy to New Deal," p. 78.

CHAPTER EIGHT

1. Numerous works stress the "clash of cultures" inherent in AES's candidacy. The best of these are Burner, *The Politics of Provincialism*; Handlin, *Al Smith*; O'Connor, *The First Hurrah*; Lichtman, *Prejudice and the Old Politics*.
2. See Peel and Donnelly, *The 1928 Campaign*; Carleton, "The Popish Plot of 1928," pp. 141–47; Miller, "A Footnote to the Role of the Protestant Churches"; Moore, *A Catholic Runs for President*; Silva, *Rum, Religion, and Votes*; Carter, "The Campaign of 1928 Re-examined"; O'Connor, *The First Hurrah*, p. 203; Eldot, *Governor Alfred E. Smith*, p. 405; Neal, *The World beyond the Hudson*, p. 279; Lichtman, *Prejudice and the Old Politics*.
3. See Lubell, *The Future of American Politics*; Kleppner, *Continuity and Change*, p. 199; Degler, "American Political Parties"; Allswang, *A House for All Peoples*; Andersen, *The Creation of a Democratic Majority*. For challenges to this interpreta-

tion, see Shover, "Was 1928 a Critical Election in California?"; Clubb and Allen, "The Cities and the Election of 1928"; Lichtman, *Prejudice and the Old Politics*, p. 215; Burnham, "The System of 1896."

4. See Bornet, *Labor Politics*, p. 275; Hofstadter, "Could a Protestant Have Beaten Hoover in 1928?," pp. 31–33; Lichtman, *Prejudice and the Old Politics*, p. 16; Burner, *The Politics of Provincialism*, p. 217.

5. Bowers, *My Life*, p. 185.

6. Democratic National Committee, *The Campaign Book of the Democratic Party*, pp. 100–125.

7. "The Democratic Platform of 1928," pp. 2611–24.

8. Kenkel, *Progressives and Protection*, pp. 151–59; Ratner, *The Tariff in American History*, pp. 47–49; Gould, *Reform and Regulation*, pp. 179–81.

9. "The Democratic Platform of 1924," pp. 2491–2505.

10. See "Washington Notes," *New Republic*, July 18, 1928, p. 225.

11. "The Republican Platform of 1928," pp. 2624–40.

12. See Patrick H. Quinn to FDR, December 11, 1924, FDR Papers, General Political Correspondence, 1920–1928, Container 6.

13. Raskob to Irénée du Pont, July 19, 1928, Irénée du Pont Papers, Series J, Box 192.

14. Fite, "The Farmers' Dilemma," p. 67.

15. Democratic National Committee, *The Campaign Book of the Democratic Party*, pp. 94–100.

16. "The Democratic Platform of 1928," pp. 2611–24.

17. Democratic National Committee, *The Campaign Book of the Democratic Party*, pp. 141–48.

18. See Hubbard, *Origins of TVA*, pp. 236–40. For a discussion of liberals' attitudes toward the problem of control of public utilities, see Gerber, *The Limits of Liberalism*, pp. 229–34.

19. Baker to Frank H. Baker, July 11, 1928, Baker Papers, Container 36.

20. Democratic National Committee, *The Campaign Book of the Democratic Party*, pp. 125–41.

21. See Bernstein, *Lean Years*, p. 196; Zieger, *Republicans and Labor*, pp. 271, 264–70; Bornet, *Labor Politics*, p. 127.

22. Green to Peter J. Brady, July 3, 1928, Graves Papers, Container 7.

23. Bornet, *Labor Politics*, pp. 86, 127.

24. Hill to Roosevelt, November 1, 1928, Eleanor Roosevelt Papers, Box 6.

25. Milton to McAdoo, July 31, 1928, McAdoo Papers, Container 339. See also Newton Baker to George Foster Peabody, July 5, 1928, Baker Papers, Box 185.

26. Pringle, "John J. Raskob."

27. Ferguson, "Party Realignment and American Industrial Structure," p. 19.

28. Smith, *Campaign Addresses*, p. 2.

29. Hoover, *American Individualism*, p. 55.

30. See Zieger, *Republicans and Labor*, pp. 61–62.

31. Hoover, *The New Day*, p. 42.

32. Ibid., p. 30. See also Mayer, *The Republican Party*, p. 411.
33. See Hoover, *The New Day*, p. 71.
34. See ibid., pp. 20 and 194; Smith, *Campaign Addresses*, p. 18.
35. Fite, "The Agricultural Issue," pp. 662–64.
36. See Wilson, "Herbert Hoover's Agricultural Policies," p. 120; Fite, *George N. Peek*, pp. 126–30; Hawley, *The Great War*, pp. 100–107.
37. Fite, "The Agricultural Issue," p. 662. See also Saloutos and Hicks, *Agricultural Discontent*, p. 403.
38. See Smith, *Campaign Addresses*, p. 39.
39. Fite, "The Agricultural Issue," p. 667.
40. Lichtman, *Prejudice and the Old Politics*, pp. 190–93; Fite, "The Agricultural Issue," pp. 669–71.
41. Hoover, *The New Day*, p. 32.
42. Smith, *Campaign Addresses*, p. 84. Stress was put on the fact that these bonds would not become obligations of the federal government, but rather of the public corporation. See AES to Samuel Untermeyer, July 14, 1927, Graves Papers, Container 74.
43. Hubbard, *Origins of TVA*, pp. 236–40; Burner, *The Politics of Provincialism*, p. 195; Hoover, *The New Day*, p. 155.
44. Smith, *Campaign Addresses*, p. 261; Bornet, *Labor Politics*, p. 175.
45. Bornet, *Labor Politics*, pp. 147, 78.
46. Zieger, *Republicans and Labor*, pp. 61–62, 100ff. Brody, *Steelworkers in America*, p. 273.
47. Bornet, *Labor Politics*, pp. 156–61, 162, 229ff., 271; Lichtman, *Prejudice and the Old Politics*, pp. 188–90.
48. Burner, *The Politics of Provincialism*, p. 196; Lisio, *Hoover, Blacks, and Lilywhites*, p. 85.
49. Hoover, *The New Day*, p. 16.
50. One of Chairman Raskob's first actions, symbolically enough, was to move Smith's campaign headquarters from the Biltmore Hotel to the General Motors Building.
51. Democratic National Committee, *The Campaign Book of the Democratic Party*, pp. 70, 72. See also Burns, "Ideology of Businessmen and Presidential Elections," pp. 230–36.
52. Roosevelt, *FDR: His Personal Letters* 2, p. 773. See also Freidel, *FDR and the South*, p. 25.
53. Roosevelt to Ward Melville, September 21, 1928, FDR Papers, Papers Pertaining to the Campaign of 1928, Container 15.
54. Roosevelt to W. H. Boshart, September 20, 1928, FDR Papers, Papers Pertaining to the Campaign of 1928, Container 22.
55. Tobin, *Organize or Perish*, p. 249.
56. See Glad, "Progressives and the Business Culture," p. 87.
57. Quoted in Tobin, *Organize or Perish*, p. 191.
58. "Should Liberals Vote for Smith?," *Nation*, September 26, 1928, p. 284.

59. Croly, "The Progressive Voter," p. 244.

60. "The Quality of Al Smith," *New Republic*, August 29, 1928, p. 32.

61. "Why Progressives Should Vote for Smith," *New Republic*, September 5, 1928, p. 58.

62. See Casey, "Scripps-Howard Newspapers."

63. Gammack, "Wall Street Likes Al Smith."

64. *Wall Street Journal*, July 3, 1928, p. 5.

65. "Smith Scores," *Wall Street Journal*, July 13, 1928, p. 2.

66. "Finance's Field," *Wall Street Journal*, November 1, 1928, p. 1.

67. Burns, "Ideology of Businessmen and Presidential Elections," p. 230.

68. See also Lichtman, *Prejudice and the Old Politics*, p. 194.

69. Baker to Cox, December 10, 1928, Cox Papers, Box 8.

70. *Declaration of Principles and Purposes of the Conference of Anti-Smith Democrats.*

71. See Brown, *Hood, Bonnet, and Little Brown Jug*, pp. 402–16.

72. See Kelley, "Deep South Dilemma"; Reagan, "Race as a Factor."

73. See McCarthy, "The Brown Derby Campaign in West Tennessee," pp. 83–84.

74. See Lisio, *Hoover, Blacks, and Lilywhites*, p. 86; McCarthy, "The Brown Derby Campaign in West Tennessee," p. 91.

75. Kelley, "Deep South Dilemma," p. 65.

76. McCarthy, "The Brown Derby Campaign in West Tennessee," p. 88.

77. See Lee, *Tennessee in Turmoil*, p. 99; Lisio, *Hoover, Blacks, and Lilywhites*, p. 85. The Republicans, too, attempted to raise southern fears about Smith's "reliability" on racial issues. Miscegenation and integration was allegedly rampant in Smith's New York, and the governor had appointed blacks to the New York City school system. See McCarthy, "The Brown Derby Campaign in West Tennessee," p. 92.

78. Key, *Southern Politics*, p. 318.

79. Reagan, "Race as a Factor," p. 17. In West Tennessee, whites who lived near areas of relatively large black populations voted heavily for Smith; in areas with fewer blacks they tended to vote for Hoover (McCarthy, *The Brown Derby Campaign in West Tennessee*, p. 95). For a cogent criticism of McCarthy's contention that race was the overriding issue in Tennessee during the campaign of 1928, see Qualls, "The 1928 Presidential Election in West Tennessee."

80. Brown, *Hood, Bonnet, and Little Brown Jug*, p. 416.

81. Hull, *Memoirs* 1, p. 131. See also Schlesinger, *The Age of Roosevelt* 1, p. 276.

82. Key, *Southern Politics*, pp. 212–14.

83. Ratner, *The Tariff in American History*, pp. 44–46.

84. Watson, "A Political Leader Bolts," p. 516.

85. Puryear, *Democratic Dissension in North Carolina*, p. 10.

86. Quoted in Watson, "A Political Leader Bolts," pp. 525, 535.

87. See ibid., p. 541; Lisio, *Hoover, Blacks, and Lilywhites*, p. 205.

88. Kilpatrick, *Roosevelt and Daniels*, p. 91.

89. Daniels, "Life Begins at 70, Draft #5," Daniels Papers, Container 768.

90. For a description of Byrd's Virginia, see Key, *Southern Politics in State and Nation*, pp. 19–35.

91. See Tindall, "Business Progressivism," p. 103; Glad, "Progressives and the Business Culture of the 1920s."

92. See Byrd to Smith, August 22, 1928, Graves Papers, Container 26.

93. "Speech—Presidential Campaign 1928," Byrd Papers, Box 357.

94. Smith and Beasley, *Carter Glass*, p. 282.

95. Glass to Daniels, July 16, 1928, Daniels Papers, Reel 51.

96. Glass to Ailsworth, July 14, 1928, Glass Papers, Box 1.

97. Glass to Daniels, July 16, 1928, Daniels Papers, Reel 51.

98. Smith and Beasley, *Carter Glass*, p. 285; Baruch, *The Public Years*, p. 214.

99. McAdoo to Claggett, July 17, 1928, McAdoo Papers, Box 339.

100. Baruch, *The Public Years*, p. 213.

101. See the long letters exchanged by McAdoo and John O. Davis on August 3, 1928, McAdoo Papers, Box 339.

102. McAdoo to Thomas J. Hamilton, October 12, 1928, McAdoo Papers, Box 340.

103. McAdoo to Cummings, November 13, 1928, Cummings Papers, Box 55.

104. Charles Warren to Roosevelt, June 15, 1928, FDR Papers, Papers Pertaining to the Campaign of 1928, Container 2. See also Bowers, *My Life*, p. 177.

105. In 1913 a wagon cost a North Dakota farmer the equivalent of 103 bushels of wheat. In 1923 the relative cost of a wagon had climbed to 166 bushels. See Saloutos and Hicks, *Agricultural Discontent*, p. 376.

106. Milton to McAdoo, July 31, 1928, McAdoo Papers, Container 339.

107. Eleanor Roosevelt to Clara Wesley, October 3, 1928, Eleanor Roosevelt Papers, Container 6.

108. Du Bois, "Is Al Smith Afraid of the South?," p. 393.

109. Ibid. See also the *New York Times*, April 15, 1927, p. 10. It appears, however, that the governor may well have entertained more enlightened views in private. When a New Yorker wrote in 1923 to ask AES to cancel a proposed boxing match between Jack Dempsey and a black fighter, he refused to take any action. This was solely a matter for the State Boxing Commission, he wrote, but "I can only say to you that I have a great faith in the document known as the 'Declaration of Independence' and one passage of it reads, 'All men are created equal.'" (AES to Hon. D. Walker Wear, June 8, 1923, Graves Papers, Container 76). See also Schlesinger, *The Age of Roosevelt* 3, pp. 426–27.

110. Democratic National Committee, *The Campaign Book of the Democratic Party*, p. 318.

111. Raskob to Irénée du Pont, July 19, 1928, Irénée du Pont Papers, Series J, Box 192; Pierre du Pont to Edward F. Hushebeck, July 7, 1928, Longwood Papers, Group 10, Box 1023–46.

112. Schlesinger and Israel, *History of American Presidential Elections*, p. 2621.

113. See Burner, *The Politics of Provincialism*, p. 200.

114. Smith, *Campaign Addresses*, pp. 107ff. and 14.

115. Ibid, p. 149.

116. See Carter Glass to Robert Ailsworth, July 14, 1928, Glass Papers, Box 1.

117. Daniels to Byrd, August 16, 1928, Daniels Papers, Container 673.

118. See Ferguson, "Party Realignment and American Industrial Structure," p. 22, on the unreliability of campaign contribution figures. Peel and Donnelly (*The 1928 Campaign*, p. 48), estimated that the Republicans raised a total of $10,062,115, while the DNC raised $7,220,681. These figures are confirmed by Fuchs, "Election of 1928," p. 2605. Merriam and Gosnell (*The American Party System*, p. 337), calculated that the total outlays of the two national committees, including amounts sent to state committees, were $6,256,111 for the RNC and $5,342,350 for the DNC. Allan Lichtman (*Prejudice and the Old Politics*, p. 195) claims that the DNC spent $7,152,512 and the RNC $9,433,604. See also Lopata, "John J. Raskob," p. 72; Pollock, "Campaign Funds in 1928."

119. See the *New York Times*, July 23, 1928, p. 4. See also Flynn, *You're the Boss*, p. 70. Merriman and Gosnell (*The American Party System*, p. 337), estimate the DNC's outlays in 1920 to have been $1,148,007, and in 1924 only $838,458.

120. Raskob to Thomas Fortune Ryan, October 17, 1928, Raskob Papers, File 602.

121. Pierre du Pont to H. B. Thompson, November 19, 1928, PSduP, Longwood Papers, File 1023-46.

122. Lopata, "John J. Raskob," p. 72.

123. Overacker, *Money in Elections*, p. 138.

124. Ibid., p. 136. Democratic figures for the 1920 and 1924 campaigns are unavailable.

125. Ibid., pp. 158–59.

126. Memorandum, "Distribution of Democratic Votes for President, 1892–1928," AES, Private Papers, PPF 221.

127. David, *Party Strength*.

128. See Lisio, *Hoover, Blacks, and Lilywhites*; Lichtman, *Prejudice and the Old Politics*, pp. 147–55; McCarthy, "The Brown Derby Campaign in West Tennessee," pp. 90–91.

129. Key, *Southern Politics*, pp. 318–29.

130. David, *Party Strength*, pp. 292–93.

131. Perkins, *The Roosevelt I Knew*, p. 46.

132. See Andersen, *Creation of a Democratic Majority*; Lubell, *The Future of American Politics*; Allswang, *A House for All Peoples*.

133. Hofstadter, "Could a Protestant Have Beaten Hoover in 1928?," p. 33.

134. Kleppner, *Continuity and Change*, p. 143.

135. Lichtman, *Prejudice and the Old Politics*, p. 125.

136. Burnham, "The System of 1896," p. 182.

137. Lichtman, *Prejudice and the Old Politics*, p. 213; Hofstadter, "Could a Protestant Have Beaten Hoover?," p. 33.

138. Burner, *The Politics of Provincialism*, pp. 179–216.

139. Peel and Donnelly, *The 1928 Campaign*, p. 122. Gilbert C. Fite argues that Smith made great inroads into La Follette's western vote and that the election of 1928 marked a strong recovery in the party's fortunes in that region. The Democrats gained 1,997,921 votes in the West over 1920, while the GOP vote increased by 1,249,319 ("The Agricultural Issue in the Presidential Campaign of 1928," pp.

669, 671). His examination, however, was limited to only a few counties, and his use of the 1920 result is open to criticism. Cox's defeat in that year was especially severe, and Smith's performance in the West is less impressive when compared to that of Wilson in 1916, and in the context of a steep decline in the farm economy since 1920.

140. Thomas J. Hamilton to McAdoo, September 20, 1928, McAdoo Papers, Container 340.

CHAPTER NINE

1. See Jouett Shouse, Speech to the Jefferson Democratic Association of Washington, D.C., June 8, 1929, Shouse Papers, Box 7.
2. See Carlson, "Franklin D. Roosevelt's Fight," p. 12.
3. See the *New York Times*, May 12, 1929, p. 22.
4. See Shouse Papers, Box 1, File F.
5. Shouse to McAdoo, March 10, 1926, McAdoo Papers, Container 324.
6. *Macon Telegraph and News* editorial "A Quiet Answer," October 26, 1930, Shouse Papers, "Newspaper Clippings, 1925–51."
7. See the *New York Times*, May 2, 1929, p. 6; FDR to Shouse, May 6, 1929, Shouse Papers, Box 1, "Correspondence 1929: Franklin D. Roosevelt letters."
8. See Smoger, "Organizing Political Campaigns," p. 118.
9. In 1961 a conservative newspaper advised the RNC that it needed a Charles Michelson to revive its flagging fortunes (Cotter and Hennessy, *Politics without Power*, p. 132).
10. Kent, "Charlie Michelson," p. 291.
11. Ratner, *The Tariff in American History*, pp. 50–54; Kenkel, *Progressives and Protection*, pp. 201–17.
12. Barclay, "The Publicity Division of the Democratic Party, 1929–1930," p. 69. These press statements are collected in the Shouse Papers, Box 7.
13. See Smoger, "Organizing Political Campaigns," p. 118.
14. See Irwin, *Propaganda and the News*, p. 291.
15. Bone, *Party Committees and National Politics*, pp. 71–72.
16. Irwin, *Propaganda and the News*, p. 292.
17. *New York Times*, February 27, 1930, p. 25. The Republicans found it impossible to consolidate their southern gains of 1928. Although some attempts were made to "reform" state Republican organizations by easing out their generally black leadership groups and replacing them with "lilywhites," these came to little. Southerners had limited their defection in 1928 to the Democratic national ticket and had generally eschewed the GOP's local tickets (Mayer, *The Republican Party*, p. 409). State Democratic organizations were quick to reassert their hegemony. In Virginia, for example, Harry Flood Byrd's organization triumphed in the 1929 state elections, and elsewhere in the South the heresy of 1928 was quickly forgotten.

The onset of the depression further ensured that Hoover's "southern strategy" would not succeed in entrenching the success of 1928. See Lisio, *Hoover, Blacks, and Lilywhites*.

18. Raskob to FDR, August 5, 1932, Raskob Papers, File 602. See also Shouse to Byrd, September 27, 1930, Byrd Papers, Box 100, Folder "Sh-Sl."

19. See Key Pittman to W. G. Great House, November 10, 1930, Pittman Papers, Container 12.

20. Jouett Shouse, Press Release, October 13, 1931, Shouse Papers, Box 7, File: "DNC Press Releases 1931."

21. "Speech to Democratic National Committee," February 1932, Raskob Papers, File 602, Box 10.

22. These figures are calculated from those found in PSduP, Longwood Papers, Group 10, File 765-11.

23. Mary Staples Porter to John W. Davis, November 18, 1931, Davis Papers, Series 4, Box 77. See also Donald S. McKinley to Raskob, June 21, 1932, Raskob Papers, File 602, Subfile 2.

24. See Raskob Papers, File 602, Subfile 4.

25. See Raskob to AES, December 2, 1930, Raskob Papers, File 602.

26. Raskob Papers, File 602, "DNC: Financial Statements."

27. *New York Times*, January 14, 1929, p. 22.

28. *New York Times*, January 14, 1931, p. 22.

29. "Speeches Delivered at the Convention of Anti-Smiths," June 18, 1929, Glass Papers, Box 39.

30. Ibid. See also Governor Dan Moody of Texas, quoted in the *New York Times*, January 16, 1931, p. 10.

31. Hull to J. M. Gardenhire, November 22, 1928, Hull Papers, Reel 6, Folder 43.

32. Byrd to Hull, January 19, 1929, Hull Papers, Folder 44A.

33. Raskob Papers, File 602, Box 8, Subfile 2.

34. See Harry Hopkins, "Goodbye to Mr. R.," p. 64.

35. Frank R. Kent, "Open Letter to John J. Raskob," January 13, 1931, quoted in the *New York Times*, January 14, 1931.

36. Raskob to FDR, March 31, 1932, Raskob Papers, File 1989.

37. See Kyvig, *Repealing National Prohibition*, p. 143.

38. Mayer, *The Republican Party*, p. 417.

39. Milton to Byrd, November 11, 1930, Byrd Papers, Box 98.

40. These percentages are calculated from the figures provided in the *Literary Digest*, May 24, 1930, p. 8. Even in 1922 a *Literary Digest* poll had shown that 61.5 percent of respondents were in favor of either modification or repeal, suggesting that the wet publicity effort was less successful than has often been assumed. See Engelman, "Organized Thirst," p. 172; Gebhart, "Movement against Prohibition," p. 172.

41. *Literary Digest*, April 30, 1932, p. 7.

42. John J. Raskob Questionnaire, November 21, 1931, Irénée du Pont Papers, Series J, Box 192, Folder: "Politics and Legislation, 1930–1931."

43. John J. Raskob, letter to members of the DNC, January 5, 1932, AES, Private Papers, Folder 162.
44. Quoted in the *Literary Digest*, December 12, 1931, p. 8.
45. See the *Washington Post* editorial "Splitting the Party," November 23, 1931, PSduP, Longwood Papers, Group 10, File 765-2.
46. See Lippmann, *Interpretations*, p. 257.
47. Undated Editorial, "Mr. Raskob's Poll," in Raskob Papers, File 602, Box 9, Subfile 2. See also the *Asheville* (N.C.) *Citizen*, quoted in the *Literary Digest*, December 12, 1931, p. 8.
48. See Raskob Papers, File 602, Box 20.
49. See Raskob's letter to the members of the DNC, January 5, 1932, AES, Private Papers, Folder 162. See also John J. Raskob, Circular Letter, April 4, 1931, Byrd Papers, Box 108.
50. Raskob's letter to the members of the DNC, January 5, 1932, AES, Private Papers, Folder 162.
51. See Kyvig, *Repealing National Prohibition*, p. 148.
52. See Farley, *Behind the Ballots*, p. 74.
53. Kyvig, *Repealing National Prohibition*, p. 151.
54. See, for example, Burner, *The Politics of Provincialism*, p. 144.
55. See Raskob to Thomas A. Doyle, July 1, 1931, Raskob Papers. File 602, Box 8, Subfile 1.
56. *New York Times*, December 11, 1928, sec. 3, p. 4.
57. Raskob Papers, File 602, Box 20, Subfile 1.
58. See Raskob to Morris Sheppard, December 23, 1931, Raskob Papers, File 602, Box 9, Subfile 2.
59. Adams, *Our Business Civilization*, p. 134.
60. Cox to Tumulty, March 13, 1931, Cox Papers, Box 40. As early as 1923 Henry Jessup noted that one of the great ironies of national prohibition was that southerners demanded that the Eighteenth Amendment should be obeyed out of respect for the sanctity of the Constitution, even as they completely ignored the Fifteenth Amendment. See Jessup, "State Rights and Prohibition," p. 63.
61. See Kyvig, *Repealing National Prohibition*, p. 132.
62. Holcombe, "Trench Warfare," pp. 921ff.
63. McAdoo to Glass, April 3, 1931, Glass Papers, Box 279.
64. Daniels to Glass, March 9, 1931, Daniels Papers, Reel 42. See also Hull to W. E. Norvell, April 30, 1931, Hull Papers, Reel 8, Folder 55.
65. Walsh to Monroe Butler, April 7, 1931, Walsh Papers, Container 382.
66. For an account of Byrd's career and influence in Virginia state politics, see Hawkes, "The Emergence of a Leader."
67. Robertson to Byrd, January 15, 1931, Byrd Papers, Box 109.
68. See Byrd to FDR, February 27, 1931, Byrd Papers; FDR to Byrd, March 2, 1931, ibid.
69. Byrd to Daniels, March 11, 1931, Byrd Papers.

70. Flannagan to Byrd, April 7, 1931, Byrd Papers, Box 105. The underline is Flannagan's.
71. Byrd to Alderman, April 8, 1931, Byrd Papers, Box 101.
72. The argument that only the convention had the power to alter party policy was frequently used by Raskob's opponents. See, for example, Josephus Daniels to Harry Flood Byrd, February 19, 1931, Byrd Papers, Box 105; McAdoo to Raskob, March 2, 1931, Raskob Papers, File 602, Box 6, Subfile 1.
73. Raskob to Byrd, April 9, 1931, Byrd Papers, Box 108.
74. Byrd to Raskob, April 18, 1931, Byrd Papers, Box 108.
75. Byrd to Flannagan, April 13, 1931, Byrd Papers, Box 105.
76. Raskob to Byrd, April 21, 1931, Byrd Papers, Box 108.
77. Byrd to Bailey, June 3, 1931, Byrd Papers, Box 102.
78. Howe to Byrd, December 18, 1931, Byrd Papers, Container 103.
79. Byrd to Breckinridge, December 31, 1931, Byrd Papers, Box 102.
80. See Byrd, "Presidential Campaign: Suggested Platform—1932" (undated), Byrd Papers, Box 359.
81. Byrd to Raskob, May 11, 1932, Byrd Papers, Box 121.
82. Raskob Circular Letter to DNC, April 4, 1931, Raskob Papers, Box 108.
83. Ibid. See also the *New York Times*, March 16, 1931, p. 16.
84. See Hicks, *Republican Ascendancy*, p. 221.
85. See Raskob, Radio Speech, *New York Times*, October 28, 1930, p. 5.
86. Shouse Speech, June 8, 1929, Shouse Papers, Box 7.
87. Shouse, "Democracy's Victory and Opportunity," p. 8.
88. Shouse, Speech in Miami, Florida, February 6, 1931, Shouse Papers, Box 7.
89. See PSduP, Longwood Papers, Group 10, File 765-2.
90. Bowers to Shouse, July 28, 1930, Shouse Papers, Box 2.
91. Flannagan to Byrd, June 26, 1930, Byrd Papers, Box 96.
92. Milton to Byrd, February 26, 1931, Byrd Papers, Box 107.
93. Quoted in Hull, *Memoirs* 1, p. 142. See also Hinton, *Cordell Hull*, p. 190.
94. Walsh to Monroe Butler, April 7, 1931, Walsh Papers, Box 382.
95. Alfred E. Cohn to Raskob, December 11, 1931, Raskob Papers, File 602, Box 20, Subfile 1.
96. Quoted in the *New York Times*, November 8, 1930, pp. 1, 2.
97. See Shouse, Speech in Miami, Florida, February 6, 1931, Shouse Papers, Box 7.
98. Tumulty to Raskob, October 20, 1930, Raskob Papers, File 602, Box 4, Subfile 4.
99. See the *Nation*, November 19, 1930, p. 539.
100. Shouse, "Watchman, What of the Night?," 252.
101. Ibid., p. 253.
102. *New York Times*, November 9, 1930, sec. 2, p. 1.
103. *Wall Street Journal*, November 11, 1930, p. 1.
104. See the *New York Times*, November 9, 1930, p. 3.
105. Baruch quoted in Schwarz, *The Speculator*, p. 256. For Traylor, see the *New York Times*, November 10, 1930, p. 1.

106. Quoted in the *New York Times*, November 13, 1930, p. 1.
107. See Clifford Allen to Carter Glass, November 14, 1930, Glass Papers, Box 245.
108. Shouse, "Democracy's Victory and Opportunity," p. 7.
109. Slichter to Raskob, November 14, 1930, Raskob Papers, File 602, Box 5, Subfile 3.
110. Quoted in the *New York Times*, November 9, 1930, p. 3.
111. Quoted in the *New York Times*, November 12, 1930, p. 13.
112. McAdoo to Garner, November 15, 1930, McAdoo Papers, Container 354.
113. Quoted in the *New York Times*, November 13, 1930, p. 6.
114. Schwarz, "John Nance Garner," p. 163.
115. See Rosen, *Hoover, Roosevelt, and the Brains Trust*, p. 290; Schwarz, "John Nance Garner."
116. Schwarz, "John Nance Garner," pp. 165, 171. For Raskob's favorable attitude to the federal sales tax proposal, see Raskob to W. B. Cassell, March 28, 1932, Raskob Papers, File 602, Box 11, Subfile 1.
117. Daniels to Garner, February 8, 1932, Daniels Papers, Reel 50.
118. Anderson, "Heaven Goes Republican," p. 368.
119. Pinchot to Raskob, December 16, 1931, Raskob Papers, File 602, Box 9, Subfile 2.

CHAPTER TEN

1. Grantham to FDR, November 12, 1928, FDR Papers, Papers Pertaining to the Campaign of 1928, Container 3, Folder: "Florida."
2. See, for example, Burner, *The Politics of Provincialism*, pp. 156, 244–52; Schlesinger, *The Age of Roosevelt* 3, p. 410; Burns, *Roosevelt*, p. 126; Davis, *FDR: The Beckoning of Destiny*, p. 712. For Roosevelt's wooing of the South, see Freidel, *FDR and the South*, pp. 10–25; Freidel, "The South and the New Deal," p. 23.
3. See Caro, *The Power Broker*, pp. 287ff.
4. Davis, *FDR: The New York Years*, p. 57.
5. See Bellush, *Franklin D. Roosevelt as Governor*, p. 76.
6. Ibid., p. 94. The Reforestation Amendment is discussed in chapter 11 below.
7. Bellush, *Franklin D. Roosevelt as Governor*, p. 94.
8. Ibid., pp. 195, 178.
9. Quoted in ibid., p. 140.
10. For a detailed account of Walker's years as mayor, see Walsh, *Gentleman Jimmy Walker*.
11. Ibid., pp. 218–42.
12. Bellush, *Franklin D. Roosevelt as Governor*, p. 301.
13. Schlesinger, *The Age of Roosevelt* 1, p. 422.
14. Walsh, *Gentleman Jimmy Walker*, p. 234.
15. Of all the northeastern political bosses, only Ed Flynn of the Bronx supported FDR's nomination in 1932. Tammany remained steadfast for Smith, as did Frank Hague of Jersey City, David Walsh of Boston, and Anton Cermak of Chicago.

Only Thomas Pendergast of Kansas City, Missouri, and Boss Crump of Memphis supported FDR before Chicago. See Dorsett, *Franklin D. Roosevelt and the City Bosses*, pp. 8–16.

16. Bellush, *Franklin D. Roosevelt as Governor*, p. 172. See also Peel and Donnelly, *The 1932 Campaign*, p. 70.

17. Davis, *FDR: The New York Years*, p. 213.

18. The most detailed account available of Roosevelt's campaign for the nomination can be found in Carlson, "Franklin D. Roosevelt's Fight."

19. Quoted in Lindley, *Franklin D. Roosevelt*, p. 322.

20. Roosevelt's speech is quoted in full in the *New York Times*, May 23, 1932, p. 6.

21. *New York Times*, May 24, 1932, p. 18.

22. See Freidel, "The South and the New Deal," p. 21.

23. See FDR to Bertron, October 1, 1930, Howe Papers, Container 41.

24. See Carlson, "Franklin D. Roosevelt's Fight," p. 145.

25. Farley to FDR, July 6, 1931, Howe Papers, Container 51.

26. Cummings to Mrs. Charles L. Donohoe, January 28, 1932, Cummings Papers, Box 62.

27. Cummings to Milton, January 20, 1932, Cummings Papers, Box 62.

28. Quoted in Israel, *Nevada's Key Pittman*, p. 96.

29. Quoted in Kilpatrick, *Roosevelt and Daniels*, p. 113.

30. Roper to Sidney McLaurin, March 1, 1932, Cummings Papers, Box 62.

31. Milton to Byrd, March 13, 1931, Byrd Papers, Box 107.

32. Taylor to Byrd, March 16, 1931, Byrd Papers, Box 110.

33. See, for example, Bernard Eichold to FDR, April 4, 1932, FDR Papers, Papers of the National Committee of the Democratic Party, 1928–1948, Container 3.

34. See Davis, *FDR: The New York Years*, p. 166.

35. Gardner to Byrd, September 19, 1930, Byrd Papers, Box 96. Roosevelt's position on prohibition does appear to have lost him the unanimous support of South Carolina's delegates to the Chicago convention. Citing the prohibition issue, the state convention refused to instruct its delegation for FDR, although the unit rule kept the Palmetto State within his camp once balloting began. See Byrnes, *All in One Lifetime*, p. 62.

36. Reed to Byrd, November 30, 1930, Byrd Papers, Box 108.

37. Roosevelt, "Our Foreign Policy," p. 581.

38. Quoted in Davis, *FDR: The New York Years*, p. 259.

39. See Stiles, *The Man behind Roosevelt*, p. 120. Although undoubtedly aimed at Raskob, FDR's general position on fund-raising dated back to at least 1926. In that year he wrote to Jesse Jones, finance director of the DNC, that "I have been opposed, on principle, to the collection of Democratic funds, either for campaign purposes or to pay off deficits, from contributions from a mere handful of very rich or moderately rich gentlemen" (see Timmons, *Jesse H. Jones*, p. 139). The circular letters, in different forms, were sent to state chairmen, county chairmen, delegates to the 1928 convention, and both successful and unsuccessful congressional can-

didates. The letters and their replies are preserved in FDR Papers, Democratic National Committee Correspondence, Container 847, "National Political Digest."

40. These figures have been calculated from the raw data collated in the "National Political Digest." They are necessarily imprecise because not all the figures are available. For some states no figures are given for votes for or against Raskob, but phrases such as "about half" and "practically all" are used. Therefore the figures and percentages cited here should be treated only as guides.

41. The above figures and percentages were all calculated from the "National Political Digest."

42. FDR to John S. Williams, February 26, 1929, FDR Papers, Papers Pertaining to the Campaign of 1928, Container 11.

43. See FDR to Cordell Hull, January 14, 1930, Hull Papers, Reel 6, Folder 44.

44. FDR to Charles McCarthy, November 20, 1930, FDR Papers, Papers as Governor of New York State, 1929–1932, Series 1, Container 53.

45. See Carlson, "Franklin D. Roosevelt's Fight," pp. 100ff.

46. See Hull, *Memoirs* 1, p. 145. See also FDR to AES, February 28, 1931, Roosevelt, *FDR: His Personal Letters* 1, p. 179.

47. Raskob to FDR, March 31, 1931,Raskob Papers, File 1989.

48. Byrd to Taylor, March 19, 1931, Byrd Papers, Box 110. See also FDR to Daniels, August 1, 1931, Roosevelt, *FDR: His Personal Letters* 1, p. 208; Shouse to FDR, September 2, 1931, Raskob Papers, File 602, Box 19, Subfile 2.

49. See FDR to H. C. Nixon, February 27, 1931, FDR Papers, Papers of the National Committee of the Democratic Party, Container 4.

50. FDR to W. C. Berryhill, March 20, 1931, FDR Papers, Papers of the National Committee of the Democratic Party, Container 356.

51. See FDR to Byrd, March 21, 1932, Byrd Papers, Box 121.

52. FDR to Daniels, April 2, 1932, Daniels Papers, Reel 59.

53. See "Proceedings of the Committee on Arrangements of the DNC, Congress Hotel, Chicago, April 4, 1932," Shouse Papers, Box 8, Folder: "DNC Proceedings, 4/4/32."

54. See Rosen, *Hoover, Roosevelt, and the Brains Trust*, p. 220. Rosen argues that the agreement of April 4 was a gigantic error on the part of FDR's "Albany group"— and especially of Louis Howe and James Farley—which, when combined with their decisions to enter the California and Massachusetts primaries, casts grave doubt upon their reputations as astute political strategists. See ibid., p. 238.

55. Cummings to Hull, April 13, 1932, Cummings Papers, Box 63.

56. *New York Times*, June 6, 1932, p. 1.

57. Baker to Shouse, June 29, 1932, Shouse Papers, Box 2, "Correspondence, January–July 1932."

58. Daniels to FDR, March 19, 1932, Daniels Papers, Reel 59. William Jennings Bryan, for very similar reasons to those put forward by Cummings against Shouse in 1932, unsuccessfully contested the DNC's designation of Alton B. Parker as temporary chairman at the 1912 convention. See Bowers, *My Life*, p. 79; Link, *Woodrow Wil-*

son and the Progressive Era, p. 12; Broesamle, *William Gibbs McAdoo*, pp. 57–58; Gould, *Reform and Regulation*, p. 167.

59. Milton to Byrd, June 13, 1932, Byrd Papers, Box 119.
60. See Davis, *FDR: The Beckoning of Destiny*, p. 348.
61. FDR to McAdoo, November 28, 1928, McAdoo Papers, Container 341.
62. Newton to McAdoo, December 1, 1928, McAdoo Papers, Container 341.
63. See McAdoo to Newton, December 10, 1928, McAdoo Papers, Container 341.
64. McAdoo to Newton, December 14, 1928, McAdoo Papers, Container 341.
65. McAdoo to Thomas J. Hamilton, January 5, 1929, McAdoo Papers, Container 341.
66. McAdoo to Milton, May 5, 1930, McAdoo Papers, Container 350.
67. See McAdoo to John L. Irvin, April 30, 1931, McAdoo Papers, Container 358.
68. See McAdoo to Brice Claggett, February 2, 1931, McAdoo Papers, Container 356.
69. McAdoo to Brice Claggett, March 3, 1931, McAdoo Papers, Container 356.
70. See Roper, *Fifty Years of Public Life*, p. 256.
71. See chapter 2 above.
72. Hennings, "California Democratic Politics in the Period of Republican Ascendancy."
73. McAdoo to McKellar, January 2, 1931, McAdoo Papers, Container 355.
74. McAdoo to Kiplinger, June 16, 1930, McAdoo Papers, Container 351.
75. See McAdoo Papers, Container 360, July, 1931.
76. McAdoo to Victor McAdoo, June 20, 1931, McAdoo Papers, Container 359.
77. See Rosen, *Hoover, Roosevelt, and the Brains Trust*, p. 232.
78. Dockweiler to Cummings, March 19, 1932, Cummings Papers, Box 62.
79. FDR to Cummings, January 25, 1932, FDR Papers, Papers of the National Committee of the Democratic Party, Container 86.
80. Handlin, *Al Smith*, p. 163.

CHAPTER ELEVEN

1. See, for example, Raskob to Daniel Balliner, February 11, 1931, Raskob Papers, File 602.
2. Howe to Shouse, November 19, 1931, Shouse Papers, Box 2.
3. See Carlson, "Franklin D. Roosevelt's Fight," pp. 145ff.
4. Roosevelt to Shouse, December 9, 1931, Roosevelt, *FDR: His Personal Letters* 1, p. 240.
5. Shouse to Howe, December 9, 1931, Shouse Papers, Box 74.
6. Quoted in the *New York Times*, February 10, 1932, p. 3.
7. "Washington Notes," *New Republic*, February 24, 1932, p. 45.
8. See "Washington Notes," *New Republic*, March 18, 1931, p. 127.
9. See Davis, *FDR: The New York Years*, p. 244.
10. See AES, "Statement . . . on Six Amendments to Be Voted on at the Next Election," October 23, 1931, AES, Private Papers, Folder 165.
11. Ibid.

12. Cramer, *Newton D. Baker*, p. 228. Chief Justice Marshall, in *Marbury v. Madison* (1819), put it thus: "The Constitution's nature . . . requires, that only its great outlines should be marked, its important objects designated."
13. AES, "Statement . . . on Six Amendments."
14. See chapter 5 above.
15. See Howe Papers, Container 51, Folder 3.
16. See the *New Republic*, February 17, 1932, p. 5; Handlin, *Al Smith*, p. 156.
17. See Rosen, "Baker on the Fifth Ballot?," p. 231. See also Shouse to G. E. Wilson, March 7, 1932, Shouse Papers, Box 3.
18. See Newton D. Baker to John H. Clarke, April 2, 1932, Baker Papers, Container 59.
19. AES, "A Financial Program for the Present Crisis," p. 3, Private Papers, Folder 190.
20. Schwarz, "John Nance Garner and the Sales Tax Rebellion," p. 177.
21. AES, "A Financial Program for the Present Crisis," p. 5.
22. Ibid., pp. 6, 8.
23. See Rosen, *Hoover, Roosevelt, and the Brains Trust*, pp. 144–145.
24. AES, "A Financial Program for the Present Crisis," p. 9.
25. This can be found in the Byrd Papers, Box 355, Folder "L."
26. Long, "Roosevelt or Smith?," pp. 17, 20.
27. Ibid., pp. 35, 37.
28. See Financial Statements, "1932 Smith for President Campaign," Moskowitz Papers, Box 4.
29. See Howe Papers, Container 53, Folder 1.
30. See Financial Statements, "1932 Smith for President Campaign," Moskowitz Papers, Box 4.
31. See, for example, Rosen, "Baker on the Fifth Ballot?," p. 231.
32. For Baker's career in both legal practice and politics, see Cramer, *Newton D. Baker*. For his years as secretary of war, see Beaver, *Newton D. Baker*; Palmer, *Newton D. Baker*; Baker, *American Chronicle*, p. 476; Sullivan, *Our Times 5*, p. 370. For a more critical assessment, see Ferrell, *Woodrow Wilson and World War I*, pp. 23–27.
33. On Baker and the open shop, see Baker to Raymond Fosdick, November 29, 1922, Baker Papers, Container 99. On Baker's Appalachian Power Company brief, see Baker to Frank H. Baker, July 31, 1931, ibid., Container 36; Rosen, "Baker on the Fifth Ballot?," p. 237.
34. See the *New York Times*, July 21, 1931, p. 20.
35. See Baker to Ralph Hayes, December 11, 1924, Baker Papers, Container 114; Beaver, *Newton D. Baker*, p. 6.
36. See Baker Papers, Container 193, Folder: "Prohibition Repeal"; AES, Private Papers, Folder 234, "Wickersham Report." The Wickersham Report and its contradictions are discussed in Kyvig, *Repealing National Prohibition*, p. 113; Rumbarger, *Profits, Power, and Prohibition*, p. 196; Allen, *Since Yesterday*, pp. 33–34.
37. See Beaver, *Newton D. Baker*, pp. 240–42.
38. Baker to Cummings, November 12, 1921, Cummings Papers, Box 51, Folder: "1921: December 3–29."
39. See Rosen, "Baker on the Fifth Ballot?," p. 236.

40. See Baker to Ralph M. Barrett, November 23, 1931, Baker Papers, Container 35.
41. Baker to Lippmann, November 18, 1931, Baker Papers, Container 148.
42. Baker to Fosdick, July 5, 1932, Baker Papers, Container 100.
43. Hayes to John H. Clarke, April 14, 1932, Baker Papers, Container 116. The emphasis is Hayes's.
44. Cramer, *Newton D. Baker*, pp. 228, 224.
45. See Baker to Fred M. Alger, October 3, 1932, Baker Papers, Container 36. See also Cramer, *Newton D. Baker*, p. 228.
46. Baker to Judge John Clarke, December 9, 1931, Baker Papers, Container 50.
47. Baker to William Dodd, March 16, 1931, Baker Papers, Container 86.
48. See the *New York Times*, July 21, 1931, p. 20.
49. Robert F. Burk argues that "some insiders" within the party even contemplated that Raskob himself might have desired the presidential nomination (*The Corporate State and the Broker State*, pp. 87–88). Burk does not, however, cite evidence to substantiate this claim. It seems highly unlikely that Raskob, or any other Democrat, would have seriously considered this possibility. Raskob was a shy and retiring man who was uneasy in public and under no illusions as to either his political popularity or his experience. Although the chairman did raise his political public profile between 1930 and 1932, this was done in order to improve his chances of persuading the party and its leaders to anoint one of the more experienced politicians discussed in this chapter.
50. See Young to National Electric Light Association, 1926, in Young and Swope, *Selected Addresses*.
51. Case and Case, *Owen D. Young*, pp. 369, 531.
52. Ibid., p. 252.
53. See Dale, *The Great Organizers*, p. 78.
54. See Young to FDR, November 1, 1928, FDR Papers, Papers Pertaining to the Campaign of 1928, Container 18; Case and Case, *Owen D. Young*, p. 601.
55. See the *New York Times*, May 10, 1932, p. 1.
56. Case and Case, *Owen D. Young*, p. 568.
57. FDR to Daniels, May 14, 1932, quoted in Kilpatrick, *Roosevelt and Daniels*, p. 116.
58. *New York Times*, May 17, 1932, p. 1.
59. See Burk, *The Corporate State and the Broker State*, pp. 86–104.
60. Freidel, *Franklin D. Roosevelt* 3, p. 235.
61. Shouse to Rosen, December 6, 1965, Shouse Papers, Box 6.
62. Hayes to Baker, March 18, 1932, Baker Papers, Container 116.
63. See Moskowitz to Philip Perlman, May 21, 1932, AES, Private Papers, Folder 568.
64. Byrd to Gardner, August 25, 1931, Byrd Papers, Box 106.
65. For Baker, see Cramer, *Newton D. Baker*; Rosen, "Baker on the Fifth Ballot?"; Rosen, *Hoover, Roosevelt, and the Brains Trust*. For Young, see Case and Case, *Owen D. Young*.
66. See Levin, "Albert C. Ritchie," p. 1–59.
67. *New York Times*, November 9, 1930, sec. 2, p. 4.

68. See Levin, "Albert C. Ritchie," pp. 91, 183.
69. Ibid., p. 199.
70. See Albert C. Ritchie, Fourth Inaugural Address, January 13, 1931, quoted in the *New York Times*, January 14, 1931, p. 22.
71. Quoted in Levin, "Albert C. Ritchie," p. 289.
72. Quoted in Oulahan, *The Man Who . . .* , p. 20.
73. See Zieger, *Republicans and Labor*, p. 127; Levin, "Albert C. Ritchie," p. 173.
74. Quoted in the *New York Times*, April 15, 1928, sec. 3, p. 4.
75. See Levin, "Albert C. Ritchie," p. 293.
76. Quoted in the *New York Times*, January 13, 1928, p. 12.
77. Albert C. Ritchie, "Lucky Strike Hour Address," April 21, 1932, FDR Papers, Papers of the National Committee of the Democratic Party, 1928–1948, Container 252.
78. See Levin, "Albert C. Ritchie," p. 104.
79. See ibid., p. 190.
80. Both Smith and Raskob kept copies of all Ritchie's major speeches in their papers. See AES, Private Papers, Folder 174; Raskob Papers, File 1966.
81. Levin, "Albert C. Ritchie," p. 347.
82. Ibid., p. 340.
83. See the *New York Times*, May 26, 1932, p. 3.
84. Ritchie, "Lucky Strike Hour Address," pp. 1, 2.
85. Ritchie, "NBC Radio Address," p. 9, May 19, 1932, AES, Private Papers, Folder 174.
86. Ritchie, "Lucky Strike Hour Address," p. 2.
87. Ibid., p. 8.
88. Ritchie, "NBC Radio Address," p. 4.
89. Ibid., p. 6.
90. See Levin, "Albert C. Ritchie," p. 358. Levin argues that Ritchie was acting alone throughout the preconvention period and that he was not privy to the strategies of the Raskob group. He does not, however, make reference to the close similarity between Ritchie's platform and that of the conservative coalition.
91. See AES, Private Papers, Folder 568. See also Moskowitz to Philip Perlman, May 21, 1932, ibid.
92. Byrd's candidacy is discussed in Tarter, "A Flier on the National Scene." See also Byrd to William Reed, October 7, 1930, Byrd Papers, Box 102.
93. Breckinridge to Byrd, October 6 and 20, 1931, Byrd Papers, Box 102.
94. Byrd to William T. Reed, October 31, 1931, Byrd Papers, Box 108.
95. See the committee's balance sheet in Byrd Papers, Box 115, Reed contributed $7,400.
96. Breckinridge to Taylor, February 11, 1932, Byrd Papers, Box 115.
97. Flannagan to Byrd, April 18, 1932, Byrd Papers, Box 115. See also Newton Baker to E. C. Folkes, September 19, 1931, ibid., Box 108; Henry Breckinridge to Byrd, October 28, 1931, ibid., Box 102.

98. Byrd to William T. Reed, July 21, 1932, Byrd Papers, Box 121.
99. Woolley to Roosevelt, January 25, 1932, Woolley Papers, Container 17.
100. See Raskob to Byrd, January 12, 1932, Byrd Papers, Box 121.
101. Flannagan to Breckinridge, February 13, 1932, Byrd Papers, Box 115.
102. Flannagan to Byrd, April 18, 1932, Byrd Papers, Box 115.
103. Byrd to Hanes, June 15, 1932, Byrd Papers, Box 116.
104. Reed to Byrd, May 16, 1932, Byrd Papers, Box 121.
105. Byrd, "Jefferson Day Address," April 13, 1932, p. 6, Byrd Papers, Box 358.
106. Ibid., p. 4.
107. Ibid., p. 6. For Byrd's prohibition plan, see chapter 9 above; Samuel Pettengill to Byrd, June 8, 1932, Byrd Papers, Box 120.
108. *New York Times*, June 29, 1932, p. 1.
109. See Hull, *Memoirs* 1, p. 150; Coben, *A. Mitchell Palmer*, p. 263.
110. "The Democratic Platform of 1932," p. 2741.
111. Ibid., pp. 2742, 2744.
112. Ibid., p. 2743.
113. See Hull, *Memoirs* 1, p. 150. At the Republican National Convention, James Wadsworth of New York pressed in vain for a wet plank. He declared with some prescience to Secretary of the Treasury Ogden Mills that "the Democrats right here next week are going to nominate Frank Roosevelt. . . . He will have a wet plank. If we don't have a wet plank, he will get in, and if he does we won't get rid of him until he dies. And thrift will never be heard of again." See Fausold, *James W. Wadsworth*, p. 228. See also Burk, *Corporate State to Broker State*, pp. 96–97.
114. Kyvig, *Repealing National Prohibition*, p. 153.
115. *New York Times*, July 2, 1932, p. 14. In 1964 Barry Goldwater called the 1932 Democratic platform "the most conservative platform of this century," and he declared that he would have been happy to run on it. See Weisbord, *Campaigning for President*, p. 113.
116. "The Democratic Platform of 1932," p. 2742.
117. Roosevelt to Daniels, May 5, 1932, Daniels Papers, Reel 59, "Roosevelt, Franklin D., 1932 Jan.–May."
118. See Timmons, *Garner of Texas*, p. 160.
119. See Byrd to Fred W. Scott, July 27, 1932, Byrd Papers, Box 122.
120. See Proskauer, *A Segment of My Times*, p. 71; Davis, *FDR: The New York Years*, p. 316.
121. See Rosen, "Baker on the Fifth Ballot?," p. 245.
122. See Rosen, *Hoover, Roosevelt, and the Brains Trust*, p. 234; Rosen, "Baker on the Fifth Ballot?," p. 245. Hearst suspected that Baker was still secretly wedded to the League of Nations, despite his February announcement. See Steel, *Walter Lippmann*, p. 294.
123. See Swanberg, *Citizen Hearst*, pp. 327ff.
124. See Levin, "Albert C. Ritchie," p. 375; Baruch, *The Public Years*, p. 240.
125. See Ralph Hayes to John H. Clarke, July 6, 1932, Baker Papers, Container 116. See also Rosen, "Baker on the Fifth Ballot?," p. 245.

126. William T. Reed to Byrd, July 8, 1932, Byrd Papers, Box 121; Byrd to Fred W. Scott, July 27, 1932, ibid., Box 122.

127. White to Hayes, July 18, 1932, Baker Papers, Container 116.

128. See Homer S. Cummings, "Memorandum concerning Certain Occurrences at Chicago on July 1, 1932," Cummings Papers, Container 64, Folder: 1932, June 13–30. See also Mullen, *Western Democrat*, p. 276.

129. Democratic National Committee, *Official Report of the Proceedings of the Democratic National Convention at Chicago, 1932*, p. 376.

130. *New York Times*, July 3, 1932, p. 9.

131. Tumulty to Cox, July 19, 1932, Tumulty Papers, Box 58.

132. Cox to Baker, July 15, 1932, Baker Papers, Container 79. See also Cox to Raskob, July 9, 1932, Raskob Papers, File 503.

133. Raskob to Byrd, July 11, 1932, Byrd Papers, Box 121.

134. Raskob to Byrd, July 6, 1932, Raskob Papers, File 602, Box 12, Subfile 2.

135. Raskob to O'Brien, July 7, 1932, Raskob Papers, Box 12, Subfile 1.

136. Of the du Pont family, only Pierre supported Roosevelt and the Democrats. His brothers Irénée and Lammot, in contrast, threw their votes and pocketbooks behind the Republican party. Yet Lammot and Irénée also contributed to the AAPA, which tended to support Democratic candidates because of the Democratic platform's strong antiprohibition plank. See Burk, *Corporate State to Broker State*, p. 102.

CHAPTER TWELVE

1. See Kerr, *Organized for Prohibition*, p. 257.

2. See Kyvig, "Objection Sustained," p. 213. For a discussion of Sabin's antiprohibition activities, see Kyvig, "Women against Prohibition."

3. James W. Wadsworth made the connection between antiprohibition and opposition to the New Deal explicit in 1935. "The common man is beginning to understand," Wadsworth declared on March 30, "that these experiments launched, presumably, for his benefit have not only failed to benefit him financially but have resulted in robbing him of a large portion of that liberty which the Constitution seeks to guarantee to him. *I feel very much about the issue as I did about the eighteenth amendment, except that I realize that it is far greater in its ramifications.*" (emphasis added, quoted in Kyvig, "Objection Sustained," p. 225).

4. See Dobyns, *The Amazing Story of Repeal*, p. 3. See also Rumbarger, *Profits, Power, and Prohibition*, p. 192. In 1975 Roy H. Lopata argued that Raskob and his colleagues in the AAPA used the "high ideals" of states' rights and individual liberties to mask their deep concern about taxation. Low taxes, Lopata argued, were an "ideal" in itself for Raskob and his friends (see "John J. Raskob," p. 30).

5. Dobyns, *The Amazing Story of Repeal*, p. 9. See also Burner, *Politics of Provincialism*, p. 100; Clark, *The Dry Years*, pp. 221–22.

6. See Kyvig, *Repealing National Prohibition*, Rosen, *Hoover, Roosevelt, and the Brains Trust*; Burk, *The Corporate State and the Broker State*.

7. Kyvig, *Repealing National Prohibition*, p. xv. See also Vose, "Repeal as a Political Achievement."

8. See Kyvig, *Repealing National Prohibition*, pp. xvii, 75 ff.

9. See ibid., p. 133. This is not to say that the effect of prohibition on taxation rates was ignored by the AAPA before October 1929. Pierre du Pont submitted to Congress a proposal to relegalize beer and wines in 1927, arguing inter alia that such a step would allow a large reduction in income taxes (see PSduP, "Proposal for Income Tax Relief and Suggestions as to a Permanent Source of Annual Revenue," 1927, Longwood Papers, Group 10, File 1023, Box 3). In May 1929 the AAPA released a pamphlet entitled *Cost of Prohibition and Your Income Tax*, which became the association's most widely distributed piece of literature. Over 200,000 copies were printed, and the pamphlet's readership has been estimated at eighty million through newspaper paraphrasing. See Kyvig, *Repealing National Prohibition*, p. 196. The point made here, however, is that the income tax argument was by no means the most important of those marshaled by the AAPA against the Eighteenth Amendment in the years before 1930.

10. Irénée du Pont to Coleman du Pont, October 16, 1926, Irénée du Pont Papers, Series J, Box 192.

11. See Kyvig, *Repealing National Prohibition*, p. 70.

12. Quoted in Fausold, *James W. Wadsworth*, p. 179.

13. The prohibition movement, too, has undergone considerable rehabilitation at the hands of recent historians. No longer is it seen as a puritanical reaction by killjoys resentful of other people's pleasures, or as a movement inspired by a displaced elite eager to regain its former role as a moral steward of society, but rather as a sincere and ambitious reform with close links to populism, business regulation, and female suffrage. See Clark, *Deliver Us from Evil*; Clark, *The Dry Years*; Rorabaugh, *The Alcoholic Republic*; Tyrrell, *Sobering Up*; Dannenbaum, *Drink and Disorder*; Kerr, *Organized for Prohibition*. For the earlier, and now questioned, "social control" interpretation of temperance and prohibition, see Gusfield, *Symbolic Crusade*. Changes in the historiography of temperance are discussed in Kett, "Review Essay." For a discussion of the evils of the saloon, see Clark, *The Dry Years*, pp. 54–63; Rorabaugh, *The Alcoholic Republic*.

14. Gebhart, "Prohibition and Real Estate Values," p. 109. Distillers were less affected because of the (suspicious) leap in demand for "medicinal and industrial alcohol," which was exempted from the Volstead Act (ibid.). It is possible that the industry itself was at least partially responsible for its misfortune. In 1918 a proposal was circulated to double the rate of federal taxation on liquor. This increment was to be placed into a sinking fund, which would enable the brewers and distillers to be compensated for the loss of their earnings once the Eighteenth Amendment became operative. This suggestion, however, was killed by the liquor industry, which preferred to fight the ratification of national prohibition rather than to concede its passage. See Steuart, *Wayne Wheeler*, p. 110.

15. See Kyvig, "Sober Thoughts," p. 6.

16. Quoted in Kerr, *Organized for Prohibition*, p. 207.
17. See Kyvig, *Repealing National Prohibition*, pp. xvii, 82.
18. Norman Clark, in his study of the rise and fall of prohibition in Washington, notes that those state senators who voted against state local option bills also tended to vote against other reforms such as female suffrage, initiative and referendum proposals, and limitation of working hours for women (*The Dry Years*, p. 124).
19. Kyvig, "Objection Sustained"; Kyvig, *Repealing National Prohibition*. For examples of unexplored connections, see Wolfskill, *Revolt of the Conservatives*, p. 39; Schlesinger, *The Age of Roosevelt* 2, p. 484.
20. See Mark Edward Lender, "The Historian and Repeal," and Vose, *Constitutional Change*, pp. 101ff., for thoughtful discussions of the present state of the historiography of the antiprohibition movement.
21. See Chandler and Salsbury, *Pierre S. du Pont*, pp. 265ff.
22. See ibid., p. 396. In 1916 a 12.5 percent munitions tax was levied upon munitions makers who earned a profit greater than 10 percent on invested capital. See Witte, *The Politics and Development of the Federal Income Tax*, pp. 81–82.
23. Ratner, *American Taxation*, p. 363.
24. Chandler and Salsbury, *Pierre S. du Pont*, pp. 406–26; Ferrell, *Woodrow Wilson and World War I*, pp. 114–16. Even Baker's terms may have been generous; on construction contracts the standard terms of government contracts during World War I allowed for a profit of 8–10 percent on contracts worth less than $250,000 and a fixed profit of not more than $250,000 for larger agreements. See Beaver, *Newton D. Baker*, pp. 63–64.
25. Chandler and Salsbury, *Pierre S. du Pont*, p. 425. At the end of the war the Du Pont Company had made a total after-tax profit of $439,000 from the American war effort (ibid.).
26. See the *New York Times*, October 17, 1920, clipping in PSduP, Longwood Papers, Group 10, File 782.
27. PSduP to Cox, October 19, 1920, Longwood Papers, Group 10, File 782.
28. For a discussion of the hopes of prohibitionists for labor productivity in the dry age see Rumbarger, *Profits, Power, and Prohibition*, pp. xxii, 155–83; Drescher, "Labor and Prohibition," pp. 43–46.
29. E. P. Sanford estimated that at least 683 million gallons of home-brewed beer, 118 million gallons of wine, and 73 million gallons of distilled spirits were produced in the 1930 fiscal year. This represented 22 gallons of alcoholic beverages per capita. In the four months between January and April 1932, over thirty-four thousand Americans were arrested for liquor offenses. See Sanford, "The Illegal Liquor Traffic," p. 40.
30. See Burk, *The Corporate State and the Broker State*, pp. 37, 68.
31. See PSduP to Smith W. Brookhart, December 17, 1923, and January 16, 1924, Longwood Papers, Group 10, File 670, Box 1, and File 946.
32. PSduP to Francis I. du Pont, August 31, 1928, Longwood Papers, Group 10, File 1023-46. Robert F. Burk provides the following reasons, in addition to taxation,

for the du Ponts' support of the AAPA: "They wanted to deal insurgency politics a decisive reversal, to test the family's national political clout, to attempt to direct a policy change outside the control of the major political parties, and to demonstrate the corporate managerial class's ability to craft public policy alternatives superior to those of partisan officeholders" (*The Corporate State and the Broker State*, p. ix). See also ibid., pp. 38ff., where Burk stresses the income tax issue more than his earlier list might suggest.

33. Stayton to PSduP, May 28, 1932, Longwood Papers, File 1023-48, Box 1.

34. See Stayton to Lammot du Pont, July 28, 1933, Longwood Papers, File 1023, Box 2.

35. See PSduP to Matthew C. Brush, July 1, 1933, Longwood Papers, File 1023-48, Box 1.

36. PSduP to Mary E. Spruance, January 27, 1926, Longwood Papers, File 1023, Box 2.

37. PSduP to L. W. Mims, August 22, 1928, Longwood Papers. File 1023, Box 4.

38. PSduP to Ella D. Cordray, March 16, 1925, Longwood Papers, File 1023, Box 4.

39. PSduP, "Constitutionality of the XVIIIth Amendment," March 1929, Longwood Papers, File 1023-18.

40. See Priest, "The Eighteenth Amendment," pp. 45–47, for a defense of this view.

41. Longwood Papers, File 1023-10. See Franklin, "What's Wrong with the Eighteenth Amendment," pp. 48–52, for a similar view.

42. PSduP to Raskob, January 16, 1931, PSduP, Longwood Papers, File 1125.

43. Ibid.

44. See Swindler, "A Dubious Constitutional Experiment," pp. 55–59. The *National Prohibition Cases* are discussed in Vose, *Constitutional Change*, pp. 91–99.

45. PSduP to Hugh E. Willis, June 1928, PSduP, Longwood Papers, File 1023, Box 4. A similar, but less radical, argument had been put in *Sprague v. United States* (1930). It was argued that Amendments 15–19 were invalid because they made substantial changes to individual rights through legislative ratification rather than by means of popular conventions. Under this argument, amendments altering basic rights could be altered only by conventions. Although U.S. District Judge William Court upheld this reasoning, it was summarily rejected on appeal by the Supreme Court. See Vose, "Repeal as a Political Achievement," p. 102. For a discussion of the use of conventions to ratify constitutional amendments, see Vose, *Constitutional Change*, pp. 112, 134–35.

46. Quoted in Burk, *The Corporate State and the Broker State*, p. 79.

47. PSduP to Cordray, March 20, 1925, PSduP, Longwood Papers, File 1023, Box 2.

48. PSduP to Little, January 7, 1927, Longwood Papers, File 765, Box 1. See also Burk, *The Corporate State and the Broker State*, p. 18.

49. See PSduP, Longwood Papers, File 1023-18. For other details of other Canadian liquor control systems, see Moffitt, "Control of the Liquor Traffic in Canada." There was another, even more statist, system of liquor control debated in the 1920s. This was the Carlisle system, named after the English city in which it was

pioneered. A board of control bought out the entire liquor industry—wholesalers, retailers, and public hotels—within an area of five hundred square miles, and then managed it itself. See Moore and Gerstein, *Alcohol and Public Policy*, p. 173. Du Pont does not appear to have considered adapting this system to American conditions.

50. See PSduP, Longwood Papers, File 1023-39 for a copy of this article, which appeared in the October 26, 1926, issue of *Current History*.

51. PSduP to Ripley, November 17, 1925, Longwood Papers, File 1075.

52. Longwood Papers, File 1023-39. See also PSduP to Leonard Mason, June 8, 1929, ibid., File 1023-34, Box 1.

53. See PSduP to Leon J. Canora, October 9, 1928, Longwood Papers, File 1023, Box 4.

54. PSduP to J. R. Raw, June 21, 1928, Longwood Papers. For a defense of this system, see Catlin, "Alternatives to Prohibition," p. 184.

55. See Longwood Papers, File 1023-18.

56. See Longwood Papers, File 1023-5, for the draft of this article. The quotation appears on p. 10 of the draft.

57. Ibid., p. 4.

58. For details of the Swedish system of liquor control, see Kinberg, "Temperance Legislation in Sweden," p. 208.

59. Longwood Papers, File 1023-5, p. 8. See also File 1023-34, "AAPA: Plans, 1929–1930," Box 2.

60. See PSduP to A. F. Hillman, July 23, 1930, Longwood Papers, File 1023-34, Box 1.

61. See Longwood Papers, File 1023-55. State licensing systems are discussed in Harrison and Laine, *After Repeal*, pp. 45ff. For discussions of postrepeal liquor arrangements, see Rubin, "The Wet War"; Clark, *The Dry Years*, pp. 242ff.; Moore and Gerstein, *Alcohol and Public Policy*; Harrison and Laine, *After Repeal*.

62. Moore and Gerstein, *Alcohol and Public Policy*, p. 65. Seven states continued prohibition after 1933, although five declared beer to be nonintoxicating. Twelve states permitted liquor to be sold only for home consumption, while twenty-nine allowed sales by the glass in "taverns" or restaurants (ibid., p. 173). See also Harrison and Laine, *After Repeal*, pp. 7ff., 43. State monopoly systems are discussed in ibid., pp. 107–72.

63. PSduP to Stayton, January 10, 1933, Longwood Papers, File 1023-48, Box 1. For the best-known discussion of the New Left view of the alliance between regulation and business, see Kolko, *The Triumph of Conservatism*.

64. See Stayton to Irénée du Pont, April 9, 1935, Irénée du Pont Papers, Series J, File 292, Box 205.

65. Stayton's biography is provided by Kyvig, *Repealing National Prohibition*, pp. 39–45.

66. In his contribution to the American Academy of Political and Social Science forum in 1923 on national prohibition, Stayton mentioned taxation only in his penultimate section. See "Our Experiment in National Prohibition," p. 37.

67. Stayton, "Memorandum of Facts," October 2, 1919. Raskob Papers, File 2168. See also Stayton, "Our Experiment in National Prohibition," pp. 30–31.

68. Quoted in Kyvig, *Repealing National Prohibition*, p. 50.

69. Stayton, "Our Experiment in National Prohibition," p. 32. For other examples of the antiprohibitionists' fear of working-class revolt, see Rumbarger, *Profits, Power, and Prohibition*, p. 293.

70. See Kyvig, *Repealing National Prohibition*, p. 46. By 1927 the AAPA claimed to have 720,000 members: see Fausold, *James W. Wadsworth*, p. 221. On Kyvig's estimation the AAPA had 550,000 members in 1932 (see Kyvig, "Objection Sustained," p. 220).

71. Kyvig, *Repealing National Prohibition*, p. 47.

72. John P. Holland to McAdoo, January 30, 1924, McAdoo Papers, Container 294.

73. See Kerr, *Organized for Prohibition*, p. 236.

74. See Carr, *The du Ponts of Delaware*, p. 303.

75. See Burk, *The Corporate State and the Broker State*, pp. 44–46.

76. See Kyvig, *Repealing National Prohibition*, p. 90.

77. See Clark, *The Dry Years*, p. 223, Kerr, *Organized for Prohibition*, pp. 265–74; Engelman, "Organized Thirst."

78. For the Anti Saloon League's travails during the 1920s, see Kerr, *Organized for Prohibition*, pp. 10, 245–60.

79. Kyvig, "Sober Thoughts," p. 14. See also Rumbarger, *Profits, Power, and Prohibition*. The AAPA's message, in Rumbarger's view, "preyed on latent fears of America's middle classes" (p. 192).

80. See Longwood Papers, Group 10, File 1023-48, Box 1, "AAPA: Wm. H. Stayton, 1934." Du Pont provided the necessary funds to keep the Repeal Associates in existence until Stayton's death in 1937. The fact that the Liberty League performed the same functions as Repeal Associates suggests that du Pont did this primarily to give Stayton financial support. This suspicion is strengthened by du Pont's prompt disbanding of the organization after Stayton's death. See Stayton to PSduP, January 2, 1936, ibid., Box 2.

81. "The Reasons for Repeal Associates," May 15, 1934, Longwood Papers, Group 10, File 1023-48, Box 1, "AAPA: Wm. H. Stayton, 1934."

82. Ibid.

83. See Stayton, "Memorandum to Advisory Committee of Repeal Associates," May 7, 1934, Longwood Papers, Group 10, File 1023-48, Box 3. The emphasis is Stayton's.

84. Stayton, "Letter No. 1," August 2, 1934, p. 1, PSduP, Longwood Papers, Group 10, File 1023-48.

85. Ibid., p. 2.

86. Stayton, "Letter No. 2," August 7, 1934, p. 3, PSduP, Longwood Papers, Group 10, File 1023-48.

87. Ibid., p. 5.

88. Stayton, "Letter No. 3," August 9, 1934, p. 1, PSduP, Longwood Papers, Group 10, File 1023-48.

89. Ibid., pp. 2–4.
90. See Stayton, "Letter No. 2.," August 13, 1934, PSduP, Longwood Papers, Group 10, File 1023-48.
91. Ibid., p. 2.
92. Ibid., p. 4.
93. Quoted in Burk, *The Corporate State and the Broker State*, p. 214.
94. Stayton, "Letter No. 4," p. 5.
95. See Stayton, "Letter No. 5," August 16, 1934, p. 1, PSduP, Longwood Papers, Group 10, File 1023-48.
96. Quoted in ibid, pp. 4, 2.
97. Ibid., pp. 2, 3.
98. Ibid., pp. 4–8.
99. Stayton, "Letter No. 6," August 21, 1934, PSduP, Longwood Papers, Group 10, File 1023-48.
100. Ibid., p. 4.
101. Stayton, "Letter No. 7," August 24, 1934, p. 1, 2–4, PSduP, Longwood Papers, Group 10, File 1023-48.
102. See PSduP to Joseph H. Lieb, September 23, 1932, PSduP, Longwood Papers, Group 10, File 1023-36.
103. Memorandum to PSduP from Frank Geesey, March 15, 1933, PSduP, Longwood Papers, Group 10, File 765, Box 1.
104. Perkins, *The Roosevelt I Remember*, pp. 237-238.
105. See PSduP, Longwood Papers, File 1173-6.
106. See PSduP, Comments to the Press, February 15, 1934, PSduP, Longwood Papers, Group 10, File 1173–6.
107. PSduP to Orville W. Underwood, November 11, 1935, PSduP, Longwood Papers, Group 10, File 765, Box 2.
108. See PSduP to Ira Nelson Morris, August 24, 1934, PSduP, Longwood Papers, Group 10, File 1173-6.
109. PSduP to FDR, June 26, 1934, PSduP, Longwood Papers, Group 10, File 1173-5.
110. Shouse, "Speech in Louisville, Kentucky, January 17, 1933," Shouse Papers, Box 12, File: "AAPA Misc., 1933."
111. See Harrison and Laine, *After Repeal*, pp. 23–30. The FACA was replaced by the Federal Alcohol Administration Act after the NIRA was declared unconstitutional in 1935.
112. Shouse, "Speech at AAPA Victory Dinner, December 5, 1933," Shouse Papers, Box 12, File: "AAPA Press Releases, 1933."
113. Harrison and Laine, *After Repeal*, p. 21. See also Ernest A. Grant, "The Liquor Traffic before the Eighteenth Amendment," p. 6.
114. Shouse, "Speech to the New England Society of Pennsylvania, December 8, 1933," p. 1, Shouse Papers, Box 12, File: "AAPA Press Releases, 1933."
115. Ibid., p. 2.
116. Ibid., p. 4.

117. One of the earliest slogans of the AAPA was "Beer and Light Wines NOW: But no Saloons EVER" (Kyvig, *Repealing National Prohibition*, p. 58).
118. Shouse, "Speech to the New England Society," p. 4.

CHAPTER THIRTEEN

1. See, for example, Fausold, *James W. Wadsworth, Jr.*, p. 253; Ferguson, "From Normalcy to New Deal," pp. 87–94.
2. Burk, *The Corporate State and the Broker State*, p. 122.
3. Quoted in Wolfskill, *The Revolt of the Conservatives*, p. 210.
4. The four most significant works on the Liberty League are Wolfskill, *The Result of the Conservatives*; Rudolph, "The American Liberty League"; Ferguson, "From Normalcy to New Deal"; Burk, *The Corporate State and the Broker State*.
5. See Wolfskill, *Revolt of the Conservatives*, p. 65.
6. Ibid., p. 103.
7. Wolfskill and Hudson, *All But the People*, p. 342. Wolfskill's and Hudson's conclusions were repeated without cavil by Roy H. Lopata in "The Business Mind and the Great Depression." Lopata's biography of Raskob ("John J. Raskob") takes a similar line. See also Cashman, *America in the Twenties and Thirties*, p. 180. FDR himself subscribed to this theory, likening the Liberty League's rich backers to a "nice, old gentleman" who had been rescued from drowning by a well-meaning friend. Instead of thanking his savior, the gentleman complained that he had lost his fine silk hat in the water (ibid., p. 200).
8. Ferguson, "From Normalcy to New Deal," pp. 87–94.
9. Lopata "The Business Mind and the Great Depression," p. 33.
10. Daniels, *Between the Wars*, p. 269. National company earnings jumped by 50 percent between 1935 and 1926, and the Dow Jones index climbed by 80 percent between 1933 and 1936 (Schlesinger, *The Age of Roosevelt* 3, p. 571).
11. Burk, *The Corporate State and the Broker State*, pp. 122, 249.
12. See Hutchins, "The Truth about the Liberty League," p. 8.
13. See chapter 5 above.
14. Quoted in the *New York Times*, June 30, 1935, p. 26.
15. See Levin, "Albert C. Ritchie," p. 423.
16. Davis to Lord Midleton, February 8, 1930, Davis Papers, Series 4, Box 65.
17. See Harbaugh, *Lawyer's Lawyer*, pp. 338–39.
18. See "Jackson Day Dinner Speeches, January 8, 1932," Shouse Papers, Box 8, File: "DNC Speeches, etc., 1932."
19. Davis to John E. Nevin, August 18, 1933, Davis Papers, Series 4, Box 92.
20. Raskob to Ellis Spreckels, November 10, 1932, Raskob Papers, File 602, Box 12, Subfile 3.
21. Raskob to Gretchen Cunningham, May 29, 1933, Raskob Papers, File 529.
22. See Raskob to Gretchen Cunningham, October 9, 1933, Raskob Papers, File 529.

23. Raskob to Gretchen Cunningham, November 21, 1933, Raskob Papers, File 529.
24. Carpenter to Raskob, March 16, 1934, Longwood Papers, Group 10, File 1173-6, Folder: "National Recovery Act 1934." See also Hutchins, *The Truth about the Liberty League*, p. 5.
25. Raskob to Carpenter, March 20, 1934, Raskob Papers, File 529.
26. See Raskob Papers, File 61, Box 1, "American Liberty League Correspondence, July–December 1934."
27. This was an organization called the Crusaders. See Raskob to Davis, August 3, 1934, Davis Papers, Series IV, Box 97. The Crusaders, too, began life as an antiprohibition organization founded by wealthy and prominent citizens. See Engelman, "Organized Thirst," pp. 190–92; Lusk (executive vice-president of the Crusaders), "The Drinking Habit," pp. 46–52; Gebhart, "Movement against Prohibition," p. 177. For a discussion of another wealthy antiprohibition group, the Voluntary Committee of Lawyers, which flirted with transformation into an anti–New Deal organization, see Vose, *Constitutional Change*, pp. 102–5, 127–32.
28. For an account of the long and often troubled gestation of the Liberty League, see Burk, *The Corporate State and the Broker State*, pp. 138–69. Raskob and his colleagues devoted many letters to the task of finding a name for their new organization. Their final decision may have been prompted by the memory of an earlier organization called the National Liberty League. Established in 1923, this organization described itself as being composed of "business men, citizens, voters and taxpayers" who supported the repeal or modification of the Volstead Act so as to permit the sale of beer and wine. The sources do not indicate whether any members of Raskob's organization were connected with this earlier group. See Don E. de Bow to AES, November 7, 1924, Graves Papers, Container 16. In another way, however, Raskob and his friends did not choose their name well. Soon after the official announcement of the formation of the Liberty League, John Davis received a letter from J. Arthur Horne of Utah. Horne wrote to say that he was the chairman of the American Liberty League, formed in April 1934 in Utah. Horne advised Davis to change his organization's name because the objectives of the two groups were scarcely compatible. "While we are both avowed champions of the rights of the people guaranteed by the Constitution," Horne wrote, "we are working for a more equitable distribution of the nation's wealth. As I understand it, you are working for the protection of accumulations of wealth" (Horne to Davis, August 24, 1934, Davis Papers, Series 4, Box 97).
29. Shouse's large salary was the subject of frequent jokes by the league's opponents. In 1936, for instance, Democratic senator Louis Schwellenbach of Washington made a speech mocking the league's forthcoming Washington dinner, at which Al Smith would announce his defection from the Democratic party. He was interrupted by his colleague from Indiana, Sherman Minton. "Is this Liberty League which the Senator is speaking about," Minton inquired in feigned ignorance, "the same thing as the Association for the Support of Jouett Shouse?" Schwellenbach continued the joke by explaining to Minton that "there has been some doubt, I

might say to the Senator, just what would be the source of the living for Jouett Shouse if his old friends . . . had not formed this particular league." See Extract from the *Congressional Record*, Senate, January 23, 1936, p. 918; FDR Papers, The President's Personal File, PPF 3146.

30. Burk, *The Corporate State and the Broker State*, pp. 168, 175.

31. Carr, *The du Ponts of Delaware*, p. 308; Hutchins, *The Truth about the Liberty League*, p. 19.

32. James M. Cox speech, Jackson Day Dinner, January 8, 1932, Shouse Papers, Box 8, File: "DNC Speeches, etc., 1932."

33. Cox, *Journey through My Years*, pp. 345ff.

34. Ibid., p. 412.

35. See Cox to FDR, April 4, 1933, FDR Papers, President's Personal File, PPF 53; FDR to Cox, March 9, 1933, ibid.

36. See Cox, *Journey through My Years*, p. 356; Schlesinger, *The Age of Roosevelt* 2, p. 203.

37. See, for example, Cox to FDR, November 7, 1940, Cox Papers, Box 35; Schlesinger, *The Age of Roosevelt* 2, p. 483.

38. See Byrd to W. T. Reed, October 4, 1932, Byrd Papers, Box 121.

39. See Patterson, *Congressional Conservatism and the New Deal*, pp. 30, 16. See also Freidel, *FDR and the South*, p. 74; Koeniger, "The New Deal, Roosevelt, and the Byrd Organization in Virginia."

40. Henry Breckinridge to Byrd, August 20, 1934, Byrd Papers, Box 129. See also Semes, "Confrontation at Charlottesville," p. 34.

41. Cramer, *Newton D. Baker*, p. 259.

42. Baker to Edward A. Filene, March 17, 1934, Baker Papers, Container 95.

43. Baker to Harry M. Ayers, June 8, 1935, Baker Papers, Container 33.

44. Baker to Louis J. Alben, November 30, 1933, Baker Papers, Container 16.

45. Baker to Frank H. Baker, June 23, 1933, Baker Papers, Container 36.

46. *New York Times*, November 22, 1934, p. 2.

47. Baker to Andrew Kelly, November 15, 1934. Baker Papers, File 61.

48. Baker to John W. Davis, January 18, 1935, Baker Papers, Container 84.

49. See Baker to Ralph W. Aigler, July 31, 1936, Baker Papers, Container 17.

50. Baker to Lippmann, January 27, 1936, Baker Papers, Container 149.

51. See the *New York Times*, November 26, 1934, p. 1; Baker to Douglas Heddon Allen, February 12, 1937, Baker Papers, Container 149.

52. See "Who's Who in the American Liberty League," Democratic National Committee Pamphlet 1936, Shouse Papers, Box 10.

53. Wolfskill, *Revolt of the Conservatives*, p. 62.

54. Burk, *The Corporate State and the Broker State*, p. 206.

55. See Irénée du Pont Papers, Series J, File 292, Box 209, Folder: "American Liberty League, October–December 1936."

56. See Irénée du Pont Papers, Series J, File 292, Box 209, "American Liberty League,

1940"; PSduP, Longwood Papers, Group 10, File 771-1, "American Liberty League: Loans and Donations, 1939, 1940."

57. See Hutchins, *The Truth about the Liberty League*, p. 14; Wolfskill, *Revolt of the Conservatives*, p. 61. Martin Fausold denies that the Liberty League's membership ever exceeded seventy-five thousand (*James W. Wadsworth*, p. 241).

58. Semes, "Confrontation at Charlottesville," p. 48.

59. Quoted in Wolfskill, *Revolt of the Conservatives*, p. 212.

60. See Kent, "Wet Their Own Powder," *Baltimore Sun*, January 15, 1935, Irénée du Pont Papers, Series J, File 292, Box 205, Folder: "February 1935." Attempts were made to circularize security holders throughout the nation to request contributions, but these were foiled by the refusal of life insurance companies and corporations to provide the league with their mailing lists. See Stayton to Irénée du Pont, May 27 and September 11, 1935, Irénée du Pont Papers, Series J, File 292, Box 206, Folder: "American Liberty League, May 1935"; Alfred Sloan to Raskob, January 15, 1936, Raskob Papers, File 61, Folder: "January 1936."

61. These were Roosevelt's veto of the Patman Bonus Bill of 1935 and his opposition to Senator Hugo Black's 1936 proposal of a thirty-hour week.

62. See Shouse Papers, Box 9, File: "American Liberty League Correspondence, 1936."

63. See Burk, *The Corporate State and the Broker State*, p. 243.

64. See Miles, *Odyssey of the American Right*, p. 32.

65. Shouse to Frederick Piper, November 14, 1936, Shouse Papers, Box 10, File: "American Liberty League, Correspondence, 1936."

66. See Wolfskill, *Revolt of the Conservatives*, p. 213.

67. See Carr, *The du Ponts of Delaware*, p. 308. See also "Report to the Executive Committee of the American Liberty League," December 20, 1934, Shouse Papers, Box 9.

68. Burk, *The Corporate State and the Broker State*, pp. 205, 216.

69. Quoted in the *New York Times*, February 1, 1936, pp. 1, 2. See also Stayton to PSduP, June 21, 1935, PSduP, Longwood Papers, Group 10, File 765, Box 2, Folder: "Political, 1935." Raskob's letter elicited derision from many of its recipients. Elmer Rice, a New York playwright, replied that "it was gratifying to learn . . . that you have acquired 'a competence for old age and the care of dependents.' I have, of course, heard rumors to that effect, but one scarcely knows what to believe these days, and it is good to learn . . . that you are not a candidate for an old age pension or any of the other hateful forms of governmental patronage." Evelyn Preston, another New Yorker, wrote Raskob in the same vein. "Your letter . . . was a great comfort to me," she declared; "you have no idea how I have been worrying about your old age. To know that you have acquired 'a competence' is such a relief." Both these letters, and many others, can be found in the Raskob Papers, File 61, Box 2, "February 1936." Raskob's letter, according to Robert F. Burk, elicited 1,703 new members and more than $30,000 in funds (*The Corporate State and the Broker State*, p. 216).

70. Irénée du Pont to W. R. K. Taylor, February 20, 1935, Irénée du Pont Papers, Series J, File 292, Box 205, Folder: "American Liberty League, February 1935."

71. PSduP to Zara du Pont, November 6, 1944, Longwood Papers, Group 10, File 765-11, "Political-Presidential Campaigns—1944."

72. Quoted in Jakoubek, "A Jeffersonian's Dissent," p. 146.

73. Ibid.

74. Ibid., pp. 120ff., and John W. Davis, quoted in Harbaugh, *Lawyer's Lawyer*, p. 354. New Deal taxation policy is discussed in Witte, *The Politics and Development of the Federal Income Tax*, pp. 98–109; Ratner, *American Taxation*, pp. 451–90. In 1934 federal income surtaxes rose to a maximum of 59 percent on net incomes greater than $1 million per year, and inheritance taxes rose to a maximum of 60 percent on estates greater than $10 million. In 1935 surtaxes rose to a maximum of 75 percent (on incomes greater than $5 million per year), and inheritance taxes jumped to a maximum of 70 percent (on estates greater than $50 million). In 1936 an undistributed profits tax, ranging from 7 to 27 percent, was also enacted. See ibid., pp. 465–74.

75. See the *New York Times*, December 9, 1934, p. 32.

76. See Irénée du Pont to Senator John Townsend, March 25, 1932, Irénée du Pont Papers, Series J, File 261, Box 192; PSduP, Longwood Papers, Group 10, File 1125, Folder: "Captain Wm. H. Stayton, 1939."

77. PSduP to Sterling E. Edmunds, December 31, 1935, Longwood Papers, Group 10, File 765, Box 2, Folder: "Political, 1935–1936."

78. Irénée du Pont to Daniel O. Hastings, April 2, 1934, Irénée du Pont Papers, Series J, File 189, Box 172, Folder: "Politics and Legislation, April 1933–1934."

79. Irénée du Pont to James H. Hughes, May 14, 1937, Irénée du Pont Papers, Series J, File 261, Box 193, Folder: "Politics and Legislation, 1936–1940." Du Pont's constitutional traditionalism was at times extreme. At the end of 1934 he arranged for the distribution to the public of copies of the Constitution. When the printers sent him the proofs of the proposed pamphlet, he found it too long. He instructed them to delete "all amendments later than the Tenth" so as to shorten the pamphlet and allow for a larger typeface (Irénée du Pont to Thomas J. Sullivan, November 6, 1934, ibid., File 292, Box 203). It seems more than coincidental that the deleted amendments were generally those extending federal power and were therefore inconsistent with du Pont's views. In any event, his actions revealed a significant attitude that the later amendments were of lesser importance than the original document and its first ten amendments. This was consistent with the doctrine of "inalienable rights" promulgated by Pierre du Pont during his AAPA days. See chapter 12 above.

80. Stayton to Irénée du Pont, December 3, 1937, Irénée du Pont Papers, File 292, Box 209, Folder: "American Liberty League, June–December 1937."

81. Quoted in Burk, *The Corporate State and the Broker State*, p. 224.

82. See Raskob to PSduP, November 28, 1934, PSduP, Longwood Papers, Group 10, File 765, Box 2, Folder: "Political, 1934."

83. See Raskob to V. G. Dunnington, November 22, 1934, PSduP, Longwood Papers, Group 10, File 765, Box 2. Raskob suggested a passing grade of 75 percent for this examination.

84. See Burk, *The Corporate State and the Broker State*, pp. 198ff.

85. National Lawyers Committee of the American Liberty League, *Report on the Constitutionality of the National Labor Relations Act*, issued September 5, 1935.

86. National Lawyers Committee of the American Liberty League, *Report on the Constitutionality of the Bituminous Coal Conservation Act of 1935*, issued December 9, 1935.

87. Schlesinger, *The Age of Roosevelt* 3, pp. 476–77.

88. National Lawyers Committee of the American League, *Report on the Constitutionality of the Potato Act of 1935*, issued December 30, 1935.

89. See Schlesinger, *The Age of Roosevelt* 3, pp. 470–74.

90. National Lawyers Committee of the American Liberty League, *The Welfare Clause in the Light of the A.A.A. Decision.*

91. See Wolfskill, *Revolt of the Conservatives*, p. 66.

92. A full list of these pamphlets, and a nearly complete collection of them, can be found in the Shouse Papers, Box 10.

93. See Wolfskill, *Revolt of the Conservatives*, p. 139. See also "Aims and Purposes of the American Liberty League (1934), Raskob Papers, File 61, "Liberty and Prosperity: An Amplification of the Platform of the American Liberty League"; Shouse Papers, Box 10, File: "American Liberty League Correspondence, 1934," p. 1, and "American Liberty League: What It Is, What It Stands For, What It Proposes to Do," Shouse Papers, Box 10, File: "American Liberty League Correspondence, 1934." See also Semes, "Confrontation at Charlottesville," pp. 36ff.

94. Shouse Papers, Box 9.

95. Ibid. See also "The National Labor Relations Act," American Liberty League Document No. 66, September 1935, Shouse Papers, Box 10.

96. American Liberty League Document No. 73, October 29, 1935, Shouse Papers, Box 10.

97. Ibid., pp. 5, 9.

98. "The New Deal vs. Democracy," June 20, 1936, American Liberty League Document No. 128, Shouse Papers, Box 10. See also "Dangerous Experimentation," American Liberty League Document No. 72, October 1935, ibid.

99. "The New Deal vs. Democracy," p. 4.

100. Ibid., p. 7.

101. "Few Tears Will Be Shed," *Baltimore Sun*, Irénée du Pont Papers, Series J, File 292, Box 208, Folder: "American Liberty League, August 1936."

102. Irénée du Pont even went so far as to attempt to interest the Ku Klux Klan in joining the league's fight against the New Deal. At the end of 1934 he wrote Hiram W. Evans, the leader of the KKK, that "perhaps it is a good time to revive [the KKK] in a cause commensurate with the one that called it into being. The preservation of the Constitution seems to be just such a cause. I believe, however, that this par-

ticular cause is one which requires fighting entirely in the open. We must make a showing of numbers which cannot be misconstrued. If every member of the Klan who believe in the principles of constitutional government, with opportunity and liberty guaranteed to all, would join the League, it would be a tremendous addition to the cause" (Irénée du Pont to Hiram W. Evans, November 20, 1934, Irénée du Pont Papers, Series J, Box 204, Folder: "American Liberty League, November 10–30, 1934"). For an account of du Pont's flirtation with the KKK, see Burk, *The Corporate State and the Broker State*, pp. 158, 166. Prominent Liberty Leaguers also financed the negrophobic Governor Eugene Talmadge of Georgia in his abortive attempt to launch a southern presidential movement in 1936. See Schlesinger, *The Age of Roosevelt* 3, pp. 520–22.

103. Kyvig, "Objection Sustained," p. 213.
104. Quoted in Semes, "Confrontation at Charlottesville," p. 47.
105. See Burk, *The Corporate State and the Broker State*, pp. 254–77, for an account of the Liberty League's decline after 1936.

CONCLUSION

1. William Cabell Bruce to Roosevelt, December 18, 1924, FDR Papers, General Political Correspondence, 1920–1928, Container 5.
2. Quoted in Schlesinger and Israel, eds., *History of American Presidential Elections*, 3:2785.
3. Burner, *The Politics of Provincialism*, p. 179.

BIBLIOGRAPHY

MANUSCRIPT COLLECTIONS

Albany, New York
　　New York State Library
　　　　Alfred E. Smith Private Papers
Charlottesville, Virginia
　　University of Virginia
　　　　Harry Flood Byrd, Sr. Papers
　　　　Homer S. Cummings Papers
　　　　Carter Glass Papers
Dayton, Ohio
　　Wright State University
　　　　James M. Cox Papers
Greenville, Delaware
　　Hagley Museum and Library
　　　　Irénée du Pont Papers
　　　　Longwood Papers
　　　　John J. Raskob Papers
Hyde Park, New York
　　Franklin D. Roosevelt Library
　　　　Democratic National Committee Papers
　　　　George B. Graves Papers
　　　　Louis McHenry Howe Papers
　　　　Eleanor Roosevelt Papers
　　　　Franklin Roosevelt Papers
Lexington, Kentucky
　　University of Kentucky
　　　　Jouett Shouse Papers
New Haven, Connecticut
　　Yale University
　　　　John W. Davis Papers
New London, Connecticut
　　Connecticut College
　　　　Belle Moskowitz Papers
Washington, D.C.
　　Library of Congress Manuscript Division
　　　　Newton D. Baker Papers
　　　　William Jennings Bryan Papers

Josephus Daniels Papers
Felix Frankfurter Papers
Cordell Hull Papers
Breckinridge Long Papers
William Gibbs McAdoo Papers
Alton B. Parker Papers
Key Pittman Papers
Joseph P. Tumulty Papers
Thomas J. Walsh Papers
Robert W. Woolley Papers

OTHER PRIMARY SOURCES

Barkley, Alben W. *That Reminds Me*. New York: Doubleday, 1954.
Baruch, Bernard M. *The Public Years*. New York: Holt, Rinehart and Winston, 1960.
Bode, Carl, ed. *The New Mencken Letters*. New York: Dial Press, 1977.
Bowers, Claude. *My Life*. New York: Simon and Schuster, 1962.
Broun, Heywood. *It Seems to Me, 1925–1935*. New York: Harcourt, Brace, 1935.
Bryan, William Jennings, and Baird, Mary. *The Memoirs of William Jennings Bryan*. Chicago: John C. Winston, 1925.
Byrnes, James F. *All in One Lifetime*. New York: Harper and Brothers, 1958.
Cannon, James. *Bishop Cannon's Own Story: Life As I have Seen It*. Durham: Duke University Press, 1955.
Columbia University Oral History Project. Reminiscences of Frances Perkins. 1955.
Cox, James M. *Journey through My Years*. New York: Simon and Schuster, 1946.
Creel, George. *Rebel at Large: Recollections of Fifty Crowded Years*. New York: G. P. Putnam's Sons, 1947.
Daniels, Josephus. *Editor in Politics*. Chapel Hill: University of North Carolina Press, 1941.
Democratic National Committee. *The Campaign Book of the Democratic Party: Candidates and Issues in 1928*. New York: Democratic National Committee, 1928.
———. *Official Report of the Proceedings of the Democratic National Convention at Chicago, 1932*. New York: Democratic National Convention, 1932.
———. *Official Report of the Proceedings of the Democratic National Convention at Houston, 1928*. New York: Democratic National Convention, 1928.
"The Democratic Platform of 1920." In *History of American Presidential Elections, 1789–1968*, vol. 3, edited by Arthur M. Schlesinger, Jr., and Fred L. Israel, pp. 2387–2402. New York: Chelsea House, 1971.
"The Democratic Platform of 1924." In *History of American Presidential Elections, 1789–1968*, vol. 3, edited by Arthur M. Schlesinger, Jr., and Fred L. Israel, pp. 2491–2505. New York: Chelsea House, 1971.
"The Democratic Platform of 1928." In *History of American Presidential Elections,*

1789–1968, vol. 3, edited by Arthur M. Schlesinger, Jr., and Fred L. Israel, pp. 2611–24. New York: Chelsea House, 1971.

"The Democratic Platform of 1932." In *History of American Presidential Elections, 1789–1968*, vol. 3, edited by Arthur M. Schlesinger, Jr., and Fred L. Israel, pp. 2741–44. New York: Chelsea House, 1971.

Farley, James A. *Behind the Ballots: The Personal History of a Politician.* New York: Harcourt, Brace, 1938.

Flynn, Edward J. *You're the Boss.* New York: Viking Press, 1947.

Forgue, Guy J., ed. *Letters of H. L. Mencken.* New York: Alfred A. Knopf, 1961.

Frankfurter, Felix. *Felix Frankfurter Reminisces.* New York: Reynal, 1960.

Gerard, James W. *My First Eighty-Three Years in America: The Memoirs of James W. Gerard.* Garden City, N.Y.: Doubleday, 1951.

Hays, Will H. *The Memoirs of Will Hays.* New York: Doubleday, 1955.

Hoover, Herbert. *American Individualism.* Garden City, N.Y.: Doubleday, Page, 1923.

————. *Campaign Speeches of 1932.* New York: Doubleday, Doran, 1933.

————. *The Memoirs of Herbert Hoover.* Vol. 2, *The Cabinet and the Presidency, 1920–1933.* New York: MacMillan, 1952.

————. *The New Day: Campaign Speeches of Herbert Hoover, 1928.* Stanford: Stanford University Press, 1928.

Hull, Cordell. *The Memoirs of Cordell Hull.* New York: Macmillan, 1948.

Ickes, Harold. *The Autobiography of a Curmudgeon.* Chicago: Quadrangle Books, 1969.

————. *The Secret Diary of Harold L. Ickes.* New York: Simon and Schuster, 1953.

Johnson, Hiram. *The Diary Letters of Hiram Johnson, 1917–1945.* Edited by Robert E. Burke. Vol. 4, *1922–1928.* Vol. 5, *1929–1933.* New York: Garland Publishing, 1983.

Johnson, Walter, ed. *Selected Letters of William Allen White, 1899–1943.* New York: Henry Holt, 1947.

Lane, Anne Wintermute, and Wall, Louise Herrick. *The Letters of Franklin K. Lane: Personal and Political.* Boston: Houghton Miflin, 1922.

McAdoo, William G. *Crowded Years: The Reminiscences of William G. McAdoo.* Boston: Houghton Miflin, 1931.

Meredith, Ellis, arr. *Democracy at the Cross Roads: A Symposium.* New York: Brewer, Warren and Putnam, 1932.

Michelson, Charles. *The Ghost Talks.* New York: G. P. Putnam's Sons, 1944.

Moskowitz, Henry, ed. *Progressive Democracy: Addresses and State Papers of Alfred E. Smith.* New York: Harcourt, Brace, 1928.

Mullen, Arthur F. *Western Democrat.* New York: Wilfred Funk, 1940.

Perkins, Frances. *The Roosevelt I Remember.* New York: Harper and Row, 1946.

"Progressive Platform, 1924." In *History of American Presidential Elections, 1789–1968*, vol. 3, edited by Arthur M. Schlesinger, Jr., and Fred L. Israel, pp. 2517–23. New York: Chelsea House, 1971.

Proskauer, Joseph M. *A Segment of My Times.* New York: Farrar, Strauss, 1950.

Raskob, John J. "Everybody Ought to Be Rich." *Ladies' Home Journal*, August 1929, p. 9.

———. "Rich Men in Politics" (as told to James C. Derieux). *Collier's Magazine*, March 5, 1932, p. 7.

———. "What Next in America?" *North American Review*, November 1929, pp. 513–18.

"The Republican Platform of 1928." In *History of American Presidential Elections, 1789–1968*, vol. 3, edited by Arthur M. Schlesinger, Jr., and Fred L. Israel, pp. 2624–40. New York: Chelsea House, 1971.

Rogers, Will. *Weekly Articles*. Vol. 3, *The Coolidge Years, 1927–1929*. Stillwater: Oklahoma State University Press, 1981.

Roosevelt, Eleanor. *This I Remember*. New York: Harper and Brothers, 1949.

Roosevelt, Elliot, ed. *FDR: His Personal Letters, 1928–1945*. New York: Duell, Sloan and Pearce, 1950.

Roosevelt, Franklin D. "Our Foreign Policy: A Democratic View." *Foreign Affairs* 6 (July 1928): 573–86.

Roper, Daniel C. *Fifty Years of Public Life*. Durham: Duke University Press, 1941.

Shouse, Jouett. "Watchman, What of the Night?" *Atlantic Monthly*, May 1931, pp. 250–58.

Sloan, Alfred P., Jr. *My Years with General Motors*. New York: MacFadden Books, 1963.

Smith, Alfred E. *Campaign Addresses, 1928*. Washington, D.C.: Democratic National Committee, 1929.

———. *The Citizen and His Government*. New York: Harper and Brothers, 1935.

———. "Housing and Slum Clearance: Another R.F.C. Joke." *New Outlook*, November 1932, p. 4.

———. *Up to Now: An Autobiography*. New York: Viking Press, 1929.

State of New York. *The Public Papers of Alfred E. Smith—Governor of the State of New York*. Albany: State of New York Publishing, 1923, 1925, 1926, 1927, 1928.

———. *The Revised Record of the Constitutional Convention of the State of New York, 1915*. Albany: State of New York Publishing, 1916.

Stayton, William. "Our Experiment in National Prohibition: What Progress Has It Made?" *Annals of the American Academy of Political and Social Science* 109 (September 1923): 26–38.

Underwood, Oscar W. *The Drifting Sands of Party Politics*. New York: Century, 1928.

U.S. Senate. Special Committee Investigating Presidential Campaign Expenditures. *Hearings*. 70th Cong., 1st sess., May–June 1928.

Young, Owen D., and Swope, Gerard. *Selected Addresses*. General Electric, 1930.

SECONDARY SOURCES

Adams, James Truslow. *Our Business Civilization: Some Aspects of American Culture.* Albert and Charles Boni, 1929.

Alexander, Charles C. "Secrecy Bids for Power: The Ku Klux Klan in Texas Politics in the 1920's." *Mid-America* 46 (January 1964): 3–28.

Allen, Frederick Lewis. *Only Yesterday: An Informal History of the 1920s.* New York: Harper & Row, 1931.

———. *Since Yesterday: The 1930s in America.* New York: Harper & Row, 1939.

Allen, Lee N. "The McAdoo Campaign for the Presidential Nomination in 1924." *Journal of Southern History* 29 (May 1963): 211–28.

———. "The Underwood Presidential Movement of 1924." *Alabama Review* 15 (April 1962): 83–99.

Allen, William H. *Al Smith's Tammany Hall: Champion Political Vampire.* New York: Institute for Public Service, 1928.

Allswang, John M. *A House for All Peoples: Ethnic Politics in Chicago, 1890–1936.* Lexington: University of Kentucky Press, 1971.

Almond, Gabriel A. "The Political Attitudes of Wealth." *Journal of Politics* 7 (August 1945): 213–55.

American Academy of Political and Social Science. *Annals.* Vol. 109 (September 1923), *Prohibition and Its Enforcement.* Vol. 163 (September 1932), *Prohibition: A National Experiment.* Philadelphia: American Academy of Political and Social Science.

Andersen, Kristi. *The Creation of a Democratic Majority, 1928–1936.* Chicago: University of Chicago Press, 1979.

Anderson, Paul Y. "Heaven Goes Republican." *Nation,* March 30, 1932, p. 368.

Apter, David E. "Introduction: Ideology and Discontent." In *Ideology and Discontent,* edited by David E. Apter, pp. 15–46. New York: Free Press of Glencoe, 1964.

———, ed. *Ideology and Discontent.* New York: Free Press of Glencoe, 1964.

Bagby, Wesley M. *The Road to Normalcy: The Presidential Campaign and Election of 1920.* Baltimore: Johns Hopkins University Press, 1962.

Baker, Ray Stannard. *American Chronicle.* New York: Charles Scribner's Sons, 1945.

Barclay, Thomas S. "The Publicity Division of the Democratic Party, 1929–1930." *American Political Science Review* 25 (1931): 68–72.

Barnes, Julius H. *The Genius of American Business.* New York: Doubleday, Page, 1924.

Bates, J. Leonard. "The Teapot Dome Scandal and the Election of 1924." *American Historical Review* 60 (January 1951): 303–22.

Beaver, Daniel R. *Newton D. Baker and the American War Effort.* Lincoln: University of Nebraska Press, 1966.

Bell, Daniel. "The Passing of Fanaticism." In *Decline of Ideology?,* edited by Mostafa Rejai, pp. 36–46. Chicago: Aldine Atherton, 1971.

Bellush, Bernard. *Franklin D. Roosevelt as Governor of New York.* New York: Columbia University Press, 1955.

Bendix, Reinhard. "The Age of Ideology: Persistent and Changing." In *Decline of Ideology?*, edited by Mostafa Rejai, pp. 294–328. Chicago: Aldine Atherton, 1971.

Bernstein, Irving. *The Lean Years: A History of the American Worker, 1920–1933.* Cambridge, Mass.: Houghton, Mifflin, 1960.

Best, Gary Dean. *The Politics of American Individualism: Herbert Hoover in Transition, 1918–1921.* Westport, Conn.: Greenwood Press, 1975.

Blocker, Jack S, ed. *Alcohol, Reform, and Society: The Liquor Issue in Social Context.* Westport, Conn.: Greenwood Press, 1979.

Blum, John M. *Joe Tumulty and the Wilson Era.* Boston: Houghton Mifflin, 1951.

Bone, Hugh A. *Party Committees and National Politics.* Seattle: University of Washington Press, 1958.

Bornet, Vaughan Davis. *Labor Politics in a Democratic Republic: Moderation, Division, and Disruption in the Presidential Election of 1928.* Washington, D.C.: Spartan Books, 1964.

Bowers, Claude. *Jefferson and Hamilton: The Struggle for Democracy in America.* Boston: Houghton, Mifflin, 1925.

Bradford, Richard H. "Religion and Politics: Alfred E. Smith and the Election of 1928 in West Virginia." *West Virginia History* 36 (April 1975): 213–21.

Braeman, John; Bremner, Robert H.; and Brody, David, eds. *Change and Continuity in Twentieth-Century America: The 1920s.* Columbus: Ohio State University Press, 1968.

Brody, David. "The Rise and Decline of Welfare Capitalism." In *Change and Continuity in Twentieth-Century America: The 1920s*, edited by John Braeman, Robert H. Bremner, and David Brody, pp. 147–78. Columbus: Ohio State University Press, 1968.

————. *Steelworkers in America: The Nonunion Era.* Cambridge: Harvard University Press, 1960.

Broesamle, John J. *William Gibbs McAdoo: A Passion for Change, 1863–1917.* Port Washington, N.Y.: Kennikat Press, 1973.

Brown, Norman D. *Hood, Bonnet, and Little Brown Jug: Texas Politics, 1921–1928.* College Station: Texas A&M University Press, 1984.

Buckley, William F, ed. *Did You Ever See a Dream Walking? American Conservative Thought in the Twentieth Century.* Indianapolis: Bobbs-Merrill, 1970.

Buenker, John D. "Essay." In *Progressivism*, by John D. Buenker, John C. Burnham, and Robert M. Crunden, pp. 31–69. Cambridge, Mass.: Schenkman Publishing, 1977.

————. "The New Era Business Philosophy of the 1920's." *Illinois Quarterly* 38 (Spring 1976): 20–49.

————. *Urban Liberalism and Progressive Reform.* New York: Charles Scribner's Sons, 1973.

Buenker, John D.; Burnham, John C.; and Crunden, Robert M. *Progressivism.* Cambridge, Mass.: Schenkman Publishing, 1977.

Burk, Robert F. *The Corporate State and the Broker State: The Du Ponts and American National Politics, 1925–1940.* Cambridge: Harvard University Press, 1990.

Burner, David. "The Breakup of the Wilsonian Coalition of 1916." *Mid-America* 45 (January 1963): 18–35.

———. "The Brown Derby Campaign." *New York History* 46 (October 1965): 356–80.

———. "The Democratic Party in the Election of 1924." *Mid-America* 46 (April 1964): 92–113.

———. "The Election of 1924." In *History of American Presidential Elections, 1789–1968,* vol. 3, edited by Arthur M. Schlesinger, Jr., and Fred L. Israel, pp. 2459–90. New York: Chelsea House, 1971.

———. *Herbert Hoover: A Public Life.* New York: Alfred A. Knopf, 1979.

———. "1919: Prelude to Normalcy." In *Change and Continuity in Twentieth-Century America: The 1920s,* edited by John Braeman, Robert H. Bremner, and David Brody, pp. 3–32. Columbus: Ohio State University Press, 1968.

———. *The Politics of Provincialism: The Democratic Party in Transition, 1918–1932.* New York: W. W. Norton, 1967.

Burnham, John C. "Essay." In *Progressivism,* by John D. Buenker, John C. Burnham, and Robert M. Crunden, pp. 70–106. Cambridge, Mass.: Schenkman Publishing, 1977.

Burnham, Walter Dean. "The System of 1896." In *The Evolution of American Electoral Systems,* by Walter Dean Burnham et al., pp. 147–202. Westport, Conn.: Greenwood Press, 1981.

Burnham, Walter Dean, et al. *The Evolution of American Electoral Systems.* Westport, Conn.: Greenwood Press, 1981.

Burns, Arthur F. "Ideology of Businessmen and Presidential Elections." *Southwestern Political and Social Science Quarterly* 10 (September 1929): 230–36.

Burns, James MacGregor. "Political Ideology." In *A Guide to the Social Sciences,* edited by Norman MacKenzie, pp. 205–24. London: Weidenfeld and Nicolson, 1966.

———. *Roosevelt: The Lion and the Fox.* London: Secker and Warburg, 1956.

Carleton, William G. "The Politics of the Twenties." *Current History* 47 (October 1964): 210–15.

———. "The Popish Plot of 1928." *Forum* 112 (September 1949): 141–47.

Caro, Robert A. *The Power Broker: Robert Moses and the Fall of New York.* New York: Alfred A. Knopf, 1974.

Carr, William H. A. *The du Ponts of Delaware.* New York: Dodd, Mead, 1964.

Carter, Paul A. *Another Part of the Twenties.* New York: Columbia University Press, 1977.

———. "The Campaign of 1928 Re-examined: A Study in Political Folklore." *Wisconsin Magazine of History* 46 (Summer 1963): 263–72.

Case, Josephine Young, and Case, Everett Needham. *Owen D. Young and American Enterprise: A Biography.* Boston: David R. Godine, 1982.

Casey, Ralph D. "Scripps-Howard Newspapers in the 1928 Presidential Campaign." *Journalism Quarterly* 7 (September 1930): 209–31.

Cashman, Sean Dennis. *America in the Twenties and Thirties: The Olympian Age of Franklin Delano Roosevelt.* New York: New York University Press, 1989.

Catlin, George E. G. "Alternatives to Prohibition." *Annals of the American Academy of Political and Social Science* 163 (September 1932): 181–87.

Cebula, James E. *James M. Cox: Journalist and Politician.* New York: Garland Publishing, 1985.

Chalmers, David M. *Hooded Americanism: The First Century of the Ku Klux Klan, 1865–1965.* Garden City, N.Y.: Doubleday, 1965.

Chandler, Alfred D., Jr. *Strategy and Structure: Chapters in the History of the Industrial Enterprise.* Cambridge: MIT Press, 1962.

———. *The Visible Hand: The Managerial Revolution in American Business.* Cambridge: Harvard University Press, 1977.

———, ed. *Giant Enterprise: Ford, General Motors, and the Automobile Industry.* New York: Harcourt, Brace and World, 1964.

Chandler, Alfred D., and Salsbury, Stephen. *Pierre S. du Pont and the Making of the Modern Corporation.* New York: Harper and Row, 1971.

Chandler, Alfred D., and Tedlow, Richard S. *The Coming of Managerial Capitalism: A Casebook on the History of American Economic Institutions.* Homewood, Ill.: Richard D. Irwin, 1985.

Clark, Norman H. *Deliver Us from Evil: An Interpretation of American Prohibition.* New York: W. W. Norton, 1976.

———. *The Dry Years: Prohibition and Social Change in Washington.* Seattle: University of Washington Press, 1988.

Clubb, Jerome N., and Allen, Howard W. "The Cities and the Election of 1928: Partisan Realignment?" *American Historical Review* 74 (April 1969): 1205–20.

Cobb, James C., and Namorato, Michael V., eds. *The New Deal and the South.* Jackson: University Press of Mississippi, 1983.

Coben, Stanley. *A. Mitchell Palmer: Politician.* New York: Columbia University Press, 1963.

———. "A Study in Nativism: The American Red Scare of 1919–1920." *Political Science Quarterly* 79 (March 1964): 52–75.

Coletta, Paolo E. *William Jennings Bryan.* Vol. 3, *Political Puritan, 1915–1925.* Lincoln: University of Nebraska Press, 1969.

Connable, Alfred, and Silberfarb, Edward. *Tigers of Tammany: Nine Men Who Ran New York.* New York: Holt, Rinehart and Winston, 1967.

Conwell, Russell H. *Acres of Diamonds.* Sydney: Angus and Robertson, 1933.

Cook, Sherwin Lawrence. *Torchlight Parade: Our Presidential Pageant.* New York: Minton, Balch, 1929.

Cotter, Cornelius P., and Hennessy, Bernard C. *Politics without Power: The National Party Committees.* New York: Atherton Press, 1964.

Cramer, C. H. *Newton D. Baker: A Biography.* Cleveland: World Publishing, 1961.

Croly, Herbert. "The Progressive Voter: He Wants to Know!" *New Republic*, July 23, 1928, p. 244.

Cross, Robert D. *The Emergence of Liberal Catholicism in America*. Cambridge: Harvard University Press, 1958.

Curti, Merle E. *The Growth of American Thought*. 2d ed. New York: Harper and Brothers, 1951.

Dabney, Virginius. *Liberalism in the South*. Chapel Hill: University of North Carolina Press, 1932.

Dale, Ernest. *The Great Organizers*. New York: McGraw-Hill, 1960.

Daniels, Jonathan. *The Time between the Wars: Armistice to Pearl Harbor*. New York: Garland Publishing, 1979.

Dannenbaum, Jed. *Drink and Disorder: Temperance Reform in Cincinnati from the Washingtonian Period to the WCTU*. Urbana: University of Illinois Press, 1984.

Darrow, Clarence. "Democracy: Its Past and Future." In *Democracy at the Cross Roads: A Symposium*, arranged by Ellis Meredith, pp. 246–61. New York: Brewer, Warren and Putnam, 1932.

David, Paul T. *Party Strength in the United States, 1872–1970*. Charlottesville: University Press of Virginia, 1972.

David, Paul T.; Goldman, Ralph M.; and Bain, Richard C. *The Politics of National Party Conventions*. Lanham, Md.: University Press of America, 1964.

Davis, John W. *Party Government in the United States*. Princeton: Princeton University Press, 1929.

Davis, Kenneth S. *FDR: The Beckoning of Destiny, 1882–1928: A History*. New York: G. P. Putnam's Sons, 1971.

———. *FDR: The New York Years, 1928–1933*. New York: Random House, 1979.

Degler, Carl N. "American Political Parties and the Rise of the City: An Interpretation." *Journal of American History* 51 (June 1964): 41–59.

Dobyns, Fletcher. *The Amazing Story of Repeal: An Exposé of the Power of Propaganda*. Chicago: Willett, Clark, 1940.

Doherty, Herbert J., Jr. "Florida and the Presidential Election of 1928." *Florida Historical Quarterly* 26 (October 1947): 174–86.

Dorian, Max. *The du Ponts: From Gunpowder to Nylon*. Boston: Little, Brown, 1961.

Dorsett, Lyle W. *Franklin D. Roosevelt and the City Bosses*. Port Washington, N.Y.: Kennikat Press, 1977.

Douglas, Paul H. "The Prospects for a New Political Alignment." *American Political Science Review* 25 (November 1931): 906–14.

Drescher, Nuala McGann. "Labor and Prohibition: The Unappreciated Impact of the Eighteenth Amendment." In *Law, Alcohol, and Order: Perspectives on National Prohibition*, edited by David E. Kyvig, pp. 35–52. Westport, Conn.: Greenwood Press, 1985.

Du Bois, W. E. B. "Is Al Smith Afraid of the South?" *Nation*, October 17, 1928, p. 393.

Eagles, Charles W. "Congressional Voting in the 1920s: A Test of Urban-Rural

Conflict." *Journal of American History* 76 (September 1989): 528–34.

——— . "Urban-Rural Conflict in the 1920s: A Historiographical Assessment." *Historian* 49 (November 1986): 26–48.

Editorial Research Reports. *Presidential Politics, 1928.* By Richard Boeckel. Washington, D.C., 1929.

Eldersveld, Samuel J. "The Influence of Metropolitan Party Pluralities in Presidential Elections since 1920: A Study of Twelve Key Cities." *American Political Science Review* 43 (December 1949): 1189–1206.

Eldot, Paula. *Governor Alfred E. Smith: The Politician as Reformer.* New York: Garland Publishing, 1983.

Engelman, Larry. "Organized Thirst: The Story of Repeal in Michigan." In *Alcohol, Reform, and Society: The Liquor Issue in Social Context,* edited by Jack S. Blocker, pp. 171–210. Westport, Conn.: Greenwood Press, 1979.

Ewing, Cortez A. M. *Congressional Elections, 1896–1944: The Sectional Basis of Political Democracy in the House of Representatives.* Norman: University of Oklahoma Press, 1947.

Fausold, Martin L. *James W. Wadsworth, Jr.: The Gentleman from New York.* Syracuse: Syracuse University Press, 1975.

Fecher, Charles A. *Mencken: A Study of His Thought.* New York: Alfred A. Knopf, 1978.

Feis, Herbert. *Labor Relations: A Study Made in the Procter and Gamble Company.* New York: Adelphi, 1928.

Fenton, John H. *Politics in the Border States.* New Orleans: Hauser Press, 1957.

Ferguson, Thomas. "From Normalcy to New Deal: Industrial Structure, Party Competition, and American Public Policy in the Great Depression." *International Organization* 38 (Winter 1984): 41–94.

——— . "Party Realignment and American Industrial Structure: The Investment Theory of Political Parties in Historical Perspective." In *Research in Political Economy,* vol. 6, edited by Paul Zarembka, pp. 4–65. Greenwich, Conn.: VAI Press, 1983.

Ferrell, Robert H. *Woodrow Wilson and World War I.* New York: Harper and Row, 1985.

Filene, Edward A. *The Way Out: A Forecast of Coming Changes in American Business and Industry.* New York: Doubleday, Page, 1924.

Fine, Sidney. *Laissez Faire and the General Welfare State: A Study of Conflict in American Thought, 1865–1901.* Ann Arbor: University of Michigan Press, 1964.

Fite, Gilbert N. "The Agricultural Issue in the Presidential Election of 1928." *Mississippi Valley Historical Review* 37 (March 1951): 653–72.

——— . "The Farmer's Dilemma, 1919–1929." In *Change and Continuity in Twentieth-Century America: The 1920s,* edited by John Braeman, Robert H. Bremner, and David Brody, pp. 67–102. Columbus: Ohio State University Press, 1968.

——— . *George N. Peek and the Fight for Farm Parity.* Norman: University of Oklahoma Press, 1954.

Flick, Alexander C. *History of the State of New York.* New York: Columbia University Press, 1935–38.

Frankfurter, Felix. "Why I Am for Smith." *New Republic*, October 31, 1928, p. 3.

Franklin, Fabian. "What's Wrong with the Eighteenth Amendment." *Annals of the American Academy of Political and Social Science* 109 (September 1923): 48–51.

Freidel, Frank. "The Election of 1932." In *History of American Presidential Elections, 1789–1968*, vol. 3, edited by Arthur M. Schlesinger, Jr., and Fred L. Israel, pp. 2707–39. New York: Chelsea House, 1971.

————. *FDR and the South.* Baton Rouge: Louisiana State University Press, 1965.

————. *Franklin D. Roosevelt.* Vol. 2, *The Ordeal.* Vol. 3, *The Triumph.* Boston: Little, Brown, 1954–56.

————. "The South and the New Deal." In *The New Deal and the South*, edited by James C. Cobb and Michael V. Namorato, pp. 17–36. Jackson: University Press of Mississippi, 1983.

Fuchs, Lawrence H. "Election of 1928." In *History of American Presidential Elections, 1789–1968*, vol. 3, edited by Arthur M. Schlesinger, Jr., and Fred L. Israel, pp. 2585–2609. New York: Chelsea House, 1971.

Galambos, Louis. *The Public Image of Big Business in America, 1880–1940: A Quantitative Study in Social Change.* Baltimore: Johns Hopkins University Press, 1975.

Galambos, Louis, and Pratt, Joseph. *The Rise of the Corporate Commonwealth: U.S. Business and Public Policy in the Twentieth Century.* New York: Basic Books, 1988.

Gammack, Thomas H. "Wall Street Likes Al Smith." *Outlook*, July 18, 1928, p. 2.

Garraty, John A. *The New Commonwealth, 1877–1890.* New York: Harper and Row, 1968.

Gebhart, John C. "Movement against Prohibition." *Annals of the American Academy of Political and Social Science* 163 (September 1932): 105–12.

Geertz, Clifford. "Ideology as a Cultural System." In *Ideology and Discontent*, edited by David E. Apter, pp. 47–76. New York: Free Press of Glencoe, 1964.

Gerber, Larry G. *The Limits of Liberalism: Josephus Daniels, Henry Stimson, Bernard Baruch, Donald Richberg, Felix Frankfurter, and the Development of the Modern American Political Economy.* New York: New York University Press, 1984.

Glad, Paul W. "Progressives and the Business Culture of the 1920's." *Journal of American History* 53 (June 1966): 75–89.

Glazer, Nathan, and Moynihan, Daniel Patrick. *Beyond the Melting Pot: The Negroes, Puerto Ricans, Jews, Italians, and the Irish of New York City.* 2d ed. Cambridge: MIT Press, 1970.

Goldman, Ralph M. *The Democratic Party in American Politics.* New York: Macmillan, 1966.

Gould, Lewis L. *Progressives and Prohibitionists: Texas Democrats in the Age of Wilson.* Austin: University of Texas Press, 1973.

————. *Reform and Regulation: American Politics from Roosevelt to Wilson.* 2d ed. New York: Alfred A. Knopf, 1986.

Graham, Otis L. *The Great Campaigns: Reform and War in America, 1900–1928.*

Huntingdon, N.Y.: Robert E. Krieger Publishing, 1980.

Grant, Ernest A. "The Liquor Traffic before the Eighteenth Amendment." *Annals of the American Academy of Political and Social Science* 163 (September 1932): 1–9.

Grantham, Dewey W., Jr. *The Democratic South*. Athens: University of Georgia Press, 1963.

Gusfield, Joseph R. *Symbolic Crusade: Status Politics and the American Temperance Movement*. Urbana: University of Illinois Press, 1963.

Gustin, Lawrence R. *Billy Durant: Creator of General Motors*. Grand Rapids, Mich.: William B. Eerdmans Publishing, 1973.

Hacker, Louis M., and Hirsch, Mark D. *Proskauer: His Life and Times*. University: University of Alabama Press, 1978.

Hand, Samuel B. "Al Smith, Franklin Roosevelt, and the New Deal: Some Comments on Perspective." *Historian* 27 (1965): 366–81.

Handlin, Oscar. *Al Smith and His America*. Boston: Little, Brown, 1958.

Hapgood, Norman, and Moskowitz, Henry. *Up from the City Streets: Alfred E. Smith: A Biographical Study in Contemporary Politics*. New York: Grossett, 1927.

Harbaugh, William H. *Lawyer's Lawyer: The Life of John W. Davis*. New York: Oxford University Press, 1973.

Harrison, Gordon A. *Road to the Right*. New York: William Morrow, 1954.

Harrison, Leonard V., and Laine, Elizabeth. *After Repeal: A Study of Liquor Control Administration*. New York: Harper and Brothers, 1936.

Hawkes, Robert J., Jr. "The Emergence of a Leader: Harry Flood Byrd, Governor of Virginia, 1926–1930." *Virginia Magazine of History and Biography* 82 (July 1974): 259–81.

Hawley, Ellis W. *The Great War and the Search for Modern Order: A History of the American People and Their Institutions, 1917–1933*. New York: St. Martin's Press, 1979.

———, ed. *Herbert Hoover as Secretary of Commerce: Studies in New Era Thought and Practice*. Iowa City: University of Iowa Press, 1981.

Heald, Morrell. "Business Thought in the Twenties: Social Responsibility." *American Quarterly* 13 (Summer 1961): 126–39.

Hennings, Robert E. "California Democratic Politics in the Period of Republican Ascendancy." *Pacific Historical Review* 31 (August 1962): 267–80.

Hicks, John D. *Republican Ascendancy, 1921–1933*. New York: Harper and Row, 1960.

Hines, Walter D. *War History of American Railroads*. New Haven: Yale University Press, 1928.

Hinton, Harold B. *Cordell Hull: A Biography*. Garden City, N.Y.: Doubleday, Doran, 1942.

Hofstadter, Richard. *The Age of Reform: From Bryan to FDR*. New York: Alfred A. Knopf, 1955.

———. "Could a Protestant Have Beaten Hoover in 1928?" *Reporter* 22 (March 1960): 31–33.

Holcombe, Arthur N. *The Political Parties of Today: A Study in Republican and Democratic Politics*. New York: Harper and Brothers Publishers, 1924.

———. "Trench Warfare." *American Political Science Review* 25 (November 1931): 914–25.

Hollingsworth, J. Rogers. *The Whirligig of Politics: The Democracy of Cleveland and Bryan*. Chicago: University of Chicago Press, 1963.

Hopkins, Harry. "Goodbye to Mr. R." *New Republic*, March 2, 1932, p. 64.

Hubbard, Preston J. *Origins of the TVA: The Muscle Shoals Controversy, 1920–1932*. Nashville: Vanderbilt University Press, 1961.

Huntley, Theodore A. *The Life of John W. Davis*. New York: Duffield, 1924.

Huthmacher, J. Joseph. *Massachusetts People and Politics, 1919–1933*. Cambridge: Harvard University Press, 1959.

———. *Senator Robert F. Wagner and the Rise of Urban Liberalism*. New York: Atheneum, 1968.

———. "Urban Liberalism and the Age of Reform." *Mississippi Valley Historical Review* 49 (1962): 231–41.

Ingalls, Robert P. *Herbert H. Lehman and New York's Little New Deal*. New York: New York University Press, 1975.

Irwin, Will. *Propaganda and the News; or, What Makes You Think So?* New York: Whittlesey House, 1936.

Israel, Fred L. *Nevada's Key Pittman*. Lincoln: University of Nebraska Press, 1963.

Jackson, Kenneth T. *The Ku Klux Klan in the City, 1915–1930*. New York: Oxford University Press, 1967.

Jakoubek, Robert E. "A Jeffersonian's Dissent: John W. Davis and the Campaign of 1936." *West Virginia History* 35 (January 1974): 145–53.

Jensen, Richard T. *Grass Roots Politics, Parties, Issues, and Voters, 1854–1983*. Westport, Conn.: Greenwood Press, 1983.

———. *The Winning of the Midwest: Social and Political Conflict, 1888–1896*. Chicago: University of Chicago Press, 1971.

Jessner, Sabine, and Sehlinger, Peter J. "Claude G. Bowers: A Partisan Hoosier." *Indiana Magazine of History* 83 (September 1987): 217–43.

Jessup, Henry W. "State Rights and Prohibition." *Annals of the American Academy of Political and Social Science* 109 (September 1923): 62–66.

Johnson, Evans C. *Oscar W. Underwood: A Political Biography*. Baton Rouge: Louisiana State University Press, 1980.

Josephson, Matthew, and Josephson, Hannah. *Al Smith: Hero of the Cities. A Portrait Drawing from the Papers of Frances Perkins*. Boston: Houghton, Mifflin, 1969.

Keller, Morton. *In Defense of Yesterday: James M. Beck and the Politics of Conservatism, 1861–1936*. New York: Coward-McCann, 1958.

Kelley, Donald Brooks. "Deep South Dilemma: The Mississippi Press in the Presidential Election of 1928." *Journal of Mississippi History* 25 (April 1963): 63–92.

Kelley, Robert. *The Transatlantic Persuasion: The Liberal-Democratic Mind in the Age of Gladstone*. New York: Alfred A. Knopf, 1969.

Kenkel, Joseph F. *Progressives and Protection: The Search for a Tariff Policy, 1866–1936.* Lanham, Md.: University Press of America, 1983.

Kent, Frank R. "Charlie Michelson." *Scribner's Magazine,* September 1930, pp. 290–96.

———. *The Democratic Party: A History.* New York: Century, 1928.

Kerr, K. Austin. "Decision for Federal Control: Wilson, McAdoo, and the Railroads, 1917." *Journal of American History* 54 (December 1967): 550–60.

———. *Organized for Prohibition: A New History of the Anti-Saloon League.* New Haven: Yale University Press, 1985.

Kett, Joseph F. "Review Essay: Temperance and Intemperance as Historical Problems." *Journal of American History* 67 (March 1981): 878–85.

Key, V. O., Jr. *Southern Politics in State and Nation.* New York: Alfred A. Knopf, 1949.

Kilpatrick, Carroll, ed. *Roosevelt and Daniels: A Friendship in Politics.* Chapel Hill: University of North Carolina Press, 1952.

Kinberg, Olov. "Temperance Legislation in Sweden." *Annals of the American Academy of Political and Social Science* 163 (September 1932): 206–15.

Kirk, Russell. *The Conservative Mind.* Chicago: Henry Regnery, 1953.

Kirschner, Don S. *City and Country: Rural Responses to Urbanization in the 1920's.* Westport, Conn.: Greenwood Publishing, 1970.

Kleppner, Paul. *Continuity and Change in Electoral Politics, 1893–1928.* New York: Greenwood Press, 1987.

———. *Cross of Culture: A Social Analysis of Midwestern Politics, 1850–1900.* New York: Free Press, 1970.

———. "Were Women to Blame? Female Suffrage and Voter Turnout." *Journal of Interdisciplinary History* 12 (Spring 1982): 621–43.

———. *Who Voted? The Dynamics of Electoral Turnout, 1870–1980.* New York: Praeger Publishers, 1982.

Koeniger, A. Cash. "The New Deal and the States: Roosevelt and the Byrd Organization in Virginia." *Journal of American History* 68 (March 1982): 876–96.

Kolko, Gabriel. *The Triumph of Conservatism: A Reinterpretation of American History, 1900–1916.* New York: Free Press, 1963.

Kyvig, David E. "Objection Sustained: Prohibition Repeal and the New Deal." In *Alcohol, Reform, and Society: The Liquor Issue in Social Context,* edited by Jack S. Blocker, pp. 211–34. Westport, Conn.: Greenwood Press, 1979.

———. "Raskob, Roosevelt, and Repeal." *Historian* 37 (May 1975): 469–87.

———. *Repealing National Prohibition.* Chicago: University of Chicago Press, 1979.

———. "Sober Thoughts: Myths and Realities of National Prohibition after Fifty Years." In *Law, Alcohol, and Order: Perspectives on National Prohibition,* edited by David E. Kyvig, pp. 3–20. Westport, Conn.: Greenwood Press, 1985.

———. "Women against Prohibition." *American Quarterly* 28 (Fall 1976): 465–82.

———, ed. *Law, Alcohol, and Order: Perspectives on National Prohibition.* Westport, Conn.: Greenwood Press, 1985.

Lane, Robert E. "The United States: Politics of Affluence." In *Decline of Ideology?,* edited by Mostafa Rejai, pp. 160–206. Chicago: Aldine Atherton, 1971.

Lee, David D. *Tennessee in Turmoil: Politics in the Volunteer State, 1920–1930*. Memphis: Memphis State University Press, 1979.

Leighton, Isabel, ed. *The Aspirin Age, 1919–1941*. New York: Simon and Schuster, 1949.

Lender, Mark Edward. "The Historian and Repeal: A Survey of the Literature and Research Opportunities." In *Law, Alcohol, and Order: Perspectives on National Prohibition*, edited by David E. Kyvig, pp. 177–206. Westport, Conn.: Greenwood Press, 1985.

Leuchtenburg, William E. *Franklin D. Roosevelt and the New Deal, 1932–1940*. New York: Harper and Row, 1963.

———. *In The Shadow of FDR: From Harry Truman to Ronald Reagan*. Ithaca: Cornell University Press, 1983.

———. *The Perils of Prosperity, 1914–1932*. Chicago: University of Chicago Press, 1958.

Levine, Lawrence W. *Defender of the Faith: William Jennings Bryan: The Last Decade, 1915–1925*. New York: Oxford University Press, 1965.

Lewis, Sinclair. *Babbitt*. New York: Harcourt, Brace and Jovanovich, 1922.

Lichtman, Allan J. *Prejudice and the Old Politics: The Presidential Election of 1928*. Chapel Hill: University of North Carolina Press, 1979.

Lindley, Ernest K. *Franklin D. Roosevelt: A Career in Progressive Democracy*. New York: Blue Ribbon Books, 1931.

Link, Arthur S. "What Happened to the Progressive Movement in the 1920's?" *American Historical Review* 64 (1959): 853–71.

———. *Woodrow Wilson and the Progressive Era, 1910–1917*. New York: Harper and Brothers, 1954.

Lippmann, Walter. *Interpretations, 1931–1932*. New York: Macmillan, 1932.

———. *Men of Destiny*. New York: Macmillan, 1927.

———. "Two Leading Democratic Candidates." *New Republic*, June 2, 1920, p. 11.

Lipsett, Seymour. "The End of Ideology?" In *Decline of Ideology?*, edited by Mostafa Rejai, pp. 47–66. Chicago: Aldine Atherton, 1971.

Lisio, Donald J. *Hoover, Blacks, and Lilywhites: A Study of Southern Strategies*. Chapel Hill: University of North Carolina Press, 1985.

Lubell, Samuel. *The Future of American Politics*. 3d ed. New York: Harper Colophon Books, 1965.

Lumley, Frederick E. *The Propaganda Menace*. New York: Century, 1933.

Lusk, Rufus. "The Drinking Habit." *Annals of the American Academy of Political and Social Science* 163 (September 1932): 46–52.

Lynd, Robert S., and Lynd, Helen Merrill. *Middletown: A Study in Contemporary American Culture*. New York: Harcourt, Brace, 1929.

McCarthy, G. Michael. "The Brown Derby Campaign in West Tennessee: Smith, Hoover, and the Politics of Race." *West Tennessee Historical Society Papers* 27 (1973): 81–107.

McCloskey, Robert Green. *American Conservatism in the Age of Enterprise: A Study of William Graham Sumner, Stephen J. Field, and Andrew Carnegie.* Cambridge: Harvard University Press, 1951.

McCormick, Richard L. "Ethno-Cultural Interpretations of Nineteenth Century Voting Behavior." *Political Science Quarterly* 89 (1974): 351–77.

——. *The Party Period and Public Policy: American Politics from the Age of Jackson to the Progressive Era.* New York: Oxford University Press, 1986.

McCoy, Donald R. "Election of 1920." In *History of American Presidential Elections, 1789–1968,* vol. 3, edited by Arthur M. Schlesinger, Jr., and Fred L. Israel, pp. 2349–85. New York: Chelsea House, 1971.

McGerr, Michael E. *The Decline of Popular Politics: The American North, 1865–1928.* New York: Oxford University Press, 1986.

MacKay, Kenneth Campbell. *The Progressive Movement of 1924.* New York: Columbia University Press, 1947.

MacKenzie, Norman, ed. *A Guide to the Social Sciences.* London: Weidenfeld and Nicolson, 1966.

McSeveney, Samuel T. *The Politics of Depression: Political Behavior in the Northeast, 1893–1896.* New York: Oxford University Press, 1972.

Margulies, Herbert F. *Senator Lenroot of Wisconsin: A Political Biography, 1900–1929.* Columbia: University of Missouri Press, 1977.

Marshall, Charles C. *Governor Smith's American Catholicism.* New York: Dodd, Mead, 1928.

Martin, George W. *Madame Secretary: Frances Perkins.* Boston: Houghton Mifflin, 1976.

Mayer, George H. *The Republican Party, 1854–1966.* 2d ed. New York: Oxford University Press, 1967.

Mencken, H. L. *A Carnival of Buncombe.* Baltimore: Johns Hopkins University Press, 1956.

——. *Making a President: A Footnote to the Saga of Democracy.* New York: Alfred A. Knopf, 1932.

——. *Notes on Democracy.* New York: Alfred A. Knopf, 1926.

Merriam, Charles E., and Gosnell, Harold F. *The American Party System: An Introduction to the Study of Political Parties in the United States.* New York: Macmillan, 1929.

Merrill, Horace Samuel. *Bourbon Leader: Grover Cleveland and the Democratic Party.* Boston: Little, Brown, 1957.

Meyer, Frank. *The Conservative Mainstream.* New York: Arlington House, 1969.

——. "The Recrudescent American Conservatism." In *Did You Ever See a Dream Walking? American Conservative Thought in the Twentieth Century,* edited by William F. Buckley, pp. 75–92. Indianapolis: Bobbs-Merrill, 1970.

Miles, Michael W. *The Odyssey of the American Rights.* New York: Oxford University Press, 1980.

Miller, Robert Moats. *American Protestantism and Social Issues, 1919–1939.* Westport, Conn.: Greenwood Press, 1958.

————. "A Footnote to the Role of the Protestant Churches in the Election of 1928." *Church History* 25 (June 1956): 145–59.

Mills, Ogden. "Our Foreign Policy: A Republican View." *Foreign Affairs* 6 (July 1928): 555–72.

Milton, George Fort. "Fifty-Fifty and Fight!" *Virginia Quarterly Review* 3 (January 1927): 23–37.

————. "Progressive Democrats in a Quandary." *Independent*, October 8, 1927, pp. 350–52.

Mitchell, Franklin D. *Embattled Democracy: Missouri Democratic Politics, 1919–1932*. Columbia: University of Missouri Press, 1968.

Moffitt, Louis W. "Control of the Liquor Traffic in Canada." *Annals of the American Academy of Political and Social Science* 163 (September 1932): 188–96.

Montgomery, David. *Beyond Equality: Labor and the Radical Republicans, 1862–1872*. New York: Alfred A. Knopf, 1967.

Moore, Edmund A. *A Catholic Runs for President: The Campaign of 1928*. New York: Ronald Press, 1956

Moore, Mark H., and Gerstein, Dean R., eds. *Alcohol and Public Policy: Beyond the Shadow of Prohibition*. Washington, D.C.: National Academy Press, 1981.

Morris, Charles E. *Progressive Democracy of James M. Cox*. Indianapolis: Bobbs-Merrill, 1920.

Morrison, Joseph L. *Josephus Daniels: The Small-d Democrat*. Chapel Hill: University of North Carolina Press, 1966.

Mosley, Leonard. *Blood Relations: The Rise and Fall of the du Ponts of Delaware*. New York: Atheneum, 1980.

Murray, Robert K. *The 103rd Ballot: Democrats and the Disaster in Madison Square Garden*. New York: Harper and Row, 1976.

————. *The Politics of Normalcy: Governmental Theory and Practice in the Harding-Coolidge Era*. New York: W. W. Norton, 1973.

Myers, William Starr. "Looking toward 1932." *American Political Science Review* 25 (November 1931): 925–31.

Neal, Don C. *The World beyond the Hudson: Alfred E. Smith and National Politics, 1918–1928*. New York: Garland Publishing, 1983.

Neal, Nevin E. "The Smith-Robinson Arkansas Campaign of 1928." *Arkansas Historical Quarterly* 19 (Spring 1960): 3–11.

Noggle, Burl. "Oil and Politics." In *Change and Continuity in Twentieth-Century America: The 1920s*, edited by John Braeman, Robert H. Bremner, and David Brody, pp. 33–65. Columbus: Ohio State University Press, 1968.

————. *Teapot Dome: Oil and Politics in the 1920's*. Baton Rouge: Louisiana State University Press, 1962.

————. "The Twenties: A New Historiographical Frontier." *Journal of American History* 53 (September 1966): 299–314.

O'Connor, Richard. *The First Hurrah: A Biography of Alfred E. Smith*. New York: G. P. Putnam's Sons, 1970.

Oulahan, Richard. *The Man Who . . . : The Story of the 1932 Democratic Convention.* New York: Dial Press, 1971.

Overacker, Louise. "Campaign Funds in a Depression Year." *American Political Science Review* 27 (October 1933): 769–83.

———. *Money in Elections.* New York: MacMillan, 1932.

Palmer, Frederick. *Newton D. Baker: America at War.* New York: Dodd, Mead, 1931.

Palombera, Joseph La. "A Dissenting View." In *Decline of Ideology?*, edited by Mostafa Rejai, pp. 243–67. Chicago: Aldine Atherton, 1971.

Patterson, James T. *Congressional Conservatism and the New Deal: The Growth of the Conservative Coalition in Congress, 1933–1939.* Lexington: University of Kentucky Press, 1967.

———. "FDR and the Democratic Triumph." *Current History* 47 (October 1964): 216–20.

Paul, Randolph E. *Taxation in the United States.* Boston: Little, Brown, 1954.

Peel, Roy V., and Donnelly, Thomas C. *The 1928 Campaign: An Analysis.* New York: Richard R. Smith, 1931.

———. *The 1932 Campaign: An Analysis.* New York: Farrar and Rinehart, 1935.

Perlman, Mark. "Labor in Eclipse." In *Change and Continuity in Twentieth-Century America: The 1920s,* edited by John Braeman, Robert H. Bremner, and David Brody, pp. 103–45. Columbus: Ohio State University Press, 1968.

Perrett, Geoffrey. *America in the Twenties: A History.* New York: Simon and Schuster, 1982.

Perry, Elisabeth Israels. *Belle Moskowitz: Feminine Politics and the Exercise of Power in the Age of Alfred E. Smith.* New York: Oxford University Press, 1987.

Petersen, Peter L. "Stopping Al Smith: The 1928 Democratic Primary in South Dakota." *South Dakota History* 34 (February 1974): 439–54.

Peterson, Merrill D. *The Jefferson Image in the American Mind.* New York: Oxford University Press, 1960.

Pollock, James K., Jr. "Campaign Funds in 1928." *American Political Science Review* 23 (1929): 59–69.

Popkin, Samuel; Gorman, John W.; Phillips, Charles; and Smith, Jeffrey A. "What Have You Done for Me Lately? Towards an Investment Theory of Voting." *American Political Science Review* 70 (1976): 415–28.

Priest, Henry S. "The Eighteenth Amendment: A Violation and Infringement of Liberty." *Annals of the American Academy of Political and Social Science* 109 (September 1923): 39–47.

Pringle, Henry. "John J. Raskob: A Portrait." *Outlook,* August 22, 1928, p. 2.

Protho, James Warren. *Dollar Decade: Business Ideas in the 1920's.* Baton Rouge: Louisiana State University Press, 1954.

Prude, James C. "William Gibbs McAdoo and the Democratic National Convention of 1924." *Journal of Southern History* 38 (November 1972): 621–28.

Puryear, Elmer L. *Democratic Dissension in North Carolina, 1928–1936.* Chapel Hill: University of North Carolina Press, 1962.

Qualls, J. Winfield. "The 1928 Presidential Campaign in West Tennessee: Was Race a Chief Factor?" *West Tennessee Historical Society Papers* 27 (1973): 99–107.

Rankin, Robert Stanley. "The Future of the Democratic Party." *South Atlantic Quarterly* 28 (July 1929): 225–35.

Ratner, Sidney. *American Taxation: Its History as a Social Force in Democracy.* New York: W. W. Norton, 1942.

———. *The Tariff in American History.* New York: D. Van Nostrand, 1972.

Reagan, Hugh D. "Race as a Factor in the Presidential Election of 1928 in Alabama." *Alabama Review* 19 (January 1966): 5–19.

Rejai, Mostafa. "Political Ideology: Theoretical and Comparative Perspectives." In *Decline of Ideology?*, edited by Mostafa Rejai, pp. 1–32. Chicago: Aldine Atherton, 1971.

———, ed. *Decline of Ideology?* Chicago: Aldine Atherton, 1971.

Rice, Arnold S. *The Ku Klux Klan in American Politics.* New York: Haskell House Publishers, 1972.

Robinson, Edgar Eugene. *The Presidential Vote, 1896–1932.* Stanford: Stanford University Press, 1934.

Roelofs, H. Mark. *Ideology and Myth in American Politics: A Critique of a National Political Mind.* Boston: Little, Brown, 1976.

Rorabaugh, W. J. *The Alcoholic Republic: An American Tradition.* New York: Oxford University Press, 1979.

Rosen, Elliot A. "Baker on the Fifth Ballot? The Democratic Alternative: 1932." *Ohio History*, Autumn 1966, pp. 226–46.

———. *Hoover, Roosevelt, and the Brains Trust: From Depression to New Deal.* New York: Columbia University Press, 1977.

Rossiter, Clinton. *Conservatism in America.* Cambridge: Harvard University Press, 1982.

Rubin, Jay L. "The Wet War: American Liquor Control, 1941–1945." In *Alcohol, Reform, and Society: The Liquor Issue in Social Context*, edited by Jack S. Blocker, pp. 235–58. Westport, Conn.: Greenwood Press, 1979.

Rudolph, Frederick. "The American Liberty League, 1934–1940." *American Historical Review* 56 (October 1950): 19–33.

Rumbarger, John J. *Profits, Power, and Prohibition: Alcohol Reform and the Industrializing of America, 1800–1930.* Albany: State University of New York Press, 1989.

Saloutos, Theodore, and Hicks, John D. *Agricultural Discontent in the Middle West, 1900–1939.* Madison: University of Wisconsin Press, 1951.

Sanford, E. P. "The Illegal Liquor Traffic." *Annals of the American Academy of Political and Social Science* 163 (September 1932): 39–45.

Sarasohn, David. *The Party of Reform: Democrats in the Progressive Era.* Jackson: University Press of Mississippi, 1989.

Schiesl, Martin J. *The Politics of Efficiency: Municipal Administration and Reform in America, 1880–1920.* Berkeley: University of California Press, 1977.

Schlesinger, Arthur M., Jr. *The Age of Roosevelt.* Vol. 1, *The Crisis of the Old Order,*

1919–1933. Vol. 2, *The Coming of the New Deal*. Vol. 3, *The Politics of Upheaval*. Boston: Houghton Mifflin, 1956–60.

———. *History of U.S. Political Parties*. Vol. 3, 1910–1945. New York: Chelsea House, 1973.

Schlesinger, Arthur M., Jr., and Israel, Fred L., eds. *History of American Presidential Elections, 1789–1968*. Vol. 3. New York: Chelsea House, 1971.

Schriftgiesser, Karl. *This Was Normalcy: An Account of Party Politics during Twelve Republican Years, 1920–1932*. Boston: Little, Brown, 1948.

Schwarz, Jordan A. "Al Smith in the Thirties." *New York History* 45 (October 1964): 316–31.

———. "John Nance Garner and the Sales Tax Rebellion of 1932." *Journal of Southern History* 30 (May 1964): 162–80.

———. *The Speculator: Bernard M. Baruch in Washington, 1917–1965*. Chapel Hill: University of North Carolina Press, 1981.

Sellers, James Benson. *The Prohibition Movement in Alabama, 1702–1943*. Chapel Hill: University of North Carolina Press, 1943.

Semes, Robert Louis. "Confrontation at Charlottesville: The American Liberty League and Its Critics, 1935." *Magazine of Albemarle County History* 29 (1971): 33–48.

Shannon, William V. *The American Irish*. New York: Macmillan, 1963.

Shover, John L. "Was 1928 a Critical Election in California?" *Pacific Northwest Quarterly* 58 (October 1967): 196–204.

Silva, Ruth C. *Rum, Religion, and Votes: 1928 Re-examined*. University Park: Pennsylvania State University Press, 1962.

Slichter, Sumner H. "The Current Labor Policies of American Industries." *Quarterly Journal of Economics* 43 (May 1929): 393–435.

Smith, Page. *Redeeming the Time: A People's History of the 1920's and the New Deal*. New York: McGraw-Hill, 1987.

Smith, Rixey, and Beasley, Norman. *Carter Glass: A Biography*. New York: Longmans, Green, 1939.

Soule, George. *Prosperity Decade: From War to Depression, 1917–1929*. New York: Rinehart, 1947.

Spencer, Herbert. *The Man versus the State*. Indianapolis: Liberty Classics, 1982.

Steel, Ronald. *Walter Lippmann and the American Century*. New York: Vintage Books, 1980.

Steuart, Justin. *Wayne Wheeler, Dry Boss: An Uncensored Biography of Wayne B. Wheeler*. New York: Fleming H. Revell, 1928.

Stiles, Lela. *The Man behind Roosevelt: The Story of Louis McHenry Howe*. Cleveland: World Publishing, 1954.

Stinnett, Ronald F. *Democrats, Dinners, and Dollars: A History of the Democratic Party, Its Dinners, Its Rituals*. Ames: Iowa State University Press, 1967.

Stone, Irving. "Calvin Coolidge." In *The Aspirin Age, 1919–1941*, edited by Isabel Leighton, pp. 130–51. New York: Simon and Schuster, 1949.

————. *They Also Ran: The Story of the Men Who Were Defeated for the Presidency.* New York: Doubleday, Doran, 1943.

Stratton, David H. "Splattered with Oil: William G. McAdoo and the 1924 Democratic Presidential Nomination." *Southwestern Social Science Quarterly* 44 (June 1963): 62–75.

Sullivan, Mark. *Our Times: The United States, 1900–1925.* Vol. 5, *Over Here, 1914–1918.* Vol. 6, *The Twenties.* New York: Charles Scribner's Sons, 1933–35.

Swain, Martha H. *Pat Harrison: The New Deal Years.* Jackson: University of Mississippi Press, 1978.

Swanberg, W. A. *Citizen Hearst: A Biography of William Randolph Hearst.* New York: Charles Scribner's Sons, 1961.

Swindler, William F. "A Dubious Constitutional Experiment." In *Law, Alcohol, and Order: Perspectives on National Prohibition,* edited by David E. Kyvig, pp. 53–66. Westport, Conn.: Greenwood Press, 1985.

Synon, Mary. *McAdoo: The Man and His Times—a Panorama in Democracy.* Indianapolis: Bobbs-Merrill, 1924.

Taft, Philip. *The A. F. of L. in the Time of Gompers.* New York: Harper and Brothers, 1957.

Tarbell, Ida M. *Owen D. Young: A New Type of Industrial Leader.* New York: MacMillan, 1932.

Tarter, Brent. "A Flier on the National Scene: Byrd's Favorite Son Presidential Candidacy of 1932." *Virginia Magazine of History and Biography* 82 (July 1974): 282–305.

Timmons, Bascom N. *Garner of Texas: A Personal History.* New York: Harper and Brothers, 1948.

————. *Jesse H. Jones: The Man and the Statesman.* New York: Henry Holt, 1956.

Tindall, George B. "Business Progressivism: Southern Politics in the Twenties." *South Atlantic Quarterly* 62 (Winter 1963): 92–106.

Tobin, Eugene M. *Organize or Perish: America's Independent Progressives, 1913–1933.* New York: Greenwood Press, 1986.

Tugwell, Rexford G. *The Democratic Roosevelt: A Biography of Franklin D. Roosevelt.* Baltimore: Penguin Books, 1957.

————. *Grover Cleveland.* New York: MacMillan, 1968.

Tyrrell, Ian R. *Sobering Up: From Temperance to Prohibition in Antebellum America.* Westport, Conn.: Greenwood Press, 1979.

Villard, Oswald Garrison. *Prophets True and False.* New York: Alfred A. Knopf, 1928.

Vose, Clement E. *Constitutional Change: Amendment Politics and Supreme Court Litigation since 1900.* Lexington, Mass.: Lexington Books, 1972.

————. "Repeal as a Political Achievement." In *Law, Alcohol, and Order: Perspectives on National Prohibition,* edited by David E. Kyvig, pp. 97–122. Westport, Conn.: Greenwood Press, 1985.

Walsh, George. *Gentleman Jimmy Walker: Mayor of the Jazz Age.* New York: Praeger Publishers, 1974.

Ware, Alan. *The Breakdown of the Democratic Party Organization, 1940–1980.* Oxford: Clarendon Press, 1985.

Ware, Susan. *Partner and I: Molly Dewson, Feminism, and New Deal Politics.* New Haven: Yale University Press, 1987.

Warner, Emily Smith, with Daniel, Hawthorne. *The Happy Warrior: A Biography of My Father, Alfred E. Smith.* New York: Doubleday, 1956.

Watson, Richard L., Jr. "A Political Leader Bolts—F. M. Simmons in the Presidential Election of 1928." *North Carolina Historical Review* 37 (October 1960): 516–43.

Weisbord, Marvin R. *Campaigning for President: A New Look at the Road to the White House.* Washington, D.C.: Public Affairs Press, 1964.

Weiss, Nancy Joan. *Charles Francis Murphy, 1858–1924: Respectability and Responsibility in Tammany Politics.* Northampton, Mass.: Smith College Press, 1968.

Wesser, Robert F. *A Response to Progressivism: The Democratic Party and New York Politics, 1902–1918.* New York: New York University Press, 1986.

White, William Allen. *Masks in a Pageant.* New York: MacMillan, 1928.

———. *Politics: The Citizen's Business.* New York: MacMillan, 1924.

Wiebe, Robert H. *Businessmen and Reform: A Study of the Progressive Movement.* Cambridge: Harvard University Press, 1962.

———. *The Search for Order, 1877–1920.* New York: Hill and Wang, 1967.

Williams, Michael. *The Shadow of the Pope.* New York: McGraw-Hill, 1932.

Wilson, Joan Hoff. "Herbert Hoover's Agricultural Policies." In *Herbert Hoover as Secretary of Commerce: Studies in New Era Thought and Practice,* edited by Ellis W. Hawley, pp. 115–44. Iowa City: University of Iowa Press, 1981.

Witte, John F. *The Politics and Development of the Federal Income Tax.* Madison: University of Wisconsin Press, 1985.

Wolfskill, George. *The Revolt of the Conservatives: A History of the American Liberty League, 1934–1940.* Boston: Houghton Mifflin, 1962.

Wolfskill, George, and Hudson, John A. *All But the People: Franklin D. Roosevelt and His Critics, 1933–1939.* London: Macmillan, 1969.

Woodward, C. Vann. *The Strange Career of Jim Crow.* 3d ed. New York: Oxford University Press, 1974.

Wyllie, Irwin G. *The Self-Made Man in America: The Myth of Rags to Riches.* New Brunswick: Rutgers University Press, 1954.

Zarembka, Paul, ed. *Research in Political Economy.* Vol. 6. Greenwich, Conn.: VAI Press, 1983.

Zieger, Robert H. *Republicans and Labor, 1919–1929.* Lexington: University of Kentucky Press, 1969.

Zwieger, Robert H. "Herbert Hoover, the Wage Earner, and the 'New Economic System.'" In *Herbert Hoover as Secretary of Commerce: Studies in New Era Thought and Practice,* edited by Ellis W. Hawley, pp. 80–112. Iowa City: University of Iowa Press, 1981.

MAGAZINES AND NEWSPAPERS

Atlantic Monthly, 1927–28.
Century Magazine, 1925–28.
Collier's, 1928–30.
Harper's Magazine, 1925–28.
Independent, 1928.
Ladies' Home Journal, 1928.
Literary Digest, 1920–34.
Nation, 1920–34.
New Outlook, 1932–34.
New Republic, 1920–34.
New York Herald Tribune, 1928–32.
New York Times, 1916–39.
North American Review, 1928.
Outlook, 1927–29.
Scribner's Magazine, 1928–32.
Wall Street Journal, 1928–33.

PAMPHLETS AND MISCELLANEOUS MATERIALS

Declaration of Principles and Purposes of the Conference of Anti-Smith Democrats. Asheville, N.C., July 19, 1928. Broadside held in the University of Virginia Library.

Dowling, Eddie. Interview with Ruthanna Hindes, May 1, 1968. Held at the Hagley Museum and Library, Greenville, Delaware.

Eldot, Paula. "Governor Alfred E. Smith: A Paradoxical Liberal." Paper delivered to the Convention of the Organization of American Historians, New Orleans, April 1979. Copy provided by the author.

Hutchins, Grace. *The Truth about the Liberty League*. International Pamphlets, No. 50. New York, 1936.

Long, Hamilton A. *Roosevelt or Smith?* Privately printed pamphlet, June 1932.

Lopata, Roy Haywood. "The Business Mind and the Great Depression: A Case Study of the Reaction of Several Members of the du Pont Family to the New Deal." Held as Accession no. 1645 at the Hagley Museum and Library, Greenville, Delaware.

National Association of Manufacturers. *Platform of American Industry, 1924*. Presented to the Annual Convention of the National Association of Manufacturers, May 20, 1924. New York Public Library Pamphlet Collections, TB p.v. 1579.

National Lawyers Committee of the American Liberty League. *Report on the Constitutionality of the Bituminous Coal Conservation Act of 1935*. Issued December 9, 1935.

———. *Report on the Constitutionality of the National Labor Relations Act*. Issued September 5, 1935.

――――. *Report on the Constitutionality of the Potato Act of 1935*. Issued December 30, 1935.

――――. *The Welfare Clause in the Light of the A.A.A. Decision*. Issued 1936.

Shouse, Jouett. "Democracy's Victory and Opportunity." Address before the Democratic Women's Luncheon Club of Philadelphia, January 15, 1931. Political Pamphlets Collection, vol. 23, Alderman Library, University of Virginia.

UNPUBLISHED DISSERTATIONS AND THESES

Carlson, Earland I. "Franklin D. Roosevelt's Fight for the Presidential Nomination, 1928–1932." Ph.D., University of Illinois, 1955.

Chatham, Marie. "The Role of the National Party Chairman from Hanna to Farley." Ph.D., University of Maryland, 1953.

Cook, Franklin Rhodes. "The Presidential Candidacy of John W. Davis." M.A., Pennsylvania State University, 1973.

Craig, Douglas B. S. "Rehearsal for Revolt: John J. Raskob and the Democratic Party." M.A., University of Virginia, 1986.

――――. "Rehearsal for Revolt: The Ideological Turmoil of the Democratic Party, 1920–1932." Ph.D., University of Virginia, 1989.

Feldman, Martin I. "An Abstract of the Political Thought of Alfred E. Smith." Ph.D., New York University, 1963.

Hanks, R. Justus. "The Democratic Party in 1920: The Rupture of the Wilsonian Synthesis." Ph.D., University of Chicago, 1960.

Henderson, Bancroft Clinton. "The Democratic National Committee." Ph.D., University of Minnesota, 1958.

Koeniger, Alfred Cash. "'Unreconstructed Rebel': The Political Thought and Senate Career of Carter Glass, 1929–1936." Ph.D., Vanderbilt University, 1980.

Levin, James Benesch. "Albert C. Ritchie: A Political Biography." Ph.D., City University of New York, 1970.

Lopata, Roy Haywood. "John J. Raskob: A Conservative Businessman in the Age of Roosevelt." Ph.D., University of Delaware, 1975.

Smoger, Gerson Harry. "Organizing Political Campaigns: A Survey of Nineteenth and Twentieth Century Trends." Ph.D., University of Pennsylvania, 1982.

Stanley, Judith Margaret. "The Congressional Democrats, 1918–1928." Ph.D., University of California at Berkeley, 1969.

INDEX

Adams, James Truslow, 191
Adamson Act, 142
Agricultural Adjustment Act, 277, 279, 283, 291
Agricultural Advisory Committee, 207
Agriculture. *See* Farm relief
Ailsworth, Robert, 172
Alderman, Edwin A., 194
Alexander, Joshua, 107
Alger, Horatio, 286
Alien and Sedition Acts, 42
Allen, Frederick Lewis, 8
Allen, William H., 114
American Bar Association, 56
American Civil Liberties Union, 119
American Federation of Labor (AFL), 68, 138, 161, 164. *See also* Trade unions
American Liberty League, 4, 5, 14, 248, 249, 251, 252, 262, 265, 269, 273, 274–95 passim, 304, 305; and historians, 274–75, 362 (n. 7); created, 281; funding, 284–85; membership, 285; documents discussed, 285, 292–94; and Republican party, 285–86; continuities with AAPA, 286–94; National Lawyers Committee, 290–93; publicity effort, 292–94
American Plan, 138
American Revolution, 53, 154, 274
Amidon, Tom, 77
Anderson, Paul, 203
Antiprohibition. *See* Association Against the Prohibition Amendment
Anti-Saloon League, 54, 250, 264
Antisdale, Louis, 24
Anti-Smith Democrats, 168–69, 178, 186

Antistatism, 10–11
Association Against the Prohibition Amendment (AAPA), 4, 14, 119, 137, 154, 234, 249–73 passim, 276, 286, 287, 292, 294, 305; and historians, 249–52, 357 (n. 32); and FACA, 271–72; and taxation, 356 (n. 9)
Associative state, 5, 128
Augusta Chronicle, 220
Ayres, William, 88

Bailey, Josiah, 196, 283
Baker, Newton D., 28, 31, 56, 61, 106, 107, 161, 168, 218, 234, 236, 241, 243, 245, 246, 250–51; candidacy for 1928 nomination, 99–100; biography, 232; philosophy, 232–33; candidacy for 1932 nomination, 232–34; and League of Nations (1932), 233–34; and New Deal, 283–84; and World War I, 357 (n. 24)
Barkley, Alben, 217
Barnes, Julius, 146–47, 277; and McNary-Haugen scheme, 335 (n. 85)
Barnett, Albert E., 98
Barton, Bruce, 264
Barton, R. M., 46
Baruch, Bernard, 36, 44, 47–48, 142, 143, 201, 245; attitude toward George White, 78
Baxter, Norman W., 239
Beck, James M., 268, 290
Bendix, Reinhard, 9
Bilbo, Theodore, 169
Bill of Rights. *See* Constitution, U.S.
Bituminous Coal Board, 291
Bituminous Coal Code, 291
Bituminous Coal Conservation Act, 291

Blacks, 35, 169–70, 174
Bliven, Bruce, 95
Blum, John M., 31
Bonds, 33, 313 (n. 17)
Bonus, 45
"Booze before bread," 192, 204, 234, 236, 239, 300
Bowers, Claude, 36, 52, 64, 69, 109, 192, 198
Braden, Spruille, 176
"Bread before booze," 199, 204, 301. See also "Booze before bread"
Breckenridge, Henry, 196, 240, 241, 247, 283
Brennan, George, 17, 22, 24, 54, 63
Breweries, 251. See also Liquor industry
Broker state, 6
Brookhart, Smith, 254
Bruce, William Cabell, 88, 298
Bryan, Charles, 60
Bryan, William Jennings, 3, 18, 39, 46, 49, 53, 54, 68, 72, 73, 84, 87, 88, 95, 100, 107, 108, 156, 158, 168, 174, 222, 262, 297, 298, 300, 301; platform proposals (1919), 20; opinion of Cox, 21; assessment of 1920 defeat, 27, 28; attitude toward Davis, 59–60; and 1924 platform, 63
Bryant and Stratton Business School, 133
Buchanan, James, 82
Bureaucracies, 42
Burk, Robert F., 6, 7, 134, 274, 276, 290
Burleson, Albert S., 16
Burner, David, 1, 9, 52, 93, 165, 179, 305
Burns, Arthur, 168
Burns, James MacGregor, 9
Business: attitudes in the 1920s, 137–47
Byrd, Harry F., 3, 175, 177, 188, 190, 198, 213, 216, 222, 235, 245, 246,

281; and 1928 campaign, 171–72; and Raskob, 187, 193–97, 240–43; and prohibition (1929–32), 196–97, 240–42; and 1932 nomination, 239–43; platform for 1932, 242–43; and New Deal, 283–84

Calhoun, John C., 82
California, 35, 219, 220, 245, 246; Democratic party in, 48, 220; 1928 primary, 98; 1932 primary, 220, 349 (n. 54)
Campaigns: of 1920, 22–25; of 1924, 51–74 passim; of 1928, 157–80 passim
Canada, 133. See also Quebec system
Cannon, Bp. James, 172, 186
Cannon, Joseph G., 19
Carlisle system, 358 (n. 49)
Carnegie, Andrew, 141
Carpenter, R. R. M., 280
Carter, Benjamin, 46
Chace, Arthur F., 235
Chadbourne, Thomas L., 22, 36, 44, 46, 47–48, 78
Chandler, Alfred D., 135
Chattanooga News, 90
Chesterton, G. K., 229
Chicago Tribune, 260
Child Labor Amendment, 43, 53, 123, 166, 277, 289
Chrysler, Walter, 281
Citizen's Union, 114
Claggett, Brice, 73, 81, 102–3, 105, 173
Clark, Champ, 33, 93
Clayton Act, 138, 139
Cleveland, Grover, 3, 4, 18, 53, 54, 73, 88, 167, 235, 266, 268, 291, 294, 297, 298, 299
Cohn, Alfred E., 199, 200
Colby, Bainbridge, 16, 202
Collier's Magazine, 155

Communism, 9, 275
Comstock, William A., 106
Condon, Thomas G., 176
Congress, 34, 62, 71, 77, 268; and
    McNary-Haugen scheme, 62; conser-
    vative coalition in, 283
Congressional committees, 76, 77
Congressional Democrats, 184, 202,
    203, 283
Congressional elections: of 1918, 27,
    77, 85; of 1920, 28; of 1922, 71; of
    1924, 71; of 1930, 188, 225
Conservatism: defined, 10–11, 308
    (n. 37)
Constitution, U.S., 42, 88, 175, 250,
    253, 254, 255, 256, 257, 268, 269,
    275, 287, 289, 290, 291, 293, 358
    (n. 45); Bill of Rights, 255, 256;
    Thirteenth Amendment, 251; Four-
    teenth Amendment, 43; Fifteenth
    Amendment, 53, 191, 345 (n. 60);
    Sixteenth Amendment, 56, 115, 237,
    262, 267, 289; Seventeenth Amend-
    ment, 115; Eighteenth Amendment:
    see Prohibition; Nineteenth Amend-
    ment, 114, 121, 236; Twenty-First
    Amendment, 254, 264, 271; General
    Welfare Clause, 266, 291
Converse, Edmund C., 32
Coolidge, Calvin, 11, 36, 59, 62, 67,
    70, 95, 132, 138, 145, 237
Cooperation statement, 200–203,
    215–16
Co-operative Club International, 40
Cordray, Ella, 257
Corporatism, 5, 40, 140; defined, 6–7
Cox, James M., 4, 5, 17, 36, 37, 39,
    40, 52, 56, 64, 71, 77, 78, 79, 81,
    82, 86, 87, 97, 105, 132, 163, 168,
    176, 178, 191, 206, 210, 229, 246,
    247, 248, 249, 253, 296, 302, 303,
    304, 305; gubernatorial record, 18–
    19; philosophy, 19; attitude toward

prohibition, 22; assesses 1920 defeat,
    26; assesses 1924 defeat, 72–73; and
    New Deal, 281–82
Creel, George, 39, 55
Croly, Herbert, 167
Crusaders, 363 (n. 27)
Culliver Bill, 55
Cultural conflicts, 1, 51–52
Cummings, Homer S., 24, 28, 81, 89,
    90, 92, 108, 173, 212, 218, 222,
    232; attitude toward Alfred Smith's
    1928 nomination, 109–10
Curran, Henry H., 264
Current History, 258
Curti, Merle, 150

Daniels, Josephus, 25, 28, 101, 105,
    172, 176, 177, 189, 192, 194, 202,
    203, 212, 217, 218, 235, 244, 301;
    attitude toward Alfred Smith's 1928
    nomination, 108–9; and 1928 cam-
    paign, 171, 175–76
Daugherty, Harry, 139
Davis, John W., 3, 4, 5, 40, 41, 47, 48,
    52, 79, 80, 82, 87, 97, 105, 130,
    132, 176, 178, 210, 226, 229, 232,
    234, 247, 248, 249, 281, 284, 287,
    288, 290, 296, 302, 303, 304, 305;
    defines liberalism, 12, 57; biography,
    56; philosophy, 56–59; on taxation,
    57; and labor, 57–58, 68; attitude
    toward McAdoo, 58–59; campaign
    for 1924 nomination, 58–59; and
    1924 campaign, 63–70; and Progres-
    sive party, 64–68; 1924 circular letter,
    65–66, 319 (n. 76); campaign strat-
    egy, 65–70, 72; campaign style, 69–
    70; analysis of 1924 defeat, 71; and
    Victory Fund, 184–86; and New
    Deal, 278–79; and depression, 279;
    and prohibition, 320 (n. 85)
Dawes Committee, 234
Debt moratorium, 203

Declaration of Independence, 11, 41, 257, 287

Delaware, 257; liquor policy, 260–61

Democratic Bulletin, 198

Democratic Economy Committee, 203

Democratic National Committee (DNC), 24, 36, 49, 73–74, 75–91 passim, 99, 104, 131, 137, 149, 176, 181–204 passim, 216, 217, 220, 240, 276, 284, 286, 292, 293, 294, 297, 301, 304; structure and history, 76–77

Democratic National Convention: of 1912, 33; of 1920, 17, 35; voting at 1920 convention, 18; of 1924, 47, 51–52, 59–63, 68, 88, 92, 97, 314 (n. 38); of 1928, 93, 101, 106, 179, 210, 327 (n. 50); of 1932, 185, 207, 214, 217–18, 220, 222, 223–24, 225, 243–47, 248, 301, 304; voting at 1932 convention, 243–47

Democratic party: and historians, 1, 4, 27, 28, 51–52, 93, 158; structure, 75–76; attitudes toward Alfred Smith's 1928 nomination, 104–11
—fund-raising: in 1912, 33; in 1920, 24–25, 70; in 1921–23, 79; in 1924, 176; in 1925–27, 80; in 1928, 176–77, 342 (n. 118); in 1932, 348 (n. 39)
—national platforms: of 1920, 19–21; of 1924, 60–63, 159; of 1928, 158–61, 168, 170, 173, 175, 179; of 1932, 243–47, 248, 269, 279, 292, 301

Democratic Publicity Bureau, 4, 182–84

Depression, 130, 183, 208, 242, 299. *See also* Economic conditions

Desvernine, Raoul, 290

Dewson, Molly, 121

Dickinson, John, 84

Dill, Clarence C., 217, 247

Disfranchisement, 108

Dockweiler, Isidore, 220, 222

Dodd, William, 38

Dodge, Cleveland, 25

Doheny, Edward, 31, 36–38, 47, 49, 50, 52, 60, 64. *See also* Teapot Dome scandal

Dominion Iron and Steel Company, 133

Douglas, Stephen A., 82

Dowling, Eddie, 154

Dreiser, Theodore, 52

Du Bois, W. E. B., 174

du Pont, Alfred, 134

du Pont, Eugene, 134

du Pont, Francis I., 254

du Pont, Irénée, 4, 6, 159, 175, 251, 253, 264, 284, 287, 289; and Constitution, 366 (n. 79); and KKK, 367 (n. 102)

du Pont, Lammot, 6, 253

du Pont, Pierre, 4, 6, 119, 130, 151, 153, 154, 175, 176, 235, 246, 250, 252–61 passim, 269, 272, 277, 281, 283, 287, 289, 290; and Raskob, 133–37, 140; political activities of (1906–20), 252–53; and prohibition (1920–25); philosophy, 254–57; and AAPA, 254–61; and prohibition (1925–33), 254–61; and constitutional reform, 255–57, 267; and right to drink, 256–57; and plans for repeal, 258–61; and New Deal, 269–71; and Repeal Associates, 360 (n. 80)

du Pont, T. Coleman, 134, 151, 250

du Pont family, 171, 251, 263, 265; support of AAPA, 264; and Liberty League, 284–85; and 1932 elections, 355 (n. 136); and historians, 357 (n. 32)

Du Pont Company, 131, 133–37, 140,

150, 151, 234, 252, 280, 281, 333
(n. 13); and World War I, 252–53;
and New Deal, 276
Durant, William Crapo, 134. *See also*
General Motors Corporation

Early, Steve, 23
Economic conditions: in 1920, 27; in
1924, 38; in 1920–29, 138, 315
(n. 46). *See also* Depression
Economy Bill, 279
Edison Electrical Institute, 284
Education, 62
Eldot, Paula, 113
Electoral college, 66, 67, 71, 100, 106,
177, 178
Electoral realignment, 177, 298, 299,
300. *See also* Fourth party system
Electoral strategy: in 1916, 22; in 1920,
22–29; in 1924, 65–70, 71; in 1928,
174–79
Employee committees, 142, 144
Employee savings and investment plans,
150. *See also* Welfare capitalism
Employee stock-buying schemes, 142
See also Welfare capitalism; Working
Man's Investment Trust
Esch-Cummins Law, 20
Ethnic vote: in 1920, 25–26
Ethnoculturalist historians, 2, 52
Excess profits tax, 44
Executive budget system, 117

Fall, Albert, 37–38
Farley, James A., 211–12, 227, 285
Farm bloc, 40
Farm Loan banks, 33, 43
Farm relief, 65, 160, 162–63, 199, 207,
242, 244, 298, 299, 300
Fay, Charles, 146
Federal Alcohol Control Administration
(FACA), 271–72
Federal Farm Bureau, 198

Federal Judiciary, 43. *See also* U.S.
Supreme Court
Federal Reserve Act, 33
Federal Reserve banks, 33, 43
Federal Reserve Board, 68, 282
Ferguson, Thomas, 7, 142, 155,
275–76
Filene, Edward A., 142, 143–44, 145,
150, 283
Flannagan, Roy, 194, 198, 240, 241
Florida: land boom, 8
Force bills, 175
Ford, Henry, 16, 36, 63
Fordney-McCumber tariff, 43, 159,
198
"Forgotten man" speech, 130, 211,
212, 221, 230, 231, 269
Fosdick, Raymond, 233
Fourth party system, 2. *See also* Elec-
toral realignment
Frankfurter, Felix, 5, 58, 64, 65, 127,
318 (n. 39)
Free silver, 53, 95, 108, 168, 262
French Revolution, 127

Galambos, Louis, 141
Gammack, Thomas, 167
Gannett, Frank, 111
Gardner, O. Max, 213, 236
Garner, John N., 200, 202, 203, 214,
220, 222, 223, 244, 246
Gary, Elbert H., 32, 141
Geertz, Clifford, 8, 9
General Electric Corporation, 118, 142
General Motors Acceptance Corpora-
tion, 136, 140, 150
General Motors Corporation, 131,
134–37, 150, 152, 234, 281; and
New Deal, 276
Gerard, James W., 104
Gilded Age, 8, 13, 22
Gilmore, Thomas, 251
Glass, Carter, 19, 77, 78, 103, 177,

192, 202, 247, 283; and 1928 campaign, 172–73
Glass-Steagall Banking Act, 203
Glazer, Nathan, 127
Gompers, Samuel, 68, 164
GOP. *See* Republican party
Gore, Thomas P., 283
Gould, Jay, 141
Grantham, Jesse, 205
Graves, Bibb, 117
Green, William, 161

Hamilton, Alexander, 33
Hampton, Frank, 95
Handlin, Oscar, 113
Hanes, John, 241
Hanna, Mark, 156
Harding, Warren G., 14, 19, 36, 138, 153, 182, 237; and 1920 campaign, 22
Hart, James, 295
Hastings, Daniel, 289
Hawley, Ellis, 2, 5, 128
Hayes, Ralph, 100, 106, 233, 235, 246
Hearst, William Randolph, 129, 214, 231, 245, 247
Heflin, Thomas, 98
Hickey, Louis W., 98
Hill, Louise B., 161
Hoey, James, 102, 103, 131
Holcombe, Arthur, 12, 192
Hooper, Ben W., 145
Hoover, Herbert, 15, 127, 138, 139, 159–80 passim, 183, 198, 203, 232, 242, 246, 286, 293, 300; and 1928 campaign, 162–65
Hoovercrats. *See* Anti-Smith Democrats
House, Edward M., 46, 70, 107
Howe, Louis McH., 24, 54, 89, 96, 102–3, 196, 214, 226
Hughes, Charles Evans, 252
Hughes, James, 289
Hull, Cordell, 89, 100, 105, 171, 177,

186–87, 190, 199, 217, 218, 244; biography, 78; as chairman of DNC, 78–79, 86; campaign for 1928 nomination, 99; and 1928 campaign, 170
Hundred Days, 279, 283
Hutton, Edward, 281

Ideology: defined, 8–10, 308 (nn. 30, 34, 35)
Illinois Manufacturers Association, 201
Immigration, 334 (n. 57)
Income tax, 45, 78. *See also* Taxation
Independent, 100
Industrial Advisory Board, 270
Inheritance tax, 45, 78, 267. *See also* Taxation
Injunctions. *See* Strikes
Internal Revenue Service, 138
International Court of Justice, 145
International Labor Organization, 145
Interstate Commerce Commission, 34, 44, 160
Investment theory, 7, 162
Irwin, Will, 183–84

Jackson, Andrew, 39, 40, 82, 282, 294; and Bank of the United States, 39
Jackson Sun, 169
Jefferson, Thomas, 11, 12, 40–43, 53, 83, 88, 100, 147, 148, 155, 175, 197, 282, 294, 298
Jeffersonian Democrats, 4
Johnson, Hiram, 58, 59
Johnson, Hugh, 62, 270
Johnston, Forney, 293
Johnston, Mercer, 166
Jones, Jesse, 80
J. P. Morgan and Company, 59

Kennsay, William F., 104, 113
Kent, Frank R., 187, 285, 294
King, Will, 107
Kiplinger, W. M., 221

Kremer, J. Bruce, 80
Krock, Arthur, 81
Ku Klux Klan (KKK), 1, 3, 31, 50, 53, 54, 63, 65, 68, 73, 81, 95, 100, 174, 367 (n. 102); 1924 Convention issue, 60–61
Kyvig, David, 4, 249–51, 264, 294, 295

Labor. *See* Trade unions
Ladies' Home Journal, 150, 152
La Follette, Robert M., Sr., 14, 64–65, 72, 144–45, 320 (n. 91). *See also* Progressive party
La Guardia, Fiorello, 203
Laissez-faire, 12
Landon, Alfred M., 124, 285
Lane, Franklin K., 26
Lansing, Robert, 58
Latin America, 166
Lea, Luke, 47
League of Nations, 15, 20, 22–23, 24, 29, 35, 44, 60, 61, 65, 66, 71, 161, 214, 233, 234, 241, 253
Legislative Investigative Commission, 115, 116
Lehman, Herbert, 104
Lenroot, Irvine, 37
Leuchtenburg, William E., 117
Liberalism, 5, 88, 194; defined, 11–13, 308 (n. 43); defined by FDR, 209
Liberty Loans, 33, 141
Lincoln, Abraham, 282
Lincoln Star, 187
Lippmann, Walter, 113, 233, 284; opinion of McAdoo, 35, 38–39
Lipsett, Seymour, 9
Liquor industry, 356 (n. 14), 357 (n. 29). *See also* Breweries
Lisio, Donald, 165
Literary Digest: 1920 poll, 16; 1922 poll, 344 (n. 40); 1923 poll, 36; 1930 poll, 188, 344 (n. 40); 1932 poll, 188

Little, Arthur, 258
Lodge, Henry Cabot, 20, 161
London Economic Conference, 282
Long, Breckenridge, 46, 48, 67, 80; and Democratic strategy, 85–86
Long, Hamilton A., 231
Long, Huey P., 247
Los Angeles, 35, 94, 220
Louisville Post, 36
Love, Thomas, 47, 77
Lusk bills, 118
Lynd, Robert and Helen, 8
Lyon, Frank, 186

McAdoo, William G., 1, 3, 4, 13, 14, 28, 29, 52, 55, 72, 89, 92, 93, 94, 100, 102, 103, 105, 108, 147, 161, 170, 174, 180, 182, 192, 202, 204, 206, 212, 213, 223, 224, 233, 247, 264, 297, 301, 304; campaign for 1920 nomination, 16–17, 19; biography, 30–50 passim; and women's rights, 32; and Wilson's campaign for 1912 nomination, 32–33; and Wilson administration, 33–35; as railroad commissioner, 34–35; and 1924 nomination, 35–39, 314 (n. 34); and Teapot Dome scandal, 37–38, 326 (n. 26); and Treasury Department during 1920s, 38, 64; political strategy, 39–40; philosophy and economic platform, 39–46; and Jeffersonian thought, 40–43; and League of Nations, 44; and railroads in 1920s, 44; and taxation, 44–45; and soldier's bonus, 45; and tariff policy, 45, 316 (n. 72); political activities after 1924, 48–50; and prohibition, 49–50; and KKK, 60–61, 63–64, 318 (n. 54); and 1924 campaign, 68–69; and DNC, 80–86; attitude toward FDR (1925), 90; activities (1925–28), 94–96; campaign for 1928 nomination, 94–96; and 1928 campaign, 173; and FDR (1932), 219–22; presidential aspirations (1932), 219–22, 245; at Chicago convention, 245–46; and historians, 313 (n. 1)

McCarthy, Charles H., 24, 216

McCormick, Richard L., 2, 7

Mack, Norman E., 55

McKellar, Kenneth, 221

McKinley, William, 156, 161

McNary-Haugen scheme, 62, 160, 163, 174, 277, 299, 335 (n. 85)

Macon Telegraph and News, 182

Madison Square Garden, 51–52, 73, 95, 97

Mellon, Andrew: taxation policies, 45, 54, 58, 63, 138, 153, 192

Mencken, H. L., 19, 21, 60, 70

Merchant marine, 34

Meredith, Edwin, 59, 99, 100, 103, 109

Me-tooism, 162, 167–68, 199, 203–4, 300, 301, 303

Michelson, Charles, 182–84, 286

Middletown, 8

Midleton, St. John Broderick, 278

Miles, Vincent K., 110

Mill, John Stuart, 13

Miller, Nathan, 113

Mills, Ogden, 202, 203

Milton, George Fort, 36, 47, 63, 69, 73, 84, 90, 92, 93, 95, 96, 103, 108, 110, 161, 173, 174, 188, 212, 213, 218, 220; and DNC, 81–82; and two-thirds rule, 82–83; and me-tooism, 199

Model License League, 251

Moley, Raymond, 230

Moody, Dan, 117

Moore, Ed, 17

Morgan, J. P., 58, 64

Morgenthau, Henry, 207

Morrison, Cameron, 117

Moses, Robert, 113, 207

Moskowitz, Belle, 100, 106, 165, 207, 231, 235, 239; and Alfred Smith, 121–22; philosophy, 122

Moynihan, Daniel, 127

Muir, Ramsay, 13

Murphy, Charles F., 17, 24, 54, 103, 115, 133

Muscle Shoals, 63, 199, 211, 232, 277

Nation, 72, 203

National Association of Manufacturers, 138, 139, 144–47, 148–49, 150, 152; 1924 platform, 144–45

National Committee for the Protection of Children, 289

National Industrial Conference, 153

National Industrial Recovery Act, 270, 271

National Labor Board, 270

National Labor Relations Act, 129, 277, 290, 295

National Lawyers Committee, 290–93

National Prohibition Cases, 256

National Recovery Administration (NRA), 270, 271, 279, 280, 283, 295

National Securities Exchange Act, 289

Nazism, 9

Neff, Pat M., 117

New Deal, 4, 5, 6, 12, 112, 113, 121, 123–26, 158, 178, 249, 251, 257, 261, 262, 265, 272, 274–95 passim, 304

New England Society of Pennsylvania, 271

New Era, 147, 152

New Freedom, 252

New Hampton Tribune, 96

New Left, 261

New Outlook, 125

New Republic, 89, 93, 95, 166–67, 227

New York and New Jersey Railroad Company, 32
New York City, 32, 37, 79, 303, 314 (n. 38)
New York County, 114
New York State Democratic Committee, 216
New York Times, 81, 84, 89, 101, 119, 126, 148, 186, 191, 201, 211, 235, 244, 246, 284
Norris, George, 164
North-South alliance, 191, 193, 194–95, 293, 297, 299, 302, 303

O'Brien, Arthur, 247
O'Connor, Richard, 113
Oglethorpe University speech, 211, 221, 269
Ohio primary (1924), 52
Oldfield, William A., 102
Olvaney, George, 103
Omaha World-Herald, 72, 189
Orcutt, G. N., 55–56
Organized labor. *See* Trade unions
Outlook, 161, 167

Palmer, A. Mitchell, 243; campaign for 1920 nomination, 17–18
Palmer raids, 18
Parker, Alton B., 17, 56, 64, 108, 218
Parker, John W., 117
Peay, Austin, 117
Peek, George N., 62, 163
Perkins, Frances, 112, 115
Perrett, Geoffrey, 19
Petersen, Peter, 1
Peterson, Merrill, 11
Pinchot, Amos, 203
Pinchot, Gifford, 117
Pittman, Key, 25, 61, 66–67, 212
Polk, Frank, 47
Popkin, Samuel, 7, 155
Populism, 3

Portland Press Herald, 47
Potato Act, 291
Presidential elections
—campaigns: in 1912, 297; in 1916, 297; in 1920, 14, 15–29 passim; in 1924, 8, 14; in 1928, 14, 157–80 passim; and race (1928), 169–70, 340 (n. 79); in 1932, 14; in 1936, 285. *See also* Roosevelt, Franklin D.
—results: in 1912, 321 (n. 123); in 1916, 321 (n. 123); in 1920, 26–28; in 1924, 71–72; in 1928, 169–70, 178–79, 342 (n. 139)
Procter and Gamble Company, 142, 143
Progressive National Committee, 166
Progressive party, 64–70 passim, 144, 179
Progressives, 23, 297; and 1928 campaign, 166–68;
Progressivism: defined, 13
Prohibition, 3, 5, 21, 48, 49, 53, 54, 65, 66, 108, 119, 154, 171, 172, 173, 175, 176, 182, 184, 187–93, 199, 204, 215–17, 219, 220, 222, 228, 234, 235, 237–38, 240, 243, 244, 289, 296, 298, 299, 300, 301, 302; and historians, 356 (n. 13)
Protective legislation, 115–16
Public Health Service, 33

Quebec system, 258–60

Railroads, 33–35, 55
Raleigh News and Observer, 108, 189
Ralston, Samuel, 54, 59
Randolph, Hollins, 36, 61, 94; and DNC, 83–84, 85, 89
Randolph, John, 127
Raskob, John J., 3, 4, 5, 12, 14, 49, 119, 128, 130, 131–56 passim, 159, 162, 163, 165, 166, 167, 168, 170, 171, 172, 175, 176, 177, 179, 181–

204 passim, 207, 211, 212, 225–47
passim, 248, 249, 257, 264, 265,
275, 276, 277, 278–81, 283, 284,
285, 290, 293, 296, 299, 301, 302,
303, 304, 305, 365 (n. 69); appointment to DNC, 131–32; biography,
133–37; and Du Pont Company,
133–37; and General Motors, 133–
37; and Pierre du Pont, 133–37; philosophy, 147–53, 336 (n. 109); and
Working Man's Investment Trust,
151–52, 336 (n. 115); and prohibition, 154, 187–93; attitude toward
political parties, 154–55; and Alfred
Smith, 154–56; renounces Republican party, 156; and funding of DNC,
(1929–32), 185–86; and 1931 questionnaire, 189–90; and historians,
190; and Home Rule plan, 190–93,
216, 228; and Byrd, 193–97; economic policy (1929–32), 197–200;
tariff policy (1929–32), 197–200;
and cooperation statement, 200–201;
and FDR (1929–32), 214–19; and
1932 nomination, 226, 352 (n. 49);
assesses Chicago convention, 246–47;
and New Deal, 279–81
Reagan, Ronald, 331 (n. 88)
Reconstruction, 169, 191, 293
Reconstruction Finance Corporation,
203
Red Cross, 288
Red Scare, 119
Reed, James A., 37, 98; campaign for
1928 nomination, 99
Reed, William T., 213, 240, 247;
defines progressivism, 242
Reforestation Amendment, 208, 229
Religious conflicts, 1, 51–52, 296
Repeal Associates, 265–69, 288, 360
(n. 80); Charter, 265
Republican National Committee
(RNC), 76, 153, 176, 281, 285

Republican party, 15, 49, 69, 72, 98,
120, 121, 131, 138, 139, 145, 153,
155, 158, 159, 162, 163, 164, 165,
171, 178, 179, 183, 199, 200, 204,
220, 221, 225, 244, 246, 249, 250,
252, 253, 296, 297, 303, 304; fund-
raising (1920), 25, 253; fund-raising
(1924), 70; structure, 75–76, 322
(n. 12); fund-raising (1928), 176–
77, 342 (n. 118); and the Liberty
League, 285–86; and the South
(1929–32), 343 (n. 17)
Ripley, William Z., 259
Ritchie, Albert C., 246, 247, 249, 255;
campaign for 1928 nomination, 99;
and 1932 nomination, 235; biography, 236; as governor of Maryland,
236–37; philosophy, 237, 242; and
prohibition, 237–38, 243, 245; 1932
economic platform, 238–39; and
New Deal, 278–79
Robertson, A. Willis, 193
Robinson, Joseph T., 112, 150, 190,
200
Rockefeller, John D., 141
Rockwell, David Ladd, 36, 47
Romantic individualism, 5
Roosevelt, Eleanor, 174
Roosevelt, Franklin D. (FDR), 3, 4, 13,
14, 24, 31, 50, 54, 85, 96, 101, 102,
105, 106, 107, 113, 118, 121, 122,
124, 125, 130, 158, 161, 174, 178,
188, 190, 196, 205–24 passim,
225–47 passim, 249, 254, 258, 269,
270, 274–95 passim, 297, 301, 302,
303, 304, 305; platform proposals
(1919), 19–20; nominated for vice-
president (1920), 21; 1924 circular
letter, 86–89, 298; suggestions for
reform of DNC, 86–91, 323 (n. 54),
324 (n. 70); and 1928 campaign,
165; 1928 circular letter, 181–82,
214–15; and historians, 204–5; as

New York governor, 207–10; and depression, 208–9; philosophy, 209, 211; and Tammany Hall, 209–10; and farm relief, 210–11; campaign for 1932 nomination, 210–18, 223–24; and water power, 211; and Alfred Smith, 213; and League of Nations (1932), 214; versus Raskob, 214–19; and Shouse, 217–18, 243; and McAdoo, 219–22; and 1932 convention, 243–47; and fund-raising, 348 (n. 39)

Roosevelt, Theodore, 153, 252

Roper, Daniel, 36, 39, 44, 47, 78, 212, 243

Rosen, Elliot, 4, 235

Rossiter, Clinton, 10

Ryan, Thomas Fortune, 25

Sabin, Pauline, 249

Sales tax, 146, 203, 230, 238, 239

Sarasohn, David, 27

Scripps-Howard newspapers, 167

Seabury, Samuel, 209–10

Sea Girt, N.J., 68

Senatorial committees, 76

Seward, William, 155

Shaver, Clem, 58, 66, 70, 90, 132; as chairman of DNC, 79–81, 84; and FDR's circular letter, 89–90

Sherman, William Tecumseh, 32

Sherman Antitrust Act, 197, 252

Shipping Board Act, 34, 138

Shouse, Jouett, 4, 71, 182–204 passim, 211, 215, 235, 236, 240, 243, 249, 264, 265, 271, 272, 282, 283, 285, 286, 288, 292, 293, 302, 304, 363 (n. 29); biography, 182; and cooperation statement, 200–201; and permanent chairmanship of Chicago convention, 217–18; and FDR, 227; and 1932 nomination, 227; and Liberty League, 292–94

Simmons, Furnifold, 95, 105, 172, 177; and 1928 campaign, 170–71

Sisson, Francis H., 138

Slichter, Sumner S., 144, 202

Sloan, Alfred, 133, 135, 141

Smith, Alfred E., 1, 3, 4, 5, 14, 18, 31, 36, 37, 39, 40, 48, 49, 53, 54, 84, 85, 86, 90, 92–111 passim, 112–30 passim, 132, 133, 137, 142, 147, 149, 153, 154, 155, 157–80 passim, 182, 188, 189, 200, 206, 207, 210, 211, 212, 213, 219, 223, 226–33 passim, 238, 239, 247, 248, 249, 275, 276, 278, 279, 281, 284, 285, 286, 302, 303, 304, 305; strategy for 1924 nomination, 54–56, 66; and prohibition, 55, 119–20; qualifications for 1928 nomination, 93–94; strategy for 1928 nomination, 100–111; attempts to woo South, 102–3; fund-raising for nomination, 104; and historians, 111–13, 329 (nn. 9, 10), 330 (n. 37); biography, 114–16; as New York assemblyman, 114–16; and Tammany Hall, 114–16; and labor reform, 115–16, 121, 123, 125–26; and women, 115–16, 121–23; philosophy, 115–30; as governor, 116–27, 207; and business, 118–20; and states' rights, 119, 124; and New Deal, 123–26; as conservative, 126–30; and Southern Democrats (1928), 168–73; and blacks, 174, 340 (n. 77), 341 (n. 109); analyzes 1928 defeat, 178; candidacy for 1932 nomination, 226–32; versus FDR, 228–32; 1932 economic platform, 230–31; at Chicago convention, 245

Smith, Katie, 103

Smoot-Hawley tariff, 183, 195, 196, 198, 199, 242

Social Security Act, 129, 295

Soldier's Bonus, 45

Soldiers' Insurance Scheme, 33
Spanish-American War, 262
Spellman, Cardinal, 103
Spencer, Herbert, 12, 13
Sprague v. United States, 358 (n. 45)
States' rights, 10, 40–43, 53, 56, 66, 119, 124, 175, 237, 259, 262–63, 279, 296
Stayton, William, 4, 252, 254, 262–69 passim, 270, 272, 281, 288, 289; biography, 262; and states' rights, 262–63; philosophy, 262–69; and Repeal Associates, 265–69, 360 (n. 80); and taxation, 267–69
Strauss, Jesse, 210
Strikes, 27, 43, 139–40, 161, 312 (n. 84)
Sullivan, Mark, 105, 137
Sumner, William Graham, 11
Swanson, Claude, 172, 282
Sweden: liquor system, 259–61
Swope, Gerard, 118, 142

Taft, William H., 139, 252
Taggart, Tom, 17, 22, 24, 54
Tammany Hall, 17, 24, 31, 33, 50, 54, 55, 73, 83, 88, 90, 93, 97, 102, 103, 107, 108, 133, 166, 173, 174, 212, 213, 214, 219, 220; and Alfred Smith, 114–15, 168; and FDR, 209–10
Tariff policy, 45, 53, 65, 66, 78, 145, 158–60, 170, 172, 183, 195, 196, 197–200, 279, 298, 302
Taxation, 65, 66, 146, 147, 160–61, 208, 230, 238, 239, 242, 250, 254, 267, 279, 280, 289, 291, 300, 310 (n. 34), 313 (n. 17), 315 (n. 66), 333 (nn. 12, 34), 357 (n. 22), 366 (n. 74)
Taylor, Tyre, 213, 216
Teapot Dome scandal, 31, 37–38, 55, 66, 97, 98, 314 (n. 41)

Temporary Emergency Relief Agency, 208
Tennessee Valley Authority (TVA), 277, 284
Texas Democratic Convention (1928), 48
Texas Seeds Bill, 266, 291
Thomas, Norman, 166
Trade unions, 35, 40, 52, 164, 334 (n. 38)
Traylor, Melvin, 202; and 1932 nomination, 235, 236
Triangle Shirt Waist Company fire, 115
Tumulty, Joseph, 24, 78, 102, 103, 131, 191, 200, 246
Two-thirds rule, 82–83, 101
Tydings, Millard F., 283

Underwood, Oscar W., 3, 36, 59, 61, 85; campaign for 1924 nomination, 52–54; philosophy, 53–54
Underwood-Simmons Tariff, 43, 78, 159, 170
Union League, 153, 172
U.S. Chamber of Commerce, 146–47, 148
U.S. Steel Corporation, 164
U.S. Supreme Court, 58, 141, 266, 267, 291
U.S. Trucking Corporation, 113, 120
United States v. William M. Butler, 291
Unit rule, 82
Urban transit: Hudson River tunnels, 32; Dallas street railways, 133

Van Buren, Martin, 101
Vanderbilt, Cornelius, 141
Van Kennan, George, 55
Van Namee, George, 104
Victory Fund, 184–86
Villard, Oswald G., 117
Vincent, John, 7

Virginia, 171–72, 187, 193, 213, 240, 242
Virginia Quarterly Review, 82
Volstead Act, 25, 65, 94, 175, 176, 188, 190, 230, 250
Voter sovereignty: and historians, 7

Wadsworth, James, 153, 250, 264, 354 (n. 113), 355 (n. 3); and McNary-Haugen scheme, 319 (n. 64)
Wagner, Robert F., 115, 123, 153
Walker, James J., 114, 209–10
Wall Street, 33, 37, 39, 43, 46, 47, 48, 49, 54, 59, 64, 66, 73, 95, 97, 124, 157, 167
Wall Street Journal, 139, 167, 200
Walsh, David I., 244
Walsh, Thomas J., 3, 18, 38, 63, 64, 87, 100, 103, 192, 199, 243; analyzes 1924 defeat, 73; campaign for 1928 nomination, 97–98
War Industries Board, 138
Warner, Charles, 149, 153
War Revenue Acts, 20
Washington, George, 33
Water power, 43, 62–63, 118, 142, 160, 164, 166, 174, 208, 211, 231, 232, 235, 244, 298
Webb-Kenyon Act, 271–72
Welfare capitalism, 10, 122, 140–44, 150, 334 (n. 56), 335 (n. 68)
Welfare state, 9, 10
West Virginia, 58
Wheat growers, 27, 138
Wheeler, Burton K., 64, 103, 217, 247
Wheeler, Wayne, 54
White, George, 24, 132; as chairman of DNC, 77–78

White, William Allen, 52, 246
Wickersham, George, 290
Wickersham Commission, 232
Wiebe, Robert H., 2, 5, 135
Willard, Daniel, 142
Willis, Hugh, 257
Wilson, Woodrow, 2, 13, 14, 22, 23, 30, 31, 35, 37, 39, 49, 52, 72, 77, 79, 106, 142, 153, 156, 158, 161, 170, 173, 177, 182, 212, 232, 240, 252, 282, 296, 297, 298, 301, 302, 303, 321 (n. 123); hopes for 1920 nomination, 16; opinion of Cox, 19, 21; agricultural policy, 27; attitude toward Davis, 59; attitude toward McAdoo, 309 (n. 6)
Winston-Salem Journal and Star, 105
Wolfskill, George, 276, 305
Women's Christian Temperance Union, 94, 257
Women's rights, 32, 35
Wood, Leonard, 93
Woodin, William H., 176
Woodson, Urey, 63
Wooley, Robert, 23, 24–25, 77, 78, 241
Work, Hubert, 178
Working Man's Investment Trust, 151, 336 (n. 115)
World War I, 33–35, 63, 251, 266, 292, 310 (n. 34), 357 (n. 24)

Young, Clement, 117
Young, Owen D., 118, 145, 150, 232, 236; biography, 234–35; and 1932 nomination, 234–35
Young Committee, 234